Social History of Africa

THE BLUEST HANDS

THE BLUEST HANDS

A SOCIAL AND ECONOMIC HISTORY OF WOMEN DYERS IN ABEOKUTA (NIGERIA), 1890–1940

Judith A. Byfield

HEINEMANN
Portsmouth, NH

JAMES CURREY
Oxford

DAVID PHILIP
Cape Town

#46992158

Heinemann
A division of Reed Elsevier Inc.
361 Hanover Street
Portsmouth, NH 03801-3912
USA
www.heinemann.com

James Currey Ltd.
73 Botley Road
Oxford OX2 0BS
United Kingdom

David Philip Publishers (Pty) Ltd.
208 Werdmuller Centre
Claremont 7708
Cape Town, South Africa

Offices and agents throughout the world

ISBN 0–325–07009–1 (Heinemann cloth)
ISBN 0–325–07008–3 (Heinemann paper)
ISBN 0–85255–650–0 (James Currey cloth)
ISBN 0–85255–600–4 (James Currey paper)

British Library Cataloguing in Publication Data

Byfield, Judith A.
  The bluest hands : a social and economic history of women
  dyers in Abeokuta (Nigeria), 1890–1940.—(Social history of Africa series)
  1. Dyers—Nigeria—Abeokuta—History 2. Women—Employment
  —Nigeria—Abeokuta—History 3. Dyes and dyeing—Nigeria
  —Abeokuta—History 4. Abeokuta (Nigeria)—Social
  conditions—19th century 5. Abeokuta (Nigeria)—Social
  conditions—20th century
  I. Title
  331.4'8673'0966923
  ISBN 0–85255–600–4 (James Currey paper)
  ISBN 0–85255–650–0 (James Currey cloth)

Library of Congress Cataloging-in-Publication Data

Byfield, Judith A. (Judith Ann Marie)
  The bluest hands : A social and economic history of women dyers in Abeokuta
(Nigeria), 1890–1940 / Judith A. Byfield.
    p. cm.—(Social history of Africa, ISSN 1099–8098)
  Includes bibliographical references and index.
  ISBN 0–325–07009–1 (alk. paper)—ISBN 0–325–07008–3 (pbk. : alk. paper)
  1. Dyers—Nigeria—Abeokuta—History. 2.
  Women—Employment—Nigeria—Abeokuta—History. 3. Dyes and
  dyeing—Nigeria—Abeokuta—History. I. Title. II. Series.
  HD6073.D92N69 2002
  331.4'8763'0966923—dc21   2001026387

Paperback cover photo: Alhaja Ajoke Soetan (Abeokuta, 1988). Photo by Judith A. Byfield.

Printed in the United States of America on acid-free paper.

06 05 04 03 02 SB 1 2 3 4 5 6 7 8 9

Copyright Acknowledgments

The author and publisher gratefully acknowledge permission to reprint Judith A. Byfield's "Innovation and Conflict: Cloth Dyers and the Interwar Depression in Western Nigeria," *Journal of African History* 38, 1 (1997), pp. 77–99. Reprinted with the permission of Cambridge University Press.

To

Funminiyi, Iwoaya, Kenya, Camara, and Lily Dahn

May your lives be rich with love and joy.

CONTENTS

ILLUSTRATIONS

ABBREVIATIONS

Abe Prof	Abeokuta Provincial Records
CMS	Church Missionary Society
ECR	Egba Council Records
NAA	National Archives—Abeokuta
NAI	National Archives—Ibadan
PRO	Public Record Office (London)

PREFACE

Tell them a story.

—Ron Takaki.

As we walked toward Dartmouth Hall, where he would deliver a talk, Ron Takaki, a professor of history at UC–Berkeley, shared some of his insights about writing with me. He told me that he did his best work when he started telling stories. The theory is there, he explained, it is not expunged, but it is deeply embedded in the stories about people's lives, actions, motivations, and accomplishments.

This story is about women indigo dyers in Abeokuta, a Yoruba town in western Nigeria, who in their effort to maintain and protect their craft offer a rich tapestry of events and personalities that illustrate the complex ways in which colonialism transformed their lives and livelihood. I did not set out to work on dyers or textiles at all when I began the journey that resulted in this book. When I first visited Nigeria in 1985, I went to see if sufficient material existed to write a dissertation on a women's tax revolt in Abeokuta in 1947. While gathering information about the revolt, I also collected data on women's economic enterprises and industries so that I could lay an economic foundation for their decision to resist a tax increase after World War II. It soon became obvious that the *adire* (tie and dye) industry loomed very large in Abeokuta's economy and among women's enterprises, so large in fact that it went from being one chapter to becoming the topic of the dissertation.

It is somewhat ironic that I write on textile producers. My paternal grandfather was a tailor, several aunts were seamstresses, and my mother was a wiz on the embroidery machine in the clothing factory where she and my father met. My father started out in this factory as a cutter, but he was managing the factory by the time I and my siblings came along. I remember visiting the factory on weekends and being surrounded by machines and bolts of cloth, with innumerable straight pins underfoot. When we left Jamaica and moved to America, textiles continued to play an important role in our lives, for my father worked as a cutter in New York's garment industry. To help cut expenses, he also taught himself to sew. He made our prom gowns, curtains, and bridal gowns for an assortment of friends and relatives, and recently he began experimenting with men's suits. Yet, my siblings and I were not taught to sew; such tasks lost out to the primacy my parents placed on academic work.

My research in Nigeria has brought me full circle. The lives and experiences of the women dyers in Abeokuta forced me to reflect on the textile workers who populated my life in Jamaica and New York. That reflection will someday take the form of another book. This book, however, belongs to the dyers of Abeokuta whose experiences opened my eyes to new questions and new ways of exploring the complex history of colonialism.

This book could not have been written without the assistance of many people. I offer a collective "thank you" to all those who have encouraged and challenged me and held my hand through this lengthy process. This study builds upon my dissertation, therefore I must acknowledge the abundant support I received and continue to receive from my thesis adviser, Marcia Wright. Over the years, she continually challenged and encouraged me through the good and the difficult times. I also learned a tremendous amount from Hollis Lynch, who encouraged my interest in Nigeria and in politics, and the late Graham Irwin, who inspired me as a teacher. Mohamed Mbodj's gentle but probing questions helped me to think like an economic historian. I am grateful to the early and continued support that Iris Berger, Toyin Falola, Jean Hay, Robin Law, Paul Lovejoy, Kristine Mann, Cheryl Johnson-Odim, and Richard Roberts supplied in large doses. I owe a special debt of gratitude to a number of friends from my Columbia University years who proved that time and distance do not have to weaken the bonds of affection, especially Aji and Tunji Adeniji, Carolyn Brown, Joseph Caruso, Ehiedu and Ifi Iweriebor, Kenneth Jones, Margot Lovett, Sheryl McCurdy, Funke Okome, Marlyse Rand, Elisha Renne, and Luvone Robeson.

I owe my greatest debt to the many people in Nigeria who contributed time, help, and friendship. This work could not have been completed without the assistance of Bola Sowemimo and Femi Adenmosun, who interpreted, translated, and transcribed the interviews. I am grateful for the cooperation and patience of those who allowed us to interview them and take hours of their time, especially Madam Wosinata Adeniji, Madam Adepate Adeniji, the late Alhaja Ajoke Soetan, and Mrs. Ronke Doherty. I am indebted to the staffs of the Nigerian National Archives in Ibadan and Abeokuta and the University of Ibadan Libraries for their generous assistance, especially Segun Faleye, Abraham Olayemi, and Efo Osifoh. Of the numerous friends and colleagues I made in Ibadan, Abeokuta, and Lagos, I owe special thanks to Professor J.F. Ade Ajayi, the late Professor S.O. Biobaku, Dr. LaRay Denzer, Professor Bolanle Awe, and Dr. Nina Mba. Over the years, many also took care of me and made sure that I felt truly at home in Nigeria, especially Dr. Fumni Ajayi, Professor R.A. Elegbe, Mrs. Lorraine Animasaun, Mrs. Ronke Doherty, Iyabo and Fassy Yusuf, Kunle and Bisi Adiniji, Yinka Ogunsanwo, and Drs. Irene and Ohioma Pogoson.

I also owe numerous debts to many people in England. Shula Marks encouraged me to work on cloth long before I fully appreciated the suggestion. She, along with Helen Calloway, Terrence Ranger, Peter Alexander, Megan Vaughn, and Obi Igwara offered friendship and collegial support. Michael Atkinson and Anthony Ingelsdorf patiently shared recollections of their tenure in the colonial service in Nigeria, while John Mack generously made the Bevin collection at the Museum of Mankind available to me. Jane Barbour very generously shared her insight and knowledge about *adire*. The staffs at the Public Records Office and Rhodes House (Oxford) were wonderfully helpful. My numerous family in England, especially Leisa Taylor, Dennis Chambers, Ashley Flash, and Ann Sotoudemehr supplied me with good food and fun; while my family in Jamaica, especially my aunts, Geraldine Byfield and Louise Simpson, reminded me I had a bed with my name on it whenever I needed to take a break.

Since July 1991, I have been at Dartmouth College. I am extremely grateful for the camaraderie and enormous support I have received from my colleagues in history, African and African American studies, and women's studies, especially Alex Bontemps, Ann Brooks, W.W. Cook, Michael Ermarth, Carl Estabrook, Douglas Haynes, Mary Kelly, Deborah King, Annelise Orleck, Leo Spitzer, and Roberta Stewart. They have made my return to my alma mater a pleasure. I have to acknowledge the reference staff at Baker Library. Patricia Carter always managed to find the most obscure references whenever I needed them, and Greg Finnegan, who has since joined the Tozzer Library at Harvard, made sure I was aware of the newest titles. I also owe a great debt to Mark O'Neil, Rohan

McFarlane, Matt Ungerer, and Lucinda Hall who patiently prepared and scanned maps and photographs.

Returning to Dartmouth has strengthened relationships that began twenty-five years ago as we all struggled through Milton's *Paradise Lost*. I especially thank Sabrina King and Carol Green for their steadfast love and friendship. I must say a word about my students. Over the years, I have had the distinct pleasure of working with a number of bright, challenging, and wonderful students. Their questions, insights, and research interests have been a source of nourishment for me. I thank them all, especially Chinwe Ajene, Nicholas Gunia, Ritika Nandkeolyar, Rachel Perry, Melanie Soares, and Xiajing Wang for sharing this intellectual journey with me.

My research could not have been conducted without the financial support of several institutions. First I would like to thank the Graduate School of Art and Sciences, the Institute of African Studies, and the Institute for Research on Women and Gender at Columbia University for supporting my first two research trips. Subsequent trips were supported by the Burke Award from Dartmouth College and a Rockefeller Humanities Fellowship from the Center for Afroamerican and African Studies (CAAS), University of Michigan. I must thank the members of CAAS for their encouragement and assistance, especially Earl Lewis, Evans Young, and Elsa Barkley Brown (now at the University of Maryland). An extra-special thank you to Matthew and Rosemary Countryman, Donna Daniels, Veronica Gregg, Cecilia Green, Stephan Meischer, Lane Clarke, and Lynn Thomas for making me feel so welcome in Ann Arbor.

This manuscript has benefited immensely from the insight and wisdom of numerous people. I especially thank Douglas Haynes, Deborah King, and Margot Lovett for reading early drafts, the editors of this series, Jean Allman and Allen Isaacman, and the anonymous readers. Your comments and suggestions helped me to think more critically and broadly about this subject.

Last, but not least, I want to thank family, my parents, Hugh and Ruby Byfield, my sister, Natalie, and my brothers Brian and Byron, whose encouragement and love have been unwavering.

INTRODUCTION

The Bluest Hands is a social and economic history of women dyers in Abeokuta, a Yoruba town in southwestern Nigeria.[1] By the second decade of the twentieth century, most dyers were producing *adire* cloth. *Adire* cloth featured a variety of patterns that were created by resist dyeing.[2] They were primarily one color, indigo blue, and Yoruba dyers excelled at indigo dyeing.[3] While dyers created some patterns on locally woven cloth, *adire* was produced primarily with imported European manufactured cloth. The strong relationship between *adire* and imported cloth was rooted in important economic transformations that occurred during the first few decades of colonial rule.

Many consumers within Nigeria considered Abeokuta the premier center of *adire* production. *The Bluest Hands* examines Abeokuta's dyeing industry between 1890 and 1939. It carefully reconstructs the historical foundations as well as the social and economic milieu in which dyers came to produce these highly desired cloths that were steeped in Yoruba aesthetics. It highlights the dynamic ways these women engaged the colonial economy in taking full advantage of new infrastructure, credit, and the increasing availability of European cloth, as well as new technology. Equally important, it explores the paradoxes of this engagement that for many became apparent only when commodity prices and credit markets collapsed in the 1920s and 1930s. The worldwide economic crisis revealed the fragility of an industry that had become dependent on international trade for its most basic supplies.

As this study periodizes the development of this industry, it challenges some of the theoretical and conceptual models scholars have

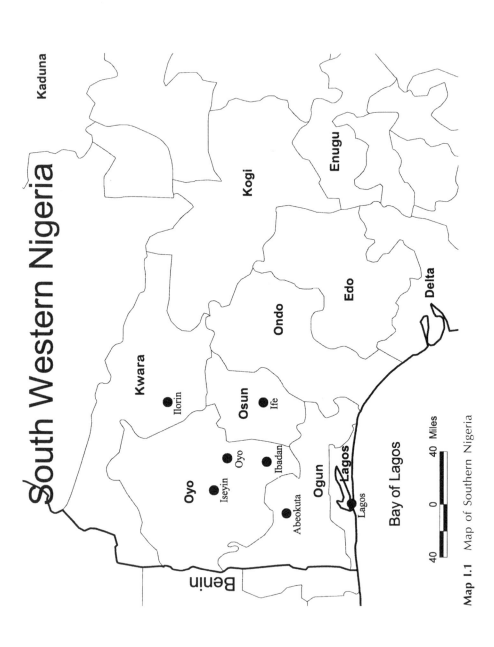

Map I.1 Map of Southern Nigeria

applied to indigenous industries, such as deindustrialization. Some scholars contend that indigenous textiles were more or less forced out by cheaper European imports. Others have suggested that Africa's productive weakness, especially in manufacturing, led African consumers to depend on imported manufactured goods.[4] The impact of European imports varied by craft, by sectors within a craft, and over time. The complexity of indigenous craft industries meant that imports did not simply depress local production, instead by working through the differences that already existed, they transformed local industry in complex ways.[5] The dyeing industry in Abeokuta was one textile sector that actually increased as the town became more integrated into the international economy.

Critics of the deindustrialization paradigm have pointed out that the volume of production and any decline have been very difficult to quantify. Furthermore, increased consumption of imported cloth did not necessarily indicate an absolute decline in indigenous cloth.[6] In order to more fully understand declines in local industries, we must examine the factors of production, such as access to threads, dyes, credit, labor, and markets. These factors were among the many that artisans contemplated as they weighed continuing in their craft against other economic options.

The deindustrialization thesis also presumes a significant degree of powerlessness and conservatism among artisans, such that artisan producers have neither the resources nor the desire to affect their circumstances. This study demonstrates that dyers built on a craft and an industry that had had a long history in Yoruba society, but their longevity was predicated on innovation and adaptation. Dyers had to constantly respond to competition from imported cloth, new technologies, new consumer tastes, new economic and political circumstances, and changes within their individual life cycles and family histories. They adopted new technology that allowed them to adjust to shifts in the availability of labor and consumer spending. They produced new designs and initiated and responded to fashion trends. Dyers' ready adaptability allowed them to navigate the economic and social changes that came with colonialism.

Dyers' actions on their own behalf were critical to the industry's expansion in the early decades of the twentieth century and to its survival during the depression. The interwar period was indeed a crisis period for dyers and this study's focus on a group of women craft producers refines our understanding of the social and economic reordering that occurred during that period. It illustrates the importance of incorporating gender into our analysis of the depression. The fall of commodity prices and the collapse of credit markets reverberated through Abeokuta's economy and led both men and women traders and producers to ask the state to intervene. The study contrasts the state's response to male producers with its response to female producers and shows how state intervention contributed to deeper gender inequities. The colonial government's decision to purchase the cocoa crop in 1939 helped to buoy men's income, but the state did woefully little to support women's industries. As a result, women's incomes continued to decline under the weight of the economic crisis. The state's actions supported the view of men as the breadwinners of the family, but such perceptions overlooked women's status as independent taxpayers and their responsibility to provide daily food and necessities for their children. This study not only illustrates how craft producers fared under colonialism, it also shows how a representative group of women producers navigated the colonial political economy.

Thankfully, this study is not the story of a dead or dying industry. *Adire* production continues in Abeokuta and other Yoruba towns. It is still made with factory-produced cloth, but now that cloth is made by Nigerian factories. Today *adire* is often multicolored. It is still a staple in the wardrobes of fashionable women and men in Nigeria and other parts of West Africa. Increasingly it is also found in the wardrobes of men and women in the cities of Western Europe and North America to which Nigerians and other West Africans have emigrated. The list of items made with *adire* has also increased. Now it is used to make bed linens, curtains, tablecloths, and other household items. *Adire* did more than just survive, it was actually thriving in the 1980s. In order to fully appreciate the artisans at the center of *adire* production, this study had to employ multiple analyses. Therefore, this study is both an economic and a social history because one cannot tell the story of how and why this industry survived or thrived without examining women's social roles and expectations in Yoruba society and their access to the state, labor, credit, and markets.

TEXTILES, ARTISANS AND HISTORY

For centuries, weavers, spinners, and dyers collectively produced cloths for subsistence and for trade between and beyond Yoruba communities. Even though cloth has long been an important sector of Nigerian economic life, historians have largely ignored the history of African textile production.[7] Art historians have paid much greater attention to the history of crafts in general, yet as recently as 1988 John

Picton argued that the present interest in textiles in African art studies
was relatively new.[8]

African art studies primarily concentrated on sculpture and on the
forms of sculpture pieces rather than their relationship to the societies
in which they were produced. Much of the analysis was devoid of
context, concentrating on regional and stylistic studies that supported
the interests of connoisseurship. By the end of the twentieth century,
African masks and figurative sculptures were less available, and consequently art dealers began to promote African textiles, ceramics, and
other objects as artworks.[9] Some contemporary producers of *adire* have
taken full advantage of the emerging art market in African textiles.
Nike Davies, for example, an internationally known Nigerian artist,
produces *adire* and batik wall hangings and other items for the international art market.[10] Yet most *adire* producers either in the past or
today did not produce these cloths as artworks to be mounted and ad-
mired. Yoruba consumers and producers recognized artistry and innovation by individual dyers and designers, but *adire* was produced to be
worn, to cover the body and clothe it in Yoruba social conventions. It
was cloth intended for mass consumption rather than for curatorial
collections.

Early art historical writings on textiles tended to be descriptive, offer-
ing varyious degrees of ethnographic and technological information.[11]
Early works on *adire* followed this model. Many were articles by European authors in magazines such as *Nigeria.* They gave brief descriptions
of the dyeing process and the materials used, and provided pictures of
adire designs.[12] Wenger and Beier expanded the analysis and located *adire*
in a broader religious and cultural context by collecting data on the deity
associated with its production.[13] One of the first major studies of *adire*
was a collection of articles edited by Jane Barbour and Doig Simmonds,
which provided much more detailed discussions of the chemistry of the
dye bath preparation, the dyeing methods, and the origin and devolution
of certain designs.[14]

In spite of the long recognition of *adire* and the importance of the
textile industry in Yoruba communities, few historians explored it in
any great detail. It is only in the last decade that several dissertations
appeared on *adire*. My own dissertation focused on *adire* production
in Abeokuta, while Caroline Keyes Adenike examined *adire* production in several Yoruba towns and carried the discussion into the
postcolonial period.[15] A brief discussion of *adire* also appeared in
Philip Shea's dissertation on the dyed cloth industry in Kano emirate
in northern Nigeria. Despite the paucity of historical works on textiles,

some early historians appreciated the importance of cloth to both regional and international trade. A.F.C. Ryder, for example, argued that cloth was central to the development of trust or credit trading between European and African merchants operating in the Niger delta in the seventeenth century.[16] Trade, however, was just one dimension of a much richer analysis historians could gather from textiles. For cloth, as Braudel argued, touches on every issue of concern—raw materials, production processes, manufacturing costs, cultural stability, fashion, and social hierarchy.[17] Therefore, there was much to glean about larger social, cultural, economic, and political changes from exploring not only how cloth was traded, but also how cloth was produced and by whom.

Recent studies on textiles have begun to place cloth in larger economic, social, and cultural contexts. These works are increasingly interdisciplinary and are models of the rich and textured analyses scholars can achieve by employing theoretical and methodological insights from other disciplines. Art historian Lisa Aronson's work is a good example of the pairing of art historical studies and economic history. Aronson shows that we can reconstruct networks and patterns of trade from examining the adoption of weaving and dyeing techniques by different societies.

Although the Yoruba town of Ijebu-Ode and the southern Igbo village Akwete are more than 250 miles apart, Akwete weavers produced a cloth, *ikakibite* or tortoise cloth, whose design was of Ijebu origin. This cloth was a prestige item in the nineteenth century, and its dissemination was the outcome of extensive trade relations in the delta region involving Ijebu and Ijo traders. Ijo traders took Ijebu cloths further east, introducing it to Igbo weavers, who replicated the designs for Ijo patrons.[18] The dissemination of the tortoise design was one thread of a larger picture of historical change in the nineteenth century that included the transition from the trade in slaves to trade in palm oil, the emergence of a new class of economic and political brokers, and changes in consumption. Aronson's work demonstrated that form and context were not mutually exclusive.

Textiles also offer ample data to study more subtle and ephemeral changes, such as changes in gender and household relations, for gender and social status correlated strongly with occupational niches. In Daboya, for example, a famous center of dyeing and weaving in northern Ghana, elite women and Muslim women spun thread, while weaving and dyeing were considered male preserves. Weavers and dyers did not farm; they were engaged in these activities full-time, while slaves performed the agricultural work. Therefore, there was a strong correlation between these occupations and free-born status.[19] The position of weavers in Daboya contrasted significantly with that of weavers in Tukulor society in Senegal, where weaving was a low-status occupation. Freemen held most of the rights to cultivate land, and so weavers were dependent on the patronage of freemen for their subsistence. Only those with sufficient land could cultivate cotton, and women of these households controlled the cultivation of cotton. Women also controlled the spun cotton and operated as patrons to weavers. As a result, women owned the weaver's product, the finished cloth.[20]

Yoruba society presents a fascinating contrast to both Daboya and Tukulor. In Yorubaland, weaving was not a male preserve. Both men and women wove, although women spun the cotton into thread. In addition, dyeing was considered a women's occupation. Weavers took threads or cloths to dyers for them to be dyed, but at the end of the production process weavers owned the final product. Thus, weavers were in a relatively stronger economic position than spinners and dyers, though weavers were dependent on these others for their raw material and secondary processing.

Craft specializations were not fixed in time, they were the "product of determinate historical changes."[21] It is precisely this susceptibility to historical developments that allows scholars to use craft specialization to examine changes in relations of power between men and women and between social groups.[22] In Maraka, for example, textile production grew as the emergence of new Muslim states in the western Sudan led to an increase in the demand for indigo cloths. Women, who were the producers of spun thread and indigo, engaged a large number of female slaves to harvest indigo, spin cotton and dye. A number of women also bought male slaves to weave for them so they could avoid paying independent weavers or using their husband's slaves. However, the nineteenth century also marked a period of increasing seclusion for Maraka women. Seclusion, coupled with the availability of slave labor, freed women from agricultural work, but it also reduced their scope for direct commercial transactions. These developments encouraged men to enter this primarily female economic sphere. Indigo began to be cultivated and processed in slave villages, thereby becoming the property of the male household head.[23] In this instance, the sweeping political, economic, and social changes of the period encouraged the emergence of new relations of production and shifts in gender relations. Roberts's close study of relations of production allowed him to reconstruct the consequences of these larger developments in multiple settings, from the regional political economy to the household.

Studies of artisan-produced textile have shown that access to labor was a central issue for all producers. Therefore, textile producers relied on multiple forms of labor recruitment. Philip Shea's analysis of dyed cloth production in the Kano Emirate showed that as dye pits came to be owned by people who were investors rather than dyers, wage labor became increasingly important. In Iseyin, Bray found that weavers primarily relied on family labor, while *adire* producers used slaves, pawns, apprentices, family, and wage labor.[24] Yet many labor historians overlooked textile and other crafts,[25] concentrating instead on labor mobilization and the organization of work in peasant and export agriculture and capital-intensive industries such as mines.[26] As a result, conditions of work and labor recruitment for craft producers were relegated to an ahistorical universe that was outside the scope of regional and international political and economic developments.

Textiles also offer an invaluable perch from which to examine social and cultural history. Cloth covered the body and was a canvas against which numerous social codes, kin relations, and cultural critiques were displayed. The Kalibari of eastern Nigeria demanded strict rules of dress for men's ensembles of a top garment and a wrapper. The rules organized men's dress into a hierarchy that paralleled the age-grade and political structure in Kalibari society.[27] In Bunu Yoruba villages, young women could wear certain cloths only after they had completed all the steps of the traditional marriage.[28] The incorporation of imported cloth often signaled new social and cultural developments. European cloth demonstrated wealth and social or political status, while European dress expressed conversion to Christianity.[29] These new forms of cloth and dress increased the options available for self- and group expression.[30] Dress was also the language of social commentary and critique.[31] Cultural nationalist movements of the late nineteenth and early twentieth centuries, for example, often called for the return to "traditional" dress. Thus, dress and the cloths from which it was constructed communicated multiple stories and relationships.

The artisans who produced these cloths were linked by multiple networks and relationships and often shared the same social universe. In Iseyin, for example, it was not uncommon for male weavers to marry women from weaving families in order to ensure the availability of handspun thread.[32] Abeokuta's dyers' association acknowledged the births, marriages, and deaths in the life cycles of its members. Some scholars noted a strong correlation between Islam and indigenous crafts, including textiles, in some Yoruba towns.[33] Where, when, and why this correlation developed and its consequences remain to be explored because it was not universal across Yoruba societies. Nonetheless, it raises intriguing questions about the intersection of religious, economic, and social networks among craft producers and may allow us to reconstruct the history of production as a dynamic process that is shaping and shaped by broader social and cultural change.

ABEOKUTA, TEXTILES, AND THE COLONIAL ECONOMY

Most economic studies of Abeokuta and Yorubaland in general have been preoccupied with the production of raw materials for European markets.[34] By the end of the nineteenth century, Abeokuta producers were exporting palm products (oil and kernels), cotton, and cocoa to Europe. As a result, most scholars concentrated on these commodities. Few examined economic activities geared to local markets,[35] and fewer still examined the local textile industry. Thus, much of our analysis of economic change and transformation relied on examining the export sector in isolation. The production of exports captured only one side of the economic transformation that occurred from the mid nineteenth century and into the colonial period. Scholars overlooked changes in local industries that relied on imports and the links between these industries, the export sector, and the world economy. The *adire* industry exposes these links because its producers relied on imported cloth and their main consumers were cash crop producers. This industry illuminates the complex and multiple ways in which Abeokuta was integrated into the world economy. Equally important, since *adire* was primarily a women's industry, it places women producers at the center of this economic analysis rather than on the periphery.

Cloth imports began to increase significantly before the imposition of colonial rule and would increase even more dramatically under colonialism. The price of export crops had direct bearing on the volume of cloth imports. In Abeokuta, as producers benefited from the sale of cocoa, in particular, much of their profit was invested in imported items, including cloth. Colonial commentators often paired the discussion of cocoa and cloth because high cocoa prices translated into large cloth imports. Abeokuta's position as a major exporter of cash crops and an importer of textiles allows us to reconstruct the complexity of the dyers' universe and to gauge opportunities available to dyers at specific moments in the history of the dyeing industry. The study illustrates that the infrastructure that facilitated cocoa production also assisted the *adire* industry. The European trading firms that bought cocoa and extended credit also sold cloth and extended credit to cloth buyers. Railway lines, roads, and steamships took out cocoa and brought cloths of all varieties to a wider consumer base.

As dyers marshaled their resources to meet the opportunities presented by these developments, they did so within a new sociopolitical context. Forms of labor mobilization they had used in the past, such as slavery and pawning, were being actively discouraged by the colonial state. Much of the political structure from the nineteenth century carried over into the twentieth century, but the configuration of power was quite different. The depth of that difference became most visible when dyers looked to the state to assist them during the interwar economic crisis. Dyers eventual confrontation with the state provided this rare opportunity to examine these women both as craft producers and political actors.

WOMEN, POLITICS, AND THE COLONIAL STATE

This study benefits from the recent scholarship that has helped to break down monolithic views of the colonial state.[36] The state comprised administrative, legal, and coercive apparatuses, and their effects on distinct social segments were highly variable.[37] There were differences of opinion between branches and levels of officials and different audiences to whom officials had to respond.[38] These cleavages could be exploited by segments of colonial society.

This work also benefits from a fuller appreciation of how African men and women in daily life simultaneously engaged with and asserted their independence of colonial institutions and ideologies. As Fred Cooper notes, struggles within the colonized population over class, age, gender, and other inequalities gave texture to peoples' lives and to their engagement with colonial institutions and ideologies.[39] Thus, politics was much more complex than resistance or collaboration.[40] It reflected multiple layers and levels of struggles that sometimes coalesced in a unity of goals and direction and at other times remained fractured and unconnected. Dyers' struggle against the colonial state was not part of a larger concerted political movement. Their discussions did not carry any strains of the strident language of anticolonialism. They focused exclusively on issues germane to the crisis in the industry. Nonetheless, their meetings with the "traditional" king, the *Alake*, and the local governing council and their protests against legislation that banned the use of new technology, caustic soda, and synthetic dye, illuminate critical dimensions of both a practical and theoretical engagement with colonialism. Their thoughts and statements as recorded in countless minutes of the local council demonstrate that these women assumed a right to a dynamic, cooperative relationship with the state. Therefore, their appearances before the council were as much to discuss strategies for saving the industry as to discuss the obligations and responsibilities between ruler and ruled.

The dyers' experiences provide an important opportunity to explore women's relationship to the colonial state and how state formation was gendered. In recent years, an impressive body of literature on colonial state formation in Africa has emerged.[41] Yet, as Kathleen Staudt argues, many writers on the state have not viewed state formation as a gendered process, or even questioned the obvious male monopolization of state power.[42] The absence of women and gender in the analysis of the state has been increasingly challenged by an important body of literature that attempts to explain and explore the different ways in which men and women experienced and were affected by the process of state formation. The collections, for example, by Parpart and Staudt, *Women and the State in Africa*, and Hay and Wright, *Women and the Law in Africa*, draw our attention to the ways colonial states were gendered. Their contributors demonstrated the collaboration between colonial officials and some African men to reassert and protect patriarchal authority; efforts by colonial governments to claim economic arenas dominated by women; as well as efforts to restrict women's political participation.[43] They also reminded us that states do not only impose, women sometimes used the state in their effort to renegotiate gender relations.[44] Similarly, they document how women also shaped the process of state formation. Through their actions, demands, and protests women reconfigured some of the best-laid colonial plans and helped to shape nationalist discourse.[45]

This study explores several of these themes. First, it examines how the colonial state in Abeokuta became an exclusively male enclave, even though the Egba Native Council did not represent the interests of all men consistently. Its priorities and policies reflected divisions by class and generation.[46] Second, the study examines the notion of the state as a resource. The first group of dyers who went to the *Alake* for help hoped to use the authority of those officials to address some of the industry's problems. The extent to which the colonial state was a resource for women dyers can be measured by contrasting actions taken on behalf of European and African men.

Finally, it examines the nature of politics and the rhetoric of the political engagement between the dyers, the British resident, and the *Alake*. This rhetoric revealed multiple layers of political imagery through which dyers and the state challenged their respective interpretations of state society relations. Colonial officials used the ideology of kinship to frame political discourse. Consequently, much of the discussion revolved around the idea of the *Alake* as the father of the community and therefore the one who knew what was best for the dyers. This discourse constructed the dyers as errant children. Dyers both challenged and accepted the terms of the debate. They agreed that the *Alake* was their father, but they expected a less authoritarian relationship with their father. Thus, the decision to ban caustic soda and synthetic dyes in spite of the dyers' concerns reflected his attempt to cross acceptable boundaries. It is in some of this word play that we can discern aspects of the ways in which women conceptualized the state.

The conflict between dyers and the *Alake* also exposed the limits of political action during this period. Dyers' grievances focused exclusively on their industry, and their implicit and explicit criticisms of the colonial state did not galvanize other groups into joining them. Nonetheless, their experience is important because it highlights the dramatic shifts that occurred by 1947 when women across Abeokuta joined forces to support the tax revolt.

METHODOLOGY AND SOURCES

Michel-Rolph Trouillot reminds us that history as social process involves people in three distinct capacities: as agents, or occupants of structural positions; as actors in constant interface with a context; and as subjects, voices aware of their vocality.[47] This study attempts to capture the dynamic interaction of these modes, but its success is mediated by the availability and the nature of the sources at my disposal. I collected the data for this book during several visits to Nigeria and England between 1985 and 1997. I combined qualitative interviews, observation data, newspapers, missionary records, and archival data in the construction of this history. Government documents were a critical source, especially minutes of Egba council meetings, district reports, provincial reports, and the testimonies and reports of the Commission of Enquiry into the *adire* industry in 1936. An important outline of the history of the *adire* industry and its organization is contained in the proceedings of the 1936 Commission of Enquiry. The goal of the commission was to determine whether the new production technology (caustic soda and synthetic dyes) that was incorporated in the 1920s was harmful to the cloths. The commission heard testimony from dyers, local (Yoruba) and foreign (Senegalese) buyers, farmers, and agents of European trading firms. In three days of testimony, the participants attempted to define the industry and the ways it had changed and to delineate the parameters of the conflict that brought them together. The testimony and reports made in conjunction with the Commission of Enquiry therefore form an important cache of information on the industry.

The Minutes of the Egba Native Council constituted a second major source. A vast body of the council's minutes survives. The minutes were written in English and are, at best, summations rather than verbatim accounts of statements made by those in attendance. Nonetheless, they indicate the major issues of the day and the opinions of council members and those who presented grievances. The information in this serial record was time-specific and a great aid in constructing a chronology of the changes in the industry. They helped illuminate the multiple layers of time and process that had been conflated in the Commission of Enquiry report. This cache of information confirms Geiger's argument that women show up in the colonial records only when there is a problem.[48]

Interviews supplemented information from the archival sources. The majority of informants were or had been dyers and *adire* makers. Since I looked primarily for women who had been dyeing during the 1920s and 1930s, most of the women we interviewed were quite elderly. All except one were born in Abeokuta. She was born in Scotland and moved to Nigeria with her Nigerian husband.[49] The interviews were conducted in their homes, which in many cases were also their places of work. I was, therefore, able to observe how they managed their business and familial obligations. Interviews with dyers were conducted in Yoruba with the assistance of Mrs. Bola Sowemimo, a Yoruba and English teacher at the Abeokuta Girl's Secondary School, and Femi Adenmosun, an M.A. candidate in the anthropology department at the University of Ibadan and an administrator at the Ogun State Cultural Center in Abeokuta.

I devised a five-part questionnaire for the interviews with the dyers. The sections explored production, marketing, lore associated with dyeing, the dyers' association, and the protests. To tease out some of the changes that had occurred in the industry, informants were asked to describe how their mothers or the women who trained them accomplished certain tasks, in contrast to how they themselves accomplished them. The most significant aspect of these interviews was the information about the protests that we could not recover. Though I was well armed with names of individuals involved in the protests and the names of the lawyers to serve as prompts, my informants could provide very little information about the protests. Some women remembered when it was illegal to use caustic soda and synthetic dye but did not recall how they responded to the bans. Only one woman recalled the protests and the abusive songs they sang to the *Alake*. Since most could not tell us much about the 1936 protest, we asked the dyers to tell us about the protest they did remember. Repeatedly we were told about the women's tax revolt in 1947–48.[50]

The silence on the 1936 protest was initially disappointing. Greater reflection on the events that the women did remember led to the realization that they were telling us which events had the most significant impact on their consciousness. In terms of their craft, the bans were the most significant events, while in terms of their political history, the 1947 tax revolt was the most significant. The gaps in our informants' memories do not invalidate the main thrust of this study, for this analysis provides the economic and political context to appreciate the significance of the 1947 tax revolt.

In addition to dyers, we interviewed several men who were stencil makers and tailors and the elderly nephew of one of the largest Egba cloth merchants during the 1920s and 1930s. We also met with several members of historically prominent Egba families (Coker, Ransome-Kuti, and Williams). These families were part of the early Christianized, educated elites in Abeokuta. These informants had never been personally involved in *adire* production, but each had relatives who had produced *adire*. They each shed light on how factors such as social and economic status and religion influenced who became dyers, and the structure and organization of their enterprise. The Nigerian interviews were supplemented with interviews in Britain with two ex-colonial officials who had served in Yorubaland in general and Abeokuta specifically. These interviews provided important information about Abeokuta and the Europeans who lived in the town during the 1930s and 1940s.

The Commission of Enquiry report, council minutes, and interviews corroborated major developments in the history of *adire*. Yet there were important divergences. Often those divergences indicated important changes that could easily have been overlooked. I was compelled to use all these sources because each added different characteristics to the project, and together they offered a detailed picture of these women producers and traders in a period of profound socioeconomic and political change.

ORGANIZATION

The dyers' story is told in six chapters. Chapter 1 calls attention to the value of indigo in Yoruba society and the multiple social and cultural features interwoven in cloth. It reconstructs the textile industry in the nineteenth century, paying particular attention to the impact of legitimate trade and the Yoruba civil wars. Chapter 2 examines the transition to the twentieth century. It focuses on the transformation of the Egba political structure and economy after Britain effectively extended its political control over most of Yorubaland after 1893. Although Abeokuta retained a nominal independence, the British continually impinged on the town's autonomy until the town's leaders were forced to cede power after an uprising in 1914. The years of autonomy under Egba United Government ironically witnessed the town's deepening integration into the international economy. This was greatly facilitated by the construction of the railway that first reached Abeokuta in 1899. The railway tremendously increased commercial activity as European firms opened stores in the town. Greater amounts of cloth and credit were available to consumers. Chapter 2 examines the fluidity of business practices as European merchants competed for customers and the importance of credit in cementing their viability and success. It also examines the complex social consequences of the town's deeper engagement with the colonial state and European merchant capital.

Chapter 3 provides an overview of the structure and organization of *adire* production in the early decades of the twentieth century. Working from the testimony of the Commission of Enquiry and the minutes of the Egba council, which offers a serial account of developments within the industry, chapter 3 documents the complex and integrated nature of *adire* production. *Adire* linked the urban and rural economies as well as many craftspeople, including potters and tailors. At its pinnacle, *adire* production involved roughly one quarter of Abeokuta's population. Chapter 3 also examines the dyers' workforce and how they organized work. Both archival sources and interviews report a variety of models, from one-person enterprises to twelve-person assembly-line production. The chapter also addresses the distribution and marketing of *adire*. Many dyers sold their own cloths at the markets, thereby constituting the first level of a complex distribution network that involved regional and long-distance traders from across Nigeria and other West African nations. Production and marketing were structurally linked in the *adire* industry and heightened dyers' sensitivity to changes that affected either side of the industry.

Chapter 4 examines the impact of the interwar depression on the *adire* industry and argues that to fully understand its consequences dyers cannot be examined in isolation. It situates dyers within a larger social and economic universe and juxtaposes dyers' strategies to offset the economic downturn against those of other economic actors. This analytical strategy allows us to see how the actions of other sectors reverberated through the dyeing industry. For example, European trading companies tightened credit in order to lessen their vulnerability but in the process put such extraordinary pressure on dyers that some women were forced out of the industry. Dyers were also deeply affected by the fall or stagnation of export commodity prices because it weakened consumer buying power. In response to these developments, dyers competed very aggressively in the marketplace for customers by sometimes reducing prices below the cost of production. They also experimented with new technology, specifically caustic soda and synthetic indigo, that held the promise of lowering production costs. The use of these products, however, caused considerable disruptions within the industry and compelled some dyers to solicit the *Alake*'s assistance.

Women dyers were not the only economic sector that saw the state as a resource during this crisis. A group of male traders also encouraged the state to take measures to address the credit crisis and the larger issue of indebtedness. Chapter 4 shows that gender profoundly shaped the ways in which the state attempted to address the issue of indebtedness. Local officials informed women traders that there was nothing they could do to assist them, but they assisted men by making it more difficult for wives to leave husbands, since a substantial portion of men's debts were related to the cost of marriage. The council's measures on debt did little to improve the economic conditions for the dyers as producers, but they had tremendous implications for dyers as women because it gave men greater control over wives.

Chapter 5 explores the dyers' response to the *Alake's* decision to ban the new technology. The dyers' protests, which included the surreptitious use of caustic soda and synthetic indigo and the hiring of literate men to represent them, precipitated a crisis of authority and brought the political changes under colonialism into sharp focus. Chapter 5 also examines dyers' attempts to constitute themselves into an effective association. They invested a tremendous amount of energy in trying to establish a dyers' association that could address some of the issues that generated tension among their ranks. This association illuminated important new dimensions in the longstanding Yoruba practice of forming commodity associations.

In spite of the dyers' efforts, the industry continued to flounder. Chapter 6 examines the conditions that contributed to their continued crisis. Their economic difficulties were the direct and indirect outcome of developments that illuminate just how precariously they were balanced within the international, regional, and local economies. While 1936 was a year of marked economic improvement, 1937 witnessed a severe downswing. This cycle proved particularly destabilizing, because dyers lost one of their largest markets during the Gold Coast (Ghana) cocoa holdups of 1937–38. They also lost their market in the Belgian Congo when the government built a textile factory that produced copies of *adire*. By 1939 colonial officials declared in the annual report that the *adire* industry had collapsed, and indeed it had lost its flagship position in Abeokuta's economy. The remainder of the chapter interrogates this collapse and situates it in a broader social and economic context.

The conclusion reiterates the need to locate the developments in the *adire* industry in a larger socioeconomic context. It suggests that a similar approach is necessary to understand why *adire* production did not disappear even after 1939, and why it achieved a renaissance in the 1980s. Similarly, it emphasizes the importance of locating dyers in a wider sea of social change that demonstrates the contradictory results of changes in the social spaces they inhabit as women, producers, wives, and mothers.

NOTES

1. Yoruba-speaking communities are also found in neighboring Benin as a result of colonial divisions at the end of the nineteenth century. Migrations since the colonial period have established significant Yoruba communities also in Togo and Ghana. See A.I. Asiwaju, *Western Yorubaland under European rule, 1889–1945: A Comparative Analysis of French and British Colonialism* (London: Longman, 1976). William Bascom, *The Yoruba of Southwestern Nigeria* (Prospect Heights, IL: Waveland Press, 1984); J.S. Eades, *Strangers and Traders: Yoruba Migrants, Markets and the State in Northern Ghana* (Trenton, NJ: Africa World Press, 1994).

2. There were two principal techniques for creating patterns when dyeing, resist and discharge. In resist dyeing, a portion of the cloth (or thread) was covered by starch or raffia thread (made from palm fibers) in order to prevent absorption of the dye. The discharge method entailed dyeing the entire cloth, then painting on a powerful reducing agent that removed the color. Margaret Trowell, *African Design* (London: Faber & Faber, 1960), 37–38. It should also be noted that tie-dyeing is not unique to Africa. Japanese *shibori* is quite similar to *adire*.

3. Other groups that practice indigo dyeing were the Hausa (northern Nigeria), Baule (Ivory Coast), and Soninke (Senegal). Other dyes were also available. Yellows were made from turmeric and kola nuts; reds from a species of guinea corn, sorghum, henna and the camwood tree; black from forest mud; and brown from various trees such as the locust bean and acacia. See John Picton and John Mack, *African Textiles* (New York: Harper & Row, 1989), 39.

4. John Thornton, "Precolonial African Industry and the Atlantic Trade, 1500–1800," *African Economic History* 19 (1990–91): 1–3. Also see Ralph Austen, *African Economic History* (Portsmouth, NH: Heinemann, 1987), 99–100.

5. Tirthankar Roy, ed., *Artisans and Industrialization: Indian Weaving in the Twentieth Century* (New York: Oxford University Press, 1993), 2. For a critique of deindustrialization, also see David Washbrook, "South, the World System and World Capitalism," *Journal of Asian Studies* 40 (1990): 479–508.

6. Marion Johnson, "Technology, Competition and African Crafts," in Clive Dewey and Anthony Hopkins, eds., *The Imperial Impact* (London: Athlone Press, 1978), 264–67. Shea also points out that increased consumption of imported cloth did not necessarily indicate an absolute decline in indigenous cloth: Philip J. Shea, "The Development of an Export Oriented Dyed Cloth Industry in Kano Emirate in the Nineteenth Century," Ph.D. diss., University of Wisconsin–Madison, 1975, 88.

7. Shea, "Development of an Export," 1. Also see Colleen Kriger, "Textile Production and Gender in the Sokoto Caliphate," *Journal of African History* 34 (3): 361–401.

8. Paul Tiyambe Zeleza, *A Modern Economic History of Africa,* Vol. 1, *The Nineteenth Century* (Dakar, Senegal: CODESRIA, 1993), 225; and John Picton, "Tradition, Technology, and Lurex: Some Comments on Textile History and Design in West Africa," in John Picton, ed., *History, Design, and Craft in West African Strip-Woven Cloth* (Washington, DC: National Museum of African Art, 1992), 13.

9. Mary Jo Arnoldi, Christraud Geary, and Kris Hardin, eds., *African Material Culture* (Bloomington: Indiana University Press, 1996), 8.

10. See Kim Marie Vaz, *The Woman with the Artistic Brush: A Life History of Yoruba Batik Artist Nike Davies* (New York: M.E. Sharpe,1995).

11. See, for example, Joanne Eicher, *Nigerian Hand-Crafted Textiles* (Ife, Nigeria: University of Ife Press, 1976); Venice Lamb and Judy Holmes, *Nigerian Weaving* (Roxford, U.K.: H.A. & V.M. Lamb, 1980).

12. One of the earliest articles was written by Mrs. F. Daniel, "Yoruba Pattern Dyeing," *Nigeria,* no. 13 (1938), 125–28.

13. Susan Wenger and H.U. Beier, "Adire—Yoruba Pattern Dyeing," *Nigeria,* no. 54 (1957), 208–25.

14. Jane Barbour and Doig Simmonds, eds., *Adire Cloth in Nigeria: The Preparation and Dyeing of Indigo Patterned Cloths Among the Yoruba* (Ibadan: University of Ibadan, 1971).

15. See Judith Byfield, "Women, Economy, and the State: A Study of the Adire Industry in Abeokuta (Western Nigeria), 1890–1939" (Ph.D. diss., Columbia University, 1993); and Carolyn Keyes, "Adire: Cloth, Gender and Social Change in Southwestern Nigeria, 1841–1991" (Ph.D. diss., University of Wisconsin–Madison, 1993). There are a number of unpublished sources, such as B.A. honors essays and master's theses in Nigeria. For example, Adesola Afolabi, "The Origin, Development and Impact of 'Adire' Dyeing Industry in Abeokuta" (B.A. honors essay, University of Ibadan, 1981).

16. Alan F.C. Ryder, "Dutch Trade on the Nigerian Coast During the Seventeenth Century," *Journal of the Historical Society of Nigeria* 3, 2 (1965): 195–210.

17. Fernand Braudel, *Capitalism and Material Life 1400–1800* (New York: Harper & Row, 1967), 226.

18. Lisa Aronson, "History of Cloth Trade in the Niger Delta: A Study of Diffusion," in Dale Idiens and K.G. Ponting, eds., *Textiles in Africa* (Bath, U.K.: Pasold Research Fund, 1980), 92–98.

19. Esther Goody, "Daboya Weavers: Relations of Production, Dependence and Reciprocity," in Esther Goody, ed., *From Craft to Industry: The Ethnography of Proto-industrial Cloth Production* (Cambridge: Cambridge University Press, 1982), 50–84; Elisha Renne, *Cloth That Does Not Die: The Meaning of Cloth in Bunu Social Life* (Seattle: University of Washington Press, 1995).

20. Roy M. Dilley, "Tukulor Weavers and the Organization of Their Craft in Village and Town," *Africa* 56, 2 (1986): 124–25. Also see R.M. Dilley, "Weaving Among the Tukulor of the Senegal River Basin: A Study of the Social Position and Economic Organization" Ph.D. diss., Keble College, Oxford, 1984).

21. Zeleza, *Modern Economic History*, 208.

22. Richard Roberts, "Women's Work and Women's Property: Household Social Relations in the Maraka Textile Industry of the Nineteenth Century," *Comparative Studies in Society and History* 26, 2 (1984): 229–50. Mona Etienne, "Women and Men, Cloth and Colonization: The Transformation of Production-Distribution Relations Among the Baule (Ivory Coast)," pp. 214–38 in Mona Etienne and Eleanor Leacock, eds., *Women and Colonization: Anthropological Perspectives* (New York: Praeger, 1980). Also see Richard Roberts, *Two Worlds of Cotton: Colonialism and the Regional Economy in the French Soudan, 1800–1946* (Stanford, CA: Stanford University Press, 1996).

23. Roberts, "Women's Work," 243–46.

24. Shea, "Development of an Export," 161. Jennifer Bray, "The Economics of Traditional Cloth Production in Iseyin, Nigeria," *Economic Development and Cultural Change* 17, 4 (July 1969): 544.

25. Kriger raises a similar concern in her study of iron workers. Colleen Kriger, *Pride of Men: Ironworking in 19th Century West Central Africa* (Portsmouth, NH: Heinemann, 1999), 13; also Zeleza, *Modern Economic History*.

26. For examples, see Bill Freund, *The African Worker* (New York: Cambridge University Press, 1988); Robin Cohen, *Labour and Politics in Nigeria* (London: Heinemann, 1974); and Fred Cooper, et al., *Confronting Historical Paradigms: Peasants, Labor, and the Capitalist World System in Africa and Latin America* (Madison, WI: University of Wisconsin Press, 1993).

27. Joanne Eicher and Tonye Erekosima, "Why Do They Call It Kalabari? Cultural Authentication and the Demarcation of Ethnic Identity," in Joanne Eicher, ed., *Dress and Ethnicity* (Oxford: Berg, 1995), 147.

28. Renne, *Cloth That Does Not Die*, 56–84.

29. Judith Perani and Norma Wolff, *Cloth, Dress and Art Patronage in Africa* (New York: Berg Press, 1999). Jean Hay, "Hoes and Clothes in a Luo Household: Changing Consumption in a Colonial Economy, 1906–1936," in Mary Jo Arnoldi, Christraud Geary, and Kris Hardin, eds., *African Material Culture* (Bloomington: Indiana University Press, 1996), 243–61.

30. Perani and Wolff, *Cloth, Dress and Art Patronage*, 46.

31. See Leo Spitzer, *The Creoles of Sierra Leone: Responses to Colonialism, 1870–1945* (Madison: University of Wisconsin Press, 1974); and Misty L. Bastian, "Female 'Alhajis' and Entrepreneurial Fashions: Flexible Identities in Southeastern Nigerian Clothing Practice," in Hilde Hendrickson, ed., *Clothing and Difference: Embodied Identities in Colonial and Post-Colonial Africa* (Durham, NC: Duke University Press, 1996), 97–132.

32. Jennifer Bray, "The Organization of Traditional Weaving in Iseyin, Nigeria," *Africa* 38, 3 (1968): 272.

33. Ibid.; also Titilola Euba, "Dress and Status in 19th Century Lagos," pp. 143–63 in Ade Adefuye, Babatunde Agiri, and Jide Osuntokun, eds., *History of the Peoples of Lagos State* (Lagos: Lantern Books, 1987).

34. See Sara Berry, *Cocoa, Custom and Socio-economic Change in Rural Western Nigeria* (Oxford: Clarendon Press, 1975); R. Galletti, et al., *Nigerian Cocoa Farmers* (Oxford: Oxford University Press, 1956); Brian Vincent, "Cotton Growing in Southern Nigeria: Missionary, Mercantile, Imperial and Colonial Government Involvement Versus African Realities, from 1845 to 1939," Ph.D. diss., Simon Fraser University, British Columbia, Canada, 1977.

35. An important exception is Babatunde Agiri, "Kola in Western Nigeria, 1850–1950: A History of the Cultivation of Cola Nitida in Egba-Owode, Ijebu-Remo, Iwo and Ota Areas," Ph.D. diss., University of Wisconsin, 1972.

36. Frederick Cooper, *Decolonization and African Society: The Labor Question in French and British Africa* (Cambridge: Cambridge University Press, 1996), 9.

37. Karen Tranberg-Hansen, "The Black Market and Women Traders in Lusaka, Zambia," in Kathleen Staudt and Jane Parpart, eds., *Women and the State in Africa* (Boulder, CO: Lynne Rienner, 1989), 143.

38. See Bruce Berman, *Control and Crisis in Colonial Kenya: The Dialectic of Domination* (Athens: Ohio University Press, 1990). Berman examines the contradictions and tensions that resulted from district officials' support of African chiefs and provincial officials' support of European settlers.

39. Frederick Cooper, "Conflict and Connection: Rethinking Colonial African History," *American Historical Review* 99 (1994): 1533.

40. Ibid., 1519.

41. See, for example, Bruce Berman and John Lonsdale, "Coping with the Contradictions: The Development of the Colonial State, 1895–1914," in *Unhappy Valley—Conflict in Kenya and Africa, book 1: State and Class* (Athens: Ohio University Press, 1992); Donal Cruise O'Brien, *Saints and Politicians: Essays in the Organisation of a Senegalese Peasant Society* (Cambridge: Cambridge University Press, 1975); Richard Roberts, *Warriors, Merchants and Slaves: The State and the Economy in the Middle Niger Valley, 1700–1914* (Stanford, CA: Stanford University Press, 1987); Anne Phillips, *The Enigma of Colonialism: British Policy in West Africa* (Bloomington: Indiana University Press, 1989).

42. Staudt and Parpart, eds., *Women and the State*, 4.

43. See Martin Chanock, "Making Customary Law: Men, Women, and Courts in Colonial Northern Rhodesia," in M. J. Hay and Marcia Wright, eds., *Women and the Law in Africa* (Boston: Boston University, 1982), 53–67; and Marjorie Mbilinyi, "This Is an Unforgettable Business: Colonial State Intervention in Urban Tanzania," in Parpart and Staudt, eds., *Women and the State*, 111–29. Also see Martin Chanock, *Law, Custom and Social Order: The Colonial Experience in Malawi and Zambia* (Cambridge: Cambridge University Press, 1985), and Elizabeth Schmidt, *Peasants, Traders and Wives: Shona Women in the History of Zimbabwe, 1870–1939* (Portsmouth, NH: Heinemann, 1992).

44. See, for example, Jean M. Allman, "Of 'Spinsters,' 'Concubines' and 'Wicked Women': Reflections on Gender and Social Change in Colonial Asante," *Gender & History* 3, 2 (1991): 176–89.

45. For example, see Nina Mba, *Nigerian Women Mobilized: Women's Political Activity in Southern Nigeria, 1900–1965* (Berkeley: University of California Press, 1982); and Susan Geiger, *TANU Women: Gender and Culture in the Making of Tanganyikan Nationalism, 1955–1965* (Portsmouth, NH: Heinemann, 1997).

46. Paul Tiyambe Zeleza, *Manufacturing African Studies and Crises* (Dakar: CODESRIA, 1997), 201.

47. Michel-Rolph Trouillot, *Silencing the Past: Power and the Production of History* (Boston: Beacon Press, 1995), 23.

48. Susan Geiger, "Women in Nationalist Struggle: Dar es Salaam's TANU Activists," *International Journal of African Historical Studies*, 20, 1: 1–26.

49. Interview with Betty Okuboyejo, 24 September 1988, Maryland, Lagos.

50. Richard Roberts offers an interesting suggestion for conceptualizing the silences that we encounter in oral testimony. His suggests that the silences are reflective of reversible social processes that did not leave an imprint on historical memory, in contrast to conclusive social changes that left a large imprint because of the dislocations they engendered. See Donald Moore and Richard Roberts, "Listening for Silences," *History in Africa* 17 (1990): 319–25, and Richard Roberts, "Reversible Social Processes, Historical Memory, and the Production of History," *History in Africa* 17 (1990): 341–49.

1

DRESS AND TEXTILE PRODUCTION IN NINETEENTH-CENTURY ABEOKUTA

In passing over the hills, some extensive and beautiful prospects presented themselves. We passed through several fine plantations of corn, yams, and cotton. . . .

(the king) wore a handsome damask cloth, thrown lightly over his shoulder, and a scarlet cloth cap with a blue tassel on the crown of it. . . .

every principal street seems . . . to be a market-place, in which native productions are exhibited for sale, such as rich cotton cloths, Moorish caps . . . reels of cotton.[1]

Circa 1830, refugees from the first wave of wars after the collapse of the Oyo empire established a new town, Abeokuta.[2] The Egba and Owu refugees who settled there created a vibrant economy that catapulted Abeokuta into a leading role in nineteenth-century Yoruba history. Like other Yoruba towns, Abeokuta was a town of farmers, traders, and craftspeople; it was also a town where cotton and textile products played important roles in the local economy.[3] The town's first European visitor, Thomas Birch Freeman, an English Methodist missionary, visited in 1842. The quotes at the beginning of this chapter, taken from Freeman's account of his trip, provide a tantalizing glimmer of the importance of cotton and textiles. They also demonstrate that local and imported cloths were integrated into the town's social and economic life.

This chapter has three main tasks. First, it examines the cultural and aesthetic values that defined the importance of cloth and dress. Visitors often commented on what Yoruba men and women wore. They described the shapes of garments, the colors, the quality of the cloths individuals wore, and the source of the fabrics—local or imported. These early descriptions help us to develop a more nuanced understanding of how European cloths became integral to Yoruba dress. The discussions about dress also illuminate the cultural frameworks and idioms Europeans and Africans used to assess, interpret, and make sense of their interactions.

Second, it utilizes data gathered from travelers' accounts as well as the diaries and letters of European and African missionaries who lived in Abeokuta during the nineteenth century to reconstruct its history of cloth production. Abeokuta's establishment and development were profoundly shaped by the Yoruba civil wars and the rise of "legitimate" trade that replaced the trade in people. The wars disrupted trade while "legitimate" trade encouraged exports of local products, including cotton, and imports of manufactured items such as cloth. Thus, the chapter's final task is to examine cloth production within the context of these developments and suggest ways in which they shaped the textile industry. By recasting Abeokuta's textile industry within the context of regional conflict and British commercial and cultural engagement, this chapter establishes a reference point from which we can appreciate developments in textile production and changes in dress in the twentieth century.

THE PHILOSOPHY OF DRESS

Dress, as Barnes and Eicher argue, is a comprehensive term for direct body changes, such as tattooing and hair styles, and items added to the body, such as clothing and jewelry.[4] Among the Yoruba, clothing and its accessories constitute the most important form of aesthetic expression.[5] Dress did not merely cover the body, it indicated one's gender, character, wealth and status, and it determined and negotiated social relationships. Yoruba popular thought often expressed the relationship between dress and social interaction, *"iri ni si ni isonilojo"*—one's appearance determines the degree of respect one receives.[6] The social importance of dress underscored the many ways in which dress conveyed Yoruba values, as the following poem demonstrates.

> Take care of your character, character is clothing, character is
> dress,
> For if we live long, long, long on earth, if we become too old to
> walk, the day we die, it is character that remains.[7]

Yoruba men and women expended considerable time and resources on
dress, since it recorded enduring statements about one's character and
station in life.

Yoruba aesthetics also appreciated freshness and improvisation;[8]
nonetheless, improvisation often took place inside parameters considered
to be "traditional." In Yoruba music, for example, popular music such as
juju incorporated new instruments but was still self-consciously traditional
in form, function, and feeling. Older forms of Yoruba music guided the
use of imported technology.[9] Dress and specifically clothing often reflected this drive toward freshness and improvisation as consumers purchased new cloths or weavers borrowed new weaving techniques. Visitors
to Abeokuta and other Yoruba towns in the nineteenth century recognized
the obvious importance of dress and recorded their observations in journal entries and travel accounts.

CLOTHING, CLOTH, AND SOCIAL CHANGE

Most visitors to Abeokuta and other Yoruba towns in the nineteenth
century gave very basic descriptions of what men and women wore. Sir
Richard Burton, the intrepid British explorer, wrote, for example

> people are tolerably well clothed. Dressy men wore *shogoto*, or loose
> cotton drawers fastened above the hips . . . and extending to the knee.
> The body was covered with a cloth gracefully thrown like a plaid over
> the shoulder.[10]

They also reported the socioeconomic distinctions that could be dis-
cerned from dress. Wealthy men wore a *tobe* (robe), an embroidered
"loose large garment, worn over the shoulders, and falling below the
knees."[11] While poor men often "dispensed with the *shogoto* and shoulder cloth retaining (only) the *diggo* or loin wrap."[12] Yet few wrote
with the astute observations recorded by William Clarke, an American
Baptist missionary, who visited Yorubaland between 1854 and 1858.
Clarke observed that Yoruba men and women took great pride in their
dress and exercised great care in the selection of styles and colors.[13]
It was clear to Clarke that Yoruba dress was not an undifferentiated

mass of cloth and accessories. Styles and colors had social meaning and significance.

Local observers such as Samuel Johnson, the nineteenth-century Yoruba historian, placed clothing styles in a historical context. Johnson argued that Yoruba clothing before the nineteenth century was very plain and purely of "native manufacture." Only the kings and chiefs wore gowns made of superior fabrics richly embroidered. In lieu of gowns, less wealthy men often wore a "sheet of cloth three yards by two" that was "wrapped around the body . . . passing under the right armpit and overlapping over the left shoulder."[14] Johnson's comments suggest that Yoruba dress was not static; it reflected changing historical circumstances.

In his discussion of Yoruba clothing during the nineteenth century, Johnson examined changing influences and styles. Men's apparel included gowns, vests that were worn under the gowns, and trousers. Johnson's discussion is especially significant because he provided details about the manufacture of these cloths as well as the consumers. The *kukumo* was a sleeveless vest without a collar and open in front. It was made of "any kind of native stuff, but that which [was] made of *alari* [crimson dye] or of *samayan* [local silk] [was] the most respectable [and] . . . the most costly."[15] Soldiers wore a sleeveless dress like the *kukumo*, which, according to Johnson, was smaller and simpler and worn with a turban wrapped around like a belt. The other vest, *ewu*, was "more commonly used in modern times." It was similar to the *kukumo*, "except that it had sleeves and was always made of white cloth." The third type, the *dandogo*, was pleated and reached the calves. This imported vest "was worn instead of the gown and only by big [wealthy] men."[16]

There were three types of gowns: *suliya, agbada,* and *girike.* The *suliya* was the smallest, plainest, and lightest and was always made of white material. The *agbada* was a larger form of the *suliya* that was always made of dyed or colored cloth. However, unlike the *suliya* that stopped at the knee, the *agbada* extended to the ankle and had a great deal of embroidery at the neck and breast. The *girike* was the largest and heaviest of the gowns. It was as ample as the *agbada*, ankle length, and heavily embroidered.

There were approximately eight types of pants (*sokoto*). Johnson asserts that the *ladugbo*, an ample pant, but somewhat tight at the knee where it ended, was the commonest. Young men and working men wore this pant; however, it eventually went out of fashion. The *aibopo*, which was loose but tightened toward the knee where it ended, "was worn by all classes." Johnson compared the *alongo* to "a bishop's gaiter," for it was tight throughout and reached below the knee. It was used chiefly by sportsmen. The *kafo* was similar to the *alongo*, but it extended to the ankle. Warriors and ruffians seemed to prefer this pant. The *kembe* was similar to the *aibopo*, but it had rich crimson embroidery around the legs. This pant was usually worn by wealthy men, such as nobles and gentlemen. The *efa* or *abenugbangba* resembled European trousers, but it was a very ample pant that stopped a little below the knee. The *wondo* was entirely like European trousers, but it too went out of style. The final type of *sokoto*, the *agadansi*, was adopted from the Nupe. This ankle-length pant was very wide, using two to three yards of cloth. It was very tight at the ankle and heavily embroidered. When the cord was drawn at the waist, "it gather(ed) into a large volume between the legs."[17] In addition to their gowns, vests, and pants, men often wore hats made from cloth or straw and turbans.

Women's apparel was much simpler than men's, consisting of two or three wrappers and a headdress. Women's clothing was not tailored and did not appear to involve the elaborate embroidery found on some men's pieces. Their undergarment, the *tobi*, a knee-length apron or petticoat, was tied around the waist with a strong cord or band. Girls began wearing the *tobi* at the onset of puberty. Art historian T.M. Akinwumi argues that unmarried women wore a wrapper, the *irobinrin*, and a small head scarf, the *idiku*, when they went out.[18] Johnson's description differs slightly; he claimed that unmarried women generally used two wrappers, but this may have been for more casual use. The under wrapper was usually a heavier cloth that women fixed above the breasts. A lighter cloth sufficed for the upper wrapper, which wrapped around the waist.[19] Married women used a third cloth, the *iborun*, as a shawl or as a covering for the head and back. The headdress, or *gele*, finished a woman's outfit. Either plain cloth or expensive material, such as velvet, constructed the *gele,* which measured 6–10 inches in width and 5 feet in length.[20] Elderly women had the exclusive right to another head scarf accessory known as the *ikaleri*. They used this to carry gifts presented to them.[21]

The importance of dress carried with it a commitment to being stylish and conscious of changing fashions. Clarke became aware of the importance of being in step with fashion when he visited an artist who was changing the pattern on several copper and brass rings. When asked why he was making these changes, the artist responded "*Obinrin* (a woman) says she wants it changed . . . it won't do now, too old."[22] Changes in fashion came from a variety of sources. Innovations in weaving and dyeing as well as the incorporation of new fabrics and garments created new styles. Yoruba men, for example, adopted the *agbada* gowns from the Hausa in the nineteenth century.[23]

New fashions reflected more than fickle trends. Fashion, as Braudel reminds us, is also a search for a new language through which each generation can repudiate its immediate predecessor and distinguish itself from it.[24] The languages represented by the variety of dress available in Abeokuta in the nineteenth century were not limited to an intergenerational dialogue. They spoke of economic opportunities and socioeconomic divisions as well as the formation of new social groups defined by their adherence to new gods and new values.

Among Abeokuta's Christian population, British styles were the norm. The earliest Christians, the Saros, were men and women liberated from the slave ships who initially settled in Sierra Leone, where they were introduced to British clothing, culture, and Christianity. The first set of Saros to arrive in Abeokuta in 1839 received permission to continue wearing European clothing.[25] Certain garments that formed the standard wardrobe of those in the mission stations became emblems of the new way of life. One such garment, singled out by an American Baptist minister, R.H. Stone, was a knee-length shirt that all boys in his mission station wore.[26]

Although certain clothes defined social groups such as religious communities, those garments did not always stay restricted to those communities. Their use became secularized and their social meaning broadened. Sarah Tucker, who wrote a history of early missionary work in Abeokuta, reported that "independently of any religious motive, some of the gay young men (of Abeokuta) affect the Mohamedan costume, and wear wide sack-like trowsers, much embroidered, and confined close around the ankle, with loose upper garment, and turban."[27] We can also see the adoption of tailored blouses or *buba*s by Yoruba women as one example of the ways in which fashion could prevail over ideology and take over a symbol that was politically potent.[28] Tailored shirts lost their status as markers of Christian convertion once women who practiced Islam and Yoruba religion also adopted them.

Dress communicated multiple layers of socioeconomic and religious information to observers. It also provided a framework through which observers interpreted those around them, although the social and cultural distance between observer and observed shaded and distorted their interpretation. For example, Reverend Stone argued that the knee-length shirts worn by the boys in his mission station were seen by all as "a badge of civilization."[29] Stone's comment reveals much more about his own assumptions and interpretations than those of the Yoruba observers. For Stone, the adoption of European clothes did more than identify one as a convert; it helped demarcate the boundary between "the civilized" and the "uncivilized."

Reading clothing for social and cultural meaning was not unique to Europeans. Yoruba men and women also applied their cultural idioms in an analysis of European dress and culture. When William Marsh, a Yoruba catechist for the Church Missionary Society (CMS), reunited with his family in Abeokuta, his European clothes drew quite a bit of attention.[30]

> one of my own sisters could not approach to me for many days because of my dress, which in some form resembles that of *Egungun*, the god who returns from the world of spirits and walks about Abbeokuta. Death is the punishment of any one who reveals the secret of "*Egungun*" to women, and the women are also to die. . . . My family begged me hard to put off my dress and not make myself a laughing stock. "I am not come to learn your custom," was the reply.[31]

The Marsh family's interpretation of William's dress requires some consideration. *Egungun* represented the ancestral spirits, but they were also the executioners of women accused of witchcraft. The dress of *Egungun* consisted of

> various colors or the feathers of different kinds of birds, or the skins of different animals. The whole body from head to foot is concealed from view; the *Egungun* seeing only from the meshes of a species of network covering the face.[32]

It is possible that William's European clothing reminded his sister of *Egungun* because it covered every part of his body (especially if he also wore a hat). William suggests that fear informed his sister's reluctance to meet him, and indeed it may have played a role since *Egungun* suggested danger for women. But the ridicule his dress also obviously invoked suggests that there were other factors in her response to his appearance.

It is possible that William's *Egungun*-like dress invited ridicule because of its inappropriateness for everyday wear. *Egungun*s appeared during funeral ceremonies,[33] during the annual festival to worship them—usually held in February after the bean harvest, and at the *Egungun* anniversary held in May or June.[34] Thus, William's European dress was not a sign of high culture to his family. Instead, it reflected ignorance of appropriate dress and composure and invited derision and social disgrace on all of them. William's reference to *Egungun* is also significant because the *Egungun* was one of two masquerades which came to specialize in satirizing the peculiarities of European colonialists. According to art historian Babatunde Lawal, Yorubas viewed European dress as ludicrous and "underdeveloped" and believed that men's clothing, in particular, suffocated the wearer because it did not let air circulate around the body like loose-fitting Yoruba clothing.[35]

Since dress was an important component of Yoruba aesthetics, the type of cloth used to construct one's outfit was equally important. The quality of the cloth indicated an individual's socioeconomic status and wealth because only those with sufficient wealth could acquire the finest cloths. Several factors defined a fine cloth: the quality of the weave, the type of thread—cotton or silk[36]—the novelty or workmanship of the design and the depth of color, especially of indigo-dyed cloths. Additional factors came into play when assessing a fine garment, such as the amount of fabric used as well as the fineness and heaviness of any embroidery.[37]

Sayings collected by Akinwumi dramatically illustrate the social significance given to different handwoven cloths.

Kijipa aso ole	*Kijipa,* a lazy man's cloth
Ofi aso agba	*Ofi,* an elder's cloth
Agba ti ko ba r'owo fi r'ofi ko ra kijipa	A poor elder incapable of possessing an *ofi* should buy *kijipa*
Nitoripe sanyan ni baba aso	Because *sanyan* is the best of textiles
Etu ni baba ewu	*Etu* is the father of garments
Alari lo ti le e	*Alari* is ranked next to it[38]

The wearer of any of these cloths clearly understood the statement that his or her dress expressed.

Dress was just one dimension of cloth's use in Yoruba society. Cloth played a crucial role in many social occasions and rituals. It was an important item in sealing social relationships such as marriage, and as Renne argues, an often underestimated item in the construction of individual and group identity.[39] Among the Bunu Yoruba, a small ethnic group west of the Niger River in the confluence area of central Nigeria, as a young woman went through the steps of marriage, each phase of the process required a particular marriage cloth. Only at the completion of the marriage ceremonies was she allowed to wear the ultimate marriage cloth called *adofi*, which served a function similar to that of the wedding band in marking her new status as a married woman.[40] The cloths involved in the marriage ceremonies were an integral part of the public acknowledgment of her new status and role as a wife.

Certain cloths played an important role in trade. In Yorubaland, the wives of the king of Oyo, the *Alafin*, had a special cloth that identified their goods on long trading trips. In describing one of these caravans, Richard and John Lander wrote "these royal ladies are distinguished from their countrywomen only by a peculiar species of cloth, which is wrapped round their goods and which no one dares to imitate on pain of perpetual slavery."[41] Punishment for imitation was severe because "the King's wives [paid] no tribute or turnpike dues whatever."[42]

Cloth, especially white cloth, was also an integral and necessary part of communication with the spirit world and deities.[43] Followers of the Yoruba god Obatala (Lord of the White Cloth) had to wear white clothing.[44] *Egungun* masquerades used *kijipa* cloths for their costumes. *Kijipa* also played an important role in rituals involving requests for various kinds of blessings.[45] Cloth was also an important component in the preparation of the body for burial and entrance into the spirit world. The types and quantity of cloth used in the burial ceremonies reaffirmed the social status and wealth of the individual during his or her time on earth. Joseph Wright, an Egba Yoruba who was freed from a slave ship about 1829 and later became a Wesleyan Methodist minister in Sierra Leone, provided a detailed description of a Yoruba chief's funeral.

> If the dead had been a man of fortune, he would be dressed by the Council. They would take all his valuable clothes and dress him carefully, with all costly apparel. The dress will make him about four feet high from the ground. Perhaps there could be twenty large pieces of costly cloth, besides those with which they lined the wall where the dead man lay. And then they would make a large coffin about five feet high and about four feet wide and properly dressed with all fine and costly cloths.[46]

The coffin would be carried about the town with thousands of people following, and when the family finally gave the signal for the body to be buried, "abundant apparel would be perfumed to line the bottom of the tomb and plenty of money would be laid at the bottom of the grave."[47]

Cloth was also a medium through which social obligations and relationships were reinforced. In Bunu, cloth was an integral part of
burials, and the community displayed specific cloths during the burials of chiefs. These were a group of five thick, red, hand-woven
cloths, called *aso ipo*, which, like the chiefs, were ranked. Four of
these cloths were woven by male and female weavers on the broad
loom historically considered the women's loom. Only men, however,
wove the highest grade cloth, the *aponuponyin*. Women could not see
the *aponuponyin*, and it had to be woven outside the village, since
Bunu society considered it extremely powerful and dangerous.[48] Renne
argues that the restrictions on the use and the production of these
cloths reflected ideas about the procreative and political powers of
Bunu men and women. The fact that only men could weave the most
potent of these red funeral cloths reinforced ideas about a hierarchy
of male and female titled chiefs headed by men.[49] Cloth also played
an extremely important role in political patronage. Gift giving, whether
at ceremonial occasions or informally, was an important mechanism
for cementing social and political alliances.

In many arenas cloth had symbolic and cultural value that exceeded
its material function. The demand for cloth on so many levels sustained
its production across Yorubaland. Certain cloths, however, possessed
greater importance than others by virtue of ritual significance, novelty,
cost, or embellishment. Yoruba communities recognized a hierarchy of
meaning and social capital in cloths, and one way of investing a cloth
with greater social capital was by dyeing it indigo.

THE VALUE OF INDIGO

In the *oriki* (appellations) to Akanni, an eighteenth century *Oba* (king)
of the town of Okuku, references to cloth and indigo were woven into
the imagery that attested to his wealth and greatness.

> Abioye, my father, Olugbola, one who takes
> the image and all its children to dance
> The beauty of cloth dyed in indigo does not fade
> Adewale, the indigo is what gives the cloth its worth[50]

Barber argued that this image of indigo-dyed cloth served as a metaphor for Akanni himself, suggesting that he was the best among cloths,
as well as the best among men.[51] The references also suggestively
point to the aesthetic value of indigo in Yoruba society. As the pas-

sage indicated, indigo bestowed enduring beauty on cloth. At one level, beauty, *ewa*, applied to "the manifestation of the well made or well done"; thus, well-dyed cloths possessed *ewa*.[52] Beauty and indigo were also symbolic on a more profound philosophical level. Indigo blue was emblematic of the Yoruba concept of *itutu* —"coolness," which according to one of Thompson's informants was "the correct way to represent oneself as a human being."[53] One was expected to maintain one's composure, dignity, the appropriate elegance and a look of dignified pride.[54] As a "cool" color, not too bright nor too dark, indigo correlated with the premium Yorubas placed on a "cool" or good character (*iwa*); and character, in Yoruba thought, determined beauty.[55] Thus, the indigo cloth image of Akanni also alluded to his character.

Indigo, as the *oriki* noted, added worth and value to cloth. Nineteenth-century Yorubas recognized at least four distinct shades of indigo, and cloths were valued in proportion to the darkness of the color. They ranged from *owududu*, the darkest, to *ofeefe*, the lightest.[56] Indigo dyed cloth, thus, functioned as a marker of status and wealth for the chiefs or wealthy men and women who could afford the most highly valued of these cloths.[57] Yet the color indigo alone did not impart value. Rather, it operated within a constellation of other factors, including the quality of the weave, the type of thread, the amount of fabric used, and the fineness and heaviness of any embroidery. Together, these elements constructed a representation of the status and wealth of the wearer.[58]

Indigo cloths also held broader collective meanings and served ritual purposes. In Bunu, indigo cloths were essential for performing the traditional marriage ceremony.[59] The indigo-saturated cloth was valued at marriages in part because of the association of indigo with fertility. Diviners took dregs from the bottom of the dye pot and ground them with other ingredients to make a medicine to counter infertility. Couples who desired children then ate this medicine mixed with ground guinea corn.[60] Indigo cloth marked not only conception; in some instances, it signified mourning. Ellis noted that women in mourning had to cover the head "with a cloth of a dark blue colour."[61]

Diviners also prescribed medicines for luck and success made from the water of exhausted indigo dye baths. One particular medicine for those who did not have money to begin trading included tobacco and indigo dye water. It was thought that "just as the dye can be obtained from the dyer, and just as the taking of, and desire for, snuff extends beyond the house of those directly concerned with its manufacture, so wealth may spread to the user of the medicine."[62] In addition, Yoruba medical practitioners thought indigo had the ability to kill germs, and they used the thick black refuse left over from the dyeing process in medicines created to treat diseases of the lower body such as gonor-rhea.[63]

Finally, indigo played important symbolic roles in Yoruba cosmology. During the ritual ceremonies through which devotees of Sango became a priest or bride of the deity, the devotee's shaved head was darkened with indigo paint.[64] Indigo was also associated with the deity *Eshu-Elegba*. Often *Elegba* is thought of simply as the trickster who causes confusion or brought about complicated situations.[65] However, his place within Yoruba cosmology was much more complex. Like *Ifa*, the deity of divination, *Eshu* assisted in the communication between the divine and the human realms, interceding on behalf of those who appealed to spiritual beings. He embodied the principles of life force, action, and individuality, and he reminded society of the unpredictable nature of human experience.[66] *Elegba*'s emblems were colored darkly with indigo and hung with white cowries that together symbolized his light and dark sides.[67]

Indigo and indigo-dyed cloth clearly functioned in multiple ways in Yoruba society and were deeply integrated into Yoruba secular, ritual, and aesthetic traditions. The preceding discussion demonstrates that indigo appeared at all stages of the life cycle. It prepared the way for marriage and conception, created possibilities for success, cured the body, and heralded the individual's departure from this life. Thus producers of indigo cloth satisfied needs and requirements in Yoruba society that went well beyond the material realm.

TEXTILE PRODUCTION IN ABEOKUTA

Textile production in nineteenth-century Abeokuta was a complex industry. It relied on the integrated activities of a wide network of producers—agricultural and craft, men, women, and children—in complementary and competing social relations. It is impossible to quantify the number of people involved in textile production and related activities. Nonetheless, nineteenth century observers give us valuable impressionistic data about the enormous cross section of people involved directly and indirectly in cloth production, its division of labor, and the quantity of output. These descriptions often indicate that tasks were gender-specific, and scholars have tended to view specialized professions and crafts as adhering to rigidly gendered social and ideological planes.[68] Yet even in occupations considered all male or all female one could find examples of women and men, respectively, who participated.[69] Each particular correlation between gender and occupation must be understood as a historically specific outcome of social and economic processes and ideological construction and change.[70]

When Richard Burton visited Abeokuta in 1861, he noted that the Egba practiced five great crafts—blacksmithing, carpentry, weaving, pottery, and dyeing.[71] His description also indicated that these industries were vertically integrated into the local economy. Abeokuta, like many other Yoruba towns, could rely on the local or regional economy to obtain the necessary resources for cloth production. Men were the main cultivators in Yoruba societies, though women visited or lived on the farms with their husbands and assisted with harvesting, processing, and transporting goods.[72] Egba farmers produced cotton that was in considerable demand in the local markets.[73] They also produced substantial amounts of indigo. We do not have descriptions of indigo plantations in Abeokuta, such as the ones Clapperton saw in Oyo in the 1820s.[74] Nonetheless, Burton observed that Abeokuta not only produced sufficient indigo for local use, farmers generated a surplus for export as well. He reported that Abeokuta exported indigo balls weighing approximately one-quarter pound that cost $2^1/_2$ strings of cowries, about $2^1/_2$ pence.[75]

Women spun the cotton into thread. It was one of the numerous tasks that punctuated a woman's day. During his first visit to Abeokuta, Reverend R.H. Stone noticed that women spun thread at night "by the light of their little bowl-lamps . . . and before morning."[76] The nineteenth-century Yoruba historian Samuel Johnson specified that the ginning, carding, and spinning of thread were performed by "women of advanced ages,"[77] however, the demand for thread required the participation of a larger pool of women.

It appears that several distribution systems existed in order to ensure a steady and adequate supply of thread for weaving and dyeing. Ojo found that in Owo, Ekiti, and parts of Oyo families practiced a system similar to the rotational credit societies, the *esusu*. All the women in an extended family contributed a definite length of yarn every market day or at other regular intervals of time. The subscribed yarn was given to one member at a time, in rotation.[78] In Iseyin, a major weaving center, women of the household were largely responsible for producing sufficient thread for the male weavers of their household. In fact, male weavers often married women from other weaving households, since these women could spin or dye and assist their husbands.[79] The nineteenth-century sources indicate that in

Abeokuta the market supplemented household production, since some weavers and dyers also purchased thread that was wound into yarn balls.[80]

Like spinning, dyeing was primarily a women's occupation.[81] It was practiced across Yorubaland, from Lagos to Ilorin,[82] in establishments of various sizes.[83] In nineteenth-century Abeokuta, dyeing occurred in many parts of town. The African-American visitor Martin Delany reported that "dyeing is carried on very generally, every woman seeming to understand it as almost a domestic necessity."[84] In Wasimi, the village of new Christians, Burton saw a number of large mortars that would have been used to pound indigo leaves. This suggested that indigo dyeing was one of the principal industries in the village.[85] By all indications, a significant number of women practiced dyeing; specialists evolved nonetheless. Existing information, however, does not allow us to reconstruct the evolution of specialization in dyeing.[86]

Burton noticed that dyers colored threads and cloths, "with every tinge from the lightest blue to what closely approaches black."[87] Indigo is a vat dye and not a direct dye. As a result, the color can be attained only through a combination of fermentation and oxidation. Dyers in the nineteenth century used a process that in its main features continued to be used by dyers in the early decades of the twentieth century. Robert Campbell, Martin Delany's travel companion, described the major features of the process:

> The beautiful blue, almost purple dye of their cloths is not from the common indigo-plant of the East and West-Indies, but from a large climbing plant. The leaves and shoots are gathered while young and tender. They are then crushed in wooden mortars, and the pulp made up in balls and dried. For dyeing, a few of these balls are placed in a strong lye made from ashes, and suffered to remain until the water becomes offensive from the decomposition of vegetable matter.[88]

Fermentation in an alkaline solution, speeded up by occasional stirring, chemically broke down indigo into its soluble form. Oxidation completed the process, and each time a dyer dipped a cloth or threads in the dye bath and dried the material, the blue color deepened. The quantity of indigo used also determined the depth of color. A very dark blue that virtually looked black required as many as 150 indigo balls.[89]

The ingredients necessary to make the dye bath were found locally. Women procured the indigo leaves from farmers or others selling them and made indigo balls;[90] they could also purchase the dried indigo balls.

The alkaline solution, *aluba*, was made from a mixture of water and wood ashes. These ashes came from local wood used for cooking fires or from the market. Some dyers also experimented with lobster shells to make the alkaline solution.[91]

It is also clear that dyeing relied on several other crafts. Carvers, mostly men, made the wooden mortars in which indigo leaves were pounded, and potters made the large open-necked clay pots dyers preferred.[92] Indeed, pottery, which was practiced by women, was another important craft in Abeokuta. Delany wrote, "crockery ware is manufactured very extensively, of almost every conceivable size and kind of vessel, for various purposes."[93]

In spite of the extensive use of indigo, dyeing was still a secondary part of the larger process of textile production. Weavers were at the apex of textile production. Both men and women wove, though men predominated in some towns and women in some others.[94] Women primarily used vertical looms that produced cloths averaging 21 inches in width. Men, using horizontal narrow looms, produced cloths averaging $4^1/_2$ inches in width. Some cloths, especially some of those for ritual use, were woven exclusively by men or by women. For example, the black marriage cloths worn by Bunu brides, *adofi*, were either woven by the bride or commissioned from another woman.[95] In general, however, both men and women produced a variety of cloths that differed in quality, design, and social significance. They ranged from *kijipa*, a coarse cloth produced on a broad loom that was generally associated with the poor, to *etu*, a prestige cloth that belonged to a category of cloths distinguished by colored patterns that were woven into the cloth.[96]

Finished cloths were tailored into ready-made clothing—such as trousers, breeches, caps, and shirts—that could be commissioned or bought in the market.[97] The tailors who made most of these garments were highly skilled craftsmen. Tailors, it has been suggested, were like sculptors, particularly in their construction of heavy gowns.[98] Most writers described tailoring as a male occupation. Clarke, for example, emphatically stated "the females never cut or sew garments"; but Johnson wrote that some women had taken up tailoring as a result of exposure to other cultures.[99] Johnson's observations suggest that the cultural prescriptions that protected tailoring as a male-specific occupation were dissolving in the nineteenth century. Indeed, women in Abeokuta had begun to sew men's breeches and caps. Women's tailoring of men's clothing became a major dispute, and in 1853 *Oro*, the spiritual figure who relayed the decisions of the senior governing council, the *Ogboni*, prohibited women from "all further interference with the making of men's breeches and caps."[100] The use of *Oro* to convey this message indicated the serious threat posed, or accomplished, by women's inroads into tailoring. The majority of tailors were men, but their predominance in this occupation was not, as Johnson maintained, a consequence of the fact that only men's dress required tailoring.[101] Political institutions in Abeokuta were mobilized to protect tailoring as a male occupational niche.

This overview shows evidence that textile production abounded all around nineteenth-century Abeokuta. The new town had access to all the relevant natural and manufactured resources to produce textiles, thus from its earliest existence cloth production played an important role in its economy. "Legitimate" trade held major implications for textile production, since British interests hoped to export cotton from Abeokuta.

COTTON, PALM OIL, AND MISSIONARY DREAMS

Palm oil was probably the most important export commodity from West Africa after the abolition of the British slave trade. Palm oil had many applications in Britain, where it was used as a lubricant for machinery and railway stock, in the manufacture of soap and candles, as a source for glycerine, and in the processing of tinplate.[102] In this new economic era contemporaries called "legitimate" trade, Abeokuta specifically and Yorubaland in general produced and exported substantial quantities of palm oil.[103] The introduction of steamship service between Britain and West Africa during the 1850s led to a dramatic expansion of trade and encouraged Yoruba traders and producers to intensify their involvement in palm oil production.[104]

Europeans also took note of other potentially viable exports such as cotton, indigo, yams, hides, sugar, tobacco, and shea butter.[105] Visitors to Abeokuta often highlighted cotton and indigo, but cotton by far consumed the major share of their attention. Due to several overlapping developments including the need for inexpensive cotton by British cotton mills, Abeokuta became the focal point of attention for early discussions around cotton production in the nineteenth century. The town's initial receptivity to the liberated Africans returning from Sierra Leone, the Saros, and missionaries contributed significantly to this attention. Henry Townsend of the Church Missionary Society (CMS) visited soon after Freeman, and Townsend's favorable report convinced the CMS to establish a station in Abeokuta rather than in Lagos.

When Townsend returned to Abeokuta in 1846 with a group of settlers, he received a warm reception.[106] Egba chiefs foresaw potential political and economic benefits, especially in regional politics, from having these Christian settlers in their midst. Tucker reported that the chiefs were especially proud of the honor of Abeokuta being the first town in which white people intended to reside and exclaimed that "the news of their arrival . . . would fly from Lagos to Ilorin, and excite the envy of all the chiefs."[107] She failed to note the chiefs' political motives in the history she prepared for broader British consumption. Abeokuta was "sunrise within the tropics"—the point from which the light of Christianity and civilization would take root and shine into the darkness that otherwise shrouded the continent, a "universal den of desolation, misery and crime."[108]

Missionary activity in Abeokuta had a strong economic component from its inception. For Thomas J. Bowen, the Southern Baptist missionary who worked in Yorubaland from 1849 to 1856, the missionary program in Africa was "summed up in one word—civilization."[109] In his estimation, the only work for missionaries was the preaching of the gospel, but commerce with Christian countries provided the greatest means of extending the gospel. Bowen's beliefs echoed those of T.F. Buxton, a leader in the British abolitionist movement who advocated marrying evangelical and abolitionist concerns with commerce. They anticipated that "legitimate" trade would bring an end to the trade in enslaved Africans and begin the process of developing a middle class in West Africa that would support Christian values.[110]

Cotton appeared to be the ideal crop on which these endeavors could be pinned. Missionary interest in cotton dovetailed with industrial considerations. By the nineteenth century, British commercial interests needed to identify new supplies of cotton and new markets.[111] Despite population increases in Britain and its corresponding rise in consumption, the technological advances in both spinning and weaving created a context in which productive capacity outstripped demand. Consequently, the industry was dependent on exporting, and cheap cotton goods predominated among the cloths exported to Europe, North America, and India.[112] Since the export market specialized in cheap cloth, manufacturers in Britain had to simultaneously keep the cost of raw cotton as low as possible and find new markets for their products. Spinners who supplied thread to weavers were the producers most enmeshed in this dilemma, since increases in the price of raw cotton could not be passed on easily to consumers. Thus, spinners were the driving force behind the search for alternative sources of cotton.[113]

There was a clear overlap in the British commercial and missionary communities regarding the economic objectives that could be pursued in West Africa. Several textile manufacturers, most prominently Thomas Clegg, a Manchester cotton spinner, sought to combine their abolitionist concerns with their commercial interests.[114] This ideological overlap materialized in concrete form in Abeokuta when Clegg joined forces with Henry Venn. Venn, the secretary of the CMS, was a leading advocate of legitimate trade and sought to implement Buxton's ideas through a program of "native agency." The program attempted to create a class of African traders, teachers and farmers who would be the main support of their own African-led church. Venn also believed that West African cotton could replace the cotton grown by enslaved labor in the United States, transform African social relations, and end slavery within Africa. Furthermore, Venn viewed the Saros as the principal agents of this social and economic transformation.[115]

In 1856 Venn and Clegg created the Industrial Institution in Abeokuta. The institution was to be both a training center for this emerging middle class and a commercial center. The institution taught brickmaking, carpentry, and dyeing; it also received and prepared the cotton for export to England.[116] Two young men managed the institution, Samuel Crowther, Jr., the son of a Saro missionary, and Henry Robbin, a young Saro who had been sent to Clegg's factory for training. The two managers worked full-time for the institution for a salary of £50 per year and did a certain amount of trading on their own. Clegg used the profits from the sale of cotton in England to purchase machinery and cotton piece goods and to cover his commission. It was anticipated that the profits from the piece goods, which were quite popular, would be put back into the institution to pay the wages of both the managers and the laborers. The profits would also be applied to the institution's training programs and missionary expenditures.[117] The "Native Agency" program tied missionary work and African social change to the commercial prospects of cotton exports and cloth imports.

In spite of their shared desire to develop cotton for the international market, Venn and Clegg did not share long-term goals. Clegg sought a new site of cotton production and was not concerned with the specifics of production, while Venn wanted production of this crop to engender social reform. Clegg, for example, extended credit to the young men he trained as buying agents. Venn was very opposed to credit because he felt it helped maintain slavery and inhibited social transformation.[118] Financial disputes also arose between Venn and Clegg.[119] By 1863 the missionaries abandoned their commercial involvement in cotton, and that aspect of the institution was absorbed by Clegg's West Africa Company. Nonetheless, the changes begun under this joint missionary and commercial initiative sank deep roots in Abeokuta and their impact would be experienced across the town's economic and social spectrum by cloth producers, men and women, enslaved and free.

SOCIAL AND ECONOMIC CONSEQUENCES OF "LEGITIMATE" TRADE

Missionary effort to promote agriculture for export initially produced remarkable results, for it coincided with Egba expansion into new farmlands. As a result of military insecurity up through the 1840s, Egba farms remained confined within a few miles south of the town's walls, but farms grew rapidly beyond the walls after 1850. The defeat of Dahomey in 1851 gave Egba farmers the confidence to begin expanding production into those territories to the south and southeast that earlier had been conquered in order to safeguard trade routes to Lagos.[120] With this expansion, a greater number of war chiefs in particular began to turn their attention to farming for export.[121]

Abeokuta cotton began to sell on the Manchester exchange in 1853.[122] Samuel Crowther, Sr., a Yoruba missionary, was put in charge of the CMS's cotton project, and his wife oversaw the buying of the cotton for the CMS in the early days. They paid 1d. per pound for cleaner seed cotton and $^3/_4$d. for lots that required a great deal of picking. When cotton required cleaning, women employed by the CMS performed the task. Samuel Crowther, Jr., who took over the operation from his father in 1854, noted that they did not pay the lower rate regularly because much of the cotton was brought in clean.[123] The cleaned cotton was then ginned and pressed into bales that weighed between 112 and 125 pounds. Richard Burton noted that Wasimi, the village of new Christians, had cotton gins and seven presses which, on average, produced 16 bales of cotton daily. Male and female carriers transported the bales from Ake to the Aro gate and beyond to Aro port on the Ogun river, a distance of approximately five miles.[124] At the Aro gate a "toll of $3^1/_2$% on the first cost of goods" was collected by the Egba trade chiefs, the *Parakoyi*.[125] From the port on the Ogun River the bales traveled by canoe to Lagos, where they were stored on the CMS wharf until they could be transported on an available steamship to Liverpool.

In the early years of cotton export from Abeokuta, only six to seven bales were sent out at a time.[126] In spite of the difficulties of transportation, cotton production continued to increase significantly, particularly as the price of cotton rose throughout the 1850s, reaching an average of 7¹/₄d. per pound in 1857.[127] Cotton which was once considered a "poor man's crop" increased in popularity as missionaries promoted its production and export and as prices improved.[128] Samuel Crowther, Jr., attested to the fact that "the cotton trade seems to have taken good hold on the minds of the chiefs and people."[129] By 1856, Abeokuta chiefs and farmers delivered more than three tons of clean, ginned cotton to the Industrial Institution.[130] Large-scale producers were sending thousands of pounds of cotton at a time. For example, Chief Ogubonna, a prominent military chief, sent 1,012 pounds of clean cotton to Mr. Clegg on one occasion, while Madam Tinubu, one of the wealthiest women traders and holder of the highest women's title, *Iyalode*, sent 3,000 pounds.[131]

The CMS's cotton venture allowed small farmers to take advantage of this emerging export market; however, the greatest beneficiaries were chiefs and traders. Cotton export reinforced socioeconomic divisions in Abeokuta. Chief Ogubonna, in particular, exemplified this relationship between cotton, wealth, and status. He held an important military title, the *Balogun of Ikija*, held extensive farmlands, owned many slaves, and was very interested in pursuing "legitimate" trade. When the British consul, John Beecroft, visited Abeokuta in 1851, Ogubonna presented him with "a load of cotton, a bag of ginger and a bag of pepper as specimens of the produce of the country and their desire to trade."[132] As a result of his influence and strong support of commerce with Europe, Ogubonna received most of the foreign visitors to Abeokuta. He kept the presents given to him by foreigners in a room in his house that resembled a small museum.[133] Ogubonna valued his economic and social relations with missionaries and relished the access they provided to imported items. He felt that England was at his disposal as a result of his engagement in cotton work; "he could order anything in England and get it without doubt," from French lamps to custom-made garments.[134] The strength of Ogubonna's relationship with Europeans was reflected in one of his appellations, *Agboke-t'oyinbo*, a man of elegant manners like a European. He earned this appellation because he imitated Europeans so much.[135]

Ogubonna exercised a substantial degree of political influence and power in Abeokuta. It was not uncommon for visitors to refer to him as "His Highness" even though he was not an *Oba* (king).[136] Ogubonna's influence exemplified the nature of politics in nineteenth-century Abeokuta and reflected the ways in which those with military power and large investments in "legitimate" trade could dominate the political land-scape.

Contrary to missionary hopes, cotton production did not undermine sla-very. In fact, it had the opposite result. Intensified agriculture increased the use of enslaved labor by traders and producers, including Christians.[137] Henry Townsend acknowledged that even missionaries used slave labor.[138] The investment in slave labor was so significant that James Johnson, a Yoruba CMS missionary, argued that "to say that Egbas Christian or hea-thens, should not buy slaves any more and use their services was equal to one undertaking to prevent the circulation of silver currency at Lagos."[139]

Enslaved men and women worked in agriculture and both local and long-distance trade. Some worked for themselves and gave their own-ers an agreed-upon fee. Betsy Desola, for example, a member of the Ake congregation of the CMS, demanded and received 15 strings of cowries (approximately $3^1/_2$ p.) daily from each of her slaves who worked on their own account. Annually she received about £2/10s. from each of these slaves.[140] From the profits of their trades, some slaves purchased their freedom. Such was the case of Amelia Taylor, who had adopted Christianity. After much saving she was able to pur-chase her freedom as well as her son's.[141] Slaves were definitely an important source of labor, but the fact that they could be exchanged for goods or money enhanced their value. All captives from the wars were put to work or sold to slave dealers, if they were not redeemed by their countrymen.[142] Nonetheless, owners' willingness to allow cap-tives to be redeemed varied. British officials in Lagos noticed that owners were often unwilling to allow female slaves to redeem them-selves.[143]

Although the population of those enslaved increased, it does not ap-pear that Abeokuta became a slave-dominated society. Contemporary es-timates suggested that between one-fifth and one-third of the population was enslaved.[144] They concurred that the free population in Abeokuta sig-nificantly outnumbered the slave population, in contrast to Ibadan, where those enslaved outnumbered freeborn. Slightly more than one-half of Ibadan's population were enslaved.[145]

Agricultural intensification also led to an expansion of and increase in the number of great households with many dependents. The proliferation of these households was a distinct feature of nineteenth-century Yorubaland, because formerly such large households had been associated only with the Yoruba aristocracy and nobility. These great households, some containing upwards of 500 people, belonged primarily to military chiefs and large entrepreneurs who commanded their own private armies.[146] They comprised lineage members, clients, and large numbers of slaves. The male heads of great households tended to have a great many wives. Shodeke, the military chief who led the displaced Egba to Abeokuta, supposedly had 600 wives,[147] Chief Ogubonna was said to have had 95 wives,[148] and the *Sagbua*, Okukenu, a senior *Ogboni* or civil chief, had 50.[149]

WOMEN AND LEGITIMATE TRADE

"Legitimate" trade had complex and sometimes contradictory consequences for Yoruba women. It expanded opportunities for wealthy and powerful military leaders to create large households with dependent and enslaved women. Nonetheless, women also played a significant role in "legitimate" trade because of their extensive participation in the economy. They were the primary producers of palm oil; they cleaned and spun cotton and dyed cloth; they were porters and traders. Thus, they helped to create and convey the town's primary exports. They also distributed and consumed its imports. Women participated from various social locations in this circuit of production and distribution. Some were enslaved while some were slaveholders. "Legitimate" trade reinforced some women's economic independence yet intensified the desire for enslaved women and created opportunities for enslaved women to regain their freedom.

Women's socioeconomic independence was admirable to some but also a point of concern for missionaries, who were trying to create a middle class that was monogamous and reflected European patriarchal ideals. To Thomas Bowen, Yoruba families lacked unity, and every wife was a free dealer who had her own property and supported her own children.[150] Bowen's call for "family unity" was a critique of women's autonomy, for his notion of family unity was embedded in an idealized male-centered and male-dominated household. Commerce, which he saw as the answer to the slave trade, was also the answer to this problem of women's autonomy.

> The increase of wealth, knowledge, refinement of feeling, and respect for family, which would result from commerce, would operate with other causes to revolutionize the present relations of husband and parent and child, and . . . would remove another or the last support of polygamy.[151]

Commerce would end polygyny, privilege monogamy, and domesticate wives.[152]

Christian households were expected to be role models, but Egba Christians did not live up to missionary expectations. James Johnson expressed his disapproval of the wife of one of the town's Egba pastors, Mrs. Allen, who did little to identify with her husband and the work of the church. She

> scarcely resides in her station . . . sometimes sleeping there only at nights or other times spending only a few hours on Sundays out of a whole week. She resides chiefly at Iporo township, where they have a house of their own, where she does her own business . . . and has her own slaves.[153]

Rather than following the examples of missionary households, where wives fully supported their husbands' work for the church, Mrs. Allen lived like a Yoruba wife.[154]

Missionary concern with household relations informed their preoccupation with cotton. Ideally, cotton production was to occur within the context of a monogamous peasant household, and its processing and trade would lead to the development of a middle class. In contrast to their hopes for cotton, missionaries condemned the palm-oil trade because it did not lead to the emergence of a middle class and left African society unchanged.[155] Furthermore, the palm-oil trade did not offer the possibility of transforming gender relations in the direction that missionaries desired because it was produced by women. Men played only a small role in its production, cutting down the palm fruit from the trees. Women did all the processing in individual and collective settings.[156] Women were the primary retail traders of palm oil in the local markets, though both men and women organized large-scale long-distance trading enterprises.

The division of labor in palm-oil production did not put men at its center in the way that cotton production did and therefore did not conform to the patriarchal relations missionaries hoped to instill. Palm-oil production and trade reinforced women's economic independence and autonomy and did so for a broader cross section of women than cotton allowed. Many enslaved women redeemed themselves and their children with their profits from palm oil.[157] Palm oil, which was the primary export during the era of "legitimate" trade, reinforced Yoruba gender ideology, which expected women to work, keep their profits, and support their children's daily upkeep.

Despite the prevailing Yoruba gender ideology, Yoruba men did not celebrate women's commercial success either. Women's economic position created tensions within Abeokuta, and within Yoruba society more generally. Law argues that these tensions were reflected in the ways in which women were more or less taxed by male masquerades. *Egungun* masquerades, which represented ancestral spirits, were used to secure money from women.[158] According to Johnson, *Egungun* festivals were "a lucky time for men," since women were obliged to pay for the feasts, but the food was consumed by the men.[159] *Egungun* was also used to reassert male authority. When a wife was uncontrollable, the husband could call on *Egungun* for assistance, and "if she dares resist, Egungun gives her a drubbing not soon to be forgotten and takes his exit with the thanks of the victorious husband."[160] In the process, *Egungun* reasserted the husband's authority and invested it with ancestral validation. As Law suggests, it is quite possible that *Egungun* was exploited by some men to cope with changes in gender relations that resulted from "legitimate" trade.[161] While "legitimate" trade contributed to expanding economic opportunities for women, those opportunities were challenged by old and new social prescriptions.

"LEGITIMATE" TRADE AND TEXTILE PRODUCTION

"Legitimate" trade affected every fiber of Yoruba society, and textile production was no exception. Statistical data document substantial increases in the volume of imported cloth. Inikori has argued that these data offer strong evidence to support the deindustrialization paradigm in the case of West African cotton textiles. In the face of import levels, cotton textile production must have been severely undermined, as was the case in India.[162] Imports had economic and social consequences on local textile industries but contemporary sources are too fragmentary to give us detailed information on how different textile sectors grew and evolved during the era of "legitimate" trade. Nonetheless, we can still identify important trends.

For most of the nineteenth century, weavers and dyers in Abeokuta primarily relied on the local economy for their resources. It does not appear that commercial cotton production in Abeokuta undermined the local textile industry, because cotton producers increased production and their surplus in order to compete in the international economy. Delany, Campbell, Stone, and Burton were in Abeokuta toward the end of this high point in cotton export, 1859–61, and their accounts clearly document a vibrant local industry.

Commercial cotton production benefited from the ongoing Yoruba civil wars, which did not end until 1892. These conflicts produced numerous captives as well as *iwofas*, persons in debt bondage, whose labor could be invested in both agriculture and commerce.[163] It is likely that cloth producers and other manufacturers also benefited from those displaced or enslaved during the conflicts. We do not have corroborating data from the mid-nineteenth century, but oral data collected from dyers indicate that some dyers used enslaved labor. One such example was Madam Jojolola, who succeeded Madame Tinubu as *Iyalode* and held the office until 1932. Jojolola was a very diversified entrepreneur, like her predecessor. She had farms, traded agricultural goods, and was a dyer. She also had numerous slaves who assisted her in all parts of her operation.[164] Her story suggests that the civil wars and "legitimate" trade intersected for cloth producers. Whether the producer concentrated entirely on cloth production or had diversified interests, the civil wars and "legitimate" trade gave textile producers access to labor and new markets.

The wars as well as trade also contributed to the diffusion of weaving techniques and designs. Many towns were destroyed during the ongoing conflicts, leading to large-scale migrations. As refugees established new towns or settled into existing towns, they adopted and added weaving techniques. After the destruction of Oyo, for example, many weavers migrated to Iseyin. These migrant weavers disseminated certain designs. Brocade was one of the designs whose diffusion during the nineteenth century is best documented. Before the nineteenth century, only weavers in Oyo and Ijebu produced brocade designs. Migrating Oyo weavers taught weavers in Abeokuta and other Yoruba towns to produce brocade designs on the treadle loom. Egba weavers also copied the Ijebu method of producing brocade on the broad-loom.[165]

Even though many textile producers may not have benefited directly from "legitimate" trade, they stood to benefit indirectly, since wealth was often invested in textiles and in locally produced prestige cloths. Locally produced cloth still played a vitally important role in Yoruba social and cultural life. Travelers' accounts of local production across the region attest to the high demand for resources to produce cloths as well as finished clothes. Some towns produced such a substantial volume of cloth that they attracted traders from across Yorubaland. Iseyin, in addition to being a major weaving center, also conducted a significant trade in indigo. Ijaye, another town extensively engaged in manufacturing cloth, bought a substantial amount of their indigo from Iseyin. Ila was another major center of cloth production, and traders from other Yoruba towns flocked to its markets as the following quote illustrates:[166]

The cultivation of [cotton] is so extensive or so exclusive and the manufacturing department on such a large scale—comparatively speaking—
the traders from Ijesa, Ilorin, Yoruba and Abeokuta flock to Ila for the
purchasing of cheap cloths.[167]

Abeokuta had a vibrant textile industry: it traded indigo locally and
exported indigo-dyed cloth to Brazil; yet it was not considered one of the
dominant centers. Abeokuta was "largely engaged in the palm oil and
cotton trade."[168] Still, our information on textile production is impressionistic and it remains difficult to quantify to any reliable degree how
local cloth production increased or decreased over the century.

In spite of the amount of cloth produced locally and regionally,
Yoruba towns also imported cloths from other parts of the world.[169]
As "legitimate" trade enhanced the social and economic position of
large traders and producers, it gave them access to new levels of consumption. One of the most desired items was imported cloth, since it
was a highly valued symbol of wealth in Yoruba culture.[170] Samuel
Crowther, Jr., reported that the *Alake* and chiefs asked him to recom-
mend merchants in England to whom they could send cotton in exchange for cloths.[171]

The price of British cloths fell over the course of the century, and
as a result a much wider cross section of West Africans were able to
purchase inexpensive imported fabrics. Manchester cloths, calico, and
shirting, as well as velvets, were seen in the markets in many towns.
By mid century Abeokuta was an important commercial center for the
distribution of imported cloth.[172] Convoys of Lagos traders would ren-
dezvous with traders from Abeokuta exchanging imported cloth for
local cloth as well as other items. William Marsh, the CMS cathecist,
captured one of these scenes. Setting out from Lagos to Abeokuta for
the anticipated reunion with his family, Marsh traveled by canoe to
Isheri, where

The Abeokuta people and people of Lagos meet for the purpose of
trading. . . . More than 400 small canoes from Abeokuta were there
and about 100 large ones from Lagos, these generally bring rum,
European cloth, beads, cowries and other sorts of articles. Those
from Abeokuta slaves, country cloth, Indian corn, yams and other
sorts.[173]

From Abeokuta, traders in large caravans took goods "to all parts of the
surrounding countries even as far as Ilorin and Sokoto."[174] In spite of the
conflicts and wars that characterized much of the nineteenth century, trad-

ers traveling in large caravans continued to move goods from the coast to the interior and vice versa.[175]

A substantial volume of British cloth was imported into West Africa in general in the first half of the nineteenth century. The amount of cotton, calicoes, and prints imported from the U.K. increased from 355,077 yards in 1820 to 16,929,026 yards in 1850.[176] Lower cost to a certain degree accounted for the popularity of these particular cloths. The price of calicoes and prints fell from $10\frac{1}{2}$d. and 1s./2d. per yard in 1817 to $3\frac{1}{2}$d. per yard in 1850.[177] They were cheaper in both price and quality than the locally woven cloth. Yoruba cloths were much more durable than the Manchester prints, and hence "the native cloths are by far the more costly."[178] To extend the life of these imports, whose colors faded quickly, dyers often redyed them for clients.[179]

Despite the rise in imports, as late as 1889 the governor of Lagos, Alfred Moloney, suggested that a substantial amount of cloth was being produced in West Africa. British officials had very little idea of how much cloth was actually produced by West African weavers. In a presentation to the mayor of Manchester and the chamber of commerce, Moloney gave his impression of indigenous textile production as part of an effort to excite the chamber about the potential of the African market.

> I may first remind you than an important, and indeed extensive, cotton native industry, both in the raw and manufactured form, proceeds along West Africa in the Wolof, Mandingo, Tehi, Ewe, and Yoruba countries—that the export of the raw product gives no idea of the industry. But when we remember the millions of cloths turned out annually for their home consumption, of which little is generally known, we must recognize with appreciation the active industry of the natives in this one growth alone, and begin to consider, in these days of keen commercial competition for Africa's markets, whether Lancashire cannot replace this industry, and be thus the means to let loose the native energy confined thereto for more extended agricultural pursuits, of such moment to that continent, and indeed to us.[180]

It's clear that Moloney thought African textile producers still had the upper hand in this contest for African consumers. He also showed that the volume of imports did not proceed on a steadily increasing trajectory. In the five-year period 1884–88, the value of imported manufactures declined steeply between 1884 and 1886 and then rebounded in 1887 and 1888.[181] In this instance, international developments no doubt contributed to the fluctuations that Moloney noted. By the 1880s trade became increasingly difficult as a result of the fall in palm oil prices and a more generalized depression in international trade. Lagos palm oil prices fell from £40 a ton in 1851 to £30 a ton in 1881 and pulled down consumer purchasing power in its wake.[182]

Local economic and political conflicts also hampered trade. Traditionally, cloth sold in Lagos was arranged in thirty folds, with each fold representing one yard. By 1891 the folds had become so narrow that thirty folds measured only fifteen yards.[183] On numerous occasions African traders and states protested these practices by closing the trade routes. The trade routes were also closed in response to the Kiriji War that erupted in 1877, the last and longest episode of the Yoruba civil wars. Abeokuta participated in many road closures, though the town was not directly involved in much of the fighting.[184] Closure of the trade routes meant that while imported goods were trapped in Lagos, production and local trade of indigenous cloths continued. In the interest of trade, Governor Moloney, with the assistance of Reverends Samuel Johnson and Charles Phillips, succeeded in bringing the main combatants together to sign a peace treaty only after the war reached a stalemate in 1886.[185] This military conflict most likely played a role in the decline in imports between 1884 and 1886. The Lagos government's expanding political role would in time end these local obstacles to trade and facilitate the exponential growth in the volume of cloth imports.

Scholars working with the deindustrialization paradigm assume a mechanical transfer of taste and preference to imported cloth. The documentary evidence from the nineteenth century demonstrates that the process was much more complex. Multiple spaces were created for imported cloths in the existing ideals and philosophy of dress. Without abandoning a desire for indigenous textiles, consumers incorporated British cloths into the Yoruba panoply of cloths. Velvet, damask, silk, and satin were used by kings, chiefs, and wealthy men and women and were often worn to impress visitors. The *Oba* of Ede met Clarke in

> four different colours of velvet in a fine coat, a rich silk robe, a pair of green Turkish trousers and a cocade hat of various colours . . . the dress in which he had proudly arrayed himself to impress me with an idea of his importance.[186]

The *Alake*s and chiefs of Abeokuta also received visitors in their finest. During Burton's visit, the *Alake* Okukenu wore a "robe of scarlet velvet . . . [and] pantaloons of purple velvet," and Chief Ogubonna wore a "fez-like cap of crimson velvet . . . necklace of red coral . . . toga of white . . . silk, striped with broad crimson bands."[187]

"Legitimate" trade supported the acquisition of these garments. In 1857 Ogubonna asked Crowther, Jr., to order a gown for him through Mr. Clegg that would distinguish him on public occasions as the *Oyinbo*'s (European's) friend. The gown he requested was indeed splendid and elaborate. It was to be made of crimson silk velvet with two epaulets, broad gold embroidery on the borders, a band in the middle of the robe, two large tassels, and a hood with a large gold tassel. He also wanted a green silk velvet cap with embroidery and tassel to match the robe. Clegg estimated that the gown would cost 1,000 pounds of clean cotton, or £20, and Chief Ogubonna promptly sent 1,507 pounds of clean cotton toward payment.[188] Europeans came to appreciate the value of imported cloth to Yoruba leaders, and they used cloth to build alliances. When the Italian trader Signore Scala met with *Alake* Okukenu in September 1856 to request permission to reside in Abeokuta, he presented him with a "superior piece of red silk velvet, silk damask, and a very long string of large red corals."[189]

So used were Clarke and other visitors to seeing chiefs in their finest dress that failure to appear well dressed warranted comment. During a visit to the village of Okeibode, Clarke was clearly taken aback by the lack of distinction of the chief's dress.

> I reached Okeibode and immediately dispatched the gate-keeper to announce my arrival to the chief. . . . In a short time a motley crowd was seen coming to gaze . . . and I tried to single out the chief as they drew near expecting as usual that he would be the most gentle-looking . . . but the reverse was true. His very appearance was filthy; his head bound up with a dirty rag, his body naked, while his only covering was a cloth drawn around his loins and dangling down his legs.[190]

The chief's casual wear made it impossible for Clarke to quickly surmise the center of power within that community. Describing the chief's appearance as "strange and savage," and mindful of the stereotypes he had learned about this community, Clarke fully expected a hostile reception. To the contrary, he was well received, leading him to conclude "this man gave me another additional lesson on the old adage, 'Trust not to appearance.'"[191]

Costly imported cloths were used for ritual purposes as well. The body of Chief Ogubonna's son, who died in battle, was wrapped in silk while it lay in state.[192] In some instances, velvets and other expensive cloths were draped on the walls of the room where the body rested and used to line the tomb.[193] Imported cloths also figured prominently among the material possessions that were redistributed after the owner's death. Reverend J.B. Macaulay was asked on one occasion to intervene in the case of a young man who was held by Kemta township's *Ogboni* because the young man refused to admit what he had done with a pair of "rich breeches and a velvet cap" that he had taken from a deceased brother. The *Ogboni* released the young man after he admitted to selling the breeches and turned over the proceeds—10 heads of cowries—to a senior brother who was more entitled to the inheritance.[194]

Imported cloths were also the cloths of everyday wear in which one worked, traded, or prayed. At the same time that these cloths made inroads it is important to note that they did not undermine the value system that dictated how cloth should be used or worn. Thus, refining our understanding of how and why the market for imported cloths increased as well as why indigenous production did not entirely collapse requires more than economic indicators.

CONCLUSION

The history of cotton and cloth exemplified the complex ways in which local and international developments were woven into Abeokuta's evolution over the course of the nineteenth century. The leaders and citizens of Abeokuta capitalized on its environmental resource base and transformed it into a vibrant center of trade and production and a power broker in regional politics. At critical junctures, the town's position within the regional political economy relied strongly on its relationship with British commercial and cultural agents. Many facets of that relationship were unequal, but, as this chapter demonstrates, how we understand those inequalities today were not evident to the historical actors at the center of these events. Ogubonna and other consumers of imported cloth did not see themselves as facilitators in the destruction of local textile industries. They saw themselves as engineers of a strong city-state with powerful allies in Britain. The fruits of that relationship were the costly and exotic fabrics and garments they procured.

The chapter also demonstrated that Abeokuta's evolution from a secure enclave for refugees to a commanding political and economic state relied on structured and culturally sanctioned inequalities in Yoruba society. Military leaders and wealthy traders used their access to enslaved labor to increase agricultural production and to protect the movement of their goods to market. Nonetheless, social inequality was fluid and malleable in the nineteenth century, and therefore access to expanding markets also gave enslaved men and women opportunities to transform their social status.

The *adire* industry built on these processes and critical cultural legacies. "Legitimate" trade established the consumer base linked to European markets that would support the *adire* industry. European traders and missionaries laid the foundations for the importation of the inexpensive cloths. Dyers also built on aesthetic traditions that valued continuity and change, and *adire* embodied both. Indigo reflected continuity while imported cloth reflected change. The level of economic expansion dyers experienced could not have occurred if *adire* had not found a place in Yoruba cultural and aesthetic traditions.

NOTES

1. Thomas Birch Freeman, *Journal of Various Visits to the Kingdoms of Ashanti, Aku and Dahomi in Western Africa* (London. Frank Cass, 1968), 221, 222, 228.

2. The Oyo empire rose to prominence during the seventeenth century and until the end of the eighteenth century extended control over much of Yorubaland as well as the kingdom of Dahomey. After its collapse, ongoing civil wars across Yorubaland last until the last decade of the nineteenth century. See Robin Law, *The Oyo Empire c. 1600–c.1836* (Oxford: Clarendon Press, 1977); A.W. Johnson, "Abeokuta," *Nigerian Geographical Journal*, 6, 2 (1963): 91. Also see S.O. Biobaku, *The Egba and Their Neighbours*, 1842–1872 (Oxford: Clarendon Press, 1957), 16. Abeokuta, which means "under the rocks," was selected in part for its defensive location.

3. Akin L. Mabogunje, *Yoruba Towns* (Ibadan: Ibadan University Press, 1962), 3. Also see Akin L. Mabogunje, *Urbanization in Nigeria* (London: University of London Press, 1968), 79–90. In contrast to nineteenth-century western Europe, Yoruba urbanization was the outcome of nonindustrial factors. Nonetheless, Mabogunje argues that they meet the criteria of urban centers because there was a greater complexity of economic activities in towns and a greater intensity of trading. They also had an elaborate system of administration.

4. Ruth Barnes and Joanne B. Eicher, eds., *Dress and Gender: Making and Meaning in Cultural Contexts* (Oxford: Berg Press, 1992), 15. This definition, they argue, takes us away from classifications that use ethnocentric and value-charged terms.

5. Justine M. Cordwell, "The Art and Aesthetics of the Yoruba," *African Arts* 16, 2 (1983): 58.

6. Babatunde Lawal, *The Gelede Spectacle: Art, Gender, and Social Harmony in an African Culture* (Seattle: University of Washington Press, 1996), 15; see also, Lawal, "Some Aspects of Yoruba Aesthetics," *British Journal of Aesthetics* 14, 3 (1974): 245.

7. Lawal, *Gelede Spectacle,* 30.

8. Robert Farris Thompson, *Flash of the Spirit: African and Afro-American Art and Philosophy* (New York: Vintage, 1984), 5.

9. Christopher Waterman, *Juju: A Social History and Ethnography of an African Popular Music* (Chicago: University of Chicago Press, 1990), 17.

10. Richard F. Burton, *Abeokuta and the Cameroons Mountain: An Exploration,* vol. 1 (London: Tinsley Brothers, 1863), 102.

11. Robert Campbell, "A Pilgrimage to My Motherland—An Account of a Journey Among the Egbas and Yorubas of Central Africa in 1859–60," in Martin R. Delany and Robert Campbell, eds., *Search For a Place: Black Separatism and Africa, 1860* (Ann Arbor: University of Michigan Press, 1969), 182–83.

12. Burton, *Abeokuta and the Cameroons Mountain,* 102.

13. William H. Clarke, *Travels and Exploration in Yorubaland, 1854–1858,* edited by J.A. Atanda (Ibadan: Ibadan University Press, 1972), 243.

14. Samuel Johnson, *The History of the Yorubas from the Earliest Times to the Beginning of the British Protectorate,* 6th ed. (London: Routledge and Kegan Paul, 1973), 110.

15. Ibid.

16. Ibid., 110–11. Johnson does not say where the *dandogo* was imported from. Also see Burton, *Abeokuta and the Cameroons Mountain,* 102.

17. Johnson, *History of the Yorubas,* 112.

18. T.M. Akinwumi, "The Commemorative Phenomenon of Textile Use Among the Yoruba: A Survey of Significance and Form," (Ph.D. diss., Institute of African Studies, University of Ibadan, 1990), 24.

19. Johnson, *History of the Yorubas,* 112.

20. Ibid. Also see Eve de Negri, "Yoruba Women's Costume," *Nigeria,* no. 72 (1962), 10–12.

21. Akinwumi, "Commemorative Phenomenon," 24.

22. Clarke, *Travels and Exploration,* 244.

23. Johnson, *History of the Yorubas,* 111; Cordwell, "Art and Aesthetics," 58.

24. Fernand Braudel, *Capitalism and Material Life, 1400–1800* (New York: Harper & Row, 1967), 236.

25. Freeman, *Journal,* 231.

26. R. H. Stone, *In Afric's Forest and Jungle; or, Six Years Among the Yorubans* (London: Oliphant, Anderson and Ferrier, 1900), 216. These shirts were sewn on a sewing machine that the Stones got after they relocated to Abeokuta during the Ijaye war c. 1860. This is one of the earliest reported sewing machines in the region.

27. Sarah Tucker, *Abbeokuta or Sunrise Within the Tropics: An Outline of the Origin and Progress of the Yoruba Mission (*London: James Nisbet, 1853), 24–25. Tucker's volume highlighted Abeokuta's importance to the Church Missionary Society strategy in Nigeria. She did not visit Abeokuta, but she drew on the accounts of explorers such as Heinrich Barth and Hugh Clapperton and missionary journals and newspapers. Also see Biobaku, *Egba and Their Neighbours,* 31.

28. Barnes and Eicher, *Dress and Gender,* 23. Akinwumi states that when the *buba* was adopted, it was initially restricted to married women: Akinwumi, "Commemorative Phenomenon," 24.

29. Stone, *In Afric's Forest,* 216.

30. The catechist was a African teacher who was to preach and minister to congregations of converts until an African pastor was provided. See Wilbert R. Shenk, *Henry Venn, Missionary Statesman* (Maryknoll, NY: Orbis, 1983), 118.

31. William Marsh, Journal, 9 June to 21 December 1845. CA 2/067.

32. Johnson, *History of the Yorubas,* 29. Also see Judith Perani and Norma Wolff, *Cloth, Dress and Art Patronage in Africa* (New York: Berg Press, 1999), 127–28.

33. Johnson, *History of the Yoruba*, 138–39.

34. Ibid., 31.

35. Babatunde Lawal, "Oyibo: Representations of the Colonialist Other in Yoruba Art, 1826–1960." AH Number 24 (Boston: Boston University African Studies Center, Working Paper Series, 1993), 10.

36. Silk in Nigeria is derived from a nonmulberry silkworm, *anaphe venata.* See M.O. Ashiru, "Silkworms As Money Spinners: Anaphe vs. Bombyx—A Status Report on Nigeria," unpublished paper presented at the Nigerian Field Society, 13 April 1988. Also see M.O. Ashiru, "Sericulture in Nigeria," *Indian Silk,* October 1979: 15–17.

37. M.T. Drewal, J. Isaac, and D. Dorward, *Yoruba Art in Life and Thought* (Bundoora, Australia: African Research Institute, La Trobe University, 1988), 2.

38. Akinwumi, "Commemorative Phenomenon," 22. Although a lazy person may be criticized and insulted, Yoruba culture recognized that the amount of property an individual accumulated did not simply depend on how hard he or she worked. William Bascom, "Social Status, Wealth and Individual Differences Among the Yoruba," *American Anthropologist* 53 (1951): 492.

39. Elisha Renne, *Cloth That Does Not Die: The Meaning of Cloth in Bunu Social Life* (Seattle: University of Washington Press, 1995), 3–6.

40. Ibid., 56–84.

41. Richard and John Lander, *Journal of an Expedition to Explore the Course and Termination of the Niger,* vol. 1 (New York: J. & J. Harper, 1832), 122.

42. Ibid., 122.

43. Renne, *Cloth That Does Not Die,* 21–37.

44. A. B. Ellis, *The Yoruba-Speaking Peoples of the Slave Coast of West Africa* (London: Chapman and Hall, 1894), 39.

45. P.S.O. Aremu, "Yoruba Traditional Weaving: Kijipa Motifs, Colour and Symbols," *Nigeria,* no. 140 (1982), 6.

46. Joseph Wright, "Joseph Wright of the Egba," in Philip Curtin, ed., *Africa Remembered: Narratives by West Africans from the Era of the Slave Trade,* 2d ed. (Prospect Heights, IL: Waveland Press, 1997), 327–28.

47. Ibid., 328.

48. Renne, *Cloth That Does Not Die,* 106–13.

49. Ibid., 106.

50. Karin Barber, "Oriki and the Changing Perception of Greatness in Nineteenth-Century Yorubaland," in Toyin Falola, ed., *Yoruba Historiography* (Madison: University of Wisconsin, African Studies Program, 1991), p. 35.

51. Ibid., 37.

52. Lawal, "Some Aspects," 241.

53. Thompson, *Flash of the Spirit,* 13.

54. Cordwell, "Art and Aesthetics," 56.

55. Lawal, "Some Aspects," 240, 245. Though outer beauty is appreciated, it is relative and its evaluation varies from person to person.

56. Caroline Keyes, "*Adire*: Cloth, Gender and Social Change in Southwestern Nigeria, 1841–1991," Ph.D. diss., University of Wisconsin—Madison, 1993, 79.

57. In an interview conducted by Elisha Renne in July 1997 in Itapa, Pa Jemitiaji, approximately 100 years old, recalled that primarily rich men used to buy a very dark, almost black, indigo dyed cloth from Ilorin called Kore. They would wear a white garment underneath, and the black cloth would gradually turn the white garment blue. Drewal also reports that in the Ijebu village of Imewuro, when the headman of the village prays for the community during an annual festival he wears a large, heavily embroidered indigo robe. Drewal, Isaac, and Dorward, *Yoruba Art,* 2.

58. Ibid.

59. Renne, *Cloth That Does Not Die*, 66–71.

60. Ibid., 74–75. Timing was critical to this therapy. The mixture was given to the woman after her menstrual cycle. After eating the corn-and-indigo mixture the couple were to have intercourse.

61. Ellis, *Yoruba-Speaking Peoples*, 160–61.

62. Anthony D. Buckley, *Yoruba Medicine* (Oxford: Clarendon Press, 1985), 155.

63. Ibid., 202–3.

64. J. Lorand Matory, *Sex and the Empire That Is No More: Gender and the Politics of Metaphor in Oyo Yoruba Religion* (Minneapolis: University of Minnesota Press, 1994), 185.

65. Jeanette Jensen Arneson, *Tradition and Change in Yoruba Art* (Sacramento: E.B. Crocker Art Gallery, 1974), 28.

66. H.J. Drewal, John Pemberton III, and Rowland Abiodun, *Yoruba: Nine Centuries of African Art and Thought* (New York: Center for African Art, 1989), 15, 25.

67. Arneson, *Tradition and Change,* 28. Also see Thompson, *Flash of the Spirit,* 27.

68. Oyeronke Oyewumi, *The Invention of Women: Making an African Sense of Western Gender Discourses* (Minneapolis: University of Minnesota Press, 1997), 68–69; and Keyes, "*Adire*: Cloth, Gender and Social Change," 211.

69. Oyewumi gives the example of female hunters even though hunting was considered a male occupation. Ibid., 69.

70. The narrow loom in West Africa is often considered the exclusive purview of male weavers, but Renne has shown that the correlation between gender and type of loom is not fixed. She found that the need to explore more income-generating activities has encouraged women in Ekiti to begin weaving with narrow looms. Elisha Renne, "The Decline and Resurgence of Women's Weaving in Ekiti, Nigeria," paper presented at the conference Artisans, Cloth and the World Economy: Textile Manufacturing and Marketing in South Asia and Africa, Dartmouth College, 23–25 April 1993.

71. Burton, *Abeokuta and the Cameroons Mountain,* 160.

72. Clarke, for example, insisted that "the males are the only class on whom this duty (farming) devolves though the females very frequently aid in harvesting and may be seen daily bringing in loads of provisions from the farm. So strong is the aversion to the native mind to this kind of female servitude that I have yet to see the first instance of a women engaged, hoe in hand, in cultivating the earth." Clarke, *Travels and Exploration,* 261.

73. Freeman, *Journal,* 231.

74. Clapperton reported that in the vicinity of Katunga (Oyo), and most other large towns, indigo was "cultivated to an extent of from five to six hundred acres." Richard Lander, *Records of Captain Clapperton's Last Expedition to Africa,* vol. 2 (London: Henry Colburn and Richard Bentley, 1830), 211. Twentieth-century sources, however, claim that indigo plantations also existed in Abeokuta. See *Proceedings of the Adire Cloth Commission,* 20, Abe Prof 4–D29 (National Archives, Ibadan—hereafter NAI).

75. Burton, *Abeokuta and the Cameroons Mountain,* 316.

76. Stone, *In Afric's Forest,* 23–24.

77. Johnson, *History of the Yorubas,* 84, 123.

78. G.J.A. Ojo, *Yoruba Culture: A Geographical Analysis* (London: University of London Press, 1966), 84. This system was still in practice in the twentieth century.

79. Jennifer Bray, "The Organization of Traditional Weaving in Iseyin, Nigeria," *Africa* 38 (1968): 272.

80. Burton, *Abeokuta and the Cameroons Mountain,* 163.

81. Many writers suggested that only women dyed. See for example, Johnson *History of the Yorubas,* 124; Campbell, "Pilgrimage to My Motherland," 184; and Ojo, *Yoruba Culture,* 85. But Lander reported that "male and female dyers were numerous in Yariba." Recently, Carolyn Keys also suggests that both men and women dyed, but by 1850 there were more women dyers. More detailed local studies of textile production in specific Yoruba towns are necessary in order to refine our understanding of the division of labor historically. See Richard Lander, *Captain Clapperton's Last Expedition,* 211; and Keyes, "*Adire*: Cloth, Gender and Social Change," 220.

82. Campbell, "Pilgrimage to My Motherland," 186; Johnson, *History of the Yorubas,* 124.

83. Clarke, *Travels and Exploration,* 272.

84. Martin R. Delany, "Official Report of the Niger Valley Exploring Party," in Martin R. Delany and Robert Campbell, *Search For a Place,* 120.

85. Burton, *Abeokuta and the Cameroons Mountain,* 76.

86. Ojo, *Yoruba Culture,* 85.

87. Burton, *Abeokuta and the Cameroons Mountain,* 163.

88. Campbell, "Pilgrimage to my Motherland," 186. For a twentieth-century description of the entire process, see Proceedings of the Adire Cloth Committee, Abe Prof 4 D29 (NAI), Appendix I: "Report on the Nature of the Adire Cloth Industry in Abeokuta"; and O.L. Oke, "The Chemistry and General History of Dyeing," in Jane Barbour and Doig Simmonds, eds., *Adire Cloth in Nigeria* (Ibadan: Institute of African Studies, University of Ibadan, 1971), 45–48.

89. Nancy Stansfield, "Dyeing Methods in Western Nigeria," in Barbour and Simmonds, eds., *Adire Cloth,* 19–20.

90. Clarke, *Travels and Exploration,* 272.

91. It was suggested that lobster shells, which were purchased from Lagos, were in use sometime after the 1860s. Minutes of Egba Native Council, 2 April 1936, 6. ECR 1/1/77, vol. 2 (NAA).

92. Georgina Beier, "Yoruba Pottery," *African Arts* 13, 3 (1980): 48. Yoruba dyers' use of clay pots stand in contrast to the dye pits that were used by Hausa dyers. See Philip Shea, "The Development of an Export Oriented Dyed Cloth Industry in Kano Emirate in the 19th Century," Ph.D. diss., University of Wisconsin–Madison, 1975.

93. Delany, "Official Report," 74.

94. Ojo, *Yoruba Culture,* 87–88. Women weavers predominated in Akoko, Owo, and Ekiti, while male weavers predominated in Ondo, Oshogbo, Ibadan, Iseyin, Oyo, and Ilorin.

95. Renne, *Cloth That Does Not Die,* 62. The *adofi* cloth could also be borrowed, rented, or given by an older women. The production of *adofi* reflected a constellation of relationships among women.

96. Keyes, "Adire: Cloth, Gender and Social Change," 77, 80.

97. Thomas J. Bowen, *Adventures and Missionary Labours in Several Countries in the Interior of Africa from 1849 to 1856,* 2d ed. (London: Frank Cass, 1968), 297; and Clarke, *Travels and Exploration,* 266.

98. Cordwell, "Art and Aesthetics," 58.

99. Clarke, *Travels and Exploration,* 245; Johnson, *History of the Yorubas,* 110. It is possible that Johnson, who produced his book at the end of the nineteenth century, was alluding to women who made European-style dresses.

100. J. B. Macaulay, Church Missionary Society journal ending 25 December 1853, 25 June 1853. CA2/065. *Oro* also carried out executions sanctioned by the *Ogboni.* When *Oro* appeared, all women had to stay indoors; any caught outside were put to death.

101. Johnson, *History of the Yorubas,* 119.

102. Martin Lynn, *Commerce and Economic Change in West Africa: The Palm Oil Trade in the Nineteenth Century* (Cambridge: Cambridge University Press, 1997), 3.

103. Clarke, *Travels and Exploration,* 263. See Kristin Mann, "Owners, Slaves and the Struggle for Labour in the Commercial Transition at Lagos," in Robin Law, ed., *From Slave Trade to "Legitimate" Commerce: The Commercial Transition in Nineteenth-Century West Africa* (Cambridge: Cambridge University Press, 1995), 144–71; and Robin Law, "'Legitimate' Trade and Gender Relations in Yorubaland and Dahomey," in Law, ed., *From Slave Trade to "Legitimate" Commerce,* 195–214.

104. Martin Lynn, "From Sail to Steam: The Impact of the Steamship Services on the British Palm Oil Trade with West Africa, 1850–1890," *Journal of African History* 30 (1989): 230–31. Also see Martin Lynn, *Commerce and Economic Change,* 41.

105. Buxton, *The African Slave Trade* (New York: Anti-Slavery Society, 1840), 199. Clarke, *Travels and Exploration,* 264; Richard Burton, *Wanderings in West*

Africa from Liverpool to Fernando Po, vol. 2 (London: Tinsley Brothers, 1863; repr. 1970), 235; Delany, "Official Report of the Niger Valley Exploring Party," 73, 127.

106. Tucker, *Abbeokuta,* 110.

107. Ibid.

108. Ibid., 4.

109. T.J. Bowen, *Adventures and Missionary Labours,* 327.

110. Jacob F. Ajayi, *Christian Missions in Nigeria, 1841–1891: The Making of a New Elite* (London: Longman), 1981, 10–19.

111. Brian Vincent, "Cotton Growing in Southern Nigeria: Missionary, Mercantile, Imperial and Colonial Government Involvement Versus African Realities, from 1845 to 1939," Ph.D. diss., Simon Fraser University, 1977, 29-30. Also see Allen Isaacman and Richard Roberts, eds., *Cotton, Colonialism, and Social History in Sub-Saharan Africa* (Portsmouth, NH: Heinemann, 1995), 3–4.

112. Tariff regulations in Europe and North America protected their finer cloths by excluding British cloth while local weavers filled India's demand for high-quality cloth. Vincent, "Cotton Growing in Southern Nigeria," 7, 46.

113. Ibid., 46–48.

114. McPhee identifies Clegg as the prime mover in the export of raw cotton from West Africa. See Allan McPhee, *The Economic Revolution in British West Africa,* 2d ed. (London: Frank Cass, 1971), 45.

115. Vincent, "Cotton Growing," 15–18. Also see Shenk, *Henry Venn.*

116. Ajayi, *Christian Missions,* 85.

117. Vincent, "Cotton Growing," 34.

118. Ajayi, *Christian Missions,* 84.

119. Vincent, "Cotton Growing," 31. Clegg took a 20 percent commission on cotton and another 20 percent commission on the cloth he sent to Abeokuta. In addition, he sent equipment that was expensive and often inappropriate, for example, horse-driven machinery to be operated in this tsetse fly infested area. As a result of these large commissions and the equipment purchases, the institution lost money and was in debt to Clegg.

120. B.A. Agiri, "Kola in Western Nigeria, 1850–1950: A History of the Cultivation of Cola Nitida in Egba-Owode, Ijebu-Remo, Iwo and Ota Areas," Ph.D. diss., University of Wisconsin, 1972, 15. Also see Biobaku, *Egba and Their Neighbours,* 27. Conflict between Abeokuta and Dahomey would flare several times over the course of the century in part because they both wanted to control of valuable areas of oil palms. Roberta W. Kilkenny, "The Slave Mode of Production: Precolonial Dahomey," in Donald Crummey and C.C. Stewart, eds., *Modes of Production in Africa: The Precolonial Era* (Beverley Hills, CA: Sage Publications, 1981), 165; Patrick Manning, *Slavery, Colonialism and Economic Growth in Dahomey, 1640–1960* (Cambridge: Cambridge University Press, 1982), 53; and Jacob F. Ade Ajayi and R.S. Smith, *Yoruba Warfare in the Nineteenth Century* (Cambridge: Cambridge University Press, 1964), 71.

121. E.A. Oroge, "The Institution of Slavery in Yorubaland with Particular Reference to the Nineteenth Century," Ph.D. diss., University of Birmingham, 1971, 186.

122. Vincent, "Cotton Growing," 32.

123. Samuel Crowther, Jr., Journal for the quarter ending 25 September 1855 (CMS, CA 2/ 037A), 8 October 1855.

124. Burton, *Abeokuta and the Cameroons Mountain,* 71. In *Iwe Irohin*, a Yoruba-English newspaper begun by Rev. Townsend, a trade report noted that 314 bales of cotton contained 41,407 pounds. Each bale thus was approximately 131.9 lbs. See *Iwe Irohin*, Appendix, 2 October 1867, 4.

125. Vincent, "Cotton Growing," 50.

126. Ibid., 32.

127. Ibid., 33.

128. Ibid., 52. Vincent suggests that prior to this cotton was primarily grown by ordinary farmers and grown as part of a mixed crop.

129. Samuel Crowther, Jr., Journal for the quarter ending 25 December 1857 (CMS, CA 2/037A).

130. Vincent, "Cotton Growing," 34.

131. Letter from Rev. A.C. Mann to the Lagos Cotton Warehouse, 5 August 1857. CMS, CA2/067. Rev. Mann reported that Tinubu also had another 3,000 pounds cleaned and ready in her store when a fire broke out, destroying the store and the cotton.

132. Henry Townsend, letter to M.H. Straith, 28 January 1857, 4–5. CMS CA 2/085. In 1853 Townsend sent a box of arrowroot to Henry Venn that was produced on Ogubonna's farm. Townsend acknowledged that he "received it from him with very great pleasure, not for its intrinsic value, but for the evidence it affords of his desire to follow agricultural pursuits." Townsend to Henry Venn, 24 October 1853, 1.

133. Stone, *In Afric's Forest,* 206.

134. Crowther, Journal for the quarter ending 25 December 1855 (CMS, CA 2/037A).

135. A.K. Ajisafe, *History of Abeokuta,* 3d ed. (Lagos: Kash and Klare Bookshop, 1948), 48. *Oyinbo* meant white men, but it was also applied to western blacks, who were called *Oyinbo dudu*. Campbell, "Pilgrimage to My Motherland," 244. It is quite possible that when Townsend described the Abeokuta chief who showed a great fondness for finery, and who was the first to build a European-modeled home with a large doorway, windows, and floorboards, he was describing Ogubonna. Henry Townsend, letter to Captain Trotter, 31 January 1849, 8. CMS CA 2/085.

136. Campbell, "Pilgrimage to My Motherland," 177.

137. James Johnson called attention to several Christian women traders who were also slaveowners. James Johnson, letter to H. Wright, 2 August 1879. CMS CA 2/056.

138. Henry Townsend, letter to Henry Venn, 31 December 1856. CMS CA 2/085.

139. James Johnson, letter to H. Wright, 29 November 1879. CMS CA2/056.

140. James Johnson to H. Wright, 2 August 1879, 5. CMS CA2/056. Johnson estimated that 50 strings of cowries were equivalent to 1 shilling. He thought owners were unconscionable for demanding such payments from their slaves while opposing efforts to raise church dues to 7½ strings per week.

141. J.B. Macaulay, Journal for the half year ending 25 March 1857 (CMS 2/065), 17 October 1856. Also see Oroge, "Institution of Slavery," 200–204; Law, "'Legitimate' Trade and Gender," 200.

142. Bowen, *Adventures and Missionary Labours,* 319–20.

143. Law, "'Legitimate' Trade and Gender," 207–8.

144. Burton estimated that one-fifth of the population was enslaved. He also identified three classes of Egbas—rich free men, poor freemen, and serfs and slaves. See Burton, *Abeokuta and the Cameroons Mountain,* 299. On the other hand, J.P.L. Davies, a wealthy Egba merchant based in Lagos, thought it was one-third. See Oroge, "Institution of Slavery" 167.

145. Oroge, "Institution of Slavery," 178. In 1870 Ibadan's total population was estimated at 100,000 people, yet 104 chieftaincy houses in Ibadan held a total of 52,000 slaves.

146. Oroge, "Institution of Slavery," 181–83. See also Bolanle Awe, "Militarism and Economic Development in Nineteenth Century Yoruba Country: The Ibadan Example," *Journal of African History* 14, 1 (1973): 65–77.

147. Henry Townsend, letter to Captain Trotter, 31 January 1849, 10. CMS CA 2/085.

148. Vincent, "Cotton Growing," 28. Slave wives were often purchased at the slave markets in Ilorin. Also see Campbell, "Pilgrimage to My Motherland," 58.

149. Henry Townsend, letter to Venn, 8 November 1850, 11–12. CMS CA 2/085.

150. Bowen, *Adventures and Missionary Labours,* 343.

151. Ibid.

152. Missionaries across the continent were concerned with household relations and saw commodity production based on the model of the "yeoman" farmer and the nurturing homebound wife as central tenets of their program. Jean and John Comaroff, "Home-Made Hegemony: Modernity, Domesticity, and Colonialism in South Africa," in Karen Tranberg-Hansen, ed. *African Encounters with Domesticity* (New Brunswick, NJ: Rutgers University Press, 1992), 37–74.

153. James Johnson, letter to H. Wright, 18 September 1879. CMS CA2/056.

154. For examples of missionary households, see Ann Hinderer, *Seventeen Years in the Yoruba Country* (London: Religious Tract Society, 1872), and Stone, *In Afric's Forest.*

155. Ajayi, *Christian Missions,* 19.

156. Robert Campbell gives a fairly detailed description of palm-oil processing in Abeokuta. See Campbell, "Pilgrimage to My Motherland," 186–87. Also see Julian Clarke, "Households and the Political Economy of Small-Scale Cash Crop Production in South-western Nigeria," *Africa* 51 (1981): 807–23.

157. Law, "'Legitimate' Trade and Gender," 207.

158. Clarke, *Travels and Explorations,* 284.

159. Johnson, *History of the Yorubas,* 30.

160. Clarke, *Travels and Explorations,* 284.

161. Law, "'Legitimate' Trade and Gender," 209. One specific *Egungun,* the *Agan,* was the executor of women accused of witchcraft. Witches were presumed to be women, and market women were thought to be the daytime counterparts of witches.

See J. Lorand Matory, *Sex and the Empire,* 54, and Belasco, *The Entrepreneur As Culture Hero* (New York: Praeger, 1980), 29.

162. Joseph Inikori, "West Africa's Seaborne Trade 1750–1850: Volume, Structure, and Implications," in G. Liesegang, H. Pasch, and A. Jones, eds., *Figuring African Trade: Proceedings on the Symposium on the Quantification and Structure of the Import and Export and Long Distance Trade of Africa in the 9th Century* (Berlin: Dietrich Reimer, 1986), 71.

163. Following Ijaye's defeat, Egba soldiers accepted many children as *iwofa*s. Stone, *In Afric's Forest,* 185. Townsend reported that many Ijaye people were captured and sold by other Ijayes as well as Egbas and Ibadans. Henry Townsend, letter to Henry Venn, 2 July 1862, 5. CMS CA 2/085.

164. Interview with Alhaja Soetan, 1 September 1988, and Alhaji Soetan, 9 August 1988.

165. Akinwumi, "Commemorative Phenomenon," 139–43; and Keyes, "*Adire*: Cloth, Gender and Social Change," 83–85. Keyes argues that this diffusion also contributed to a standardization of loom construction and size. These brocade designs also spread to the Nupe and Hausa in the north and to the Ijo and Ibo in the east. See Judith Perani, "Nupe Costume Crafts," *African Arts* 12, 3 (1979): 52–57; and Lisa Aronson, "Ijebu Yoruba Aso Olona," *African Arts* 25, 3 (1992): 52–63.

166. Clarke, *Travels and Exploration,* 263.

167. Ibid., 152.

168. Burton, *Abeokuta and the Cameroons Mountain,* 316; also see Clarke, *Travels and Exploration,* 263–64.

169. Cloths reached Yorubaland via the trans-Saharan trade as well as coastal trade. See Marion Johnson, "Cloth on the Banks of the Niger," *Journal of the Historical Society of Nigeria* 6, 4 (1973): 353–63; Marion Johnson, "Calico Caravans: The Tripoli–Kano Trade After 1800," *Journal of African History* 12, 1 (1976): 95–117; and Keyes, "*Adire:* Cloth, Gender and Social Change," 87.

170. Rev. Stone noted that cotton was the material of which the clothing of the masses was made, but on state occasions, the rulers and rich men appeared in garments of silk and silk-velvet. Stone, *In Afric's Forest,* 30.

171. Samuel Crowther, Jr., Journal for the quarter ending 25 June 1856. CMS, CA 2/037A.

172. Clarke, *Travels and Exploration,* 266. Also see Richard and John Lander, *Journal of an Expedition,* 67; Bowen, *Adventures and Missionary Labours,* 297; Burton, *Abeokuta and the Cameroons Mountain,* 133. During the seventeenth and eighteenth and the first half of the nineteenth century, cloth from Bengal was the most prominent, but by the second half of the nineteenth century British cottons became the most important. Anthony Hopkins, *An Economic History of West Africa* (New York: Columbia University Press, 1973), 110; also see Inikori, "West Africa's Seaborne Trade," 63–64.

173. William Marsh, Journal 9 June–21 December 1845, 11 June 1845. Church Missionary Society, CA2/067.

174. Clarke, *Travels and Exploration,* 264.

175. Since traders traveling in small groups were extremely vulnerable to attacks and kidnapping, caravans were of tremendous sizes, numbering in the hundreds and

even thousands, according to some estimates. In some instances, chiefs provided armed men to protect the caravan, and wealthy traders often had their own armed retainers to protect their goods in transit. Henry Townsend, Letter to Captain Trotter, 31 January 1849, 7 (CMS CA 2/085); Clarke, *Travels and Exploration,* 22; Bowen, *Adventures and Missionary Labours,* 332; and E.A. Oroge, "Institution of Slavery in Yorubaland," 181–83.

176. Colin Newbury, "Prices and Profitability in Early Nineteenth-Century West African Trade," in Claude Meillassoux, ed., *The Development of Indigenous Trade and Markets in West Africa* (London: Oxford University Press, 1971), 93. Also see Inikori, "West Africa's Seaborne Trade" 79.

177. Newbury, "Prices and Profitability," 94.

178. Clarke, *Travels and Exploration,* 272.

179. Keyes, *"Adire:* Cloth, Gender and Social Change," 90.

180. Alfred C. Moloney, "Cotton Interests, Foreign and Native in Yoruba, and Generally in West Africa," *Journal of the Manchester Geographical Society* 5 (1889): 256. Moloney was governor of Lagos colony from 1886 to 1891, but previously he had served on the Gold Coast and in the Gambia. See Olufemi Omosini, "Alfred Moloney and His Strategies for Economic Development in Lagos Colony and Hinterland, 1886–1891," *Journal of the Historical Society of Nigeria* 7, 4 (1975): 657–72.

181. Moloney gave the following figures for the value of British cloth imported into Lagos.

| 1884 | £225,112 | 1885 | £193,782 | 1886 | £138,183 |
| 1887 | £177,128 | 1888 | £192,896 | | |

See Moloney, "Cotton Interests," 258.

182. Hopkins, "Economic Imperialism," 586. Also see Susan Martin, *Palm Oil and Protest: An Economic History of the Ngwa Region, South-eastern Nigeria, 1800–1980* (Cambridge: Cambridge University Press, 1988), 45–46.

183. Hopkins, "Economic Imperialism," 594.

184. Ayandele argues that Abeokuta's military involvement in the war ended by 1879. E.A. Ayandele, *The Missionary Impact on Modern Nigeria, 1842–1914: A Political and Social Analysis* (London: Longman, 1981), 44.

185. Omosini, "Alfred Moloney and His Strategies," 662. Also see S.A. Akintoye, *Revolution and Power Politics in Yorubaland, 1840-1893:* Ibadan Expansion and the Rise of Ekitiparapo (New York: Humanities Press).

186. Clarke, *Travels and Exploration,* 114.

187. Burton, *Abeokuta and the Cameroons Mountain,* 142, 279. Clapperton also noted that the king of Oyo was richly dressed in a scarlet damask tobe, ornamented with coral beads, with a blue damask cap thickly studded with coral beads. Lander, *Captain Clapperton's Last Expedition,* 195.

188. Samuel Crowther, Jr., Journal for the quarter ending 25 December 1857. CMS, CA 2/037A.

189. Rev. J.B. Macaulay, Journal for the half year ending 25 March 1857 (CMS, CA 2/065), 20 September 1856. Also see Robert Smith, "Giambattista Scala: Adventurer, Trader and First Italian Representative in Nigeria," *Journal of the Historical Society of Nigeria* 7, 1 (1973): 67–76.

190. Clarke, *Travels and Exploration*, 125.

191. Ibid.

192. Stone, *In Afric's Forest,* 195.

193. Joseph Wright, "Narrative of Joseph Wright," 327–28. Also see Campbell, "Pilgrimage to My Motherland," 199.

194. Rev. J.B. Macaulay, Journal entry for 16 June 1858. CMS, CA 2/065. A "head" was roughly equivalent to 4s./2d., so he had obtained £2/1/8 for the breeches. See Sarah Tucker, *Abbeokuta: Sunrise Within the Tropics,* 26, and Clarke, *Travels and Exploration,* 268, for a discussion of currency and conversion rates.

2

"THE KING OF ENGLAND WAS THEIR WALL": STATE AND SOCIETY DURING THE EARLY COLONIAL PERIOD

As we saw in Chapter 1, "legitimate" trade and Britain's expanding political power established some of the preconditions for the takeoff of *adire* production. This chapter examines the consolidation of these processes as Britain assumed political control over Abeokuta and the rest of Nigeria. It examines British–Egba relations between 1893 and 1914 and delineates critical factors that shaped changes in Abeokuta's political and economic structures. At the center of this discussion is the Egba United Government (EUG). The EUG, which was nominally independent, existed from 1898 to 1914. Although it was independent, the EUG was continually being transformed in order to carry out what Fields calls "the grass-roots work" of the colonial state, enforcing order and control while lending a veneer of legitimacy to the process of colonial imposition. The establishment and gradual transformation of the EUG effectively created a model of indirect rule well before the concept was systematized by Lord Lugard.[1] Abeokuta's political development during this period supports Field's argument that Lugard's system did not establish something entirely new; rather, it tidied up in many ways what already existed.[2] Yet Abeokuta's experience also shows the gradual evolution of theories surrounding "native administrations."[3] As the EUG evolved, it instituted many economic changes that put Abeokuta in line with developments taking place throughout Nigeria.

Abeokuta's stature as a commercial center increased during this period because it became one of the major centers of cocoa production and an important consumer of imported items, including cloth. In time, the price of cocoa and the volume of imported cloth became indices of the town's economic well-being.[4] Several factors contributed to Abeokuta's important economic role—the initiative of local farmers, new infrastructure, the expansion of markets, and the availability of credit. The economic changes discussed in this chapter are pivotal to understanding the transformations that occurred in textile production during the twentieth century. Collectively, these developments broadened the consumer base that would later support the *adire* industry and bring dyers into the web of international trade.

The political and economic changes also set in motion a range of social developments that held important implications for women more broadly as well as women producers. The chapter also calls attention to the ways in which the town's economic and political transformations were gendered by demonstrating where and how women were affected. It also highlights how various groups of women took advantage of these changes to reconfigure some of their roles and expectations.

THE EGBA UNITED GOVERNMENT

The decision by the Lagos government to assert its control over Yorubaland opened a new phase in Yoruba history. It began with the bombardment of Ijebu in 1892. Abeokuta was spared similar destruction because important Egba Saro in Lagos and Abeokuta helped shape a treaty that offered a measure of protection for the city-state's autonomy. Abeokuta chiefs signed a treaty in 1893 in which they guaranteed open trade routes through Egba country. In the treaty the Lagos government recognized the town's independence and its borders "upon the strict observance of the Treaty."[5] This agreement in theory retained Egba control over its political economy.

The treaty was signed by the *Alake*, Sokalu, as well as the three men who held the reins of power—Sorunke, the *Balogun* of the Egbas; Osundare the Nlado, a senior *Ogboni* official; and Ogundeyi, the *Mogaji* of Iporo, a military chief.[6] These three figures represented Abeokuta's complex political structure. In order to appreciate the importance of these signatories as well as the significant changes to come under the creation of the EUG, it is necessary to briefly trace the evolution of the town's political structure.

The Egba and Owu refugees who founded Abeokuta did not establish it as a single town, but as a collection of towns in close juxtaposition.[7] The town comprised four main quarters—Egba Ake, Oke Ona, Gbagura, and Owu, reflecting the three original Egba provinces and the large influx of refugees from Owu. Together these quarters held approximately 150 to 200 separate townships,[8] and each township tried to reproduce its old political structure. Each town had an *Oba* (king) at the pinnacle. There were three main branches in the political structure: the *Ogboni*, which corresponded to the civil government and included older men and women; the *Ologun*, the military offices; and the *Parakoyi*, the trade chiefs.[9] Within each province, one *Oba* was recognized as the senior *Oba* of that province. The senior *Oba* of Egba Ake was the *Alake*, in Oke Ona the *Oshile*, in Gbagura the *Agura*, and the *Olowu* in Owu. In spite of efforts to recreate the townships, many of the old political offices did not survive the transition, and some titles lapsed or became less important.

The grave insecurity of the first two decades gave the military chiefs unprecedented influence and authority in Egba politics and encouraged the formation of all-Egba or federal structures. A federal *Ologun*, a military apparatus, was created after 1832, headed by Shodeke, the military chief who led the Egba to Abeokuta.[10] They also attempted to create a federal *Ogboni* in which officers were drawn from various townships. In theory, the federal *Ogboni* should have included all the townships. In practice, however, all the officers named were from Egba Ake sector, therefore dooming this attempt at a federal civil arm of government. As a result, each quarter maintained its own civil authority.[11]

By the mid-1850s, gradual steps were taken toward establishing a centralized government under one *Oba*, the *Alake*. Missionary encouragement, particularly that of Reverend Henry Townsend, was an important element in this development. Yet for most of the nineteenth century the *Alake*s could not consolidate power or control the actions of wealthy chiefs and traders.[12] Their weakness was reinforced by the fact that they did not have a revenue base. The *Alake* did not exercise any control over the town's economic development, or revenue collection or distribution. The revenue from customs duties on imports and exports that were collected at any town gate belonged to the chief who controlled that area, not to the *Alake*.[13] Decentralized control over revenue collection reinforced the *Alake*'s position as a figurehead over a highly fractured polity. As a result, *Ogboni* chiefs and military chiefs like Ogubonna often overshadowed the *Alake*s.

Abeokuta's political system was also very flexible and expanded to incorporate new social groups. As Christian converts gained economic wealth, they were allowed to take titles. In 1860 John Okenla was given the military title *Balogun* of the Christians, after his Christian army, composed primarily of slaves, fought in the Ijaye war.[14] Other leading converts, including the CMS printer, Robert Fisher, joined the *Ogboni*. Some missionaries were dismayed by this development, since joining the *Ogboni* required certain rituals and practices that were against missionary teachings,[15] but by taking titles and joining the *Ogboni* these men effectively carved out a role for themselves in the indigenous political structure.

As the Muslim community grew, influential members of that community also took titles. The first *Balogun* of the Muslims was named around 1860.[16] Women were also among the new political brokers of this period. The *Parakoyi* was often described as an all-male institution, but in 1878 Betsy Desola, a Christian convert, large-scale entrepreneur, and slaveowner was named *Iyalode* of the *Parakoyi*.[17] One of the most important women to emerge during this period, however, was Madam Tinubu, the *Iyalode* of the Egbas. She had a substantial trade in cotton, as we saw in Chapter 1, as well as palm oil and ammunition. Tinubu was given the title in 1864 as reward for her support during the Dahomean invasion of that year.[18] It is clear, then, that political power in Abeokuta for much of the nineteenth century was diffuse and expansive.

The three signatories of the 1893 treaty with Britain reflected the town's competing power brokers. Little changed in Egba politics until 1897, when a political crisis paved the way for the Lagos government to intervene.[19] In March 1897 the Governor, Sir Henry McCallum, and a contingent of troops visited Abeokuta in order to put the government "on a sounder footing."[20] The crisis revolved around Aboaba, Sorunke's successor as *Balogun* of the Egbas, who tried to monopolize the tolls. Supporters of the *Alake* called on the Lagos government to intervene. Governor McCallum arrested Aboaba, fined him £200, and deported him to Ibadan.[21] McCallum then threatened to interfere actively in the town's affairs if its political structures were not reorganized.[22] From this reorganization the Egba United Government (EUG) was created.

The EUG made the *Alake* the central figure of authority. He was assisted by an eight-member salaried council that included the three other sectional *Oba*s as well as a senior *Ogboni* representative, a senior war chief, a senior Muslim chief, and a Christian chief.[23] The reigning *Alake,* Sokalu, died just three months after the formation of the EUG, and he was succeeded by Gbadebo, the son of *Alake* Okukenu. As a result, the EUG is primarily associated with Gbadebo's reign.

The EUG established a new political template for Abeokuta. This new Egba government had a firm financial footing. It controlled the collection of export tolls as well as tolls on imported spirits. It also had a small administrative staff, many of whom were Saro/Christian men.[24] The EUG modeled itself after the colonial state and began to centralize its authority by establishing ministries that assumed functions previously carried out by *Ogboni* and *Parakoyi* chiefs. For example, a government prison was built so that criminals did not have to be held in *Ogboni* houses. By 1908 the EUG employed about 350 people. It had a secretariat, treasury, audit office, customs department, judicial department, public works department, medical and sanitary department, police, printing office, post office, forest and agricultural office, and education department.[25] It also carried out development programs such as road construction and vaccinations.[26] The bureaucratization process was largely facilitated by the employment of Reverend J.H. Samuel (who later changed his name to Adegboyega Edun) as secretary in 1902.[27]

As the administrative structure increased, the size of the council also increased. By 1912 there were thirty-five members on the council. The majority of new members sat on the council as representatives of townships—in all twenty-two townships were represented. These chiefs acted primarily as a liaison between their townships and the council, expressing the interests of their township while defending and explaining government policy.[28] Even though the council kept expanding, women chiefs were not invited to join.[29] Furthermore, it appears that following Madam Tinubu's death in 1887, her title, *Iyalode* of the Egbas, lapsed for several years. Informants suggest that her successor, Madam Jojolola, was appointed during the reign of *Alake* Gbadebo, therefore sometime after 1898.[30] However, Madam Jojolola did not begin to appear in government documents until 1918, and her appointment was not noted by the town's chroniclers.[31] Nonetheless, it appears that some titled women continued to function in the township *Ogboni* councils. The 1906 Report on the Native Laws of Egbaland noted

> Women . . . hold Political position, as *"Olori Erelu"* (Chief of the women in the township). *"Olori Erelu"* is not present when serious matters are discussed at Township councils. The Head trading woman in a township is called *"Iyalode"* (Mother of the public). *"Iyalode"* may attend minor meetings, and her opinion is consulted on matters affect-

ing trade. . . . Women hold considerable influence politically, and behind the scenes bring great influence to bear on the Chiefs in almost every big palaver.[32]

As the EUG streamlined the Egba political structure and privileged the position of the *Alake*, this centralized political space became an exclusive male enclave with women leaders confined to minor meetings, trading matters, or behind-the-scene politiking. The centralization of the Egba state resulted in a much lower political profile for women at the same time that it facilitated economic transformations that benefited many women.

TRANSFORMING THE EGBA ECONOMY

On Saturday, 14 December 1902, the governor of Lagos and an entourage of distinguished men and women met at Iddo terminus in Lagos to take an inaugural rail journey to Abeokuta. The first leg of the journey ended at Aro, the important terminus for riverine trade, now also a railway terminal. There the governor's party was met by the *Alake*, Gbadebo, the *Olowu* (*Oba* of Owu), the *Alagura* (the *Oba* of Gbagura), members of their council, and thousands of Egba people. At Aro, they joined another train that took them across a new bridge and into Abeokuta proper to the new station, Ibara Gate Station.[33]

During his speech heralding the occasion, the governor noted that the "wall of the town had been allowed to fall into disrepair because the *Alake* and Council knew that the King of England was their wall."[34] While the governor highlighted the protection the king of England guaranteed to the *Alake*, another speech maker, the Honorable C.A. Sapara Williams took the discussion in a slightly different direction. Williams stressed that even though the governor had often expressed his sympathy for Africans and his desire to protect their interest, it was most "desirable that the native Government should be continued, and the integrity of its independence maintained."[35] Williams clearly preferred British respect for Abeokuta's independence over British paternalism.

The speeches, the circumstance, and the participants involved richly captured the profound political as well as socioeconomic changes that had taken place in Abeokuta by the beginning of the twentieth century. By 1900 Abeokuta was recognized by all as an independent polity, yet it was enveloped by the Yoruba protectorate, and the town's leaders relied on the protection of the king of England. The *Alake* was now the head of a government, the Egba United Government, which Williams characterized as a "federal compact . . . under the inspiration of a natural and legitimate life."[36] This new government was a significant development from the days when "authority was left to be usurped by the man who was most powerful and exerted the strongest influence."[37] From this new position, the *Alake* and his council were able to "induce their people to allow the railway the come to Abeokuta," thus ensuring "development and the good and welfare of the country."[38]

The developments that brought these men together at Aro reflected the rise of British colonialism and the recasting of Abeokuta's political, economic, and social developments according to the aims and imperatives of colonialism. The imagery of the Egba walls being allowed to disintegrate reflected more of British hope and anticipation than reality. In order for the colonial state to rule effectively, the walls of the old Egba state could not be allowed to fully dissolve. Pieces of that state had to be molded into a new political mosaic, for the colonial state was a consumer of power generated within the customary order.[39] The pieces of the old Egba state that remained were essential to the economic transformation that accelerated as the railway extended beyond Lagos.

English merchants had anxiously awaited the pacification of the interior. Merchants like John Holt who did a brisk business in palm produce had been extremely frustrated each time the Egbas and Ijebus interrupted trade at their will. In 1892 Holt argued, "we don't want any fighting, but we must get the upper hand over these people and command the peace of the district from which my trade is derived."[40] Once British control was established, they were eager to see the railway reach Abeokuta. An early plan called for the railway to terminate at Otta, but Manchester traders expressed strong dissatisfaction.

> The (Manchester) sub-Committee cannot approve the present purpose to construct the line only to Otta, unless it is intended to extend it, without delay, at least to Abeokuta, because a length of 20 miles of line cannot afford an adequate test of the paying capabilities of the railway. It is strongly recommended, thereupon that the work should be pushed on as fast as possible to the first objective viz., Abeokuta.[41]

Lagos traders also strongly supported the railway going to Abeokuta, because there was so much trade between the two cities. They estimated that "the greatest bulk of the trade of Lagos in cotton goods, provision and sundries is absorbed by Abeokuta alone."[42] Both European and African traders clearly anticipated substantial economic rewards from direct access to Abeokuta.

The Egba United Government carried out its own program for expanding the town's infrastructure concurrent with the arrival of the railway. A wide road, begun in 1899, ran through the center of town and extended to the railway station in Aro. More concerted efforts began after the turn of the century, when trained personnel were employed.[43] In 1901 the EUG began widening and leveling roads using forced labor.[44] Much of this construction occurred in the rural districts to the south and southeast of Abeokuta town. Through the Department of Roads the EUG provided skilled road overseers, while the local population supplied labor.[45] The networks of roads contributed significantly to the establishment of new markets and an overall increase in the volume of trade. In Yorubaland, in general, the network of new roads had a much more direct effect on the growth and location of markets than the railway, although several important markets evolved around railway stations.[46]

In addition to road construction, the *Alake*, who was also patron of the Farmers' Association at Abeokuta, traveled throughout the town and its rural areas encouraging farmers to pursue export production. On 10 April 1903, for example, he visited Opelifa, a district well known for its production of palm oil and kernels. He was accompanied by the *Olowu*, the *Agura*, the Moslem chief, and the government secretary, as well as Cyril Punch, the railway commissioner, and B.J. Profit, the local agent of John Holt & Co. The aim of this visit was

(1) to inspect the kernel cracking machine purchased by the Egba Government, and placed at Opelifa for the use of the farmers free of charge; (2) to inspect the new roads from the different farm-villages to the rail-line at Opelifa that had been ordered by the Egba Government; (3) to hold a meeting of farmers and others, and encourage cotton growing; and (4) to establish a fifth-day market near the rail-line in the interests of farmers and traders.[47]

Gbadebo also made an important appearance at the Lagos Agricultural Show that was inaugurated on 11 November 1903.[48] Cyril Punch had encouraged many people to participate and many Egba farmers, "especially the Christian farmers . . . sent cows, sheep, palm nuts, yams, cotton, coffee, cocoa, maize and fowls."[49] Those who attended the show viewed cotton gins sent out by the Cotton Growing Association, kernel-cracking machines, and other labor-saving devices. Egba spinners and weavers also gave a "practical exhibition of their art."[50] Gbadebo's visits to trade shows and villages were complemented by the establishment of new markets near the rail line, the appointment of a government representative or *Parakoyi* to control and regulate them, and the construction of roads to important market centers.[51] The EUG was clearly trying to create the transportation and marketing infrastructure that would enhance production and trade.

Gbadebo's efforts to promote export production showed good results in part because commodity prices increased at the beginning of the century. Between 1900 and 1907, the price of palm oil rose from £19/1s. to £30 per ton.[52] Palm-oil and palm-kernel production increased steadily throughout the period. Between 1909 and 1913, Nigeria exported 81.9 metric tons of palm oil.[53] Prices collapsed at the beginning of World War I with the loss of the German market and German traders.[54] Britain had always imported five-sixths of Nigeria's palm oil, but Germany was the main market for palm kernels.[55] Thus, initially the loss of the German market was a severe blow.

Prices improved by the end of 1915 as the British market readjusted to absorb the bulk of Nigerian palm oil and kernels. Palm produce prices remained high in Liverpool until 1920, but prices in Nigeria were low. This was due to the shortage of shipping space during the war.[56] Although palm products remained important commodities, their share of the export market declined during the first four decades of the century. They fell from 82 percent of total exports from Nigeria in 1900 to 31 percent in 1937.[57] In Abeokuta, export peaked in 1915 but declined thereafter because farmers paid more attention to other crops, in particular, gbanja kola and cocoa.[58]

It was not apparent that cocoa was to be the crop of the future when Nigerians began investing in it.[59] Historians credit J.P.L. Davies with establishing the first cocoa farm in Nigeria by 1880.[60] Davies's success encouraged a cross section of Lagos society to follow suit. He was soon joined by other merchants, civil servants, army clerks, lawyers, numerous clergy, and petty traders, who established the first major center of cocoa production in Agege and southern Egbaland.[61]

World-wide cocoa consumption increased sevenfold during the first four decades of the twentieth century. By 1936 the center of cocoa production in the world had shifted to West Africa, with the Gold Coast and Nigeria producing 50.5 percent of total world exports.[62] Between 1900 and 1920 the volume of cocoa exported increased from 202 tons to 17,155.[63] Although Abeokuta was one of the first areas engaged in cocoa production, much of the dramatic increase occurred around Ibadan and Ife. Of the 92.8 acres of cocoa planted in 1900, 41.6 were in Ibadan. By 1920 the total acreage devoted to cocoa farms reached 12,452, and of that 6,515 (52.3 percent) were in Ibadan and 3,695 (29.6 percent) in Ife.[64]

Berry attributes much of the increase in cocoa production in the decade preceding World War I to the favorable terms of trade for cocoa farmers, though prices fluctuated significantly.[65] In 1907 and 1908, for example, the price of cocoa averaged £3/19s. and £2/15s. per cwt. respectively.[66] Before World War I, however, prices had fallen to between £1/12s. and £2/7s. per cwt. They improved slightly during the war to between £1/17s. and £3/8s. per cwt.[67]

Expansion of cocoa and gbanja kola production virtually coincided in Abeokuta. Although cultivation of gbanja kola had begun in the nineteenth century, the big expansion of kola nut cultivation came after 1910. In 1910 the Nigerian Department of Agriculture obtained large quantities of seed from Ghana for sale to farmers. They also established a nursery for seeds at Agege. By 1918 the trees had reached maturity and started producing nuts that proved more profitable than the trade in cocoa.[68] The profitability of gbanja kola was due to the lower labor requirements in its production. It cost farmers twice as much labor to maintain cocoa trees as it did to maintain kola trees.[69] In the older cocoa-growing areas, kola was initially planted along with cocoa. As cocoa trees died, they were often replaced with kola trees because kola was more tolerant of the poor soil conditions.[70] Kola nut production increased steadily in Abeokuta. By 1918 Agege, Otta, and Abeokuta together exported 77 tons of gbanja kola to northern Nigeria.[71]

Abeokuta's economic picture changed significantly during the first two decades of the twentieth century. The palm-oil industry, though still important, had lost its premier position. It competed with kola and cocoa for farmers' attention. Kola competed effectively against cocoa in the areas of earlier cocoa cultivation, while new regions of the Egba territory were brought into cocoa cultivation. In spite of price fluctuations throughout the period, the terms of trade remained favorable, inducing farmers to expand the acreage under cultivation.

Abeokuta's new economic and political landscape contributed to rising incomes for both men and women. The end of the internal conflicts allowed more freedom of movement and secure conditions for cultivation. Cocoa production provided incomes for an expanding base of producers as well as wage laborers. Women made up an important segment of the buyers who purchased small quantities of cocoa from farmers and transported it to bulking centers.[72] The expanding kola nut market brought revenue to farmers as well as the women who dominated its retail trade. By custom, women owned the palm kernel, so the demand for palm-kernel oil was also a new economic avenue for them. This expansion of the agricultural economy increased the consumption of all imported goods, but most especially cloth.

CLOTH AND ECONOMIC EXPANSION

Abeokuta's changing economy brought much more money into circulation and allowed for greater consumption of manufactured items, both local and imported. European merchants arrived in Abeokuta soon after the railway reached the town, for this was the entrée they had long awaited. As early as 1888, Thomas Welch, John Holt's business partner in Lagos, visited Abeokuta to survey the possibilities of opening a store there.[73] Once the railway reached Abeokuta, several firms stayed and opened stores, but some firms moved even further inland before the railway actually reached cities north of Abeokuta.[74] John Holt noted that "some people have already gone to Ilorin in anticipation of the railway's arrival."[75]

The Lagos government first sublet land in the railway area to European firms, and by 1902 several European merchants were concluding contracts to lease land from the Egba government.[76] The earliest European firms were John Holt & Co., G.L. Gaiser, Paterson Zochonis & Co., the Lagos Stores Ltd., and a small shop owned by a Mr. Le Gros.[77] European merchants were initially welcomed by petty traders and consumers, "who had hitherto patronized the native merchants [but] now preferred buying from and selling direct to the European merchants."[78]

Abeokuta did indeed prove to be an important center both for the purchase of produce and for the sale of imported goods. William MacGregor, the governor of Lagos from 1899 to 1904, estimated that Abeokuta produced about one-third of all produce exported through Lagos and consumed one-quarter of the total imports.[79] John Holt's agents considered it a more important place for trade than Ibadan because of the volume of trade conducted there.[80] Their conclusions were based on observation and interaction with traders in other cities. After conducting a tour of other Yoruba towns, Holt's agent H.J. Rawlings reported that "There is a big goods trade to be done in the town of Ede itself but it is a credit trade. The people of Ibadan and the towns north are apparently as poor as church mice but all seem to be trading on borrowed capital."[81]

All the firms did a brisk business in cloth and competed to supply Nigerian consumers. The estimation of income levels had a direct impact on the quality of cloth that was traded. Rawlings pointed out that

Paterson Zochonis do a good trade with the Gambari (Hausa) caravans in a cheap croydon which they sell at 3/9 per 20 yards pce. . . .
The brocades you are sending to Up-country are too good to enable
us to do much in them. The Gambari trade which constitutes a great
proportion of the Ibadan Cotton business, consists almost entirely
of cheap baft, croydon and brocades but they must be very cheap.[82]

Rawlings insisted that a print should not cost more than $2^3/_4$d. per yard,
velvets 10d. and sateen 5d., and white brocades $2^1/_2$d. at first cost.[83] These
prices allowed the trading firms to maintain a profit margin regardless of
shifting commodity prices. In order to make it easier to respond to changing market circumstances, Holt suggested that they grade or standardize
the quality of the cloth. He argued that

> The main object of standardising a line is to enable a merchant, in
> the case of a big advance in the price of cotton, to substitute, quite
> openly and without resorting to any trickery, a second quality, when
> the price of the original quality became too high for the market.
> For instance, in the case of H.V. Croydon, we think it should be
> advisable to have three qualities (each at a different price). . . . It
> would thus enable you to offer to a trader who comes along and
> asks for our H.V. Croydon and finds the price too high (remarking
> perhaps at the same time that the French Co. are selling something
> just as good at 3d to 6d per pce below us) a substitute, bearing the
> same stamped heading, with the addition of Quality No 2, or other
> distinguishing mark.[84]

In addition to trying to tailor the quality of the cloth, firms tried to
meet and shape demands in a number of ways. Rawlings noted that "during June there is a big festival called the *Egungun* at Ibadan and Oshogbo
during which a lot of money changes hands. The goods in demand are
Rum, Velvets and Bright Coloured Prints."[85] Consequently, he tried to
increase their stock of these cloths at this time of the year. He also had
the company send out inexpensive speculation patterns of prints and
printed velvets to see what consumers desired.

There was a clear relationship between export production and consum-
erism. As more people participated in export production, they were able
to afford imported items, especially cloths, whose prices were tailored to
meet most income levels. Imported cloths, especially cotton prints, also
benefited from tolls that were in their favor. The 1904 schedule of tolls
published by the Egba government showed that the toll on imported cot-

ton prints was calculated in cowries and was less than the toll on domestic cloth and even certain food items.[86]

Articles	Amount	Rate of Duty
Cloth—		
Velvet and domestics	per bale of 50 pieces	2s./6d.
Prints	per piece	strings 5
Coconuts	per bag	strings 10
Guinea fowls	each	strings 10
Kola nuts	per bag	6d.
Sewing machines	each	6d.

Millions of yards of cloth came from the United Kingdom, Germany, and Holland as well as other European countries, but by far the greatest exporter was the U.K. By the first decade of the century, the value of cotton goods imported into Nigeria from the U.K. alone reached £1,000,000 [87] The following chart shows the value of imported cotton goods from the UK between 1900 and 1911.

Year	1900	1901	1902	1903	1904
Value (£)	327,919	—	415,398	372,308	345,865

Year	1905	1906	1907	1908	1909
Value (£)	344,841	739,915	1,036,807	934,753	950,061

Year	1910	1911
Value (£)	1,184,133	1,083,432

In less than a decade, between 1910 and 1918, the value of cotton piece goods imported into Nigeria increased by more than 100 percent, from £1,322,707 to £2,804,379.[88] In actual yardage, Nigerian consumed 40 million square yards of cloth annually between 1895 and 1906. By 1912 cloth consumption had increased to nearly 100 million square yards, and with some fluctuations, it more or less remained at that level until 1917.[89]

Since the Egba government was a separate entity, it kept accounts specific to Abeokuta. *Egba Government Gazettes* between 1907 and 1915 recorded a remarkable increase in the value of cotton goods imported into the town, although it does not help us to calculate the actual yard-age.[90]

Year	1907	1908	1909	1910	1911
Value (£)	64,133.1.7	—	77,341.0.5	99,247.3.5	139,328.19.4

Year	1912	1913	1914	1915
Value (£)	108,653.9.2	107,028.19.2	94,016.9.9	107,862.10.7

TOTAL (£) £797,611.13.6

Textiles were the most important single item of the import trade. The increasing variety in both the quality and the price of textiles shows the dedication with which European trading firms tried to reach Nigerian consumers. Those who marketed a cloth that had widespread popularity could profit immensely. Since most cotton goods, cloths as well as yarns, were known by their trademarks, firms protected their trademarks vigilantly. In a case that went to the Lagos Supreme Court in 1900, the plaintiff, the Lagos Stores, sought an injunction against Blackstock from infringing on their trademark. Lagos Stores had a popular yarn that was considered of high quality and was known as Ankuri in the local trade. The yarn, which was similar to the local *alari* yarn made from silk, was especially popular among Hausa traders. Blackstock copied the label, altering only the Arabic that appeared in the center of the label.[91] Protecting trademarks and by extension market shares, as well as anticipating market trends, enabled the European traders to profit greatly from cotton goods.

Cotton goods reached consumers through an elaborate network of traders. There were a few African merchants, such as J.H. Doherty, who had sufficient capital to import goods directly from England. The majority obtained their goods from the European firms and resold them through their own stores or in the markets. Some African merchants had stores in several towns, for example, A.M. Mustafa, who had stores in Lagos and Abeokuta.[92] Most large merchants had one primary base of operations. In Abeokuta, one of the largest merchants was J.B. Majekodunmi, whose family could be traced back to the original Egba homesteads. He was a general merchant, but cloth was a substantial part of his business. Majekodunmi obtained cloth from the European firms such as G.B. Ollivant and John Holt and Co. and sold it to consumers, smaller retail traders, and dyers from his store in Ikereku.[93] Retail traders sold cloth in the numerous markets throughout Abeokuta to consumers who purchased smaller quantities.

Credit supported the vast networks of export and import trade. The *Alake* had warned against introducing the credit system in Abeokuta so as to avoid difficulties and complications over debt; nonetheless, European merchants conducted an extensive amount of business on credit.[94] Several forms of credit were employed, reflecting the firms' dual roles as importers and exporters.[95] African traders who dealt in imported merchandise had to provide some form of surety, either cash or property, that could be used as collateral before they were allowed to take goods.[96]

The other form of credit was advances. In the nineteenth century, advances were in the form of goods given to African traders, who used them to purchase produce from African farmers.[97] In the twentieth century, advances increasingly were in cash, which made its way down to producers through a hierarchy of buyers. Cash advances eclipsed advances in commodities fairly early in southern Yorubaland. In 1887 Governor Alfred Moloney of Lagos reported that all palm kernels and much palm oil were bought for cash. As the use of cash increased, traders less frequently resorted to the old system of bartering merchandise.[98] Sterling silver circulated freely along with cowries, but cowries were increasingly limited to use in the internal markets or for small purchases.

The entire structure of trade depended on credit, since it was essential to both the dissemination of imported goods and the collection of Nigerian produce. Yet there were constant complaints about the credit system, and colonial officials were always extremely concerned about the amount of credit extended. In an effort to establish a ceiling on credit, the Lagos Chamber of Commerce presented a petition to the Legislative Council in 1903 calling for the enactment of a law that would limit the amount of credit firms could give the customers to £25.[99] This effort was directed at European firms as much as African traders, since firms feared that if they refused to extend credit to an African trader, another firm would.[100] The attempt to limit credit apparently did not succeed, because in the 1907 Annual Report, the commercial intelligence officer drew attention to the "unreasonably large credits allowed to irresponsible middlemen."[101]

Firms tried to set guidelines on the amount of credit extended and their collection, but agents in the field often acted on their own discretion. Holt informed his Lagos agent in 1908, Stephen Ayles,

I have come to the conclusion that it would be better for us to have no credit at all for produce, with anybody, rather than go on in this foolish manner. . . . I must insist upon your reducing all these produce credits to a safe basis, by which I mean that the credit must be covered by weekly payment, after each market day. . . . Either the produce or the cash must come back to you. . . .

You state that you have cut down the Lagos advances, but have not yet touched Abeokuta. . . . [I] don't want you to run away with the idea that in giving out credit you are selling our goods. You are simply placing your liberty in the hands of your creditor.[102]

The amount of credit extended to Abeokuta traders varied considerably, as the following list from John Holt & Co. shows

Abeokuta Credit List—John Holt & Co.[103]

17 January 1908

Kuforigi Brothers	£750	Laoriyan	£50
Badaru	£400	Mrs. Franklin	£50
Shobeyo	£75	S. Morin	£100
Onipedi	£200	Gbademosi	£80
Kembi	£150	Abudu Barawa	£100
D.O. Thomas	£250	John Olukulu	£250
E.S. John	£100	J.B. Majekodunmi	£1,000

28 May 1910[104]

Madame Oja	£25	Bakare Laloko	£50
Sani Idowu	£50	Sani Egun	£20
Yesufu Agola	£50	Reduced from	£100
Onipedi	£100	Reduced from	£200
Kuforiji Bros.	£200	Reduced from	£300

Although Holt clearly expressed his preference for small accounts,[105] and for produce credit to be settled following every market and goods credit to be settled monthly,[106] the repayment schedule varied. Agents sometimes took as long as nine weeks to settle an account. Frustrated, Holt pushed his agents to collect outstanding credit at the end of every six weeks.[107]

Holt also insisted that when Ayles wanted the firm to authorize credit or credit increases for anyone, he had to provide a good reason along with a history of the candidate's turnover in the past. He also had to vouch for the client's reliability and receive a security. In spite of his instructions, it was clear that Ayles and his assistants often gave credit beyond the traders' authorized limit. For example, a trader by the name of Onipedi had a limit of £200 but had an outstanding account of £379. In frustration, Holt wrote, "It is evident . . . that no matter what limits we give you, you take no notice of them, or you are unable to prevent your assistant from disobeying your orders."[108]

The communication between Holt, Deemin, Ayles, and Rawlings demonstrated the difficulties of establishing and maintaining prudent business practices while rushing to expand trade and competing for the business of African traders and consumers. In spite of Holt's conviction that his agents were too liberal with credit, it was clear that credit was the glue that held both the import and export sides of commerce together.

Although women conducted much of the retail trade in Abeokuta, it is noteworthy that very few women traders were discussed in these records, and that the amounts loaned to them were significantly lower. For example, Rawlings noted that "Madam Oja is one of our oil traders and wants to sell our gin in the markets where she buys oil for us. She uses her own cash for produce. She trades in goods with Gaiser and Millers and has paid them well." In spite of her commendable record, she was only given £25 credit by Holt & Co.[109] It is quite possible that many women bought from African merchants since they may not have had the capital or the connections to establish a relationship with the European firms. The European firms also had a long-established tradition of working primarily with male traders, and that tradition apparently continued when they expanded their operations to Abeokuta.

THE CONTRADICTIONS OF ECONOMIC EXPANSION

Abeokuta's increasing engagement with the international economy and the proximity of European traders created some of the tensions the *Alake* had feared. While the Egba government reported that trade increased year after year, Egba merchants suffered from bankruptcies and crippling indebtedness. European merchants competed directly with independent African middlemen who had previously controlled the bulking and transportation of goods to the coast. The local merchants appealed to the EUG and the British commissioner for assistance, but they were told that "no check must be put in the way of trade."[110] The situation of African middlemen in Abeokuta was not unique. Across southern Nigeria, the position of African middlemen became precarious soon after the turn of the century. As European

firms moved further into the interior, they undermined African merchants and established direct access with a smaller-scale class of
trader.[111]

African traders were also subject to subtle and sometimes blatant forms
of racism. Several of Holt's agents had money stolen from them, and
Holt admonished them for being "too careless in trusting these black fel-
lows with our property. . . . They do not remember that the blackman is
on the qui vive to rob."[112] Holt's attitudes were hardly unique. An article
in *West Africa* noted that educated Africans sometimes had trouble obtaining credit because "the fact of his being educated or civilized [made]
him at once an object of suspicion and distrust to the [European] merchant on the score of his being too sharp."[113] African employees of the
firms were also subject to discriminatory practices. D.D. Africanus Coker,
who was from Sierra Leone but worked for Holt's in Nigeria and Gabon,
reported some of the unfair treatment he received. For example, European staff members were given all their necessary comforts, but "you
will see the Africans without even a chair, a table or a bed although both
are working for the same firm and are both perfect strangers in the
place."[114]

Economic expansion also brought European traders into conflict
with the independent Egba state. In 1903 a major conflict erupted over
the tolls that European traders paid the Abeokuta government and were
to begin paying the Ibadan government in June.[115] The conflict exposed tensions between local autonomy, the needs of the colonial state,
and merchant capital. Abeokuta was the showcase of an evolving colonial policy that argued for the "strengthening of native institutions
and the consolidation upon a firm basis of the native State form."[116]
Sir William MacGregor, who was the governor of Lagos at the time,
"identified himself conspicuously with this policy."[117] Although
Frederick Lugard is credited with developing the system of indirect
rule, it is clear that Governor MacGregor—who was in Lagos during
the same period that Lugard was in northern Nigeria—shared similar
ideas. MacGregor also recognized that these states had to have a system for collecting revenue.[118] Tolls, which had been collected during
the precolonial period, still appeared the most expedient way of gen-
erating revenue. In 1900 Governor MacGregor and the Egba government negotiated import and export tariff agreements whereby goods
in transit were exempted from duties, but fifty-six import items, mostly
manufactured in Europe, and thirty-three export items, primarily local
agricultural products, were subject to duties.[119] EUG revenue increased
from £3,000 in 1900 to £16,000 by 1902,[120] and it was used for salaries, road construction, and other projects.

European traders argued vociferously against the tolls, claiming that they had already paid duty on trade items in Lagos. Tolls, they insisted, led to corruption and extortion, and most of the revenue collected was wasted on luxuries for the chiefs. In addition, tolls interfered with trade and gave too much power to native chiefs, allowing them to set up their own little kingdoms. They suggested instead that the Lagos government subsidize the interior chiefs out of Lagos revenue, reduce the Lagos local expenditure, or increase the customs duties.[121]

This dispute exposed the divergent concerns of European merchants and the colonial state. Whereas merchants were primarily concerned with expanding trade, the state had to balance its support for economic expansion against the need to maintain political order. Thus, the colonial state could not be the "obedient servant of capital."[122] Local autonomy was the linchpin of the alliance between the Yoruba states and the Lagos government that allowed the colonial state to maintain order while the colonial economy revolutionized their societies. This alliance was most effective with rulers like the *Alake,* who was characterized as loyal, cheerful, and cooperative.[123] In the interest of maintaining political order, the colonial state supported the Egba state in this conflict with merchant capital.

Governor MacGregor's support did not mean, however, that he and the *Alake* shared one interpretation of autonomy. He envisioned the EUG as a protected government, rather than one that was independent. In a statement to the Aborigines Protection Society in 1902, MacGregor wrote, "It would be a most dangerous idea to put into the heads of a protectorate State that they are an independent sovereign Power. They are not independent as a State, although they are held responsible for the maintenance of peace and order in their provinces."[124]

The Egbas, on the other hand, did not understand their status as protected; they understood autonomous to be synonymous with independent. Furthermore, their independence was protected by treaty. Thus, the EUG and Egba traders saw the 1903 outcry against their tolls as an attack on their independence and an effort aimed "at reducing the rulers of the interior to the same condition as the chiefs of Lagos."[125] Abeokuta traders protested against the European traders in several ways. They held mass meetings and boycotted European stores.[126] Traders and *Parakoyi* chiefs met and passed a resolution to take their trade directly to Lagos rather than trade with those Europeans in town who agitated against the tolls.[127] Although a letter to the *West African Mail* suggested that most people as well as chiefs were against the tolls, most newspaper responses contradicted this claim.[128]

The conflict was finally resolved when the *Alake* and the EUG agreed to several concessions. They agreed to appoint a trained auditor and to publish annual estimates of revenue and expenditures and the auditor's report. They also agreed not to increase the tolls without the sanction of the secretary of state, and to allow free transit to the railway through the Abeokuta territory for all non-Abeokuta goods, and full rebate on goods reexported. All export duties were abolished as well as the tolls on agricultural produce and local trade commodities.[129] This conflict left an unpleasant pall over relations with European merchants. An editorial in the *Lagos Weekly Record* noted

> For the native, the lesson taught by the toll agitation is one calculated to fill him with regret and disappointment. The agitation has served to awaken him to the fact that he has been labouring under a delusion. He had always thought that his interests and those of the merchants were one and identical; but he has now learnt to his dismay that occasions may arise when the merchant will try to thrust him aside and take all the advantage to himself. This unfortunate revelation must of necessity create a feeling highly detrimental to trade.[130]

The toll agitation was only one of several issues that exposed the tensions between Egba and European merchants as well the tensions between European merchants and the EUG. Each issue that exposed conflicts involved the Lagos government and ultimately advanced the colonial state's increasing leverage in Egba affairs. As the number of European businesses in Abeokuta increased, for instance, the Lagos government actively sought the right for the railway commissioner to establish a court for the recovery of debt.[131] The struggle between the Egba and Lagos governments over the right to hear debt cases also reflected the struggle between competing merchant groups to control trade. European firms with their large capital base were able to extend credit, a powerful incentive for shifting commercial alliances, but they also needed speedier recourse in the event of default than was possible in the customary Egba proceedings.[132]

The EUG rejected the Lagos government's proposals to hear debt cases but reorganized the judicial system in order to systematize the judicial process and prevent individual chiefs from holding private courts. They established courts in the *afins* (palaces) of each sectional king that included a set of judges and a literate clerk.[133] It was not until 1904 that the Lagos government effectively superimposed itself on Egba judicial affairs through an agreement that ceded jurisdiction to the British government "for nineteen years in all cases where one or both parties to the suit are not natives of the Egba country, and in all cases of murder and manslaughter."[134]

While the Egba government struggled to maintain its independence, it also faced internal opposition as the town's economic and political structures changed. Often opposition flared when the EUG exercised its new powers as the central authority. In 1903, for example, the people of Kemta township revolted when the Alake set aside a judgment made by a Kemta *Ogboni* chief and then attempted to arrest him. Railway Commissioner Cyril Punch called on the Lagos government to send troops to support the *Alake*. The troops were accompanied by Governor MacGregor, who, according to Ajisafe,

> only blamed the Kemta people for taking such aggressive steps without complaining to the Commissioner in Abeokuta. "If in the future," he said, "you have a grievance against your authorities you should either write to the Alake and Council or send a deputation to them and state your grievance; if you receive no satisfaction from them, you should appeal to the Foreign Government. It is for this cause the British Representative is stationed here.[135]

MacGregor's statement clearly indicated that he did not see the Egba state as a sovereign entity. Furthermore, the Lagos government had an assumed right to intervene in Egba affairs.

On each occasion when the Lagos government intervened to support the *Alake* they demanded more concessions in return. In 1907, for instance, protests flared following the death of an elderly man whom the Egba police arrested for sedition. In return for quelling the protests, Governor Egerton demanded that the Egba government accept a permanent British commissioner.[136] Despite the fact that the Egba government was malleable, successive governors chafed at their independence, none more so than Lord Lugard, who became governor general in 1912.

The Lagos government seized the opportunity to end Abeokuta's anomalous status when a road construction campaign initiated by the EUG sparked disaffection and protests in 1914. A chief of Ijemo township, Ponlade, was arrested for not providing labor for roadwork.[137] His subsequent death while still in custody led to protests as people from Ijemo demanded a full investigation into Ponlade's death and the dismissal of certain EUG officials. Unable to quell the protesters, the *Alake* turned to the Lagos government for help. On 8 August, troops went to arrest the leaders of the protests, and in the process thirty-seven people were killed, including several of the chiefs they were to detain.[138] Lord Lugard was in Britain at the time, but it was well known that he wanted to end Abeokuta's nominal independence. His deputy took advantage of this crisis to bring Abeokuta firmly under British control. In exchange for the promise of continued British support, the *Alake* had to renounce Egba independence and abrogate the treaty of 1893.[139]

ECONOMIC EXPANSION AND SOCIAL CONFLICT

The political and economic changes that unfolded under the EUG had contradictory consequences for men and women. The development of the trade in cocoa, palm kernels, and kola increased trading opportunities for both men and women. Yet both men and women were subject to forced labor as the state oversaw the construction of roads to carry these goods to markets. Politically, a centralized government was created that had a clear line of authority and a revenue base, but it continually relied on the Lagos government to use the threat of force or actual force to support its authority. This new government, while inclusive in some ways, marginalized women from the political arena, so that women in the twentieth century had a much lower political profile than had their predecessors in the nineteenth century.

The political and economic developments of this period also engendered a range of social changes. The remainder of this chapter will focus on some of these changes, especially as they affected gender roles and social control. It will also highlight the ways in which the economic and social processes influenced changes in consumer tastes and preferences. All these developments had direct bearing on the textile industry more broadly and *adire* producers specifically.

Expanding economic opportunities, especially cocoa production, placed labor at a premium. Workers were needed to plant, harvest, process, or transport a much larger volume of commodities. Within the cocoa sector, a close relationship between the independent church movement and cocoa production gave clergy-planters distinct advantages over other producers and allowed African churchmen to dominate the plantations in Agege. Whereas obtaining sufficient labor was a constant problem for planters, those associated with the independent churches were able to recruit labor through their religious communities. For example, when planters were in need of labor, interior churches coopted their young men to work at Agege.[140] Although early planters had established plantations, most cocoa was produced on small farms.[141]

For smaller producers, marriage was an important labor strategy. J.J. Ransome-Kuti, who was superintendent of the Abeokuta Church Mission in Soren-Ifo, a rural district, found that as the price of produce increased "people rushed to accumulate wives so as to get helpers in the field."[142] This rush to get wives did not abate even though the bride price increased substantially. The demand for labor made it difficult for Ransome-Kuti to persuade members to send children to school or to give up "extra wives."

European presence and the expanding economy also contributed to a general perception that there was as a breakdown in social control over dependent women and men. The 1906 Report on Egba Native Law argued that

> the family system is breaking down, owing to the influx of civilisation, which has produced the following effects: *a)* The parents' hold over grown-up children, formerly absolute, is now practically extinct, except from a moral point of view; *b)* Husbands not having absolute power over their wives as heretofore, seduction and adultery are more prevalent; *c)* Children will not allow themselves to be pledged for debt, as has been customary; *d)* The chiefs and elders of the country do not now receive the same respect from the younger generation, and their personal influence is greatly reduced.[143]

Many commentators called specific attention to the increasing number of divorces and suggested that it had become a social revolution in the interior countries.[144] Divorce invited attention because it became an option for many more women at a moment when the demand for labor was at a premium. Yoruba sociologist N.A. Fadipe specifically attributed the great state of flux in native marriage to the diffusion of foreign ideas, the process of rapid economic growth, and the advance of the railway.[145] Many women and girls visited the railway camps in pursuit of trade and established relationships with men employed in the camps. The camps provided a sanctuary from lineage authority, new relationships, and economic opportunities as well as an alternative judicial space, since they fell under the railway commissioners' jurisdiction.[146]

Records show that many who wanted to renegotiate their status took advantage of the railway commissioners' judicial and political authority. Communication between the railway commissioners and the *Alake* shows that the commissioners effectively established themselves as a court of appeal for those who did not expect a favorable hearing in the Egba courts. They wrote to the *Alake* on behalf of claimants who did not want to be forced into marriage, or who wanted to leave a marriage because of ill-treatment. They helped settle disputes over bride-wealth that often posed an obstacle in divorce settlements as well as disputes over debts. The *Alake*, on the other hand, wrote to the commissioners on behalf of the deserted fathers and husbands. In the process of inserting themselves into local disputes, the commissioners further undermined the autonomy of the EUG.[147]

Slaves also went to railway commissioners for assistance. The slave trade in Egba territory was abolished in 1901, but slavery was not abolished. Nonetheless, slaves were entitled to self-redemption.[148] There were letters from the Railway Commissioners on behalf of slaves who wanted to redeem themselves or family members trying to redeem an enslaved relation. For example, the following letter was written by Acting Railway Commissioner L. Norton Blackwell on behalf of a slave woman, Barikisu.

> I have the honor to request that the woman Barikisu's case may be enquired into. She states that the brother Eweobaja of her late mistress Omikunle wishes to sell her now, and took her round the town to several houses. She states that her husband . . . redeemed her from her late mistress in the presence of witnesses before her death for 15 bags. In this case she should receive certificate of freedom, and Eweobaja's action for endeavoring to sell her enquired into.[149]

We do not have the outcome of this case, but Barikisu's story illustrates how some Abeokuta residents tried to use the commissioners' authority. Many slaves, however, did not seek self-redemption; instead, they elected to run away. Some fled to Lagos, while others established their own free villages in rural areas of Egba territory.[150] Slave flight was such that a severe labor shortage developed from the end of the nineteenth century. Many people had to work their farms themselves, and in some years crops went unharvested.[151]

The demise of slavery contributed to the expansion of the *iwofa* system, a type of debt bondage. Under the *iwofa* system, creditors extended loans. In lieu of paying interest on the loan, the borrower, or a substitute, worked for the lender until the loan was repaid. The *iwofa* system held certain advantages for creditors, particularly when a dependent relation or a slave substituted for the borrower. A borrower usually worked for the creditor for a specified number of days a week, but the younger relation (or slave) who substituted for the borrower lived with the creditor until the loan was repaid. Thus, the creditor could dispose of his or her labor at all times.[152] While farmers and manufacturers increasingly relied on the *iwofa* system for labor in the twentieth century, they had more difficulty controlling this labor force. As the 1906 Report made clear, many children refused to serve, or they ran away repeatedly. Farmers also noted that *iwofa* "absolutely refuse to do transport work, and if pressed they run away to the railway."[153] These reports confirm that the *iwofa* system provided a very insecure form of labor. Since some dyers relied on both slave labor and *iwofa*, it is highly possible that dyers like farmers experienced labor difficulties during this period of rapid economic growth.

The political and economic changes that unfolded from the last decade of the nineteenth century allowed various dependent groups in Egba society to exercise greater degrees of autonomy over their lives. The improving economic picture after the turn of the century as well as the expanding opportunities for small-scale traders and the expanding wage labor sector facilitated capital accumulation that could be used for self-redemption, divorce, agricultural investment, or consumption. The increasing volume of textile imports into Nigeria was an important indicator of both the rapid expansion of trade and the increasing consumer base.

Dress naturally reflected these larger changes that were unfolding. In Abeokuta and Lagos, towns that had a long history of Christianity and educational institutions, young people increasingly wore European dress on formal occasions such as weddings and in everyday wear. European dress came to indicate one's wealth, achieved or anticipated social status, and modernity. The social importance of European dress and the quality of one's attire were articulated in the degree of detail found in some of the wedding announcements. For example,

> The Bride . . . wore a gown of Broach Satin of cream colour with a Court Train of moire quilted draped from the shoulders and slung through the back covered over with Tulle embroidered veil. . . . Her page . . . was adorned in blue velvet Fauntlery suit trimmed with pink lace and sash with Tam o, Shoes, and stockings to match. . . . The maids of honor . . . were attired in richly trimmed dresses of mixed ashes and pink coloured silk. . . . The Bridesmaids. . . were all attired in uniform costume of elegant silk striped muslin coloured Pink trimmed with lace and Satin with cream straw hats of ribbon and Satin flower trimmed to match.[154]

Both British and Nigerian commentators expressed a range of opinions about the evolving dress styles. There were those who clearly applauded the adoption of British fashions. Many missionaries believed that converts who did not drink tea or wear European clothes could not be genuine Christians.[155] This equation was reflected in the story of Lapido Lateju who was sent to school in London by Prince Ademuywa of Lagos to study religious instruction and tailoring. A British supporter prophesied that on his return

> he will penetrate the heart of Africa, preaching the faith and fitting out all his black and woolly haired converts with frock coats cut in harmony with the leading Piccadilly fashions, and finished with all the sartorial elegance of a West-end garment.[156]

Those who encountered Lateju would be draped in new material and spiritual dress.

Other observers condemned the practice. A Mrs. Fry, for example, who had many positive things to say about Yoruba dress, thought the growing tendency to adopt European dress and style was deplorable, arguing that it was unsuitable to climate and customs.[157] Frederick Lugard also disliked the practice, but for a different set of concerns. Africans wearing European clothes transgressed the social, cultural, and racial divide Lugard sought to maintain. He pointedly deplored missionaries who encouraged European dress as a visible sign of conversion as well as those missionaries who did menial work. He thought that they carried the ideal of the equality of man too far and in the process "destroyed missionary influence for good and lessened the prestige of Europeans."[158]

Nigerian commentators also criticized the use of European dress, but their criticism was part of a broader cultural nationalist critique of imperialism. The newspapers, especially the *Lagos Weekly Record* and the *Lagos Standard* instituted a vigorous campaign of cultural consciousness that sought to stimulate a greater interest in African history, language, and culture.[159] This discussion was sparked by colonial policies and the increasing signs of racism as Britain extended its control over Nigeria. The CMS, for example, abandoned Venn's goal of developing an African-led church and increased the number of white missionaries in Nigeria and in supervisory positions. This led to the creation and expansion of independent African churches. Nigerians in the civil service also began to face a color bar. In a number of instances, less-qualified Europeans were promoted over Nigerians, and there were disparities in salaries and benefits. There were also attempts to create racially segregated communities and churches.[160]

Educated Nigerians were especially affronted by these developments and began to reevaluate their enthusiasm for European culture and their dismissal of African institutions and practices that had been denigrated by Europeans. Discussions flowered about the use and study of the Yoruba language, especially in schools, and around dress, polygyny, the education of women, and secret societies.[161] This reevaluation was encouraged by the writings and speeches of Edward Blyden, one of the earliest and most prolific writers on Pan-Africanism, who visited Lagos and the hinterland in 1890 and 1895 and served as agent for native affairs from 1896 to 1897.[162] Like Blyden, some began to study local culture seriously. In 1903 the Lagos Native Research Society was founded, and an important body of histories and oral traditions was recorded. Some dropped their European names and adopted African names.[163] Inspired by the dress reform movement in Sierra Leone, some also abandoned European dress and began wearing native dress. European dress was characterized as unsuitable for the African climate and a symbol of mental bondage.[164] European names and dress became concrete reminders of their ambivalent cultural and social positions: "every African bearing a foreign name is like a ship sailing under false colours, and every African wearing a foreign dress in his country is like the jackdaw in peacock's feathers."[165]

Some critics argued that the adoption of European dress also contributed to other social ills. They claimed, for example, that it was accompanied by an unsettling frivolity especially among young women. An editorial in the *Lagos Standard* lamented that educated, Christian girls were being raised with no useful skills, utterly consumed with finding a desirable partner, and almost manic in their passion for dress—hats, dresses, and gloves. Their lives did not contrast favorably with their "sister in the interior, who is brought up in some useful occupation, is betrothed in childhood, and has her life mapped out for her."[166] This characterization presented women in the interior as very docile, which certainly contradicted the other popular image of them as freewheeling, quick-to-divorce women.

Dress became the metaphorical canvas against which the conflicts arising from British imperialism were projected. European dress was contrasted with Yoruba dress to highlight gender and generational tensions over the actions of educated young women. The two styles of dress also became signifiers in a larger debate about race, class, and identity. Most discussions of the cultural nationalist movement of this period highlight men's participation, but there were some women who also shared this critique of European dress and cultural values. A number of women began to question the Victorian ideal of women's economic dependence. Abigail Macaulay, the daughter of Bishop Samuel Crowther and the wife of Reverend Thomas Macaulay, traded to supplement her husband's small salary even though the CMS pressured her to stop.[167] The daughters of Richard Blaize, the wealthy Egba Saro merchant, made names for themselves by wearing traditional dress on special occasions. One daughter, Mrs. Gibson, wore an "unusual combination of *adire* 'tie dye' wrapper and differently patterned European prints as *buba*-like overblouse, headtie, and shawl . . . (while) her sister . . . combined, hand-woven cloth, *adire* and European prints."[168] This reevaluation of European culture primarily affected a small group, and it was not supported by all within that group. Some, in fact, regarded it as a fad.[169] Nonetheless, it marked a critical moment in Nigerian political and cultural history.

While some Christian elites turned to Yoruba dress as a way to reconnect with "traditional" Yoruba culture, Yoruba dress was not static. It too was changing. More people wore shoes;[170] women and girls adopted the *buba* or blouse, in the process creating a new standard for "traditional" dress. The photographs at the end of the chapter capture some of the changes in dress. Photos 2.1 and 2.2 illustrate the dramatic range in dress styles by the end of the nineteenth century. The African men and women at the governor's house (2.2) are fully attired in Victorian costume. Only skin color differentiates them from the Europeans in the picture. The "typical" Yoruba woman, as a caption on the photograph calls her, does not have shoes on and she wears three wrappers reminiscent of Samuel Johnson's description of women's dress. The cloth across her shoulders appears to be handwoven and of a dark indigo dye, and the bottom wrapper also appears to be handwoven. Her headdress, however, appears to be an imported plaid cloth. Photo 2.3 illustrates the new norm of "traditional" dress. Both women's tops are tailored. Their wrappers are not tailored, and both appear to be made from imported cloth. The woman on the left finished her outfit with a smaller hand-woven wrapper, while the other woman's complete outfit shows a tie-and-dye pattern. All the men's garments, on the other hand, appear to be of made of European cloth and tailored in European styles.

Practical considerations encouraged the use of some imported cloths. Manchester prints and calico were not durable, but they were affordable. They were also lighter and more comfortable. As Renne argues, European cloth was associated with *olaju*, enlightenment. Among other things, imported cloth expressed people's identification with a wider "civilized" world. [171] The ways in which these cloths were finished by dyers and worn suggest that they also connected consumers to Yoruba history and aesthetics. Cloths like *adire* allowed consumers to be simultaneously "modern" and "traditional." Untailored

Photo 2.1 Guests at Governor Moloney's Party. "An At Home in Government House Given by Sir Alfred Moloney" ca. 1889. (Copyright The Bodleian Library, University of Oxford. John Holt Papers. MSS Afr. S. 1789. Reprinted with permission.)

Photo 2.2 "Typical" Yoruba Woman, ca. 1890. (Copyright The Bodleian Library, University of Oxford. John Holt Papers. MSS Afr. S. 1789. Reprinted with permission.)

Photo 2.3 "Suman and Bride at Lagos 24 July 1910." Unfortunately, the original caption did not identify Suman or his bride. (Copyright The Bodleian Library, University of Oxford. Sir Edmund Oswald Teale, MSS Afr. S. 384, Box II. Reprinted with permission.)

wrappers and dyed indigo cloths placed women at the beginning of the twentieth century in the same cultural universe with women at the mid nineteenth century, but they had modernized that universe through the use of imported cloths, tailored blouses, and resist patterning.

CONCLUSION

The political terrain changed considerably between 1898 and 1914. The *Alake* became the central figure in the political structure, but his consolidation of power was entangled with expanding British power. By 1914 the Egba government was no longer independent. It was now fully under the thumb of the colonial government. The *Alake* retained his position, and very little changed, since the abrogation of the treaty virtually overlapped with the beginning of World War I. The colonial state waited until 1918 to impose significant political changes and taxation. [172] While it existed, the Egba United Government helped solidify the processes that supported the expansion of the dyeing industry. The railway and the expansion of roads brought Abeokuta much more fully into the circuits of international trade. Abeokuta residents exported cotton, palm produce, and cocoa and they imported "rice from India, . . . coffee from Brazil, . . . sugar from Germany, . . . tobacco from Virginia, . . . cotton goods from Manchester, . . . cutlery from Sheffield and . . . coffins from Liverpool."[173] Abeokuta clearly lived up to the commercial expectations of the European trading companies.

These developments put labor at a premium but created a social revolution that weakened access to sources of labor that producers had previously enjoyed. The expansion of trade and wage labor gave dependent men and women opportunities to assert their interests. In this millieu, local industries had to adjust to new labor conditions, new commercial conditions, and changing tastes. Indigenous industries in some Yoruba towns suffered under the new circumstances,[174] but Abeokuta's dyers were able to take advantage of the new economy. Using inexpensive Manchester cottons, they produced a product that appealed to the aesthetic taste, the nationalist sentiments, and the purses of consumers in Yorubaland as well as other parts of West Africa.

NOTES

1. Frederick Lugard, *Dual Mandate in British Tropical Africa,* 5th ed. (Hamden, CT: Archon Books, 1965).

2. Karen Fields, *Revival and Rebellion in Colonial Central Africa* (Portsmouth, NH: Heinemann, 1997), 39. Also see Crawford Young, *The African Colonial State in Comparative Perspective* (New Haven, CT: Yale University Press, 1994), 141–81.

3. Mahmood Mamdani, *Citizen and Subject: Contemporary Africa and the Legacy of Late Colonialism* (Princeton, NJ: Princeton University Press, 1996), 62–108.

4. Ekundare argues that cotton goods "represented the most important single item of importation" into Nigeria. See R.O. Ekundare, *An Economic History of Nigeria 1860–1960* (New York: Africana, 1973), 212.

5. Letter from Governor G.T. Carter to the Marquis of Ripon, 18 January 1893, in C.W. Newbury, ed., *British Policy Towards West Africa: Select Documents 1875–1914* (Oxford: Clarendon Press, 1971), 131. Also Agneta Pallinder-Law, "Government in Abeokuta 1830–1914: With Special Reference to the Egba United

Government 1898–1914," Ph.D. diss., Götesborgs University, 1973, 59. The treaty, however, forced Abeokuta to relinquish control of several towns near Lagos. See Harry A. Gailey, *Lugard and the Abeokuta Uprising: The Demise of Egba Independence* (London: Frank Cass, 1982), 28.

6. A.K. Ajisafe, *History of Abeokuta,* 3d ed. (Lagos: Kash and Klare Bookshop, 1948), 87; Agneta Pallinder-Law, "Aborted Modernization in West Africa? The Case of Abeokuta," *Journal of African History* 15, 1 (1974): 73; S.O. Biobaku, "The Egba Council 1899–1918: Part 1," *ODU—Journal of Yoruba and Related Studies* 2 (1956): 17.

7. Akin L. Mabogunje, "The Changing Pattern of Rural Settlement and Rural Economy in Egba Division, South Western Nigeria," M.A. thesis, University College, University of London, 1958, 13.

8. S.O. Biobaku, *The Egba and Their Neighbors 1842–1872* (Oxford: Clarendon Press, 1957), 88; and Earl Phillips, "The Egba at Abeokuta: Acculturation and Political Change, 1830–1870," *Journal of African History* 10, 1 (1969): 117–31.

9. There were two other categories of titles, the *Olode,* or the scouts, and the *Olorogun,* an early township militia. Biobaku suggests that chieftaincy titles corresponded to the life cycle. A young man could begin as an *Olode,* then branch into the *Parakoyi* if he was a trader or *Olorogun/Ologun* if he was a successful farmer and still young enough to bear arms, and when he became an elder, join the *Ogboni.* S.O. Biobaku, *A Window on Nigeria* (Lagos: Nelson, 1994), 55.

10. This was not the first time the Egba had created a federal militia. In 1780 the Egba launched a revolt against Oyo, their overlord. A militia, which had emerged from the farmers' associations, led the revolt. It appears that this militia was the antecedent for the later military apparatus. See Ajisafe, *History of Abeokuta,* 6, and Biobaku, *Egba and Their Neighbors,* 9.

11. Biobaku, *Egba and Their Neighbors,* 21.

12. Another major effort to create an effective centralized government came in 1865, when George William Johnson created the Egba United Board of Management (EUBM). Johnson envisioned a government of traditional rulers with a powerful civil service of educated African men as officials and advisers. The *Bashorun,* Somoye, was the president-general of this body, which included both *Ologun* and *Ogboni* chiefs and Johnson as its secretary. They established a regular postal system between Abeokuta and Lagos as well as a Customs Department to levy export duties in place of the tolls which had been collected at the gates. The EUBM never dominated Egba politics, even though it had the support of some important chiefs who sympathized with its effort to centralize power. It lost its most important patron when *Bashorun* Somoye died in 1868. The EUBM further declined in significance after 1874, when Johnson moved to Lagos, returning to Abeokuta only occasionally. See E.A. Ayandele, *The Missionary Impact on Modern Nigeria, 1842–1914: A Political and Social Analysis* (London: Longman, 1981), 46; and Pallinder-Law, "Aborted Modernization," 72.

13. Richard F. Burton, *Abeokuta and the Cameroons Mountain: An Exploration,* vol. 1 (London: Tinsley Brothers, 1863), 126.

14. E.A. Oroge, "The Institution of Slavery in Yorubaland with Particular Reference to the Nineteenth Century," Ph.D. diss., University of Birmingham, U.K., 1971, 233–39.

15. Jean H. Kopytoff, *A Preface to Modern Nigeria: The "Sierra Leonians" in Yoruba, 1830–1890* (Madison: University of Wisconsin Press, 1965), 127. Burton, *Abeokuta and the Cameroons Mountain,* 158. It was alleged that several European missionaries, including Henry Townsend, also joined the *Ogboni.* See R.E. Dennett, "The Ogboni and Other Secret Societies in Nigeria," *Journal of the African Society,* October 1916, 22.

16. S.O. Biobaku, personal communication, Lagos, 26 August 1996.

17. James Johnson to H. Wright, 2 August 1879. CMS, CA 2/056. Relatively little has been written about the *Parakoyi.* Belasco suggests that their emergence among the Egba represented an innovation tied to the growth of coastal trade. Fadipe, Biobaku, and Belasco all state that *Parakoyi* were male title holders. See N.A. Fadipe, *The Sociology of the Yoruba* (Ibadan: University of Ibadan Press), 255; Biobaku, *Egba and Their Neighbors,* 6; and Bernard Belasco, *The Entrepreneur As Culture Hero: Preadaptations in Nigerian Economic Development* (New York: Praeger, 1980), 67.

18. S.O. Biobaku, "Madame Tinubu," in *Eminent Nigerians of the Nineteenth Century* (Cambridge: Cambridge University Press, 1960), 38–39. Oladipo Yemitan, *Madame Tinubu, Merchant and King-Maker* (Ibadan: Fastprint, 1987).

19. The men who signed the treaty dominated the political arena only for a few more years following the agreement. Sorunke and Osundare died in 1895 and Ogundeyi in 1897. Ajisafe, *History of Abeokuta,* 88.

20. Pallinder-Law, "Government in Abeokuta," 64.

21. Ajisafe, *History of Abeokuta,* 90. McCallum deported Aboaba's secretary, Emmanuel Coker, to Ibadan as well.

22. Gailey, *Lugard and the Abeokuta Uprising,* 31.

23. Pallinder-Law, "Government in Abeokuta," 65. Pallinder-Law argues that this was the most novel feature of the reorganization. For various religious reasons, *Obas* were not allowed to meet previously.

24. For example, William Allen was named the superintendent for native affairs, the Lagos government's representative; C.B. Moore, a Brazilian repatriate and prosperous trader, was named treasurer; P.P. Martins, another Brazilian repatriate, was named secretary; and Rev. David Ogunsola Williams was made colonial chaplain and advisor to the king. See Ajisafe, *History of Abeokuta,* 90 and Pallinder-Law, "Aborted Modernization," 74.

25. Pallinder-Law, "Aborted Modernization," 75–76.

26. The EUG began a vaccination program, and two young men were sent to the Lagos government for training. Ajisafe, *History of Abeokuta,* 93–94.

27. Samuel, an ordained Wesleyan minister, had been on the Lagos Board of Education and principal of the Wesleyan Boys High School. He had the full support of Gov. MacGregor when he was named secretary. Pallinder-Law, "Government in Abeokuta," 91–93. Also see Ajisafe, *History of Abeokuta,* 122–24.

28. Pallinder-Law, "Aborted Modernization," 75–76.

29. Pallinder-Law, "Government in Abeokuta," 187–209. Pallinder-Law compiled a helpful list of all the council members between 1898 and 1914.

30. Interview with Afusatu Arogundade, 28 August 1996, Kemta, Abeokuta.

31. One of the earliest references to Madam Jojolola was in "Testimony of the Commission of Enquiry into the Disturbances into Abeokuta Province," 11 November 1918, 212. N.A.I., CSO 16/20 C92/1918. Afusatu Arogundade.

32. "A Report on the Native Law of Egbaland, 1906," 15. MSS. AFR.S. 1913. Cyril Punch Papers, Rhodes House.

33. The Aro Station was officially opened a year earlier. At that time Abeokuta residents did not want it to go into the town because they did not want to take employment away from women and carriers in general. See "The Ceremony at Abeokuta," *Lagos Weekly Record*, 9 March 1901.

34. "Opening of the Abeokuta Branch Line of the Lagos Railway," *West Africa*, 25 January 1902, 92.

35. Ibid. Sarapa-Williams was born in Freetown in 1855. His father was Ijesha, though he had strong Egba connections. He was a British-trained barrister and a member of the Lagos Legislative Council from 1901 to 1915. He also served on the committee which compiled a report on the Yoruba in 1906. See Anthony G. Hopkins, "A Report on the Yoruba, 1910," *Journal of the Historical Society of Nigeria* 5, 1 (1969): 69.

36. Ibid.

37. Ibid.

38. Ibid.

39. Fields, *Revival and Rebellion,* 31.

40. John Holt to Thomas Welch, 17 February 1892. MSS.AFR.S.1525, 19/4, Rhodes House. Holt began his African career working in a retail store in Fernando Po in 1862. He subsequently purchased the store, which did most of its business in hardware and textiles. He used the profits from the store to get into the produce trade. See Cherry Gertzel, "John Holt: A British Merchant in West Africa in the Era of Imperialism," Ph.D. diss., Oxford University, 1959, 98–110.

41. Letter from Thomas Barker, secretary, Incorporated Chamber of Commerce, Liverpool, to the Manchester subcommittee, 14 December 1895. MSS.AFR.S 1525, 9/1, Rhodes House.

42. "Lagosian On Dits," *Lagos Standard*, 8 April 1896. Also see "Lagosian On Dits," *Lagos Standard,* 8 January 1896.

43. Pallinder-Law, "Government in Abeokuta," 88. Edun hired a trained European engineer to head road construction in Egbaland.

44. Ajisafe, *History of Abeokuta,* 94, 117.

45. Pallinder-Law, "Government in Abeokuta," 114. The order in council dated 27 July 1905 stated "it is expedient that a Department for the construction and main-tenance of Public Roads be organized" and furthermore that "it shall be lawful for the Alake or proper Officers appointed by him to call upon the Chiefs and Headmen of Townships, and of villages, to take steps and be responsible for the supply of labor necessary to construct and keep in order such roads as are authorized by the Alake and Council to be made." Letter from A. T. Somoye, Clerk of Council ECR 1/1/73 (National Archives, Abeokuta—hereafter, NAA).

46. B. W. Hodder and U. I. Ukwu, *Markets in West Africa: Studies of Markets and Trade Among the Yoruba and Ibo* (Ibadan: University of Ibadan Press, 1969), 38–39. The expansion of roads sustained and probably increased the demand for transport labor. The first trucks were introduced in 1910, but until the supply of trucks was adequate, the increased volume of trade was carried to the markets or railway stations by men and women. *Egba Government Gazette,* 1911 (NAA).

47. "Agriculture and Trade at Abeokuta," *West African Mail,* 10th April 1903, 64.

48. "Lagos Agricultural Show," *West African Mail,* 24 December 1903, 996.

49. Missionary letter 14, from Rev. Ernest Fry, November 1903, 4. CMS 72372.r79, Rhodes House. Fry served in Abeokuta from 1899 until his death in 1906. He was accompanied by his wife, Phillis, who stayed on in Nigeria until 1915. Together they wrote thirty missionary letters, which kept their friends and supporters in England apprised of their activities.

50. "Lagos Agricultural Show," *West African Mail,* 24 December 1903, 996–97. A photograph of the weavers on exhibit at the trade show was later made into a postcard. The card features a male and a female weaver and the caption "Native Industry Looms Egba." MSS.AFR.S.384(6), Rhodes House.

51. "An Egba Trader's Protest, *West Africa,* 1 August 1903, 113.

52. Sara Berry, *Cocoa, Custom and Socio-economic Change in Rural Western Nigeria* (Oxford: Clarendon Press, 1975), 23; Annual Report, Southern Provinces—Nigeria, 1907 (NAI).

53. Richenda Scott, "Production for Trade," in Margery Perham, ed., *The Native Economies of Nigeria,* vol. 1 (London: Faber & Faber, 1946), 224. Total net exports of palm oil 1909–13 was 81.9 metric tons; 1924–28, 128.1; 1929, 132.9; 1930, 136.7; 1931, 118.8. See Chapter 5 herein for further discussion of changing commodity prices.

54. The resident noted that with the outbreak of the war, trade almost totally collapsed, as the merchants stopped buying oil and kernels. See Report on the Abeokuta Province for the Six Months Ending 30 September 1914. Abe Prof. 2/2—289/1914 (NAI).

55. In 1913, for example, Germany bought virtually Nigeria's entire crop of palm kernels (2 million pounds). Palm kernel oil was used in the production of margarine and toilet soap. Durant F. Ladd, *Trade and Shipping in West Africa* (Washington DC: United States Shipping Board, 1920), 72. See A. Osuntokun, *Nigeria in the First World War* (London: Humanities Press, 1979), 21–25.

56. In 1916 palm oil hit a record price of £44 per ton in Liverpool. Osuntokun, *Nigeria in the First World War,* 60. Martin reports that produce often piled up at the Nigerian ports. Susan Martin, *Palm Oil and Protest: An Economic History of the Ngwa Region, South-eastern Nigeria, 1800–1980* (Cambridge: Cambridge University Press, 1988), 57.

57. Margery Perham, *The Native Economies of Nigeria*, vol. 1, Introduction. The decline, though gradual, began in a rather dramatic fashion. In 1902, the palm-oil industry accounted for 91.2 percent (in value) of the total exports of Lagos colony; by 1911 the figure had fallen to 79 percent.

58. Babatunde A. Agiri, "Kola in Western Nigeria, 1850–1950: A History of the Cultivation of Kola Nitida in Egba-Owode, Ijebu-Remo, Iwo and Ota Areas," Ph.D. diss., University of Wisconsin, 1972, 129–32.

59. J. B. Webster, "The Bible and the Plough," *Journal of the Historical Society of Nigeria* 4, 2 (1963): 429.

60. Ibid., 428. Davies captained a ship which traded between Freetown (Sierra Leone), Lagos, and the Niger, and it is suspected that during his travels he learned of the nascent cocoa cultivation. By 1880 Davies had established a cocoa plantation with seedlings he obtained from Fernando Po. His plantation was located in Ijan on the Lagos lagoon in order to facilitate transportation. Also see Berry, *Cocoa, Cus-*

tom, 40, and Anthony G. Hopkins, "Innovation in a Colonial Context: African Origins of the Nigerian Cocoa-Farming Industry, 1880–1920," pp. 83–90 in Clive Dewey and Anthony G. Hopkins, eds., *The Imperial Impact: Studies in the Economic History of Africa and India* (London: Athlone Press, 1978).

61. Webster, "Bible and the Plough," 429–30. Also see S. A. Dada, *J.K. Coker, Father of African Independent Churches* (Ibadan: Aowa Press, 1986). Many of the most enthusiastic advocates of cocoa production were Christian clergymen and members of the independent African church movement. J. K. Coker, considered the father of the independent church movement, was Davies's brother-in-law and one of the major cocoa producers in Agege.

62. Scott, "Production for Trade," 247.

63. Berry, *Cocoa, Custom,* 221. Also see Scott, "Production for Trade," 250. There was a dramatic increase in production between 1912 and 1916 and between 1917 and 1921.

64. Berry, *Cocoa, Custom,* 222.

65. Berry, *Cocoa, Custom,* 80, 221. These figures show the tons of cocoa exported from all of Nigeria:

1914	1915	1916	1917	1918	1919	1920	1921
4,939	9,105	8,956	15,442	10,219	25,711	17,155	17,944

66. Annual Report—Colony and Protectorate of Lagos, 1908, 105 (NAI). Cwt., a hundredweight, was equivalent to 112 pounds. Price per ton was approximately £70 in 1907, £48 in 1908.

67. Osuntokun, *Nigeria in the First World War,* 60.

68. Akin L. Mabogunje and M.B. Gleave, "Changing Agricultural Landscape in Southern Nigeria: The Example of Egba Division, 1850–1950," *Nigerian Geographical Journal* 7, 1 (1964): 12.

69. Agiri, "Kola in Western Nigeria," 136.

70. Mabogunje and Gleave, "Changing Agricultural Landscape," 12.

71. Agiri, "Kola in Western Nigeria," 111. Of that total, 72 tons came from Agege/Otta and 5 tons from Abeokuta.

72. Julian Clarke, "Households and the Political Economy of Small-Scale Cash Crop Production in South-western Nigeria," *Africa* 51, 4 (1981): 819–20. Also see Daryll Forde, "The Rural Economies," in Margery Perham, ed., *The Native Economies of Nigeria,* 98–99. Forde estimated that women constituted 50 percent of these traders, who were called pan or basket buyers.

73. Gertzel, "John Holt," 532. Their partnership lasted from 1887 to the turn of the century.

74. By 1921 eighteen European firms had offices in Abeokuta. The list included the African and Eastern Trade Corp., John Holt & Co., London & Kano Trading Co., W. B. MacIver & Co., Miller Brothers Ltd., and G. B. Ollivant. See Annual Report Southern Nigeria, 1921 (NAI).

75. Letter of John Holt to T. Bedford Glasier, 31 January 1908. MSS. AFR.S. 1657/5. James Deemin Papers, Rhodes House. Deemin joined John Holt in 1883 and worked with the company until his death in 1939. He served in several locations in West Africa—Nigeria, Cameroons, Dahomey, Gabon—and finally in Liverpool after he left the African coast. See "Autobiography of James Deemin," in P.N. Davies,

ed., *Trading in West Africa, 1840–1920,* (New York: Africana Publishing, 1976), 93–136.

76. Pallinder-Law, "Government in Abeokuta," 96; and Letter from Cyril Punch, railway commissioner, to the assistant colonial secretary in charge, Secretariat Lagos, in Letter Book 1900–1903, Abe Prof. 9/2 (NAI).

77. "An Egba Traders' Protest," *West Africa,* 1 August 1903.

78. Ajisafe, *History of Abeokuta,* 122.

79. Sir William MacGregor, "Lagos, Abeokuta, and the Alake," *Journal of the African Society* 12 (July 1904): 479.

80. Letter of John Holt to H.J. Rawlings, 31 May 1910, 5. MSS. AFR.S.1657/1. James Deemin Papers, Rhodes House.

81. Letter of H.J. Rawlings to John Holt, 28 May 1910, 2–3. MSS. AFR.S.1657/5. James Deemin Papers, Rhodes House.

82. Ibid., 4.

83. Ibid., 6. Gertzel argued that African merchants in Lagos who dominated retail trade pioneered the trade in new types of cheap, heavily starched cottons of inferior quality. Gertzel, "John Holt," 538.

84. Letter of John Holt to H.J. Rawlings, 31 May 1910, 2-3. MSS. AFR.S.1657/1. James Deemin Papers, Rhodes House.

85. Letter of H.J. Rawlings to John Holt, 28 May 1910, 5–6. MSS. AFR.S.1657/5. James Deemin Papers, Rhodes House. Most traders were concerned with just the export of cloth, but some encouraged British manufacturers to export ready-made clothes in popular West African styles. Errol Macdonell, the British consul in Liberia, forwarded a letter to the *West African Mail* in which the author recommended "the export of 'ready-made' jumpers or blouses for native female attire." The contribution included a sketch of the blouses, measurements, as well as two pictures of women wearing similar blouses. "Openings for Trade in Liberia," *West African Mail,* 6 November 1903, 852.

86. "Tolls in the Egba Territories and Ibadan Province," *West African Mail,* 26 February 1904, 1219. A string was equal to 40 cowries.

87. See General Imports into the Colony and Protectorate of Southern Nigeria, *Blue Books,* 1900–1909 (NAI). It is difficult to compute these amounts and values with consistency. Most years they recorded the amount of imported cloth by packages, but in 1905 they recorded it by yards—33,062,275 yards. Record keeping changed again in 1912. They began to record the cloth by type—e.g., gray bafts, bleached cotton piece goods—and the amount by weight, for example: Cotton Piece Goods Dyed in the Piece—1,968,273.47 lbs = £155,884.

88. Ladd, *Trade and Shipping,* 78.

89. Marion Johnson, "Cotton Imperialism in West Africa," *African Affairs* 73 (1974): 186.

90. The *Egba Government Gazette,* which began publication in 1904, gave monthly totals of the number of packages of cotton goods and their value as well other economic indices. (Ajisafe, *History of Abeokuta,* 100). Many people appreciated the economic information provided by the *Gazette,* which was printed in both English and Yoruba. See "In Abeokuta," *Lagos Weekly Record,* 19 August 1905. The *Gazette* ended with the imposition of formal colonial rule in Abeokuta in 1914, but it was resurrected as the *Egba Administrative Bulletin*

after 1920. The *Bulletin,* however, did not provide these helpful economic reports.

91. "Trade Marks Action," *Lagos Standard,* 26 June 1901.

92. Allister Macmillan, *The Red Book of West Africa: Historical and Descriptive Commercial and Industrial Facts, Figures and Resources* (Ibadan: Spectrum Books, 1993), 115.

93. Interview with Chief Adura Majekodunmi, 21 June 1988, Ikereku, Abeokuta.

94. The *Alake* argued that a no-credit system would not lead to a rapid expansion of trade, but it would put trade on a sound and sure basis and prove beneficial all round. "European Commercial Enterprise at Abeokuta," *Lagos Weekly Record,* 13 September 1902.

95. See Scott, "Production for Trade," 266f. Of the eleven main European firms trading in cocoa in Nigeria in 1939, nine also did business in imported merchandise. Of those nine, five had stores in Abeokuta: UAC, G. B. Ollivant, Companie Française de L'Afrique Occidentale, John Holt, and Paterson Zochonis & Co. See also Annual Report, Colony of Nigeria, 1921 (NAI).

96. "Trade on the Credit System," *West Africa,* 4 July 1903, 4. Bauer argues that this transaction was not really on credit terms. The true credit was only the difference between the nominal credit limit and the cash deposit. Most of these customers, he argues, should be considered "registered" or regular customers who had ledger accounts with the firm. See P.T. Bauer, *West African Trade: A Study of Competition, Oligopoly and Monopoly in a Changing Economy* (Cambridge University Press, 1954), 61–62. This form of credit will be discussed further in Chapter 5.

97. C.W. Newbury, "Credit in Early Nineteenth Century West African Trade," *Journal of African History* 13, 1 (1972): 81–95. Newbury argues that the dramatic increase in trade between Europe and West Africa after 1850 was based on advancing credit to African traders because the old system of "ship-to-shore barter trade with immediate payment in kind" could not adapt to the new demands in trade.

98. Anthony G. Hopkins, "The Currency Revolution in South West Nigeria in the Late Nineteenth Century," *Journal of the Historical Society of Nigeria* 3, 3 (1966): 482. Writing in 1936, Gurney noted that the "barter system of trading with the natives has disappeared and the crops are paid for in cash." F. Gurney, Report on Economic and Commercial Conditions in the British Dependencies in West Africa, November 1936–March 1937, 16–17 (Dartmouth College). Also see Walter Ofonagoro, "The Currency Revolution in Southern Nigeria 1880–1948," Occasional Paper No. 14, African Studies Center, UCLA, 1976.

99. "Trade on the Credit System," *West Africa,* 4 July 1903, 4.

100. Ibid. In 1908 Holt's agent did stop giving out credit for produce in Lagos, and African traders were able to get credit from other firms, especially Miller Bros. Letter of John Holt to James Deemin, 20 July 1908, 33. MSS.AFR.S.1675/3. James Deemin Papers, Rhodes House.

101. Annual Report, Colony and Protectorate of Lagos, 1907, 104 (NAI).

102. Letter of John Holt to Stephen Ayles, 28 February 1908. MSS.AFR.S.1657/1. James Deemin Papers, Rhodes House.

103. Letter of John Holt to Stephen Ayles, 17 January 1908. MSS.AFR.S.1657/1. James Deemin Papers, Rhodes House.

104. Letter of H.J. Rawlings to John Holt, 28 May 1910. MSS.AFR.S.1657/5. James Deemin Papers, Rhodes House.

105. Letter of John Holt to Stephen Ayles, 6 March 1908. MSS.AFR.S.1657/1. James Deemin Papers, Rhodes House.

106. Letter of John Holt to James Deemin, 7 February 1908, 3. MSS.AFR.S.1657/2. James Deemin Papers, Rhodes House.

107. Letter from the Director of John Holt and Co. Ltd. to H.J. Rawlings, 31 December 1912. MSS.AFR.S.1657/1. James Deemin Papers, Rhodes House.

108. Letter of John Holt to Stephen Ayles, 17 January 1908. MSS.AFR.S.1657/1. James Deemin Papers, Rhodes House.

109. Letter of H.J. Rawlings to John Holt, 28 May 1910. MSS.AFR.S.1657/5. James Deemin Papers, Rhodes House.

110. Ajisafe, *History of Abeokuta,* 95.

111. Anthony Nwabughuogu, "From Wealthy Entrepreneurs to Petty Traders: The Decline of African Middlemen in Eastern Nigeria, 1900–1950," *Journal of African History* 23, 3 (1982): 369. Also see Felicia Ekejiuba, "Omu Okwei, The Merchant Queen of Ossomari: A Biographical Sketch," *Journal of the Historical Society of Nigeria* 3, 4 (1967): 633–46.

112. Letter of John Holt to James Deemin, 20 July 1908, 18–19. MSS.AFR.S. 1657/3. James Deemin Papers, Rhodes House.

113. "Trade on the Credit System," *West Africa,* 4 July 1903, 4.

114. Letter of D.D. Africanus Coker to John Holt & Co., 28 March 1921 in P.N. Davies, ed., *Trading in West Africa, 1840–1920,* (New York: Africana, 1976), 166.

115. Ibadan wanted to collect tolls at the Iddo Gate, which was situated at the railway. Previously toll was not collected at this gate regularly, since most trade went to the Ejinrin market via other gates. Caxton, "The Tolls Question," *West African Mail,* 10 July 1903, 418.

116. "Native Rulers in West Africa: No. 1—the Alake of Abeokuta, Capital of the Egba Province of Yoruba (Lagos Protectorate)," *West African Mail,* 29 May 1903, 246.

117. Ibid.

118. Carland argues that indirect rule was also shaped in important ways by residents who continued to serve in northern Nigeria after Lugard left in 1906. Charles Temple, for example, argued strongly for making the resident the heart of the indirect rule system, and Richmond Palmer, who created the first native treasury in Katsina, secured the resident's power by giving him veto power over expenditures. See John M. Carland, *The Colonial Office and Nigeria, 1898–1914* (Stanford, CA: Hoover Institution Press, 1985), 71–72.

119. Governor MacGregor also used the toll issue to force the Egba government to allow the railway commissioner to live inside the town in Ibara. He threatened not to allow them to collect the tolls unless they agreed to this provision. Pallinder-Law, "Government in Abeokuta," 73.

120. "The Question of Tolls in the Hinterland," *West Africa,* 18 July 1903, 60.

121. Ibid.

122. Bruce Berman and John Lonsdale, "Coping with the Contradictions: The Development of the Colonial State 1895–1914," in *Unhappy Valley, Conflict in Kenya and Africa* (Athens: Ohio University Press, 1992), 80. Also see Mamdani, *Citizen and Subject,* 22–24; Anne Phillips, *The Enigma of Colonialism: British Policy in West Africa* (Bloomington: Indiana University Press, 1989), 10; and Fields, *Revival and Rebellion,* 30.

123. "Native Rulers in West Africa."

124. Quoted in "The Lagos Native Councils and Forest Ordinances," *Lagos Weekly Record,* 6 December 1902.

125. "The Lagos Tolls—Meeting of Native Merchants and Traders," *West Africa,* 1 August 1903.

126. "Demonstration at Abeokuta," *West African Mail,* 17 July 1903, 446. Attendance was estimated at 10,000 people. Mass meetings were also held in Ibadan. *West African Mail,* 24 July 1903, 470–72.

127. "Mass Meeting at Abeokuta," *Lagos Weekly Record,* 11 July 1903.

128. "The Tolls Question. The Situation in Abeokuta," *West African Mail,* 14 August 1903, 550.

129. "British West Africa. Lagos—the Tolls Question, Letter from the Colonial Office," *West African Mail,* 24 July 1903, 470; and "The New Tolls Tariff for Abeokuta and Ibadan," *Lagos Weekly Record,* 16 January 1904.

130. "The Tolls Agitation and Its Lessons," *Lagos Weekly Record,* 1 August 1903.

131. Cyril Punch (railway commissioner), Letter Books 1900–1903, No. 60/1901, 25 April 1901, and No. 72/1901. Abe Prof. 9/2 (NAI).

132. In order to recover a debt under precolonial Egba law, the creditor obtained permission from a chief to hire a licensed distrainer, *ologo. Ologos* stationed themselves in the debtor's compound and made a nuisance of themselves by singing abusive songs, refusing to allow people to enter or leave, seizing food, and killing chickens. In addition to the debt, the debtor was also responsible for any destruction caused by the *ologo.* See Fadipe, *Sociology of the Yoruba,* 164.

133. Pallinder-Law, "Government in Abeokuta," 94.

134. Ajisafe, *History of Abeokuta,* 100. Serious cases involving foreigners as well as civil cases involving claims exceeding £50 were to be heard by the chief justice of Lagos sitting with two Egba assessors. A two-tier judiciary was also established in Abeokuta. In addition to Egba courts, a new mixed court was created in which the railway commissioner and two EUG council members or special magistrates would hear cases of lesser matters concerning foreigners. Pallinder-Law, "Government in Abeokuta," 97. This agreement was soon followed by the opening of native courts.

135. Ajisafe, *History of Abeokuta,* 98.

136. Gailey, *Lugard and the Abeokuta Uprising,* 37.

137. Osuntokun, *Nigeria in the First World War,* 104; and Ajisafe, *History of Abeokuta,* 110–12.

138. "Report of the Commission of Enquiry into the August 1914 Killings." Abe Prof 7/2 (NAI). Although the military commander of the contingent claimed that the crowd made threatening advances on his men, it appears from much of the testimony that his explanation was at best dubious. The callousness of the

whole episode was underscored by the fact that no inquest was held on the victims. They were buried without identification in a single trench, and the commission report was never published. Osuntokun, *Nigeria in the First World War,* 107.

139. See Gailey, *Lugard and the Abeokuta Uprising,* Ch. 5; Osuntokun, *Nigeria in the First World War*, ch. 4.

140. Webster, "The Bible and the Plough," 433.

141. Clarke, "Households and the Political Economy," 819.

142. I.O. Delano, *The Singing Minister of Nigeria: The Life of Canon J.J. Ransome-Kuti* (London: United Society for Christian Literature, c. 1940), 27.

143. C. Partridge, "Native Law and Custom in Egbaland," *Journal of the African Society* 10, 40: 423–24.

144. "The Social Disruption Going On in the Hinterland," *Lagos Weekly Record,* 8 July 1911.

145. Fadipe, *The Sociology of the Yoruba,* 91.

146. In 1899 George Denton, the acting governor of Lagos, effectively forced the Egbas to cede 200 yards on either side of the railway line to the British government in a 99-year lease. In addition, the EUG ceded judicial control over matters pertaining to the railway and its substantial personnel (8,000). Pallinder-Law, "Government in Abeokuta," 73.

147. See Judith Byfield, "Women, Marriage, Divorce and the Emerging Colonial State in Abeokuta (Nigeria) 1892–1904," *Canadian Journal of African Studies* 30, 1 (1996): 32–51.

148. The resolution on slavery gave specific guidelines on self-redemption and distinguished between slaves born in Egbaland and those born elsewhere. Home-born slaves could pay £5/10s. to redeem themselves, but slaves born elsewhere had to pay £10. Copy of Resolution, Egba Council Records, 3/1/13 (NAA).

149. Letter from acting railway commissioner L. Norton Blackwell to the superintendent of native affairs, Abeokuta, 30 October 1901, 124. Abe Prof 9/2—Letter Book 1900–1903 (NAA).

150. Railway Commissioner H. Kopke to the colonial secretary, 12 May 1900. Abe Prof 9/3—Administrative Minute Book Relating to Egba Affairs, 1900–1904 (NAA).

151. Rev. Ernest Fry, Missionary Letter 14, November 1903. Agiri, "Kola in Western Nigeria," 46.

152. Fadipe, *Sociology of the Yoruba,* 191. Also see Judith Byfield, "Pawns and Politics: The Pawnship Debate in Western Nigeria," in Toyin Falola and Paul Lovejoy, eds., *Pawnship in Africa: Debt Bondage in Historical Perspective* (Boulder, CO: Westview Press, 1993).

153. "The Report of the Inspector of Forests on the Agricultural Prospects of the Egba Country," *West Africa,* 29 November 1902.

154. *The Lagos Standard,* 12 December 1900. For an important discussion of the Lagos Christian elite, see Kristin Mann, *Marrying Well: Marriage, Status and Social Change Among the Educated Elite in Colonial Lagos* (Cambridge: Cambridge University Press, 1985).

155. Ayandele, *Missionary Impact,* 243.

156. "Prince Ademuyiwa's Idea," *Lagos Standard,* December 12 1900.

157. Mrs. Phillis Fry, "The Yoruba People, Their Peculiarities of Dress, European Dress Affected," *West Africa,* 18 June 1904.

158. Lugard, *Dual Mandate,* 589; Fields, *Revival and Rebellion,* 49.

159. Fred I.A. Omu, *Press and Politics in Nigeria, 1880–1937* (Atlantic Highlands, NJ: Humanities Press, 1978), 107.

160. Ayandele, *Missionary Impact,* 247–49.

161. Titilola Euba, "Dress and Status in 19th Century Lagos," in Ade Adefuye, Babatunde Agiri, and Jide Osuntokun, eds., *History of the Peoples of Lagos State* (Lagos: Lantern Books, 1987), 159; Omu, *Press and Politics,* 108–15; and Philip Zachernuk, *Colonial Subjects: An African Intelligentsia and Atlantic Ideas* (Charlottesville: University Press of Virginia, 2000).

162. Omu, *Press and Politics in Nigeria,* 136. Also see Hollis Lynch, *Edward Wilmot Blyden, Pan-Negro Patriot, 1832–1928* (Oxford: Oxford University Press, 1964), 232–35.

163. Ayandele, *Missionary Impact,* 251–60. Two well-known personalities from Abeokuta who changed their names were Rev. J.H. Samuel, secretary of the EUG, who changed his name to Adegboyega Edun, and G.W. Johnson, former secretary of the Egba United Board of Management, who became Oshokale Tejumade Johnson.

164. "Outward Adornment," *Lagos Standard,* 11 March 1896, and Euba, "Dress and Status," 159.

165. Rev. Mojola Agbebi, "The Spiritual Needs of the Africans," *Lagos Standard,* 31 July 1895 (Supplement). Ayandele credits Agbebi, formerly David Brown Vincent, with approximating the cultural nationalist ideal the most. From 1891 onward he refused to work for any Christian mission because he thought it was a curse to work for any foreign mission. While in Liberia in 1894, he changed his name and started wearing Yoruba dress. He wore traditional dress when he toured the U.S. and Britain during 1903 and 1904 lecturing on African customs. In Lagos he was the leader of the Native Baptist Church. Ayandele, *Missionary Impact,* 254–55.

166. "Our Girls," *Lagos Standard,* 31 January 1900.

167. Mann, *Marrying Well,* 79.

168. Euba, "Dress and Status," 160. Elite women also joined the debate on polygyny. A few women publicly defended Yoruba marriage and polygamy. Increasingly elite women also questioned the economic dependence that had become an expected part of Christian marriage and respectability. They began to advocate greater economic independence and tried to improve the educational and employment opportunities for girls. Mann, *Marrying Well,* 89–91.

169. "Consistent Inconsistencies," *Lagos Standard,* 1 April 1896.

170. Fry, "Yoruba People," Fry noted that canvas shoes had proliferated steadily among the men, and women and girls were beginning to wear them on state occasions.

171. Elisha Renne, *Cloth That Does Not Die: The Meaning of Cloth in Bunu Social Life* (Seattle: University of Washington Press, 1995), 173. For a discussion of

the nuances and contextual meanings associated with *olaju,* see J.D. Peel, "Olaju: A Yoruba Concept of Development," *Journal of Development Studies* 14, 2 (1978): 139–65.

172. Osuntokun, *Nigeria in the First World War,* 126–33. Also see "Rising in Egbaland," CO 583/67, #44709, PRO.

173. "A Plea for the More General Pursuit of Agriculture As a Calling," *Lagos Standard,* 23 May 1900.

174. Ibid. The contemporary author specifically identified salt making, blacksmithing, and weaving as industries in jeopardy.

3

ARTISANS AND EMPIRE: THE STRUCTURE AND ORGANIZATION OF *ADIRE* PRODUCTION

Complex changes occurred in the textile sector as Yoruba towns were transformed to meet the political and economic priorities of the colonial state. Some towns, such as Iseyin, remained important weaving centers, but weaving clearly declined in others.[1] It is unclear whether or the extent to which weaving declined in Abeokuta, but by the 1920s it was overshadowed by the dyeing industry. Dyeing had become a separate industry; and it was virtually synonymous with *adire* production because *adire* was the main focus of most dyers' business. *Adire* production was independent of weavers and spinners and had its own distinct set of linkages to the local, regional, and international economies. This chapter looks specifically at the organization of *adire* production and lays out the roles that the agricultural sector, allied textile workers, and foreign and indigenous merchants played in the production and distribution of these cloths. A detailed picture of *adire* production is crucial to an understanding of the dramatic and varied impact of caustic soda and synthetic dyes.

There is little data for an accurate chronology of the changes that occurred in dyeing before the introduction of caustic soda in the 1920s. Much of the available information about *adire* resulted from interactions between dyers and colonial officials as they debated the difficulties the industry began to experience in the 1920s. In those discussions, the period before the introduction of caustic soda was generally considered a "golden era," when production and distribution were believed to have functioned smoothly. Thus, the description of the industry in its pre–caustic soda period extrapolates from the subsequent discussions between dyers and officials. All the parties engaged in these discussions created slightly different versions of the golden past in order to underscore their causal analysis of the problems the industry faced. There were also conflicting accounts about the development of *adire* itself. Nonetheless, the competing stories are valuable because they provide different perspectives on the integration of *adire* into the local, regional, and international economies as each was reshaped by colonialism.

ARTISANS AND COLONIAL POLICY

Both colonial officials and missionaries were aware of some of the changes unfolding in textile production as well as other artisan crafts by the beginning of the twentieth century. Missionaries, in particular, tried to encourage craft production and urged colonial officials to support technical schools in Africa where artisan producers could be "properly" trained. Their campaign to shape a policy included organizing exhibits across England where African specialists demonstrated weaving, dyeing, carving, ironworking, and leatherworking to the British public. These exhibits encouraged a reevaluation of African craft producers and an appreciation of their skills. They also educated the British public about missionary activities in Africa and secured continuing support for missionary programs.[2]

Within Nigeria, craft production received official scrutiny, but there was no clear consensus on policy. Lord Lugard, for example, was a strong proponent of "cotton imperialism" when he was high commissioner of northern Nigeria. He advocated crushing the local weaving industry so that the cotton historically woven locally would be transported as raw cotton to England, and the redundant weavers would turn to growing cotton for export. Lugard imposed caravan tolls on local textiles and abolished tolls on British imports in 1906 in order to hasten the demise of the local industry. Lugard's successor did not support this policy and abolished the toll on domestic cloth the following year.[3]

Craft producers were often included in agricultural shows. The Lagos Agricultural Show on 11 and 12 November 1903 was both an attempt to promote certain crops and to demonstrate "civilisation and its advantages."[4] Organizers featured a number of labor-saving devices such as cotton gins and kernel-cracking machines as well as livestock, samples of cotton, and exhibits of weavers and spinners at work. Agricultural shows like the Lagos show were primarily display opportunities and did not reflect any concrete attempts by colonial officials to assist craft producers. Nonetheless, by the interwar period some discussions of assisting the local textile industries surfaced. In a 1917 memorandum on the planting and preparation of indigo, the author compared indigo production in Bengal and northern Nigeria. He concluded that the Bengali product was of a better quality and experimented with ways of adapting their method to Nigeria.[5] In spite of these signs of interest, colonial officials made very little effort to become knowledgeable of or involved in local textile production. Trade and agricultural production were their paramount concerns, thus the majority of changes that unfolded in dyeing and other sectors of textile production were initiated by artisans themselves.

ADIRE—EVERY MISTAKE IS A DESIGN

Adire was distinguished by the design that was created on the cloth by various resist methods. Producers covered sections of the cloth with an agent, a paste or threads, that resisted or prevented the dye from being absorbed. Most dyers insisted that they did not do resist dyeing on *aso oke*, handwoven cloth. Weavers generally brought threads to the dyers to dye.[6] But Madam Soetan recalled that some women created patterns on handwoven cloth with needles and raffia (palm fiber) threads.[7] These conflicting accounts suggest that limited resist dyeing was done with handwoven cloth, and from its early history *adire* was primarily produced with imported cloth. There were several advantages to using imported cloths. Imports were generally cheaper than handwoven cloth, and they were lighter and thus much more flexible and maneuverable.[8]

Many dyers suggested that *adire* first developed in the compound of the town's second *Iyalode*, Madam Jojolola. It has also been suggested that *adire* was introduced in Abeokuta by Saros who had learned it from the Mende in Sierra Leone, and from there it spread to other parts of Yorubaland.[9] Although Madam Jojolola's compound was one of the largest dyeing compounds in the town and the Saros practiced dyeing, there is evidence that resist dyeing was not unknown to Yoruba dyers. Its earliest application was on threads, a technique scholars call *ikat*. These threads were then woven into cloths that often had a striped design, thus the dyeing technique could have been easily overlooked by observers.[10]

There were several resist techniques. *Adire-oniko* was one of the oldest forms and involved manipulating the cloth by tying and folding.[11] Folding was by far the simplest method. The cloth was folded horizontally, vertically, or diagonally and raffia thread was tied at intervals to maintain the folds. Tying, while quite simple, sometimes proved an extraordinarily time-consuming process. Women could spend several hours or days on one piece of cloth.[12] In the pattern called *alakete* (man's hat), the designer tied raphia around small circles about the size of a fingertip. Each circle was only centimeters apart. When the tying was finished, the cloth had the shape of a traditional Yoruba men's hat, hence its name. Sometimes small pebbles or guinea corn seeds were tied into the cloths, a technique known as *adire-eleso*. Before the arrival of sewing machines, all stitched designs, *adire-alabere*, involved sewing raffia into the cloths manually with needles.[13] The arrival of industrial sewing machines opened another opportunity for innovation in designs. Sewing machines were imported as early as the 1880s.[14] Machine-sewn designs, however, were still considered new as late as the 1930s.[15]

The second class of *adire*, *adire-eleko*, was similar to batik. Designers applied a paste made from corn or cassava flour to sections of the cloth.[16] They used a feather to paint the pattern on one side of the cloth. Usually one or two young girls worked on a piece of cloth. They subdivided the cloth into sections and painted several different "pictures" on each. The cloths were then hung outside for three days to allow them to dry completely.[17] The first major innovation in *adire-eleko* occurred around 1910, when stencils were introduced. The first stencils were made from the metal lining of tea chests; patterns were cut into the lining.[18] Stenciling was first practiced in Lagos and Abeokuta and thereafter moved further inland from those two localities.[19]

Dyers and cloth designers usually had several designs in their repertoire. Nonetheless, each town came to specialize in a particular method. Abeokuta became well known for both mechanical methods and stencils, while Ibadan was better known for hand-painted cloths.[20] It is likely that the rise of stencils gave a further boost to the industry in Abeokuta, since patterns could be produced much more quickly.

Pattern designers drew inspirations from a number of sources. For example, a special cloth commemorated the city of Ibadan. This cloth, *Ibadandun*, included drawings that represented the city's town hall, Mapo Hill.[21] Special designs were also created to acknowledge important events. Specialty cloths commemorated the coronation of *Alake* Ademola in 1920, Abeokuta's centenary celebrations in 1930 as well as the silver jubilee of

England's King George V in 1935.[22] These speciality cloths sometimes introduced innovations in designs. The centenary cloth, for example, introduced calligraphy to designers.[23]

Many motifs especially in *adire-eleko* came from Yoruba religion, mythology, and folklore. The deity Yemoja, for example, was a popular design in part because women often appealed to her for children.[24] The deity Obalufon was symbolically represented by the wall gecko and the cricket. Weavers reduced cricket motifs to linear shapes, and these shapes were incorporated in *adire-eleko*.[25] Designs also drew upon common things in everyday society such as combs, earrings, cocoa pods, tomatoes, eggs, snakes, and the leaves used in certain initiation rites.[26]

A great deal of energy was invested in creating new designs, for just as fashions get outdated, designs became old. Mrs. Ronke Doherty recalled that her great-aunt was a leader in innovating new designs.

> Each time I came on holidays, and those girls who were training under her . . . would tell me "Asabi, go to Iya (mother). Tell her you want *eleko* cloth." The moment I said that, she knew somebody must have whispered it to me because it was a new design which had not gone to the market yet and nobody else had it.[27]

Dyers and their assistants created through experimentation.

> She experiments, and those girls they experiment too. They'd come up and say "Iya look, this person has been playing with a piece of cloth. Look what came out of it." And she would say, "All right, get on."[28]

Sometimes designs resulted from mistakes or unexpected occurrences—hence the popular saying among dyers, "Every mistake is a design."[29]

Adire producers brought new sets of economic relations to the dyeing industry and transformed dyeing's position within the indigenous textile sector. Dyeing was no longer subsidiary to weaving. Dyers dominated the production and marketing of *adire* and were considered the owners of this new trade. It is important to consider the social and economic backgrounds of dyers and explore the ways in which status and wealth shaped the organization of production.

A SOCIAL PROFILE OF DYERS

Dyeing was a skilled occupation with its own hierarchy based on age, wealth, and mastery of the craft, and dyers recognized distinc-

Photo 3.1 Elelo Design—Tied and Finished Product. (Photo by Judith A. Byfield, 1988.)

tions and divisions within their community. Dyers possessed the knowledge of the formula and process of dyeing, which was by far the most intricate and highly skilled part of production. A dyer owned her means of production because she owned her own pots. Owning pots was predicated on having sufficient capital to purchase the necessary ingredients and raw materials. Dyers' responsibilities expanded because *adire* production required multiple operations—tying, dyeing, and marketing.

In the nineteenth century, dyers dyed cloths and threads that were brought to them, or they bought and dyed threads in order to resell them. With the production of *adire*, however, dyers were obliged to organize the capital to purchase cloth in addition to the ingredients to make the dye bath. Furthermore, dyers had to organize the labor to design, dye, and market their wares. Dyers evolved from finishers of cloth to autonomous managers of production. This new industry made them producers, owners, and traders of the final product. Women flocked to learn the intricacies of dyeing as *adire*'s popularity grew. In time, tensions emerged between those who wanted to maintain a measure of exclusivity and those who sought to break into this lucrative craft. But these tensions were not apparent in the early decades of the century.

Adire producers came from across Abeokuta's social spectrum. Elite and nonelite women dyed. Madam Jojolola, the *Iyalode*, belonged to the ranks of the traditional elites and made a significant part of her fortune from her dyeing business. *Alake* Ademola's mother was a major dyer in Ikereku township. The wives of J.B. Majekodunmi, the Egba merchant, also produced *adire*. Similarly, Mrs. Ransome-Kuti's mother, who came from the Ilesha royal family, was a dyer.[30] Dyers also represented the full religious spectrum in the early decades of the century. J.B. Majekodunmi's wives were part of the Christianized elite.[31] Madam Jojolola remained a follower of Yoruba religion. She was a priestess of Sango, while Alhaja Soetan, who married into Jojolola's compound was Muslim.[32] Although the vast majority of dyers were women, the records indicate that there were a few male dyers. The *Balogun* of Ikereku, already an elderly gentleman in 1936, was identified as a "man dyer." He was popularly known as *Baba Alaro*, father of the dyeing industry.[33]

Dyeing was considered an inherited craft, which meant classically that succeeding generations of dyers learned the skill from their mothers or relations. Barbour reported that all her informants belonged to a family in which other members were involved in the cloth trade, and "very often their mother had handed on her skills to them."[34] Being born into the trade conveyed status and distinction and held certain advantages. It meant that training began at a very early age, and one could inherit or be associated with a well-established business. Madam Wosinatu Adeniji argued that "apart from this dyeing business there was no other business that I could have been involved in. I started watching my mother dyeing at the age of seven, and by the age of ten I had been involved in it."[35] Being born into the trade even carried an advantage when purchasing cloth, or at least allowed one to demand consideration on the price. Describing a trip to Itoku market to buy *adire*, Mrs. Doherty recalled,

they generally referred to her (great aunt) as Iya Ago-Oko, mother in
Ago-Oko. She made some beautiful and innovative designs too. The
last time I went to Itoku and I wanted the native dye one woman
charged me a mighty lot. I said, "I belong to the cult, and my great
aunt was this old lady. She said "that was my mother." She had trained
her.[36]

Women also had access to training through other avenues—apprenticeships or the *iwofa* (pawning) system. Mrs. Doherty's grandmother, for
example, had several people training under her. Some of them were *iwofa*s
and some had married into the compound. For a number of women who
did not come from dyeing families, marriage was an important avenue.
In Yoruba society marriage was virilocal, which meant wives moved into
their husbands' compounds.[37] This arrangement worked especially well
for women like Alhaja Tukuru, who had an interest in the craft, but was
not born into the trade:

> My mother sells kolanut and my father weaves *aso oke*. . . . my sister
> who got married into Jojo's compound whom I came to live with taught
> me to dye and I also got married into the same compound.[38]

By virtue of her sister's marriage into Jojo's compound, both siblings
learned to dye and were able to continue living and working together,
since Alhaja Tukuru married into the same compound. Regardless of the
route through which they entered a dyeing compound, new generations
of dyers learned the formula and the necessary skills through years of
practice in the employ of an established dyer. They also carried the tell-
tale mark of their craft, blue hands.

> when you were dyeing well and using good dyes, your hands were
> black for weeks, in fact, you could not get them clean at all.[39]

PREPARING THE DYE BATH

Information gathered for the Commission of Enquiry showed that the
dye bath preparation remained largely unchanged from the nineteenth
century until the introduction of caustic soda and synthetic indigo. This
data is invaluable because it provided much greater detail than nineteenth-
century sources did and specifically highlighted the length of time required to complete each stage of the processes involved in creating the
dye bath. Appreciating the preparation time is important, because time
was one of several factors that encouraged dyers to adopt the new technology.

Photo 3.2 Preparing the Cassava Paste. (Photo by Judith A. Byfield, 1988.)

The report noted that indigo leaves were plucked when the plants were approximately two years old. They were pounded into a pulpy mass and then rolled into balls. The balls were then sun-dried for two or three days or baked in special kilns before they were sold to dy-

Photo 3.3   Applying Paste with a Stencil. (Photo by Judith A. Byfield, 1988.)

ers.[40] To prepare the dye bath, the indigo balls were mixed with an alkali solution called *aluba* for approximately 3 to 4 days. *Aluba* was made from a mixture of water and ashes. Ashes used in the *aluba* came from palm fiber, cocoa pods, and specific woods such as epin, *ficus asperifolia*.[41] The ashes were mixed with exhausted water from the dye pots and molded into balls about the size of a tennis ball. They were then baked in a kiln for approximately twelve hours. Once the ash balls were ready, dyers placed them in a pot that had holes at the bottom. Water was added to the ashes, and the mixture percolated from the upper pot set into a lower pot. When the *aluba* was ready, the indigo balls were broken up and stirred into the solution. The mixture then soaked for five to seven days until the dye (*aro*) was ready.[42] Once the dye bath was ready, it was good for only about five days. The process Yoruba dyers used produced a faster color because a greater proportion of indigo white, the soluble form of indigo, resulted from the long fermentation period.[43] Short fermentation periods left a greater quantity of the insoluble indigo blue on the cloth. Since indigo blue was absorbed only on the surface of the cloth, the color ran as soon as it was washed.

Although the fermentation method of preparing the dye produced a better dye, it was time-consuming. If dyers processed their own ashes, they needed approximately fourteen days to complete all the stages, otherwise they needed eight to eleven days for the preparation of the *aluba* and the fermentation of the indigo. In addition to the long preparation time, the process was difficult to control. Pots often spoiled. The overall quality of the dye was determined in part by the length of the fermentation process, the quality of the indigo leaves and the processed indigo balls, and the types of ashes used. The quality of the dye bath was also affected by dyers' own beliefs and experiences. Both Alhaja Soetan and Alhaja Tukuru married into Madam Jojolola's compound, which was renowned for the quality of its dyeing. They argued that the dye was ready after the fifth day. However, another dyer, Madam Ayinde, argued that the dye was ready after the third day.[44] Such differences affected the quality of dye that individual dyers achieved.

The inability to guarantee a good pot of dye even after meticulous preparation encouraged certain restrictions on the times when a woman could dye. Alhaja Soetan noted that in the old days it was believed that "women menstruating should not move near [the dye] because . . . if such women should touch the dye, [it] would not be effective." Dyers also called upon divine intervention to ensure a good pot of dye. In the event a pot of dye was not coming out well, the Yoruba deity Iya Mapo was appeased with a meal of *ekuru*. *Ekuru*, a dish made from beans, was placed around the dye pot and "after that the dye would come out well."[45]

Iya Mapo protected all exclusively female trades like dyeing, pottery, oil pressing, and soap making. Wenger and Beier suggest that indigo was closely linked with her worship. From Iya Mapo's *oriki*, or praise poem, which they collected, it is clear that she was also associated with wealth.

Iya Mapo Atiba,
You are the owner of Oyo. You are fighting all about.
You have collected many warriors at the foot of the hill.
The white cloth will not permit them to escape in the night.
Iya Mapo, look at me as I am: completely naked.
If I have twenty slaves, I am still completely naked.
If I have thirty *iwofa* I am still completely naked.
Nobody can count your thousands.
You took two thousand cowries to the dance.
You took two thousand cowries to the dancers.
Only if they did not perform well, would you take
your two thousand home again.
You could buy all the meat in Igbeti market
You can help like a king.[46]

The *oriki* compares Iya Mapo's wealth with that of kings, suggesting vast wealth. Compared to simple people, no matter how wealthy they thought they were, her wealth was much more substantial. But if they performed well, she generously shared her wealth.[47] Homage to Iya Mapo thus offered insurance against a spoilt pot of dye, as well as the promise of great profit. Even with Iya Mapo on their side, the entire dyeing process was long and demanded judgment at every step. Ultimately successful dyers possessed the knowledge of what to do and the ability to make the right calls.

THE ORGANIZATION OF *ADIRE* PRODUCTION

Dyers employed several models of organization in their effort to maximize production. A casual observer would have trouble distinguishing the different models because many dyers lived or worked in large compounds with other dyers. Often this was the result of Yoruba residential patterns. Compounds were named residential units, which in the past consisted of a single large building, containing a series of rooms arranged around a large central courtyard.[48]

Members of the compounds would have included patrilineally related men and their wives, children, and slaves, as well as *iwofa*s. Nonetheless, women retained strong relationships with their natal compound. Upon marriage, a woman moved to her husband's compound, but if he died or they separated or divorced, she and their children could return permanently to her natal compound.[49] Residence patterns in compounds did not adhere to rigid rules. Some compounds had more than one descent group, and some descent groups were divided among a number of compounds. Since compounds were polygynous settings, it was often the case in dyeing compounds that several wives shared the common courtyard. Adepate Adeniji reported that they had up to twelve women dyeing in their compound, but not all were wives in the compound. Their group included at least one woman who was a daughter of the compound.[50] This did not appear to be uncommon. Alhaja Lasaki told us that her mother dyed "at her father's compound. . . . she never dyed in my father's compound."[51] Another informant, Alhaja Raji, reported that women from other areas used to dye in her mother's compound and then return to their homes at the end of the day. This would suggest that in cases where a dyer was isolated, she sought out companionship by working in a compound with other dyers. [52]

While dyers shared their work space in a compound, each dyer was an independent producer. In Madame Jojolola's compound (commonly

Photo 3.4 Dyer with Cloths That Have Been Dyed and Are Draining. (Photo by Judith A. Byfield, 1988.)

referred to as Jojo's compound), the women worked under a small shed erected behind the house (Photo 3.4). The shed was a simple structure, a piece of zinc supported by four wooden posts. One could see other small clusters of dyers, as several households shared this open area. Four dyers worked under the shed, each with her own set of pots.

Since dyeing compounds were centers of production, they were also centers of consumption. Cloth traders who had a special relationship with dyers stopped by to chat or to arrange large orders. Food sellers of everything from bread to rice and stew stopped in the compounds to offer their goods. Those selling *elu* and other items the dyers needed also visited the compounds regularly. Dyers shared conversation with those who passed through their workplace and observations on things that transpired around them. They also helped each other during moments of crisis or emergencies as Adepata Adeniji explained:

> I nearly had one of my babies right beside the dye pot, but for the quick intervention of the other dyers. I was moved away a bit before I had the baby boy. I was perfectly okay and the baby. The other dyers continued with my work.[53]

Yet in the midst of this camaraderie each dyer was an independent producer.

The shared workspace blurred the horizontal and vertical divisions among *adire* producers. Master dyers were older women who had established themselves as autonomous managers and producers. These women owned their dye pots. Often they had assistants to whom they passed on their skills and knowledge. These assistants—*iwofas*, apprentices, and children—constituted a category of dependent workers. *Iwofas*, primarily young girls, lived and worked with the dyers until the loan was repaid. Often the loan was not repaid until the girl was married and her fiancé assumed responsibility for the loan as part of the bride-price. Apprentices were often (but not exclusively) relatives who were sent to live with the dyer in order to learn the craft.[54] The apprenticeship period varied. Salawu Sadiku stated that it usually lasted from six months to a year, and Afusat Karimu said her mother's apprentice stayed two to three years.[55] Alhaja Bakare suggested that age played a significant role in determining the length of the apprenticeship.

> It depends on the child's smartness and intelligence, and age because we had older people coming to learn to dye. Older people can use up

to three or six months but for the under age they spent up to ten years with us.[56]

Dyers' children formed the last group of dependent workers. They assisted their mothers in all aspects of *adire* production until they left her household.

Each subgroup of dependent worker had a different social connection to the dyer, but they were all in the employ of a master dyer, and their efforts helped create her profits. Their training often began with learning the simple tasks. Alhaja Lasaki began by fetching water, rinsing cloths, removing raffia, and loosening the already dyed cloths.[57] Alhaja Bakara first learned to tie different patterns.[58] Alhaja Tukuru's first task was to collect designed cloths from tailors, while Madam Ayinde first learned to buy and break *elu* and cut a bundle of cloths in $2^1/_2$-yard pieces, the size of a wrapper.[59] As their training progressed, they were given greater responsibility and acquired greater expertise and mastery of the craft. However, they were not autonomous, independent producers.

Most dependent workers earned their independence upon marriage. Many of my informants noted that they began to dye for themselves once they moved into their husband's compound.[60] Marriage, however, did not always assure a young dyer's independence. Testimony from the Commission of Enquiry suggests that women who married into dyeing compounds were sometimes incorporated into their mother-in-law's workforce. One of the complaints lodged in 1936 was that wives of sons had begun to dye independently and compete with their mothers-in-law.[61]

Among those women who were independent, autonomous managers of *adire* production, there were significant variations in the scale of their enterprises. These differences indicated some socioeconomic distinctions. In describing the leading dyer in their compound, Adepate Adeniji said

> Madam Bankole was one of the leading dyers in our compound. She was a native of Abeokuta . . . a Christian. She was born in this compound. . . . She had about six pots of dye because she had many *iwofa* and helpers.[62]

Dyers assessed the scale of each other's enterprises by the number of pots of dye simultaneously in operation and the number of people on her workforce. It appears that approximately four pots represented a small enterprise.

Some women specialized in dyeing. Salawu Sadiku's mother had only two pots, and she did not design the cloths. She purchased cloth and then gave it to women who specialized in tying or to tailors.[63] Because of the size of her operation, she was naturally not forced to restrict herself to dyeing. Larger-scale dyers also elected to restrict their activities to dyeing. Alhaja Biliahu's mother, for example, had eight pots and ten assistants. Nonetheless, she did nothing but dye.[64] Other dyers performed both tying and dyeing. Family obligations sometimes played a role in determining whether a dyer performed both tasks. Alhaja Lasaki told us, "I used to [tie] when I had the time, but usually I give to people to tie especially when I started having children."[65]

The data suggests that there was no one model of organization. Less wealthy dyers relied on familial labor and actively participated in the production of cloths. Dyers like Madam Aroga who worked by herself put in a very long day.

> I used to wake up at five o'clock in the morning to prepare breakfast, clean the house, and take care of the children. After that I would start dyeing. In the afternoon I would give my children money to buy their lunch and at five o'clock I would close for the day to go . . . and prepare dinner.[66]

Wealthier women supplemented family labor with slaves, *iwofa*s, and later paid laborers. Alhaja Soetan remembered that there were about forty women who dyed in Jojolola's compound and most had about four pots, but that Madam Jojolola had many more pots because she had a number of slaves and *iwofa*s working for her.[67] *Alake* Ademola's mother had twenty-eight pots and about forty women who worked for her.[68] Women with a workforce used various strategies to organize large-scale production. Some created a factory type of organization with different degrees of specialization. Mrs. Doherty's great-aunt prepared the dye bath herself and did the actual dyeing. She had her trainees concentrate on tying the cloths.[69] Alhaja Raji's aunt, who taught her to dye, had about ten pots. She was assisted by apprentices as well as eight *iwofa*s. Each *iwofa* was responsible for specific tasks so that while "some were busy dyeing, some tying, some (were) fetching water, and some cooking for the others."[70] Alhaja Raji's description matched the description of the organization of the industry given by the agent of G. B. Ollivant in 1936. He stated that "Under the old method the workers learnt one part of the dyeing process only and mastered that completely—some preparing the vats, others superintending the dipping, etc."[71]

This factorylike production took on grander proportions in some compounds, such as Madam Jojolola's. Madam Jojolola's compound earned its reputation as a major *adire* compound in the early decades of this century. In 1988 both the men and the women in this compound were still involved in *adire* production, and the compound had retained its reputation as one of the biggest dyeing compounds in Abeokuta. This compound earned its reputation in part from the coordinated production of its members. Alhaji Oladunwo Soetan, a great-grandson of Madam Jojolola, learned to sew and apply stencil designs as a young man.[72] In 1988 he was no longer actively designing cloth, but he supervised several men who worked for him. Customers brought cloth to him to be designed, and once that process was completed, the cloths were given to dyers who worked in another part of the compound.[73] Membership in this compound carried certain advantages. Its high name recognition attracted customers, as did the convenience of having both the stenciling and dyeing performed in the same compound.

Dyers were ultimately skilled craftswomen and autonomous managers of their enterprises. All dyers were not equal; those with greater access to capital and labor held distinct advantages over dyers who did all their own production. Wealthier producers who controlled a workforce did not have to participate personally in dyeing. They could focus their attention on being managers. They had the time and capital to nurture social and economic relationships and to explore opportunities to diversify their business so that *adire* became only one of several ventures. Madam Jojolola, for example, was also a cloth trader. She specialized in selling white cloth to other dyers.[74]

ADIRE'S ECONOMIC LINKAGES

Adire production was considered a women's industry, but men also participated in specific aspects of the industry. A 1926 assessment report of the town estimated that at least one quarter of the town's population was involved in *adire*. The assessment indicated the complex structure of the industry and its linkages with other sectors of the economy. The report listed the principal trades in the town and enumerated the segments of the textile industry. The findings of the report allow us to make some important observations about the *adire* industry in relation to the other sectors of textile production.

Photo 3.5   Madame Jojolola's Compound. (Photo by Judith A. Byfield, 1988.)

The total population of the town was 50,717—10,605 men, 19,970 women, and 20,142 children. Approximately 5.5 percent (1,094) of the women in Abeokuta were dyers, and 5.3 percent (1,064) were *adire* makers and sellers. Altogether then, approximately 11 percent of the townswomen were directly engaged in *adire* production.[75] The claim by officials that 25 percent of the population was somehow involved in *adire* was plausible, considering the fact that farmers, potters, tailors, and cloth traders also contributed to the industry.

The report gave a detailed tally of other textile and clothing producers—weavers, dressmakers, and tailors. The report did not mention spinners at all, suggesting that the number of spinners was negligible. The number of spinners was undoubtedly affected by the widespread use of European threads, for the author noted that weaving was nearly all done with European manufactured cotton. The report also illuminated the great disparity between the number of *adire* producers and textile workers in other sectors. *Adire* producers outnumbered all other categories of textile makers. The fact that there were four times as many dyers as weavers underscores dyeing's independence from weaving, for it is unlikely that 248 weavers would have been able to keep 1,094 dyers sufficiently occupied. See Table 3.1.

Table 3.1
Textile Workers in Abeokuta in 1926, by Township

Township	Adire Makers	Adire Sellers	Dyers	Weavers	Dress-makers	Tailors
Owu	65	0	144	10	0	62
Gbagura	127	3	96	28	1	135
Oke Ona	507	75	342	63	21	154
Egba Alake	365	53	512	147	12	397
Total	1,064	131	1,094	248	34	748[76]

While the assessment report provided a great deal of important information, there were some major omissions. The general categories of the report failed to capture some of the specialization in the industry. It is unclear, for example, whether the category of *adire* makers included only those specialists who created designs but did not dye, or if it also included those dyers who also tied cloth. The report also failed to specify gender within occupations. It is probably safe to assume that women composed the majority, if not all, of the *adire* makers, sellers, and dyers. Nonetheless, information on gender would help us understand how gender roles changed as the textile industry changed. For example, we would be able to discern whether weaving was still done by men and women or if the increasing reliance on European threads affected male and female weavers differently. Likewise, it would have been helpful to know how many men became adire stencil designers.

Nonetheless, the report helps us to appreciate that while weaving continued, it was dyeing that flourished in this new era. The vast majority of dyers lived and worked in Abeokuta town, the center of economic and political life. Dyeing still continued in the rural areas, but with fewer dyers. This pattern was confirmed in an assessment report carried out in Owode district in 1929, which found 190 dyers. In the report, the assistant district officer, J.B. Carey, commented that there was a colony of dyers in many of the larger villages, but the majority of all handicraft work was done in town.[77]

Though dyeing was primarily an urban occupation, dyers still depended on the rural economy for indigo. At the same time, changes were unfolding in indigo production that were clearly related to the expansion of cash crops. Indigo grew wild, and it was reported that whenever farmers came across it, the plants were allowed to remain.[78] Indigo was also cultivated. Farmers planted it near cassava, which shaded the young plants. By the 1930s, the main areas for indigo production were the Kemta, Itoko, and Ijemo farms to the north and northwest of Abeokuta.[79] It appears that the concentration of indigo production in these districts reflected the changing agricultural landscape in Abeokuta. As more acreage was devoted to the tree crops, particularly cocoa, more intensive food production occurred in the districts to the north and northwest.[80]

Rural producers processed the indigo leaves into indigo balls. Twentieth-century sources, however, disagree on precisely who carried out this operation. Writing in 1957, Wenger and Beier noted that collecting the leaves and making indigo balls was a woman's job, but the Commission of Enquiry Report in 1936 stated that men prepared the indigo balls.[81] It is possible that when there was greater demand for indigo, men as well as women produced indigo balls, but more significantly, the disparity suggests that important changes had taken place during the twenty years between the two data points. Sources that described men processing indigo balls suggest that they were working on indigo plantations. In 1928 and 1936, charges were leveled that the indigo balls were adulterated, and farmers were summoned to the council. During the 1936 meeting, the *Olori Parakoyi* of Ilugun gave a brief but informative description of the scale of indigo ball production.[82]

> My father was an Itoko man and I was born there. He was engaged in the business of preparing indigo for sale. We were then thirty-four hands working for our father and solely engaged in the production of indigo. At times for three consecutive months we would do no work other than that of preparing indigo for our father.[83]

From this brief description of the size of the workforce and the amount of time they committed to preparing indigo balls, it is clear that the *Olori*'s father cultivated indigo on a substantial scale. During the inquiries, passing references were made to indigo plantations in Kemta, Itoko, and Iporo farm areas.[84] It is quite likely that on farms where indigo grew wild or there were few plants women prepared the indigo balls for sale, but on farms where indigo was planted commercially a workforce of agricultural workers was employed to both attend to and process the indigo leaves.

While men and women produced indigo balls, women specialized in preparing the balls of ashes used in breaking down indigo into its soluble components.[85] Some dyers purchased these balls from specialist producers, but some prepared their own ash balls.[86] Women produced the clay pots in which the dye bath was prepared. Dyers had to purchase indigo balls, ashes, and clay pots from their producers or from traders who specialized in these items.

Adire producers also had to have the capital to obtain cloth. Since most *adire* was produced on imported cloth, producers were directly linked to the networks of European commercial capital. Using the amount of European cloth sold in Abeokuta as a guide, colonial officials estimated that at its height the *adire* trade was valued at more than £500,000.[87] *Adire* makers bought their cloth from several sources. They could purchase cloth from cloth traders who had stalls in the markets or from large Egba merchants who had their own stores. Merchants like J.B. Majekodunmi purchased cloth from G.B. Ollivant, John Holt, and UAC, which he sold to dyers from his store in Iberekodo.[88] J.B. Majekodunmi's wives and numerous other dyers bought cloth from his store.[89] Some dyers had what were known as attachment cards, which allowed them to buy cloth directly from the European firms on credit.[90] For these preferred customers the firms would extend credit as much as three or even six months.[91] Chief Majekodunmi, who worked in his uncle's stores as well as European stores, confirmed that cloth merchants would not have given small traders three or six months credit.[92] Only the big traders received such terms. The women who obtained such credit terms formed an important entrepreneurial segment within the industry. They bought sufficient cloth to meet their own production demands and to sell to other dyers.

Large-scale dyers who operated at this level also functioned as conduits between European commercial capital and local producers. These dyers extended credit to other dyers or individuals who could not open credit arrangements with the European firms. Madam Jojolola was known to give extensive credit to other traders.[93] By extending credit these women acquired labor, specifically *iwofa*s. The *iwofa* system cemented productive relations between international capital and local producers, for as these women extended credit, they obtained labor which enabled them to increase the volume of their production.

A different credit structure operated for the retail buyer. Sometimes a number of small dyers pooled their resources and bought cloth in bulk. Otherwise, they purchased their cloth from cloth sellers in the market or from dyers who were cloth retailers. Most informants insisted that they did not buy their cloth on credit, but credit options existed if they needed it. Those who bought their cloth retail could purchase it on credit if they were regular customers of the dealer. They were allowed two market days, approximately nine days, to pay their debt.[94]

ALLIED WORKERS

In addition to these forward and backward linkages to European commercial capital and the agricultural sector, other crafts were linked to *adire*. These were effectively allied workers. These allied workers were involved in the tying and designing of cloth, one operation that dyers did not have to control.

Some women specialized in designing cloths. During the hearings in 1936, one dyer stated that she generally gave most of the cloth away to the persons who were solely engaged in sewing.[95] Women who specialized in tying and sewing took in work for others, but they also purchased cloths for themselves and gave them out to be dyed. As dyers got older and more frail and the tasks involved in dyeing, such as lifting and carrying water containers and lifting wet cloths, became too strenuous, many limited their activity to tying cloths. Wosanti Adeniji and her cowife Adepate were both dyers. When they were younger, the Adeniji compound was bustling with several dyers at work. By 1988, both women were in their seventies and by their estimation too weak to continue dyeing, so they spent most of their day tying designs. In fact, no one was dyeing in Adeniji compound anymore.

Although designing the cloths was primarily the preserve of women, men were involved in this sector in very specific ways. *Adire* provided a tremendous amount of work for many tailors. Alhaji Bada apprenticed with a tailor from Kemta, one of the central townships for *adire* production. In addition to making garments, they did a lot of *adire* designs. His teacher had so much work that he managed a shop with ten sewing machines and eight assistants.[96] It was reported that these machine-stitched designs were done by boys and young men. The patterns were produced at great speed, and some questioned the quality of the designs.[97] The fact that *adire* patterning was done by young boys and apprentices suggests that the relatively simple sewing involved provided ample practice for these trainees while bringing in income to their teachers.

The relationship between tailors and *adire* makers appears to have grown out of their shared production of clothing for traditional Yoruba dress. In Yorubaland, tailoring and embroidery were done by men historically, and their involvement in machine-sewn designs seems to have been an extension of their work as tailors and embroiderers of traditional clothes.[98] Early dressmakers, who were usually women, tended to concentrate on Western-style garments.[99] There were many more tailors than dressmakers: The 1926 assessment report enumerated 748 tailors, in contrast to 34 dressmakers.

Men also made stencils and applied the stencil designs. As mentioned earlier, the first stencils were made from the metal lining of tea chests and patterns were cut into the metal. As stencils became more popular, they could be purchased ready-made.[100] Stencil designers often had a workforce as well to assist them. Alhaji Olumran apprenticed with a stencil designer. His teacher made his own stencils and produced more than one hundred from which clients could choose. Ten people worked for his teacher, and they included relatives as well as apprentices. His teacher watched and oversaw the whole operation while some of them mixed the paste and others applied it to the cloth.[101] Men who produced the stencil designs and the machine-stitched designs worked on consignment. Women took cloth to them and paid them for their services.

The final step in the process involved creating a sheen on the cloth. *Adire* producers used several methods. One method involved applying a cover of pure synthetic dye (not mixed with caustic soda) to the cloth.[102] A second method was to iron the cloth with a coal iron.[103] A third method, beating the cloth with a wooden mallet, became the primary task of another set of allied workers. The cloth was folded lengthwise so that the side without the pattern showed, sprinkled with water, and placed over a board. Usually two beaters worked on a cloth, pulling it along the board and hitting it with their mallets.[104] Beating is still a current method. Before the cloths were put up for sale, many dyers sent their *adire* to a compound which specialized in beating.[105] These specialist beaters, all women, spent their entire workday beating *adire*.

Beating is another major point of discrepancy between the more recent accounts of *adire* production and those contained in archival materials. Alhaja Owomipe insists that they did not beat *adire* in the

old days.[106] Earlier descriptions of *adire* found in Egba Council minutes, the reports prepared for the Commission of Enquiry and the Proceedings of the Commission of Enquiry, are silent on this process.
Given the consistent silence of the reports on this point, it is unlikely
that beating was overlooked; it is more likely that this finishing process was relatively new in Abeokuta. Several dyers reported that they
began beating cloth when a new kind of *adire* called Kampala developed in the 1960s.[107]

A later development of this practice in Abeokuta may in fact reflect one of many differences in the history of dyeing in different
Yoruba towns. In a 1935 report on local crafts in Yorubaland, the author of the section on Oyo and Ibadan noted that the darkly dyed
cloths "are often glazed by being beaten by wooden mallets; this is a
separate craft carried on by men, and may have a Hausa origin as I
believe it is more common in the North."[108] His description was very
similar to that offered by Richard Lander in the nineteenth century.
When perfectly dry, the dyed cloths "are laid on a large flat block of
wood, smoothed by hatchets and knives, and a man beats them with a
wooden instrument, not unlike an English cricket-bat, till they become
sufficiently smooth and glossy.[109] Lander also noted that Oyo dyers
used dye pits, another practice usually associated with the dyeing industry in Hausaland. Although beating the cloths was in practice in
parts of Yorubaland before 1960, further research will be needed to
confirm when it came to Abeokuta.

THE ORGANIZATION OF TRADE

As the 1926 assessment report showed, few people specialized in selling *adire*. Most dyers sold their own cloths in the markets or entrusted
them to their assistants to sell. It appears that buyers from all levels,
wholesale to retail, purchased *adire* from Abeokuta markets. Relatively
few customers made their purchases from the compounds. Today, Itoku
market is the only market where *adire* is sold, but informants claim that
in the old days, consumers could purchase *adire* from several other markets—Iberekodo, Obada Oko, Adedotun, Sodeke, and Lafenwa.[110]

From both archival and oral sources, it is clear that market days were
especially dramatic. Women often hid new creations from their competitors with the hope of creating a flurry of interest among buyers. Dyers
closely guarded new designs and brought them out only on market day.[111]
A new design provided only a slight advantage because by the next market day other dyers would have copied it.

Part of the excitement of market days was related to the number of traders from other parts of Nigeria and West Africa who journeyed to Abeokuta to buy *adire*. Improved transportation and the wealth generated from cocoa and kola brought people from other parts of Nigeria to Yorubaland and encouraged Yoruba traders to establish new market networks. Steamship travel as well as the railway contributed significantly to the movement of goods and people along the coast and within Nigeria respectively. Hausa migrants formed one of the most important ethnic groups to visit Yorubaland in general and Abeokuta specifically. There had been a number of Hausa slaves in Abeokuta before the twentieth century, but the development of the kola trade through Lagos and later the production of kola in Yorubaland brought increasing numbers of Hausa traders from the north. Hausa men also came as migrant laborers and worked on both kola and cocoa farms. Most of those who came as migrant workers also purchased kola nuts for resale in the north.[112] Cohen argues that most of the kola trade between southern and northern Nigeria in the 1930s and 1940s was carried out by small-scale Hausa dealers. They bought the nuts from Yoruba women in the rural markets or directly from farmers.[113] Since one did not need a large outlay of capital to begin, transportation was comparatively easy and demand very wide, "almost every Hausa on the move between the South and the North—migrant laborers, cattle dealers, malams, porters, petty traders—bought kola with the money he had and took it back to the North."[114]

In addition to purchasing kola, it is probable that Hausa migrants purchased *adire* cloth and helped establish a market for it in northern Nigeria.[115] *Adire* fit well within the Hausa preference for indigo-dyed cloth. Little work has been done on the *adire* trade to northern Nigeria, but Shea suggests that it was very popular by the midcolonial period. Dyers in Kano city also began to produce *adire* between 1920 and 1940.[116]

Yoruba traders also took advantage of the improved transportation and cocoa wealth to create new markets for *adire* in the Gold Coast. Yoruba traders had been going to the famous market town Salaga, in northern Gold Coast, since the nineteenth century. These traders, primarily from Ilorin, accompanied Hausa caravans on the overland trip, which took them through northern Dahomey and Togo on their way to Salaga. After the British imposed colonial rule over the Asante, a number of Yoruba traders moved south and established Yoruba communities in Kumasi, Accra, and Sekondi. They were later joined by Yoruba members of the West African Force who had fought in the Asante–British wars and decided to settle in the Gold Coast.

The ex-soldiers joined the traders in exporting kola to Nigeria and importing Nigerian cloth. Initially these traders imported *aso oke* (hand-woven cloth) primarily from the northern Yoruba towns of Oyo, Iseyin, Ilorin, and Shaki, but by 1910 they began to import *adire* from Abeokuta on a large scale. As a result of the success of the kola-textile business, many Yorubas migrated to the Gold Coast between 1900 and 1920. The cloth was shipped by sea from Lagos to Sekondi, then transported overland to markets throughout the Gold Coast.[117]

Yoruba traders did not create this market for indigo cloth. The northern part of the Gold Coast, which constituted part of the old Gonja empire, encompassed some important indigo-dyeing towns, such as Daboya. Daboya was integrated into the Sudanic trade routes and was famous as a center of dyeing and production of fine woven cloths from the late eighteenth century.[118] Yoruba traders in the Gold Coast were thus tapping into an already established market for indigo cloth.

New markets for *adire* were created in Onitsha (eastern Nigeria), Senegal, and the Belgian Congo. Either Igbo migrants to Yorubaland or Yoruba traders may have been the conduits of its dissemination to Onitsha. Elderly informants reported that from the early part of the nineteenth century *adire* was used by many Igbo speakers as mourning cloth.[119] Equally little is known about the development of the *adire* market in Senegal. It may have begun as an extension of the trade in the Gold Coast. Sudarkasa found that while cloth and kola were the major items of trade, some informants also purchased livestock for resale in the Kumasi markets. They also traveled further north to Ouagadougou (Burkina Faso), Mali, and Niamey (Niger) to purchase cattle, which were then walked to the south. It is possible that these long-distance Yoruba traders in the Gold Coast played a crucial role in introducing *adire* to markets in Senegal.[120] It is also highly likely that the French trading firm in Abeokuta, Companie Française de L'Afrique Occidentale, played a significant role in introducing *adire* to Senegalese consumers. The Senegambia has a long history of producing as well as importing indigo cloths. In Senegal, local indigo-dyed cloth competed with imported indigo cloth from Pondicherry (India) as early as the seventeenth century. French merchants were the critical conduits in this trade, exchanging Pondicherry guinée cloth for captives and gum.[121] Thus, it is likely that Companie Française continued the practice of exporting indigo cloths to the Senegalese market.

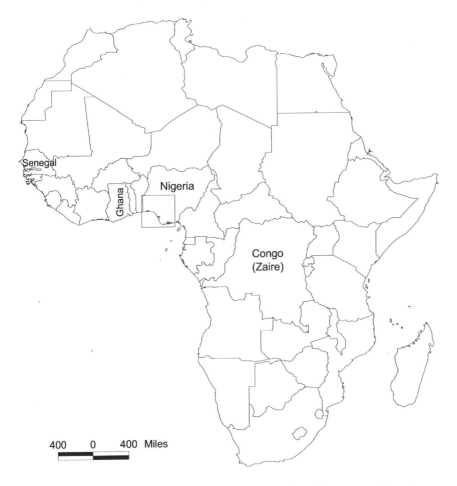

Map 3.1 Main Markets for *Adire*, 1918–39. (Produced by Evans Map Room, Dartmouth College, July 2001.)

The market in the Congo was most likely created by Yoruba traders who followed Yoruba migrant workers. In the 1890s the British government agreed to allow King Leopold of Belgium to recruit West Africans to work in the Congo. Recruitment agents in Elmina, Lagos, and Freetown signed on hundreds of workers to go to the Congo to work as laborers on the railway or in the lower echelons of the civil service. The many accusations of brutality at the hands of Belgian supervisors kept the number of migrants to the Congo small, but their

presence nonetheless encouraged others to explore its commercial opportunities.[122] However varied the agency and process by which these
markets became established, it is evident that by the 1920s Abeokuta
was integrated into a regional West African market that cut across
imperial and linguistic borders.

The records consistently reported that the largest buyers were
Senegalese wholesale merchants. It is not known when Senegalese
merchants began to frequent Abeokuta markets. One merchant interviewed by the Commission of Enquiry claimed that he had been making buying trips to Abeokuta since 1918.[123] During the industry's boom
period, Senegalese buyers visited Abeokuta every fifteen days.[124]
Senegalese traders featured prominently in the records partly because
dyers were displeased that they paid a part of the fees that interpreters received. This conflict between dyers and interpreters resulted in
fairly detailed descriptions of the organization of this element of long-
distance trade. Senegalese merchants traveled to Lagos, where they
stayed with a Senegalese host. From Lagos their hosts sent them on
to Abeokuta, where they lodged with the host's contacts, who were
usually Egba.[125]

The Senegalese buyers usually spent nine days in Abeokuta, visiting
the markets every day. Their Egba hosts served as interpreters or provided the Senegalese with interpreters to assist them. Interpreting was a
lucrative activity; interpreters earned 6d. on each wrapper a Senegalese
purchased. Senegalese buyers sometimes bought as many as 2,000 wrappers in one day. One interpreter claimed that they could realize as much
as £200 but more often they received between £25 and £50, still a substantial amount. The fee was divided equally between the host in Lagos
and the host in Abeokuta.[126]

The presence of Senegalese hosts in Lagos appears to substantiate
Austen's argument that colonialism provided opportunities for the expansion of Muslim trade networks in West Africa.[127] Many questions
remain about this trading diaspora in Lagos and the factors that facilitated the movement of merchants from Senegal. The brief evidence in
the Commission of Enquiry report suggests that the organization of
trade among the Senegalese merchants followed the pattern of other
long-distance traders, such as the Hausa cattle and kola traders.[128] The
hosts in Lagos and Abeokuta corresponded to the landlords who
housed cattle and kola traders. In Cohen's and Hill's studies the land-
lords/hosts belonged to the same ethnic group as the visiting traders,
and they were all men.[130] In Abeokuta, however, Egba landlords, and
in some instance Hausas, housed the visiting Senegalese and Gold

Coast buyers. Both men and women were hosts. One female host was identified, and she lodged Gold Coast traders. In a council meeting in 1936, Chief Sodipo of Iporo explained how he came to lodge Gold Coast traders:

> My mother, Adeyoyin, was a dyer and many people from the Gold Coast used to lodge at her place to buy adire cloths prepared with native materials. Before they left the Gold Coast, the saying used to be "Go to Adeyoyin, Molaja's mother, to buy adire." From that time on the caravans used to come and lodge with me in my house.[130]

Chief Sodipo's description suggests that hosts who were dyers also sold their cloths to the visiting merchants. Such dyers had the first opportunity to dispose of all their own dyed cloths. One host went so far as to create a market in front of his house, so that merchants who lodged with him did not have to go to the established markets. Invariably, this gave the dyers in his compound an unfair advantage over the dyers who took their *adire* to the established markets.[131]

It is clear from the evidence that dyers were only the first rung of that distributive network that gradually reached out to the rest of West Africa. The network involved several levels of merchant capital. There were small traders who purchased *adire* for resale in Yoruba markets. Long-distance merchants traveling from Senegal and the Gold Coast represented another level of capital accumulation. These traders obviously traveled with significant amounts of cash that allowed them to cover the cost of transportation and boarding as well as substantial purchases of cloth. The brief descriptions of trade in the Commission of Enquiry report and the minutes of the Egba council indicate that the distribution of *adire* cloth was complex and requires greater examination.

CONCLUSION

Ample reasons existed for believing that before the depression of the 1930s, *adire* contributed to an extremely profitable era. Alhaja Soetan, who began dyeing before the crisis took hold, noted that *adire* "was even more profitable than [in] our mothers' time."[132] *Adire* production had evolved into a complex enterprise with overlapping layers of specialists and autonomous manager/producers. Dyers were the pivotal actors in both its production and its distribution. During its golden era *adire* was a vibrant and lucrative industry which attracted new generations of specialists. It appealed to women across the social and economic spectrum of Egba society. Those who had access to substantial capital acquired the tools and the labor to experiment with various organizational models, such as factorylike specialization. Those without much capital or labor produced as much as they could by themselves.

Adire production put dyeing at the center of a complex set of economic relationships that integrated important segments of the urban, rural, regional and international economies. The relative economic importance of dyeing in the larger Egba economy shifted as women gained independent access to cloth. Dyeing was the economic equivalent of cash crops for women producers. Control and ownership of the means of production and a finished product elevated these women from allied workers to autonomous producers and competitors in the local and regional cloth market. An appreciation of the dyers' new structural position becomes most apparent when dyeing in Abeokuta is contrasted with the organization of the dyeing industry in Kano, particularly with regard to dyers' ownership and control of the final product.

Kano's dyeing industry expanded rapidly in the nineteenth century. Some dyers owned their dye pits, but many did not. Some of the dyers who did not own dye pits rented pits while others made up part of an increasingly mobile labor force which could be hired as casual workers. Many of the latter were itinerant religious students. Dyers who owned dye pits dyed cloths brought to them by traders and hired additional labor from the pool of itinerant dyers as the need arose. Toward the end of the nineteenth century, increasing numbers of wealthy cloth traders began to invest in production by constructing their own dye pits. This altered the nature of ownership within Kano's dyeing industry. Increasingly wealthy cloth traders became dye pit owners (some owned ten or more pits) and hired itinerant dyers to dye their cloth. Many of these businessmen/traders also owned large guest houses for visiting traders. Dye pits became such valuable investments that by the end of the nineteenth century, they could be sold, rented, or pledged against debt.[133] As cloth traders moved into dyeing, fewer Kano dyers owned the means of production, and increasingly control of the industry shifted toward wealthy cloth traders.

The reverse occurred in Abeokuta. Dyers maintained their control over the means of production and became cloth traders. The scope of Egba dyers' enterprises expanded because they owned and traded the cloth they produced. The following question arises: Why didn't Kano dyers become autonomous producers? The relative cost of production may have contributed significantly to the different ways in which these two sets of dyers were integrated into the colonial economy.

In Kano, the construction of dye pits and the purchase of cloths were major investments. Dye pits were a long-term investment which could not be disposed of easily if demand declined. Rather than construct new pits indiscriminately, pit owners often used rented pits to dye their extra cloth. Investment in indigenously woven cloth, the primary material dyed by Kano dyers, was frequently larger than the investment in pits. However, cloths could be sold easily and disposed of in a short period of time. Thus, Kano cloth traders—the middlemen between weavers, dyers, and consumers—were in a stronger economic position than dyers and better able to expand the range of their enterprise and become autonomous producers of dyed cloth.[134]

The cost of operating dye pots was much lower than the cost of running dye pits. Egba dyers required much lower initial capital to establish their dye pots, and their industry was based on the availability of inexpensive cloth. Although their rate of accumulation was probably significantly lower than that of Kano cloth traders who owned dye pits, the lower capital investment required to operate dye pots and purchase inexpensive European cloth allowed Egba dyers to become autonomous producers. As the colonial economy evolved in Kano, the owners of cloth increasingly became owners of pits, while those trained in the craft of dyeing became casual workers. In Abeokuta dyers became owners of cloth and in the process strengthened their economic position during this period.

The picture that is presented in this chapter is undoubtedly the outcome of many changes and transformations. Though it does not take us through the specifics of each development, it establishes the baseline from which we can appreciate the perceptions that characterized the industry before its decline. Those perceptions informed the lengthy debates which followed in the wake of the introduction of caustic soda and synthetic dyes into the dyeing process. This picture also illuminates the ways in which *adire* production bridged the precolonial and colonial economies. These practitioners of this longstanding craft were able to take advantage of the opportunities offered by the expansion of European capital, the colonial infrastructure, and cash crop production. They fit within an economic and cultural niche that was still expansive before the shock waves of the worldwide depression began to register.

NOTES

1. Jennifer Bray, "The Organization of Traditional Weaving in Iseyin, Nigeria," *Africa* 38, 3 (1968): 270–80. Also see "A Plea for the More General Pursuit of Agriculture As a Calling," *Lagos Standard,* 23 May 1900.

2. Annie E. Coombes, *Reinventing Africa: Museums, Material Culture and Popular Imagination in Late Victorian and Edwardian England* (New Haven, CT: Yale University Press, 1994), 181.

3. Marion Johnson, "Cotton Imperialism in West Africa," *African Affairs* 73, 290 (1974): 182.

4. "Lagos Agricultural Show," *West African Mail,* 24 December 1903.

5. Memorandum on Planting and Preparation of Indigo" (Lagos: Government Printer, 1917). MN/XI, 1-4 (NAI).

6. Several offered the information that weavers used to go to the dye baths and soak the threads themselves and then pay the dye-bath owner for allowing them to soak the threads. Interview with Salawa Sadiku, 29 August 1996, Kemta, Abeokuta.

7. Interview with Madam Soetan, 20 August 1996, Itoku Market, Abeokuta. Mack and Picton also reported that even in the 1960s, one could still find a few women in the rural areas wearing resist-dyed handspun cotton cloth with simple patterns. The patterns were made by sewing sticks and stones into a cloth before dyeing. See John Picton and John Mack, *African Textiles* (New York: Harper & Row, 1989), 152.

8. Adesola Afolabi, "The Origin, Development and Impact of 'Adire' Dyeing Industry in Abeokuta," B.A. honors essay, University of Ibadan, 1981, 23–24.

9. O.A. Badejogbim, "The Relationship Between Environment and Culture: Adire Industry in Southern Nigeria As a Case-Study," B.A. honors essay, University of Ibadan, 1983.

10. Carolyn Keyes, "*Adire*: Cloth, Gender and Social Change in Southwestern Nigeria, 1841–1991" Ph.D. diss., University of Wisconsin–Madison, 1993, 89. Also see Picton and Mack, *African Textiles,* 38.

11. Keyes, "*Adire*: Cloth, Gender and Social Change," 90. Also see Esther Afolabi, "Yoruba Adire, Its Potentials and Future," B.A. honor's essay, University of Ife, 1983. I thank Babatunde Lawal for sharing this essay with me.

12. In the commission report, it was noted that crochet cotton was sometime used in place of the raffia. See Proceedings of the Adire Cloth Committee, 1936, Appendix I—Report on the Nature of the Adire Cloth Industry in Abeokuta. ABE PROF 4/ D29 (NAI), 4.

13. In an 1889 address, Governor Moloney of Lagos described a cloth produced in the upper Gambia region that was very similar to *adire-alabere.* "*Fattah*: It is a pagne of light blue, mid blue, and dark blue colors on one side, and altogether dark blue on the other side. This is effected by stitching seams all over the pagne previous to dyeing, the seamed parts presenting a striped light colouring after the dyeing process is complete." Alfred C. Moloney, "Cotton Interests, Foreign and Native in Yoruba, and Generally in West Africa," *Journal of the Manchester Geographical Society* 5 (1889): 261.

14. Kristen Mann, personal communication.

15. F. Daniel, "Yoruba Pattern Dyeing," *Nigeria,* no. 13 (1938): 126. The 1936 *Adire* Commission also reported that "attempts have also been made more lately to form patterns by machining the cloth before dyeing" (Appendix 1, p. 4) and these variations are known as "machine *Adire*." R.J. Pokrant, "The Tailors of Kano City," in Esther Goody, ed., *From Craft to Industry* (Cambridge: University Press, Cambridge, 1982), notes that machines did not reach Kano until World War I.

16. Adire Cloth Committee, Appendix I, 3. It is interesting that the Commission of Enquiry reported only corn-based paste in 1936 while Nancy Stanfield, who did her research on *adire* in the late 1960s and early 1970s mentions only cassava paste. It is possible that within those thirty years, cassava paste eclipsed corn paste concomitant with cassava becoming a staple food item in the Yoruba diet. Nancy Stanfield, "Dyeing Methods in Western Nigeria," in Jane Barbour and Doig Simmonds, eds., *Adire Cloth in Nigeria* (Ibadan: Institute of African Studies, University of Ibadan), 16.

17. Stanfield, "Dyeing Methods," 17.

18. Museum of Textiles, *Adire: Indigo Cloth of Nigeria.* Text by Susan Barkley (Toronto Museum of Textiles, October 1980).

19. Susan Wenger and H.U. Beier, "Adire—Yoruba Pattern Dyeing," *Nigeria,* no. 54 (1957): 213.

20. Jane Barbour, "Adire Cloth in Nigeria," *Nigerian Field* (U.K.) 55, 1–2 (April 1990): 66.

21. Literally Ibadandun means "Ibadan is sweet." Colloquially it expresses "we enjoy Ibadan" or "Ibadan is pleasant." Mapo Hall is an imposing building with Greek columns on Mapo Hill in Ibadan. It was the seat of the colonial government. See Wenger and Beier, "Adire," 221; and Jane Barbour, "The Origin of Some Adire Designs" in Jane Barbour and Doig Simmonds, eds., *Adire Cloth in Nigeria* (Ibadan: Institute of African Studies, University of Ibadan, 1971), 51–54.

22. George Jackson, "The Devolution of the Jubilee Design," in Jane Barbour and Doig Simmonds, eds., *Adire Cloth in Nigeria* (Ibadan: Institute of African Studies, University of Ibadan, 1971), 83.

23. Keyes, "*Adire*: Cloth, Gender and Social Change," 93.

24. P.S.O. Aremu, "Yoruba Adire-Eleko Fabrics," *Nigerian Field* 44, 3/4 (1979): 100.

25. P.S.O. Aremu, "Yoruba Traditional Weaving: Kijipa Motifs, Colour and Symbols," *Nigeria,* no 140: 8.

26. Picton and Mack, *African Textiles,* 157; and Afolabi, "Yoruba Adire," (B.A. Honors Essay, University of Ife, 1983) 49–56.

27. Interview with Mrs. Runke Doherty, 3 October 1988, Ibara, Abeokuta.

28. Ibid.

29. Interview with Olanike Oladunjoye, 21 July 1996, Lagos.

30. Interview with Dolupo Kuti, 7 September 1988, Sapon, Abeokuta.

31. Interview with Chief Adura Majekodunmi, 21 June 1988, Ikereku, Abeokuta.

32. Interview with Alhaji Soetan, 9 August 1988, Kemta, Abeokuta.

33. Minutes of Egba Native Council, 2 April 1936, 6. ECR 1/1/77, vol. 2 (NAA). Unfortunately, he was not identified by name, only by title. We have some indication of his age from the fact that he spoke of knowing the *Alake*'s mother very well.

34. Barbour, "Nigerian Adire Cloths" Baessler-Archive, n.s. 18: 365.

35. Interview with Madame Wosinatu Adeniji, 30 May 1988, Ikereku, Abeokuta.

36. Interview with Mrs. Runke Doherty, 12 November 1988, Ibara, Abeokuta.

37. J.S. Eades, *The Yoruba Today* (Cambridge: Cambridge University Press, 1980), 59–61.

38. Interview with Alhaja Falilat Tukuru, 23 August 1988, Kemta, Abeokuta. Alhaji Soetan also reported that his mother taught his wives to dye.

39. Comment by Mr. Sheldon, agent of G.B. Ollivant. Extract from the Minutes of Egba Council, 20 September 1928. ECR 1/1/77 (NAA).

40. Adire Cloth Committee, Appendix I, 1. Also see Stanfield, "Dyeing Methods," 21.

41. Adire Cloth Committee, Appendix I, 2. Keyes argues that dyers preferred ashes from high-alkali hardwood trees, the same trees used in smelting iron. Keyes, "*Adire*: Cloth, Gender and Social Change," 23.

42. Adire Cloth Committee, Appendix I, 2.

43. O.L. Oke, "The Chemistry and General History of Dyeing," in Jane Barbour and Doig Simmonds, eds., *Adire Cloth in Nigeria* (Ibadan: Institute of African Studies, University of Ibadan), 30–32.

44. Interview with Madam Sidikat Ayinde, 21 June 1988, Abeokuta; with Alhaja Soetan, 6 September 1988, Kemta, Abeokuta; with Alhaja Tukuru, 23 August 1988, Kemta Abeokuta. Nancy Stanfield was also told that the dye bath was ready after three days. Stanfield, "Dyeing Methods," 19.

45. Interview with Madam Sidikat Ayinde, 21 June 1988 and 5 August 1988, Itoku, Abeokuta.

46. Wenger and Beier, "Adire," 225. Every fourth day was her day of worship and women brought her sacrifices of *ekuru* made of beans and *adun* made of maize and peanuts. On Iya Mapo's day of worship, dyers would stop work and spend the day celebrating and worshiping.

47. It would be worthwhile to collect other *oriki*s of Iya Mapo and explore the references to Atiba. Atiba was the son of Alafin Abiodun, who extended Oyo's power to its greatest extent in the late eighteenth century and consolidated Oyo's control of trade routes to the Atlantic. Atiba was later crowned the first *Alafin* of New Oyo in 1837. See Peter Morton-Williams, "The Oyo Yoruba and the Atlantic Trade 1670–1830," *Journal of the Historical Society of Nigeria,* 3, 1 (1964); and J.A. Atanda, *The New Oyo Empire: Indirect Rule and Change in Western Nigeria, 1894–1934* (London: Longman, 1973).

48. Eades, *Yoruba Today,* 45.

49. Madam Jojolola is one example of a woman who returned to her natal compound. Descendants claim that she returned because her co-wives were envious of her wealth. Interview with Alhaji Oladunwo Soetan and Alhaja Ajoke Soetan, 11 November 1988, Kemta, Abeokuta.

50. Interview with Adepate Adeniji, 29 June 1988, Ikereku, Abeokuta.

51. Interview with Alhaja Falilat Lasaki, 31 August 1988, Totoro, Abeokuta.

52. The point is worth further investigation in order to assess how widespread this practice may have been and whether the women had to be in some manner connected to the compound. Interview with Alhaja Raji, 28 October 1988, Lagos.

53. Interview with Adepate Adeniji, 1 June 1988, Ikereku, Abeokuta.

54. Interview with Alhaja Raji, 28 October 1988, Lagos; and with Alhaja Soetan, 1 September 1988, Kemta, Abeokuta.

55. Interview with Afusat Karimu, 1 September 1996, Kemta, Abeokuta; and with Salawu Sadiku, 29 August 1996, Kemta, Abeokuta.

56. Interview with Alhaja Bakare, 27 June 1988, Itoku Market, Abeokuta.

57. Interview with Alhaja Lasaki, 8 August 1988, Totoro, Abeokuta. Obtaining water was both tiring and time-consuming. They drew water from a standing pipe as well as a spring. Interview with Salawu Sadiku, 29 August 1996, Kemta, Abeokuta. Abeokuta town had pipe-borne water from 1914. A.K. Ajisafe, *History of Abeokuta,* 3d ed. (Lagos: Kash and Klare Bookshop, 1948), 110.

58. Interview with Alhaja Bakara, 27 June 1988, Itoku Market, Abeokuta.

59. Interview with Alhaja Tukuru, 23 August 1988, Kemta, Abeokuta; and with Madam Sidikat Ayinde, 21 June 1988, Itoku, Abeokuta.

60. Interview with Madam Sidikat Ayinde, 21 June 1988, Itoku, Abeokuta; with Alhaja Lasaki, 8 August 1988, Totoro, Abeokuta; and with Alhaja Bakare, 27 June 1988, Itoku Market, Abeokuta. Each explicitly expressed this. Marriage was also the primary avenue through which girls pledged as *iwofa*s gained their independence. Usually as a part of their bride price, the fiancés paid the debt owed to the loan giver.

61. Adire Cloth Committee, 7.

62. Interview with Madam Adepate Adeniji 29 June, 1988, Ikereku, Abeokuta.

63. Interview with Madam Salawu Sadiku, 29 August 1996, Kemta, Abeokuta.

64. Interview with Alhaja Biliahu, 30 August 1996, Kemta, Abeokuta.

65. Interview with Alhaja Falilat Lasaki, 8 August 1988, Totoro, Abeokuta.

66. Interview with Madam Aroga, 23 June 1988, Ikereku, Abeokuta.

67. Interview with Alhaja Ajoke Soetan, 1 September 1988, Kemta, Abeokuta.

68. See Minutes of Egba Council Meeting, 2 April 1936, 7. ECR 1/1/77 (NAA). And Minutes of Egba Council Meeting, 26 May 1932, 13. ECR 1/1/56 (NAA).

69. Interview with Mrs. Runke Doherty, 12 November 1988, Ibara, Abeokuta.

70. Interview with Alhaja Raji, 28 October 1988, Lagos Museum, Lagos.

71. Mr. Sheldon, the Ollivant agent, spoke with some authority because he had carried out extensive research into the *adire* industry in 1926–27 when problems began to surface. Adire Cloth Committee, 35–36.

72. Interview with Alhaji Oladunwo Soetan, 9 August 1988, Kemta, Abeokuta.

73. Alhaji Soetan was the senior son of Alhaja Soetan's late husband. There were approximately six women dyeing in the direct vicinity of this compound in 1988, although their relationship to Madam Jojolola was not ascertained (9 August 1988).

74. Interview with Alhaja Ajoke Soetan, 1 September 1988, Kemta, Abeokuta.

75. F.C. Royce, Report of the Re-Assessment of Abeokuta Town, 1926. CSO 26/19855 (NAI). The report provided a breakdown of occupations in each township and

in each of the four quarters in Abeokuta. In order to obtain this data, forms were distributed to each compound head, who had to fill in the name and occupation of each adult man and woman in the compound. To discourage false reporting, police visited some compounds to verify the data. In cases where information was withheld, compound heads were fined 5 to 10 shillings.

76. Ibid.

77. Assessment Report, Owode District, Egba Division, Abeokuta Province, 33–35. CSO 26/24873 (NAI).

78. "The Report of the Inspector of Forests on the Agricultural Prospects of the Egba Country," *West Africa,* 29 November 1902.

79. Adire Cloth Committee, Appendix I, 1.

80. By the time Mabogunje did his work in the 1950s, the major yam-producing region was to the northwest because of soil deterioration in other sections of the division and because of the incompatibility between yam and cocoa. Cassava was grown throughout the division because it grows well in poor soil conditions. It was grown primarily in the north-central districts. A.L. Mabogunje, "The Changing Pattern of Rural Settlement and Rural Economy Egba Division, South Western Nigeria," M.A. thesis, University College, University of London, 1958, 88–100.

81. Adire Cloth Committee, 20.

82. The title *Olori Parakoyi* meant the head of the *parakoyi* or trade association.

83. Minutes of Egba Council Meeting, Thursday, 30 April 1936. ECR 1/1/74, vol. 1 (NAA).

84. Adire Cloth Committee, 20.

85. Wenger and Beier, "Adire," 223.

86. Nancy Stanfield collected data in Ibadan, and there she found dyers who had their own kilns and prepared their own ash balls. Stanfield, "Dyeing Methods," 20. The data in the Commission of Enquiry Report clearly discusses a market relationship between dyers and the women who prepared the ashes.

87. Minutes of Egba Council Meeting, 20 September 1928, 2. ECR 1/1/77 (NAA).

88. Interview with Chief Adura Majekodunmi, 14 June 1988, Ikereku, Abeokuta.

89. Interview with Chief Adura Majekodunmi, 21 June 1988, Ikereku, Abeokuta.

90. Interview with Alhaja Raji, 28 October 1988, Lagos.

91. Minutes of Egba Council Meeting, 20 September 1928, 4. ECR 1/1/77 (NAA).

92. Chief Majekodunmi also worked for G. B. Ollivant and John Holt. Interviews, 14 June 1988 and 21 June 1988, Irereku, Abeokuta.

93. Nina Mba, "Women in Southern Nigeria Political History," Ph.D. diss., University of Ibadan, 1978, 25.

94. Interview with Madam Adepate Adeniji, 25 May 1988, Ikereku, Abeokuta.

95. Adire Cloth Committee, 6. I had several *adire* samples created for me in Abeokuta in 1988. The samples were tied by women who had once dyed, but they

said as they got older dyeing became too strenuous. They did not tie cloths full-time; they only did it occasionally.

96. Interview with Alhaji Samshedeen Bada, 2 September 1996, Kemta, Abeokuta.

97. Daniel, "Yoruba Pattern Dyeing," 126. Daniel thought that this new type of *adire* was inferior.

98. Samuel Johnson, *History of the Yorubas from the Earliest Times to the Beginning of the British Protectorate,* 6th ed. (London: Routledge and Kegan Paul, 1973), 119. This contrasts with northern Nigeria, where both men and women sewed. Secluded married women were heavily involved in tailoring. Hand-embroidered caps known as *zanna bukar* were increasingly regarded as women's work, but women also assisted in other aspects of production, such as button holing and some hand weaving. Pokrant, "Tailors of Kano City."

99. Betty Wass, "Yoruba Dress: A Systemic Case Study of Five Generations of a Lagos Family," Ph.D. diss., Michigan State University, 1975, 101.

100. Interview with Alhaji Surakatu, 28 June 1988, Igbein, Abeokuta. Alhaji Surakatu also informed us that during the Nigerian civil war men began making their own stencils again.

101. Interview with Alhaji Olumran, 2 September 1996, Kemta, Abeokuta.

102. Memo from Compagnie Française to A.E.F. Murry, resident, Abeokuta Province, 7 July 1936. ECR 1/1/42 (NAA). It was said that Gold Coast customers preferred the sheen to the matte color.

103. Interview with Alhaja Owomipe, 28 August 1996, Kemta, Abeokuta, and with Wasilat Animasaun, 1 September 1996, Kemta, Abeokuta.

104. Stanfield, "Dyeing Methods," 22–24.

105. In Hausaland, beating—a male dominated sector—was always an integral part of the preparation of dyed cloth. Specialized beating centers were always found close to dyeing centers. See Philip J. Shea, "The Development of an Export Oriented Dyed Cloth Industry in Kano Emirate in the Nineteenth Century," Ph.D. diss., University of Wisconsin–Madison, 1975, 169–75.

106. Interview with Alhaja Owomipe, 28 August 1996, Kemta, Abeokuta.

107. Interview with Alhaja Falilat Tukuru, 23 August 1988, Kemta, Abeokuta and with Alhaja Owomipe, 28 August 1996, Kemta, Abeokuta. Betty Oyeboyoje reported that Kampala were *adire* cloths dyed in bright colors, not indigo. Its name developed after Nigerian delegates at the Kampala peace talks wore outfits made with brightly colored tie-dyed cloth. Interview, 24 September 1988, Lagos.

108. Stanley Millburn, "Notes on the Development of Local Crafts and Industries," MSS. AFR.S. 1167, Rhodes House (Oxford). The section on Oyo Province with specific reference to Oyo and Ibadan was prepared by K.C. Murray of the Nigerian Education Department.

109. Richard Lander, *Records of Captain Clapperton's Last Expedition to Africa.* Vol. 2 (London: Henry Colburn and Richard Bentley, 1830), 212.

110. Interview with Madam Adepate Adeniji, 25 May 1988, Irereku, Abeokuta, and with Alhaja Falilat Tukuru, 23 August 1988, Kemta, Abeokuta. Dyers considered Itoku the main market and claimed that its five-day market set the market schedule. The order of market days was Itoku, Sodeke, Lafenwa, Iberekodo, and Isaba/Kuto which conflicted with the next Itoku market day. Interview with Alhaja Bakare,

11 November 1988, Itoku Market, Abeokuta. Iberekodo originated at one of the town gates in the nineteenth century and was the site of what Mabogunje (Akin L. Mabogunje, *Urbanization in Nigeria* [New York: Africana Publishing Corp., 1971. Second printing.]) called an interkingdom market, which usually met every nine days. Lafenwa, which opened next to the railway line, was a more recent creation. More research on the origin and development of these markets is necessary.

111. Interview with Mrs. Runke Doherty, 3 October 1988, Ibara, Abeokuta.

112. Babatunde A. Agiri, "Kola in Western Nigeria, 1850–1950: A History of Cultivation of Cola Nitida in Egba-Owode, Ijebu-Remo, Iwo and Ota Areas," Ph.D. diss., University of Wisconsin, 1972, 174.

113. Ibid., 148. In order to increase profits, some farmers employed their wives to process and take the nuts to market, since the price was higher for the processed nuts. By the end of the 1930s, Yoruba women dominated the kola trade.

114. Abner Cohen, "Politics of the Kola Trade: Some Processes of Tribal Community Formation among Migrants in West African Towns," *Africa,* 36, 1 (1966): 20. In the 1930s and 1940s a number of Hausa communities developed in Yoruba towns—Ibadan, Shagamu, Abeokuta, Agege, Ifo, Ijebu—to accommodate the needs of Hausa traders and migrants.

115. Wenger and Beier, "Adire," 212.

116. Shea does not supply any dates, but I think we can assume that he is referring to the late 1920s-1930s. See Shea, "Development of an Export," 120, 245.

117. Niara Sudarkasa, "The Economic Status of the Yoruba in Ghana Before 1970," *Nigerian Journal of Economic and Social Studies* 17, 1 (March 1975): 93–97. Also see J.S. Eades, *Strangers and Traders: Yoruba Migrants, Markets and the State in Northern Ghana* (Trenton, NJ: Africa World Press, 1994).

118. Esther Goody, "Daboya Weavers: Relations of Production, Dependence and Reciprocity," in Esther Goody, ed., *From Craft to Industry* (Cambridge: Cambridge University Press, 1982).

119. Communication from anonymous Heinemann manuscript reader.

120. Sudarkasa, "Economic Status of the Yoruba," 97.

121. Richard Roberts, "West Africa and the Pondicherry Textile Industry," in Tirthankar Roy, ed., *Cloth and Commerce: Textiles in Colonial India* (Walnut Creek, CA: Alta Mira Press, 1996), 143.

122. S.J.S. Cookey, "West African Immigrants in the Congo, 1885–1896," *Journal of the Historical Society of Nigeria* 3, 2 (December 1965): 261–270.

123. *Adire* Cloth Committee, 25. He said he had been coming to Abeokuta for about eighteen years.

124. Minutes of Egba Council Meeting , 3 April 1936. ECR 1/1/77 (NAA). The speakers contrasted that period with 1936, when the Senegalese visited every thirty days rather than fifteen.

125. An interpreter who gave testimony to the commission stated that he had between three and ten guests per month. Adire Cloth Committee, 12–16.

126. Ibid. There was an ongoing debate over who actually paid this fee. The dyers argued that they were ultimately charged this amount, while the interpreters argued that the buyer paid this fee.

127. Ralph Austen, *African Economic History* (London: James Currey, 1987), 132.

128. See Abner Cohen, *Custom and Politics in Urban Africa: A Study of Hausa Migrants in Yoruba Towns* (Berkeley: University Press of California, 1969); and Polly Hill, "Landlords and Brokers: A West African Trading System," *Cahiers d' Études Africaines* 6 (1966): 349–66.

129. Ibid.

130. Minutes of Egba Council Meeting, 2 April 1936. ECR 1/1/77 (NAA). The records also identified several hosts who lodged Senegalese buyers, but no women's names appeared in those records.

131. Minutes of Egba Council Meeting, 3 September 1931. ECR 1/1/54, vol. 2 (NAA). This case will be discussed in greater detail in Chapter 4.

132. Interview with Alhaja Ajoke Soetan, 1 September 1988, Kemta, Abeokuta.

133. Shea, "The Development of an Export," 185–86.

134. Ibid., 186.

4

INNOVATION AND CONFLICT IN THE *ADIRE* INDUSTRY

From 1927 onward it became clear that the *adire* industry faced extremely difficult conditions. The industry experienced a dramatic decline that was largely shaped by falling commodity prices and the worldwide depression, which began in earnest in 1929. The economic crisis redefined the social order of dyers and dyeing. As competing social groups struggled to enhance or protect their economic positions, dyers were left vulnerable, and the gains they had made as producers and women since the end of the nineteenth century became increasingly threatened. Conflicts also surfaced among dyers as those dyers who shared the privilege of age and wealth tried to assert their control over the industry.

To provide the fullest picture of the impact of the depression on dyers, this chapter uses two approaches. First, it examines strategies other economic sectors in Abeokuta tried to implement in order to protect their interests. The colonial state embarked on revenue collection reforms, European trading firms tried to restrict credit, while male Egba traders tried to open new avenues for credit. All these initiatives affected *adire* producers directly and indirectly both as producers and as women. The discussion illuminates dyers in their capacity as actors in constant interface with a context that was multilayered—international, regional and local, and gendered.[1] The discussion also highlights the capacity of dyers and other actors to change the context in which they struggled.

Second, the chapter examines the dyers' economic and political strategies to adapt to the economic crisis and the consequences of their efforts. The most far-reaching initiative was the incorporation of new technology (caustic soda and synthetic dyes) in the dyeing process.

The new technology had a dramatic impact on the dyeing industry. It exacerbated old tensions and created new ones while allowing dyers to increase production and cut costs. Caustic soda and synthetic dye also made the entire preparation of the dye bath easier. The new ease in preparation proved to be a double-edged sword, for while it allowed dyers to produce more at a lower cost, it also encouraged new women to enter the industry. These newcomers, branded interlopers, increased competition for a market that was declining and helped to generate a level of conflict within the industry that necessitated outside intervention.

The analysis in this chapter uses multiple lenses to explain the crisis dyers experienced in the 1920s and 1930s. It concurs with studies that demonstrate that industries fully enmeshed in the international economy through markets or credit were extremely exposed and therefore the most vulnerable to the cycles of the crisis.[2] In the case of *adire* producers, they were exposed and threatened on both fronts, markets and credit. It also demonstrates that the magnitude of the crisis as well as their responses individually and collectively cannot be fully appreciated in isolation. Dyers' actions and reactions were shaped by the complex redefinition of the commercial and social worlds in which they operated. Most studies on the depression focus on male-dominated economic sectors and do not consider the ways in which women or gender relations were affected by the crisis. This chapter offers a different perspective, since it examines the economic crisis through the experiences of women producers and highlights the ways in which gender shaped men's and women's experiences of the depression, as well as the options and strategies at their disposal.[3]

THE CREDIT CRUNCH: SOCIAL AND ECONOMIC REALIGNMENTS

The year 1929 marked the beginning of the depression in most history books, but it has been argued by economic historians of Africa that the depression can be traced back to the outbreak of World War I.[4] Beginning in 1914, the barter terms of trade (the price of imports in relation to the price of exports) widened significantly and failed to close. This gap widened when prices fell during the slump in 1920. At the beginning of 1920, palm kernels, for example, one of the major export items from Abeokuta, sold for £35 per ton, but by the end of April the price had dropped by 40 percent. By 1922 kernels sold for £10.5 per ton and rebounded only slightly to £11 per ton in 1923.

Through 1923, the British Residents in Abeokuta described trade as being at a "dull level."[5]

As prices fell, producers of the three major cash crops in West Africa—palm oil, cocoa, and ground nuts—tried to increase production in order to maintain their incomes. This strategy was somewhat successful for cocoa and groundnut farmers, because the markets for these commodities expanded over the decade and were able to absorb the production increases. The market for palm oil, on the other hand, did not expand. As a result, the incomes of cocoa and groundnut producers remained relatively high while those of palm-oil producers continued to fall.

In the 1930s the decline in the barter terms of trade for African producers continued, although a sharp drop in import prices cushioned the decline of export prices to some extent.[6] This gap in the barter terms of trade reverberated through the domestic economy in profound ways. African producers were forced to work harder and harder to maintain their buying power. In his *Report on the Taxation and Economics of Nigeria 1934,* S.M. Jacob, the government statistician, showed that prices of exports in 1926 were roughly half what they were in 1920 and 1934 export prices were again half of 1926 levels.[7]

The downturn in trade also reduced the availability of credit. Martin argues that the most distinctive features of the slump which began at the end of the 1920s were a generalized deflation and a contraction of credit.[8] This contraction of credit may have been exacerbated in Abeokuta after 1929, but it began earlier. All producers and traders were forced to reassess their activities and develop strategies to protect their interests. The following sections examine some of the strategies pursued by European traders, Egba men, and the colonial state. The strategies outlined here demonstrate that as each group plotted its own protection, economic as well as social relations in Abeokuta were altered. In addition, the state played a central role in mediating the realignments that occurred.

EUROPEAN TRADERS

As prices slumped at the beginning of the decade and stayed depressed, European firms used the occasion to reform their credit practices. They began limiting the number of people to whom they extended credit and the length of the credit period. The economic crisis also propelled the European firms in Abeokuta to attempt to reach a greater number of producers and consumers directly rather than through layers of middlemen. In 1925 the firms began opening retail shops throughout Abeokuta town. One commentator described the extraordinary impact this move had on commercial life in the town.

> There was a time when any visitor to Abeokuta, taking a walk round to Ibara in business hours could not help being impressed by the volume of trade which he saw being done in all the shops. Customers are to be found here and there in small or large groups paying at the counters or bundling up their goods to say *au revoir en entendant* to the clerks. To-day there is a sudden change, the whole atmosphere is pervaded with dullness and inactivity; the shops have been denuded of their usual customers and the agents and staff with hardly busy hands are settling down quietly to enjoy sweet commercial repose. The reason for such a sudden change from heat to cold is easily detectable; the barrier which had hitherto held up the European Merchants against ingress into the town has been unconditionally removed, and their clipped pinions having been restored they are determined to make the air feel the weight of their bodies. European shops are to be found strewn all over the nooks and crannies of the town, the petty traders are chased from the fields and threatened with complete extinction.[9]

European merchants anticipated that retail stores would achieve multiple objectives: allow the European traders to reach more consumers, reduce the number of bad debts, and damage the business of the "native" middleman.[10]

Egba middlemen bitterly opposed the retail shops, but the Resident argued that he was powerless to prevent the firms from establishing shops throughout the town. The issue was not prevention. Rather, by choosing not to intervene on behalf of African traders in this latest episode of the longstanding competition between African and European traders, the colonial government, by default, assisted European merchants. The long depression was therefore a period of major realignment among European and African traders, with European traders gaining new advantages.[11] There was considerable realignment within the European commercial community as well, as firms consolidated or were taken over. By 1920, four firms controlled between two-thirds and three-quarters of the import and export trades in West Africa—the Niger Company, A&E (African and Eastern Trade Corp.), Compagnie Française de l'Afrique Occidentale (CFAO), Société Commerciale de l'Ouest Africain (SCOA). In 1929 the Niger Company and A&E merged to form the commercial giant United Africa Company (UAC).[12]

The Resident justified the colonial government's indirect support of European merchants by arguing that the bulk of the population of Abeokuta as well as shopowners from whom the Europeans rented benefited from the proliferation of European stores.[13] While further research will be necessary to discern how many people received rents from the European firms and who these individuals were, it is quite clear that the *Alake* gained substantially. Council records show that he was a large landowner in Abeokuta town and multiple-year leases with firms such as John Holt and UAC brought in annual rents ranging from £30 to £60 per annum.[14]

Egba traders looked upon the expansion of European stores and the efforts to limit credit with alarm. Credit had been central to the economic expansion that occurred in the first two decades of the century. Colonial officials, on the other hand, saw the restrictions on credit as a blessing in disguise. Captain Royce, the assistant district officer, in 1926 argued that the retail shops would have the desirable effect of driving back into farming a number of young men who had no capital and little education but were able in the past to obtain credit from European firms.[15] While the expansion of retail stores did curtail credit for some, it did not have the impact that colonial officials desired. In the 1927 annual report, the Resident complained that the methods of trading still left much to be desired. The European firms gave out large quantities of goods on credit to a native trader who was generally covered by a surety, although the surety was sometimes not even of great value. The trader in his turn gave out goods on credit in smaller quantities, such that "a hundred pounds worth of goods may be divided among twenty or more people."[16]

Although clerks in the retail shops were supposed to sell on a strictly cash basis, goods were often given out on credit. They dispensed goods on the sale or return system, so that on the 25th of each month customers had to pay for the items taken on credit or return the unsold stock. Firms winked at the practice as long as the stock was correct at the end of the month. Invariably, some customers were unable to meet their obligations and falsifying returns of sales became a "necessary concomitant of the system."[17] By 1928 firms were less tolerant of the system, and the annual report noted that the situation was improving, for the stores were exercising greater control over their credit customers.[18] The effort to restrict credit developed unevenly, but by the end of the 1920s it was increasingly successful.

EGBA MEN

The crisis in credit forced introspection on the issue of indebtedness in the town. There had been a notable increase in the number of insolvent debtors. In council meetings, members spoke of houses being dismantled and the parts sold in order to pay debts.[19] Attention was also focused on marriage, since it was one of the main reasons that men went into debt. Many men resorted to the *iwofa* system to raise money needed for marriage. Since many husbands were debtors, there was great concern that their wives remain bound to their marriages. If there was a divorce the husband wanted the bride-price to be refunded to him immediately and in total so that he could retire his debt.

Divorce became especially integrated into the larger debate on debt, and several resolutions on refunding bride-price were passed in the 1920s.[20] High divorce rates in Abeokuta compounded the problem, because in many cases the bride-price was not refunded and former husbands remained pawns, still in debt, and without wives. Acquiring another wife involved further indebtedness. As one chief pointed out,

> In many cases he [the husband] will pawn himself in order to raise a loan for payment of the dowry. He serves his master and having got the woman in his house, finds her deserting him and claiming divorce at the instigation of a seducer. This usually constitutes a great hardship to the husband, for he is not only deprived of the services of a wife to look after him and give him food on his return from the farm, but he has actually to continue to serve because the seducer is unable to refund him his money to get another wife.[21]

The *Alake*, Ademola, attempted to redress this situation by altering an old Egba custom, *dipomu*, through which he detained women in the palace until their bride-price was refunded.[22] Previously, *dipomu* had been a system that enabled men or women who were experiencing a crisis to seek refuge in the palace. The system in practice under Ademola, however, was limited to women involved in matrimonial disputes. They were brought to the palace either by their parents or their husbands. The courts could also sentence a woman to *dipomu* for refusing to accept the husband chosen by her parents, or for being unable to refund her bride-price after a divorce.[23]

Between 1927 and 1931, 605 women were held in *dipomu*. The records show that the number of women held increased dramatically as the economic crisis deepened.

Year	1927	1928	1929	1930	1931
Dipomu	20	91	162	156	176

The records also listed the amount most women had to pay in order to secure their freedom and finalize their divorces. Fifteen judgments were missing, but of the 590 judgments listed, 262 women had to repay amounts between £1 and £10, 250 women owed between £11 and £20, and 78 owed more than £21. Approximately 38% of the women eventually paid their judgments and left (225), but 45 were returned to their husbands, 50 were redeemed by close family members and 168 were redeemed by persons to whom they were not related. Some women (51) absconded and 53 were discharged as a result of illness, pregnancy, or court order.[24]

The *dipomu* system was just one of several measures that were imposed to stem the high rate of divorce. The *Alake* and council passed rulings that stipulated that divorce cases had to be presented in court. They also imposed an eight shilling summons fee when filing for a divorce.[25] It was hoped that the courts would distinguish between what were considered sound reasons for divorce and what the council referred to as frivolous divorce. Besides the economic considerations, these initiatives around divorce were also efforts to reassert control over Egba women and junior men. Council members complained that as a result of European civilization, parents had lost control of their children. This perception was not new; it echoed those perceptions reported in the 1906 Report on Native Law and Custom in Egbaland.[26]

The *Alake* also sympathized with husbands and shared their concern with the loss of control over wives and daughters. He recalled that in the old days, a girl who ran away from her husband would have been shackled and returned to him. He used the example of one of his sisters who did not want her husband and ran off to Ibadan. She was brought back to Abeokuta in shackles and returned to her husband. She was shackled during her first pregnancy and finally left him for good after her third child.[27] Under British rule, parents could no longer resort to such measures, and in the minds of some council members the lack of such coercive measures contributed to the high divorce rate. The chiefs also complained that young men had lost respect for them and were having adulterous liaisons with the wives of *Oba*s or wooing girls away from their betrothed.[28]

It is clear from the council discussions that gender and intergenerational conflicts were heightened by the larger economic crisis. Control over wives and dependents, and by extension control over labor, assumed greater urgency, since producers had to control and reduce their expenditures while increasing the volume of production. While the depression created a difficult economic climate, council members and other wealthy men were also using these divorce discussions to protect their access to women. In 1925, 1929, and 1932, the *Balogun* of the Christians, D. Sowemimo, proposed a motion "that [the] amount of dowry returnable to the Egba Native Courts should be reduced and be limited to a certain amount."[29] He elaborated that he knew several women who were very dissatisfied in their marriages but could not divorce their husbands because of the high bridewealth.[30] One of his supporters acknowledged that the depression was a factor in this motion, because previously a woman and her seducer would not have had trouble returning the bridewealth, "but now-a-days there is no money in the town."[31]

The majority of council members opposed the *Balogun*'s motion and expressed little sympathy for women seeking divorces. One opposing member argued "if the present rule is slackened, it will give an undue free scope to our wives to do whatever they like."[32] In addition, they argued that husbands who spent a large amount of money would not recoup their expenditure after a divorce.[33] Legislation to limit the bride-price to £15 was not passed until 1936, although the depression had already pushed bride-prices as low as £12 in 1934.[34]

It is important to recognize that the lengthy discussions on divorce and bride-wealth represented one side of the question of debt. They specifically represented concerns paramount to men. Despite the volumes of documents on pawning and debt, very little addressed the ways in which the debt and credit crisis affected women. Men and women did not assume debts for the same reasons. The examples drawn from the major issues in Abeokuta during this period suggest that many men incurred debts in the pursuit of additional wives, as well as from economic investments, while women primarily incurred debts through the maintenance of their economic activities. However, in order to control their debt burden, men demanded greater social control of women. In this instance the state was an important resource for wealthy Egba men who could use their access to the state to enforce patriarchal relations that protected their economic position.

As the debate on divorce continued and the council tried to create a formula to ensure that husbands at least got back the money they may have borrowed to pay the bride-price, other segments of Egba society attempted to open new avenues of credit by demanding changes in the land laws. The principle of private property had taken root in Abeokuta from as early as the 1870s. Nevertheless, when European firms first began to lease property in Abeokuta at the turn of the century, the Egba United Government (EUG) made it illegal for anyone to sell or mortgage houses or land to foreigners. Such transactions were only legal between "natives of Egbaland."[35] Individuals could lease houses and land to non-Egbas, but only with the consent of the *Alake* and council. The bill also stipulated that houses, real estate, household furniture, and tools of a tradesman could not be seized for debt.[36] All the components of this bill were later incorporated into the 1913 Sale of Land Order that extended the ruling by stipulating the number of years that land and buildings could be leased—thirty years in the case of agricultural land and twenty-one years in the case of building land.

The original ordinance was intended to confine Europeans to Ibara, prevent them from entering the center of Abeokuta, and limit the amount of credit Europeans extended to Egba middlemen and consumers. It was feared that rights to sell or mortgage land to foreigners would have resulted in large-scale alienation of Egbaland to Europeans.[37] Lord Lugard, the governor general of Nigeria, consented to this ordinance particularly because it placed a decided check on European acquisition of land.[38]

In 1922 a group of Egba middlemen and traders petitioned the *Alake* and council to rescind the parts of the land ordinance that forbade the sale or mortgage of land to foreigners. This petition generated lengthy debates in the council. A number of council members sympathized with the arguments put forward by traders who were trying to raise capital in the depressed climate. The traders argued that Europeans would be prepared to extend more credit, if they knew they would be able to claim traders' properties. They argued that some of them had substantial properties that could be used as collateral. There were a number of houses in the town valued between £1,000 and £2,000 and yet their owners could not use them as collateral to raise even a £10 loan. It was also pointed out that the large number of dismantled houses was a direct result of the inability of house owners to use their property as collateral. They contrasted the situation in Abeokuta with that of Lagos, where, they argued, prosperity was directly attributed to the fact that Lagosians could do whatever they liked with their property. Lagos traders could mortgage their properties and raise as much as £1,000 for the purpose of trading.[39]

This agitation to change the land ordinance met strong opposition. Opponents feared that the repeal of this provision in the ordinances would result in even greater indebtedness followed by the loss of properties to foreigners. They argued that unscrupulous members of the community would take advantage of these changes to sell properties that did not belong to them. Cautious council members demanded that the proposal should be limited to individual property in the town. Family lands and houses as well as properties in the rural districts were excluded from the final proposals that were submitted.

The desire of Egba traders to use land as collateral fomented a major debate on land tenure in Egbaland.[40] The timing of this debate suggests that the depression may have been a watershed period in the transition to credit backed by landed property. This transition held important implications for future class and gender relations. The discussion was most forcefully pursued by an important segment of male traders and middlemen, although some women would benefit from the greater commercial value of land.

Yoruba society recognized women's right to own property.[41] In the more southerly city-states like Abeokuta and Lagos, women inherited land from both patrilineal and matrilineal lines. Research on Lagos has shown that women also took advantage of changes in land tenure and purchased individual property.[42] Wealthy women in Abeokuta, including some dyers such as Madam Jojolola, also owned land and two-story houses.[43] In spite of opportunities to own land, few women obtained alienable individually owned land and houses. Women who inherited land often delegated their rights to their son or a male relative. In some cases male relatives unscrupulously obtained property held by female family members. Women also had limited access to information and resources that would have enabled them to purchase land. As land became increasingly scarce and a valuable resource, the majority of women lacked ownership of individual property and by extension access to credit and the capital needed to trade.[44] The land debate certainly had implications for dyers, since they needed access to credit. Yet we have no record that dyers either as a body, individually, or as members of other associations attempted to participate in this important debate.

THE COLONIAL STATE

The colonial state was not a disinterested party in the discussions on the expansion of the European stores, divorce, or land reform. Local officials had a vested interest in enhancing the position of the European firms and in protecting the interests of Egba men. The state was also an autonomous actor with its own interests and priorities. A complex array of issues and interests guided the policies and actions of different levels within the colonial state. Two actions in particular warrant attention because they worked in tandem to deepen the economic crisis for many in Abeokuta, specifically the debate over the *iwofa* system and taxation.

The credit crisis was exacerbated by the state's decision to modify the *iwofa* system (pawning). As we saw earlier, the *iwofa* system was a mechanism to obtain both labor and credit. However, many colonial officials insisted that *iwofa* was just a variation on slavery. After World War I, the League of Nations began to explore the progress that had been made against slavery, and this spotlight on slavery opened a major debate on pawnship in Nigeria. In spite of their strong feelings against the *iwofa* system, colonial officials recognized its importance to the Yoruba economy. Any encouragement of the institution posed a dilemma, however, for the British government hoped to use its position in the League of Nations to challenge other African states, particularly Liberia, where slavery or other social institutions that could be said to resemble slavery still existed. In an attempt to reconcile the importance of pawnship in Yoruba economies with the leadership role that Britain hoped to play in the League of Nations, child pawnship was banned in 1927, and the entire institution made illegal after 1938.[45] The actions taken on pawnship had a significant impact on the Egba economy, for it threatened to curtail a major source of credit precisely at the time when other avenues of credit were contracting.

The colonial state also faced its own economic distress as a result of the depression. The crisis exposed the narrow revenue base of the colonial government. The state relied primarily on duties on the shipment of goods—i.e., import and export duties and railway fees—as well as direct taxation in northern Nigeria and parts of western Nigeria. To protect its own financial position, the colonial government tried to impose tax collection in new parts of the colony or improve tax collection in areas such as Abeokuta where the tax system was already in place.

The tax structure in Abeokuta included a flat tax and a graduated tax, a special assessment. The special assessment was to be paid by men and women whose annual income was over £40, while those who earned below that paid the flat rate. The flat rate was fixed at 5s. for men and 2/6s. for women. Colonial officials often expressed disappointment with the slow pace of collection, constant claims of over-assessment, and the failure to punish tax defaulters.[46] In 1924–25, it was decided that the *Bale*, the head chiefs in the villages, should be responsible for collecting the taxes, and they in turn would report to specially appointed district heads. They also created a chain of responsibility in the town. Heads of compounds reported to the township heads, who reported to the *Oba*s, who reported to the *Alake*. To motivate them to collect taxes, the chiefs got a percentage of the total tax receipts.[47] The amount they received varied according to their township and rank. For example:

Egba Alake		**Oke-Ona**	
Ogboni	£312	*Ogboni*	£91
Ologun	£164	*Ologun*	£72
Parakoyi	£49	*Parakoyi*	£26[48]

The chain of responsibility extended the reach of the colonial treasury into every compound, for the compound heads were to ensure that individuals in their compounds paid their taxes on time. The reform in tax collection was coupled with a major tax assessment in 1926.[49]

In spite of these reforms, Residents complained that the system was still not working efficiently, and by 1934 the heads of residential compounds were made responsible "for the payment of the tax in his compound to the nearest penny."[50] Tax reform remained a constant feature of colonial policy during the years of the depression. In spite of Residents' complaints about the inefficiency of the system, annual gross receipts did not change dramatically between 1928 and 1938.

Year	**Gross Tax Collected**	**Year**	**Gross Tax Collected**
1928–29	£35,317	1933–34	£35,411
1929–30	£36,304	1934–35	£35,083
1930–31	£36,945	1935–36	£36,172
1931–32	£33,994	1936–37	£36,264
1932–33	£36,204	1937–38	£35,274[51]

Egba tax payers paid a high cost for the state's success in keeping the tax receipts fairly constant in spite of the depression, for as Jacobs pointed out in his report, the tax rates did not reflect the decline in incomes. All producers had to work much harder to meet their unchanging tax bills.

ADIRE IN CRISIS

Adire was locked into the international economy indirectly through its consumers. Many *adire* consumers produced cash crops, and as prices fell, so did their disposable income. It was estimated that the value of the *adire* industry fell from £500,000 before 1928 to £150,000 by the mid-1930s.[52] The cost of a wrapper fell from between 5s. and 6s. before 1928, to 2s./6d and 3s. by 1936.[53] Part of the decline in the value of the industry reflected the use of cheaper cloth imported from Japan, but the fall in prices also reflected dyers' attempts to cut costs and prices as the buying power of consumers fell.[54] Colonial officials noted the direct correlation between the declining sales of *adire* and the fall in commodity prices, specifically cocoa. This trend was particularly highlighted in the Gold Coast markets. Annual reports noted the gradual decline of the *adire* trade between Abeokuta and the Gold Coast beginning in the 1920s. In 1924 a plague in Lagos interrupted the trade in dyed goods between Abeokuta and the Gold Coast. The 1927 report noted that the industry was in a bad way because dyers were making very little profit (although Gold Coast traders made considerable profit), and the 1928 report remarked that trade with Gold Coast traders had fallen off considerably.[55]

The downward trend characterized much of the first half of the 1930s, although there were some moments of optimism. The 1930 annual report stated "the dyeing trade . . . has suffered also due mainly to the reduced demand for dyed cloth from the Gold Coast."[56] Yet in February of that year, the UAC announced plans to establish a regular trade in *adire* cloth between Abeokuta and the Gold Coast. The proposal was presented as an attempt to help Egba dyers sell at a profit, but it clearly benefited UAC in two ways. First, it held out the possibility of maintaining the cloth trade that was so vital to the trading companies. It also allowed UAC to compete with African traders who had dominated this regional trade.[57] UAC's effort to oust African traders was not lost on one commentator, who remarked:

> by this new venture in my opinion the European firm will gain an insight once again into our staple trade and will try to hold the entire monopoly as is done in produce and merchandise. . . . In short, the whole project as it appears to me is like this: The natives purchase cloths intended for adire from European firm at "the dictated prices" and the European firm re-purchases the adire clothes from the natives at the "dictated prices" to re-sell again to the natives at the "dictated prices."[58]

Adire sales improved slightly in 1931, "sales . . . to dealers from the Gold Coast and Senegal have been most encouraging in the last few months,"[59] but they subsided the following year and did not pick up again until 1936.

While the relationship between cocoa prices and *adire* was clearly established, it is less clear how *adire* sales performed in relation to Senegalese commodities. "Lagos" cloth was quite popular in Senegal,[60] and dyers identified Senegalese merchants as their major buyers. However, colonial officials did not give as much attention to trade with Senegal as they gave to trade with the Gold Coast. Part of the difference in attention was due to the fact that Senegal was a French colony. It would also be useful to know where the Senegalese traders originated, and whether they supplied *adire* exclusively to the Senegalese market or to other parts of French West Africa. We know very little about how the depression affected the markets these traders supplied, except that the number of Senegalese traders visiting Abeokuta also declined over the same period.[61] The declining number of buyers from these areas indicated that markets outside Nigeria were contracting as well.

Dyers were directly tied to the international economy through their reliance on cloth and credit from European firms. As European firms tried to protect their position by tightening credit, dyers were immediately affected. One of the principal grievances dyers expressed against the European trading firms was the dramatically reduced period they were given to pay their debt. Some dyers, who had been allowed up to six months to pay for the items they had taken on credit, were now forced to pay for them in twenty-five days on the sales and return system. The shortened credit period combined with declining consumer sales left many dyers in debt to the trading firms.

DYERS RESPOND

As the colonial state, Egba men, and European traders strategized to offset the impact of the depression, their initiatives affected dyers and other women economically and socially. The economic impact was the most crucial for dyers, for both the decline in incomes and the general crisis in credit reverberated throughout the industry. The need to care for their families, pay taxes, and replenish the tools of their trade forced dyers to make adjustments. They began to innovate and experiment with new methods and procedures. Like other producers, dyers tried to increase production and lower costs. They tried a number of strategies that revealed the direct and indirect ways in which the industry was exposed to the cycles in the international economy. Several points of tension among dyers also began to surface. As they competed for a shrinking market, their heterogeneity was highlighted, particularly along the lines of socioeconomic status and age.

Dyers adopted a number of individual cost-saving measures that heightened tensions among them. Many began reducing the amount of cloth in a wrapper. Rather than using the standard five yards, many began to reduce the length of the cloths to four or even three yards. This gave them the leeway to lower prices and therefore attract customers. Unfortunately, this strategy created havoc, because it undermined any uniformity in the size of the cloths as well as prices and placed dyers who used five-yard pieces at a distinct disadvantage.[62] Some began to sell on credit and were left in a bind when their customers could not pay in time for them to settle their accounts with the stores. This happened to several women in the *afin*, the *Alake*'s palace. The women sold their cloth on credit, and when they could not recoup their money, the *Alake* was forced to help them pay their bills at the European stores. Other dyers opted to sell their cloths below cost, to the detriment of everyone.[63]

Competition for buyers reached a frightening crescendo as the decline continued. Dyers leveled charges and countercharges of inappropriate actions against each other. Older dyers were accused of not passing along their knowledge to younger women. Some dyers were accused of overwhelming buyers as they tried to select cloths and of trying to divert customers from other rival dyers. One dyer reported to the council,

> whenever any customer or the travelers who used to come from other countries to Abeokuta to buy adire cloths for trade in the Gold Coast come to the market and stands before an adire seller to buy, several other adire sellers would take their own individually and rush to the intending purchaser offering him to buy theirs and began to draw him until the purchaser becomes confused and has to buy at the lowest price possible.[64]

Some dyers completely circumvented competition in the market by taking their cloths to the Abeokuta compounds where the visiting Senegalese merchants stayed.[65] One group of dyers went so far as to meet the Senegalese buyers in Lagos.[66]

The intense competition undermined dyers' solidarity as well as their livelihood, but it benefited buyers. It was reported that the buyers from

Ogbomosho had spies in Abeokuta who visited the various markets and gauged the fluctuation in prices. When the buyers came to Abeokuta, their agents would advise them on the prices to offer sellers. Buyers also timed their arrival for the end of the month when dyers were compelled to sell their cloths in order to balance their account with the European firms.[67] The sale and return system clearly contributed to what can be characterized as panic selling on the part of dyers. In order to maintain good relations with the European firms, dyers discounted their cloths and forfeited a portion of their profits.

NEW TECHNOLOGIES—CAUSTIC SODA AND SYNTHETIC DYE

In the struggle to remain solvent, many dyers began to experiment with caustic soda. The records state that caustic soda was introduced in 1924 by Mr. I. A. Sodipo, the agent for the Union Trading Company, though its use did not become extensive until after 1928.[68] Individual dyers learned of it in different ways. Chief Majekodunmi recalled that the firms sent agents to the dyers' compounds to instruct them in using caustic soda.[69] Alhaja Raji had a vivid recollection of her first encounter with caustic soda.

> My mother died very young, so I had to live with my father's sister, who taught me to dye. I was even the first person to drop the caustic soda in the pot because I was an extrovert and very forward. On the third day the dye came out well, so dyers started using caustic soda.[70]

Adepate Adeniji recalled that Madam Bankole introduced the women in their compound to caustic soda.[71] Some dyers were cautious in the beginning. Many dyers unfortunately got injured because they did not know the appropriate proportion of caustic soda to use. Between 1926 and 1927, the agent of G. B. Ollivant, Mr. Sheldon, conducted experiments with caustic soda and disseminated information to dyers on the correct amount of soda to use.[72]

Despite the concerns, caustic soda had particular qualities that made its use salient to the times. Some argued that it allowed them to dye more cloths in one pot of dye. Dyers claimed that they could dye twenty cloths in one pot of dye made with caustic soda, as opposed to five cloths in a pot of dye made by the fermentation method. Caustic soda was also an important addition to the dyeing process because the quality of the available indigo had declined, and it had become in-

creasingly difficult to get ashes. Ash makers had turned to more lucrative ventures, and dyers were in fact paying a higher price for
poorer quality ashes.[73] Soda brought the dye out of the leaves quicker
than the wood ash solution and made it last longer.[74] It had become
difficult to obtain indigo as well because many farmers had stopped
growing indigo, and indigo makers had resorted to adulterating the
indigo balls with leaves from other trees. The shortage of indigo further encouraged the reliance on synthetic indigo when it was introduced in 1932. By the mid-1930s, indigo was being imported into
Abeokuta from Conakry and Dahomey.[75]

Caustic soda and synthetic dyes offered several important benefits.
They allowed dyers to circumvent the obstacles in obtaining quality ingredients. Moreover, they helped dyers to increase the volume of production. Caustic soda and synthetic dyes helped relieve some dyers of their
debt burden. Some women claimed that before the importation of caustic
soda and synthetic dye they were always greatly in debt to the European
firms. The new ingredients were also easier to use and did not require as
much labor as the old method. Altogether, they lowered production costs
and allowed dyers to lower prices.

While there were many benefits associated with the new technologies, the simplified production process had an unintended result. It
"admitted to the industry people who were not skilled dyers."[76] In spite
of *adire*'s difficulties, the industry still appeared to offer opportunities for income generation. Opportunity coupled with an easier production process encouraged many women to try their hand at dyeing.
Older, long-established dyers bristled at the number of untrained
women who entered the industry. Their entrance reflected a measure
of deskilling and leveling of the craft, and the older women held them
responsible for their economic difficulties. During the Commission of
Enquiry, some dyers recalled that in the old days there were not so
many dyers but their daughters-in-law, as well as daughters of firewood sellers, had since joined them. They argued that these younger
women, many of whom lacked sufficient capital and training, were
responsible for the decline of the trade.[77]

Consumers' declining buying power contributed significantly to the crisis in the *adire* industry, but the industry was also damaged by complaints about the quality of the dyed cloths. Dyers' experimentation with
the new technology created quality-control problems throughout Abeokuta
and weakened consumer confidence. Consumers registered their complaints by returning cloths to traders or by buying their *adire* from other
towns.[78] The problems consumers encountered were directly related to

the new ingredients. The use of too much caustic soda damaged the cloths. Many dyers had also switched to cheaper grades of cloth that did not hold up well to frequent washing.[79] Still, the major complaint had to do with the fastness of the dye. This problem became more pronounced after synthetic dyes were introduced. Several possibilities could account for the poor fastness of the dye: (1) insufficient time in the dye bath, (2) inadequate proportions of caustic soda and natural indigo, and (3) the quality of the synthetic dye.

The first synthetic indigo introduced into Abeokuta was manufactured by Badische Anilin and Soda Fabrik, the largest manufacturers of synthetic indigo in the world. A government analyst found that unlike natural indigo or ordinary synthetic dyes, which were vat dyes, these were direct dyes. They were dissolved in water until the required strength was reached, unlike the vat dyes, which were achieved by chemical reactions. The color that resulted from direct dyes was not a true indigo blue; it had a distinct reddish tinge, and it was not fast.[80]

It appears that a synthetic vat dye later came onto the market. If used with caustic soda or a mixture of caustic soda and natural indigo, the synthetic vat dye produced a dye bath with the same qualities of natural indigo dye bath. The dye was blue, without a reddish tinge, and it was fast. But some dyers were not using the synthetic vat dye appropriately. Experiments conducted by Compagnie Française de L'Afrique Occidentale in 1936 showed that some dyers were using synthetic dyes alone without the caustic soda. Some dyers also underdyed the cloths before dipping it into the synthetic dye. This solution of only synthetic dye produced a dark blue glossy sheen, called a sucretin cover, on the cloths. The sheen was very popular among consumers, but without benefit of the caustic soda that fixed the dye to the cloth or adequate time in the caustic-soda-based dye bath, the dark blue color disappeared with the first washing. Unfortunately, dye baths made with caustic soda did not produce the sucretin cover.[81] Dyers' experiments with synthetic dyes both to reduce costs and respond to consumer tastes damaged the town's solid reputation for high quality dyeing.

Despite the fact that the new ingredients proved to be a double-edged sword, in a remarkably short period of time most dyers had made the switch. Some contemporaries suggested that Abeokuta dyers set the example for dyers in other parts of Yorubaland.[82] The transition was primarily facilitated by the conjuncture of declining incomes and tightened credit. The state's decision to restrict pawnship also contributed to the incorporation of the new technology. Wealthier dyers, who often included *iwofa*s in their labor force, were particularly affected by the ban on child *iwofa*s. In response to suggestions that the women return to the fermentation method, Mrs. Coghill Richards, the daughter of the *Iyalode* Madam Jojolola stated:

> In those days when our own ashes was in use with the indigenous dye [elu] we had pawns and other servants to assist us in the trouble which its preparation entailed, but we have not such advantage now-a-days; can a woman of our standing afford to take the trouble of carrying ashes about?[83]

The new technology thus became an essential feature of their effort to increase the volume of production with a smaller workforce.

DYERS AND THE *ALAKE*

As the crisis deepened and the industry floundered, it became clear that these individual approaches were hurting more than they were helping. They contributed to the tensions and competition among dyers, and they did not affect some of the structural developments that preyed on the industry. As early as 1925, some dyers turned to the *Alake*.[84] They wanted him to help them regulate the industry. Although Yoruba women traders and producers traditionally established market associations, it was clear that even if a dyers association existed, it did not control its members. Those women who first approached the *Alake* wanted his sanction in order to strengthen their authority to regulate the activities of other dyers.

European firms also approached the *Alake* at the same time to encourage him to intervene in the industry. The firms had a vested interest in helping the industry thrive because they were dependent on the revenue generated by the cloth trade. In a 1933 communication, the UAC agent informed the Resident that if it were "not for the dyeing industry the firms would not be liable to support establishments at Abeokuta."[85]

A public meeting with interested parties was held in 1927. There the agents for the European firms, principally Mr. Sheldon, who represented G. B. Ollivant, called on the dyers to address the poor quality of the dyed cloths. Sheldon argued that caustic soda was not bad as long as it was used properly. All parties concurred that the women needed to form an association that could police the quality of the cloths and the actions of the dyers. Sheldon, the Resident, and the

Alake urged dyers to combine and set a standard for the depth of color of the dyed cloths and establish prices for the various designs. They also urged the women to punish any member who did not obey their rules and regulations. In addition, the *Alake* promised to recognize only those dyers in the association.[86] Even with the support of the *Alake*, the Resident, and the European traders, dyers were unable to create an effective association. The very next year, 1928, they met with the council again requesting help to reorganize the industry for "every dyer is carrying on the trade as she like(s) in the absence of rules and regulations."[87]

The testimony from the council records indicates some of the underlying reasons why it seemed virtually impossible for the dyers to organize themselves as a cohesive group. At this point, there was still a conflict among dyers over which process produced a better-quality dye. The *Alake*, in a bid to resolve this dispute, financed a contest between the two methods. Pots of dye using both methods were prepared and the women were to determine which method was better. The results of this test were not reported, but later references to the test suggest that council members believed the cloth dyed in the natural indigo bath was the superior product.[88] In addition to the conflict over the dye bath method, dyers were also torn apart by the intensity of the competition for buyers. It appears that dyers also lacked a structure through which policies regarding the dyeing process, quality control, and behavior in the markets could be established and enforced. In 1928 an attempt was made to create such a structure. Several women in each quarter were appointed "head dyers" and it was their responsibility to determine whether the dye baths in their area were of good quality. The head women were also to meet monthly with the *Alake* to keep him abreast of all developments, and the older dyers were encouraged to train the newer ones.[89]

The suggestions, however, did not bring dyers any closer to an association in part because of the competition, and the changing composition of dyers. One commentator noted that

The whole trouble is because the proper traders are not allowed to carry on the trade alone, there has since been a mixture of the children of wood cutters, pepper sellers, *agidi* sellers, native cake sellers, cassava flour sellers, etc., with the children of the proper *adire* traders; these cannot manage the business to profit, because they have no training for such trade from their parents and they have consequently spoilt the trade for the owners of the trade.[90]

As the dyeing process was simplified, the new women who entered the trade circumvented the established avenues of entrance. They did not come through apprenticeships or the *iwofa* system, and even if one married into a dyeing compound, she did not start off as a part of her mother-in-law's workforce. These new people were operating outside the hierarchies of learning and control.

The proposals to "organize the industry" were in essence efforts to reassert the control of the older, long-established dyers ("the owners of the trade"), and the primacy of those who were skilled craftswomen. One of the main spokeswomen for the *Alake*'s intervention was Mrs. Coghill Richards, the daughter of Madame Jojolola. She and her peers wanted to rein in "the interlopers," such as children of firewood sellers, who were not born into the industry, did not enter it through their tutelage, and often did not have sufficient capital to sustain themselves and therefore had to sell at any price.[91] The *Alake* was also inclined to intervene in their favor because these women represented his mother's generation of dyers and the heyday of the industry. He noted

> Formerly our parents used to be prosperous through their *adire* trade. When my own mother was coming to Ake, she had 40 female servants who were carrying on the *adire* trade for her. The youngsters used to learn to trade under them without any difficulty.[92]

He implied that by a return of control to senior dyers, new women would be properly trained and therefore redress the primary reason for the decline. His suggestion, while loyal to senior dyers, was limited because it did not acknowledge the credit crisis or the depression.

In spite of the emphasis on the control and regulation of dyers, the women did not identify the newcomers to the industry as the only problem. Dyers also complained to the *Alake* about the actions of interpreters. Interpreters assisted the Senegalese buyers with their purchases in the market. It was brought to the *Alake*'s attention that the interpreters charged 6d. on each cloth that was purchased. Dyers argued that they ultimately paid that 6d. rather than the Senegalese merchants. The *Alake* and council subsequently banned the collection of this fee by the interpreters.[93]

The dyers' most pressing problem was the change in the credit structure. They made it clear that the changes in the credit system contributed more to the industry's decline than poorly dyed cloth. One dyer stated that

Speaking about the quality of the dye in use now-a-days, I may say it is not so bad as compared with the credit system which has practically spoiled the *adire* trade. In the early days of the trade with European firms, after buying the Croydon on credit we were allowed to balance our accounts in six months time. But now-a-days we are requested to balance up in 25 days' time, the results is that nearly every dyer has plunged herself into debt.[94]

As a result of the sales and return system, some dyers left the industry altogether and some pawned their children in order to raise money to balance their accounts.[95] Egba dyers were not the only ones to complain about the sales and return system, but they clearly hoped the *Alake* would reverse the firms' credit policy.[96]

While the sales and return system had a negative impact on dyers in general, it was not universal. Class mediated the affect of the credit crisis. The women who were most immediately threatened by the shortened credit period were the wealthier traders who had had access to long-term credit. Many of these women combined cloth trading with *adire* production. The shortening of the credit period complicated their dual roles. It would have been difficult for these women to collect all the money owed to them from their retail customers in order to settle their accounts with the trading firms on the 25th of each month. The shortened credit period also restricted their capacity to give credit to others, as did the state's effort to curtail the *iwofa* system. Smaller dyers who bought their cloth from retail cloth traders in the local markets were not directly affected by the sales and return system.

These class differences do not minimize the general perception of the magnitude of the problem posed by the sales and return system. The sales and return system was a tight-money policy that restricted credit by shortening the repayment period precisely when the market was moving into its most sluggish period. Dyers could not offset the potential slow turnover of trade because of the 25-day turnaround imposed under the sales and return system. This great pressure to sell all their stock before the 25th of the month contributed to the panic selling on the part of some dyers and depressed prices for all dyers.

In spite of the general crisis in credit, dyer's complaints about the sales and return system were essentially ignored. The *Alake* informed them that they had to follow the credit policies of the Europeans, even though he was quite conversant with the financial difficulties that dyers in his own compound experienced.[97] He had loaned some of the women in his compound money to pay their bills with European traders. The

Alake's advice to the women on credit reflected the limitations of his power. Whether or not he sympathized with the dyers, he could not enact any policy adverse to the European trading firms. The firms were a powerful constituency in Abeokuta. Michael Atkinson, who served as an assistant district officer in Abeokuta province, argues that there were really "three *Alake*s in Abeokuta, Ademola himself, the Resident, and the District Manager of the United Africa Company, Mr. Mason."[98] Furthermore, the firms were outside Ademola's purview as a local functionary of the colonial state. The colonial state's commitment to a free-trade policy would have made the colonial government look askance at any suggestion to intervene directly in the economy.

While the *Alake* could not take action against the trading firms, he could take action against the dyers. As complaints about the quality of the cloths continued, the *Alake*, at the Resident's urging, banned the use of caustic soda. This decision also had the strong support of the European trading firms. Dyers were given three months from February 1929 to dispose of all the caustic soda in their possession. Synthetic dyes were subsequently banned as well. The Resident argued that the ban on caustic soda was justified, since the continued use of caustic soda damaged the cloth and threatened to drive customers away. Therefore "it is the duty of the *Alake* and Council to improve the trade by making some rules."[99] Mrs. Coghill Richards angrily responded to his assertions, "it was the Authorities who rule[d] that no one must have pawns again, with the result that there is nobody to assist us to carry ashes for the dye."[100] Implicit in her comment is the notion that the council's actions were hypocritical, not the result of genuine concern about the plight of the dyers. In her estimation, although dyers needed labor, the colonial state had banned the use of child pawns. Yet in spite of their rhetorical promises to help the industry, the main arena of concern—credit—was left untouched.

This hypocrisy can only be understood by placing dyers in relation to other sectors of the economy. The selected areas where the *Alake* and Resident were willing to intervene and those areas they refused to address reflected the state's economic priorities. Both by direct intervention or maintained silence, the state privileged the colonial treasury and European traders. Dyers, like other West African producers, were left to fend for themselves as best they could during the crisis.

CONCLUSION

The depression and the decline of the *adire* industry were inextricably linked. These women producers felt the impact of the depression because *adire* was fully enmeshed in the international economy. A significant proportion of their consumer base was involved in export agriculture; thus the fall in commodity prices weakened the industry's consumer base. Many dyers were directly or indirectly tied to credit lines from the European firms, and as a result the contractions in credit eroded dyers' access to credit. Dyers, like other segments of society, were caught in a vortex of actions and reactions as they struggled to maintain their livelihoods.

In the struggle to stave off the worst of the depression, key social, economic, and political relationships were realigned. European firms made headway in their struggle against African middlemen gaining greater access to African consumers. Men of propertied means tried to convert their property into greater access to capital, while other men tried to ensure that wives stayed securely bound to their marriage. These realignments fashioned a new social order and commercial milieu in which dyers were being increasingly disadvantaged.

The economic crisis also brought to the surface a number of tensions among dyers and highlighted the changing social composition of the industry. The new technology made it easier for new people to establish themselves as independent dyers. The change in credit terms also affected the social composition of the industry. It forced out women who could not obtain money to cover their debt at the end of the month. The new credit terms may also have forced out wealthier dyers. It jeopardized their retail cloth business and their ability to extend credit, as well as their *adire* business. Nonetheless, these women would have had more options than poorer dyers.

Although the depression in large measure set the context of the crisis the dyers experienced, it is rather amazing how little the ensuing discussion of the difficulties the industry faced reflected any acknowledgment of the systemic breakdown of international trade. Dyers assigned blame to the change in credit and the new women who had entered the industry. The state—the *Alake* and the Resident—helped limit the discussion by emphasizing that the new technology and the absence of a strong dyers' association were at the root of the problem. It must be acknowledged that these were important issues to address. The competition between dyers for customers and the conflict over newcomers were significant obstacles to concerted actions to defend an economic interest. However, the silences in their narrative of the crisis also served a purpose. It absolved the colonial state from taking any wide-ranging actions in the economy, particularly actions which would have benefited African producers. It is not a coincidence that the credit crisis was ignored. Any attempt to address the credit issue would have put the state in a more managerial role in the economy, contrary to free-trade notions, and could have put the state in conflict with European capital.[101]

The colonial government's practice, though not necessarily its explicitly articulated policy, was to do little to aid colonial producers through the depression while ensuring that these producers continued to pay for the privilege of colonial rule. This was clearly expressed in Jacob's discussion on taxes. Since taxes ostensibly went to government services, by 1932 (measured by the value of the agricultural commodities they sold) Nigerians were paying twice as much for government services as in 1926, and three times the amount paid in 1920.[102]

By examining the unfolding crisis dyers faced in this broad context, the chapter allows us to see how the confluence of gender, age, and wealth enabled some actors to reshape the context so as to protect themselves while marginalizing others. This is particularly apparent when one considers the actions of the Egba Council. The *Alake* and council could not set priorities that were independent of the colonial state or the interests of European capital, but within the purview that they controlled, they had the capacity to advocate and create policies that protected the social and economic interests of men generally and wealthy men specifically. Their efforts to create new avenues of credit by using land as collateral, restrict divorce, and leave brideprice unrestricted enhanced the position of senior, wealthy men in the society, which was the social profile of the men who composed the council. Dyers, like the majority of women in Abeokuta, did not have the type of access to the council that allowed them to define or create policies in their own image. The magnitude of the economic crisis created a context and climate for a host of realignments, but the chapter makes clear that those with access to the state even in limited capacities were able to shape the nature of some of those changes to their advantage. Women's political marginalization meant that they could not protect the social gains they had achieved in the early decades of the century, and neither could they shape economic policies that considered their interests. Thus the depression was much more than an economic watershed, it facilitated changes in both class and gender relations.

NOTES

1. Michel-Rolph Trouillot, *Silencing the Past: Power and the Production of History* (Boston: Beacon Press, 1995), 23.

2. Ian Brown, ed., *The Economies of Africa and Asia in the Inter-war Depression* (London: Routledge, 1989), 1.

3. Martin's work on the Ngwa region of eastern Nigeria is an important exception to this tendency. See Susan Martin, *Palm Oil and Protest, An Economic History of the Ngwa Region, South-eastern Nigeria, 1800–1980* (Cambridge: Cambridge University Press, 1988), and Martin, "Gender and Innovation: Farming, Cooking and Palm Processing in the Ngwa Region, South-eastern Nigeria, 1900–1930," *Journal of African History* 25, 4 (1984): 411–27.

4. Susan Martin, "The Long Depression: West African Producers and the World Economy, 1914–45," in Ian Brown, ed., *The Economies of Africa and Asia in the Inter-war Depression* (London: Routledge, 1989), 77.

5. Annual Report, Abeokuta Province, 1920/21, 38. CSO 21/309 (NAI). Annual Report, Abeokuta Province, 1923, 13. CSO 26/1,09234 (NAI).

6. Martin, "The Long Depression," 78–80.

7. S.M. Jacob, Report on the Taxation and Economics of Nigeria 1934 (Rhodes House, Oxford), 88. The report was suppressed after its completion in 1934, but Jacob circulated a few copies of the original in 1966. In his discussion of the Nigerian economy, Jacob mistakenly claimed that Nigeria's internal economy did not suffer from the depression because he assumed there was very little interaction between internal markets and the export market. Nonetheless, he provides important information about the Nigerian government's tax policies and the impact of those policies on Nigerian producers.

8. Martin, "The Long Depression," 79.

9. *Egba National Harper,* September 1926, 3.

10. Annual Report, Abeokuta Province, 1925, 23–24. CSO 26/2-11875, vol. 3 (NAI). Also see *Egba National Harper,* September 1926, 4.

11. Very similar developments were going on in eastern Nigeria. Felicia Ekejiuba shows that African middlemen lost substantial ground to European traders during the depression, and Igbo women traders who had done well in the period between 1910 and 1930 were eclipsed by male traders. See Felicia Ekejiuba, "Omu Okwei, the Merchant Queen of Ossomari: A Biographical Sketch, " *Journal of the Historical Society of Nigeria*, 3, 4 (1967): 633–46. Also see A.I. Nwabughuogu, "From Wealthy Entrepreneurs to Petty Traders: The Decline of African Middlemen in Eastern Nigeria, 1900–1950," *Journal of African History* 23, 3 (1982): 365–79.

12. D.K. Fieldhouse, *Merchant Capital and Economic Decolonization: The United Africa Company, 1929–1987* (Oxford: Clarendon Press, 1994), 10–11.

13. Annual Report, Abeokuta Province, 1926 , 29–30. CSO 26/2, 11875, vol. 4 (NAI).

14. See Minutes of Egba Council Meetings, 23 October 1930 and 11 December 1930, ECR 1/1/45, vol. 2 (NAA). Also see Minutes of Council Meetings, 5 February 1931 and 5 March 1931, ECR 1/11/45, vol. 3 (NAA).

15. Annual Report, Egba Division, 1926. ECR 1/1/37 (NAA).

16. Annual Report, Abeokuta Province, 1927, 22–23. CSO 26/2, 11875, vol. 5 (NAI).

17. Ibid. The Resident also noted that this "demoralizing" system of credit also occurred in produce buying.

18. Annual Report, Abeokuta Province, 1928. CSO 26/2 11875, vol. 6 (NAI).

19. Minutes of Egba Council Meeting, 14 August 1922. Abe Prof. 6/4–6/22B (NAI). Members told of houses valued at £400 being dismantled and the parts sold for £60 in order to pay a debt as low as £10.

20. Although the terms *bride-price* and *dowry* were used interchangeably in the documents, bride-price was the primary mechanism in contracting a marriage. Native Court Rule—Refund of Dowry, 29 June 1922. ECR 1/1/73 (NAA).

21. See Minutes of Egba Council Meeting, 15 July 1935, ECR 1/1/67, vol. 2 (NAA). The number of divorce cases heard in native courts for 1927, 1928, and the first half of 1929 totaled 8,267. The number of adultery cases for the same period totaled 2,031. Copies of Correspondence, 2 July 1929. A. P. P. 3/1/26 (NAA).

22. Annual Report, Abeokuta Province, 1920/21. Addendum to Political Report on Egba Division. CSO 21/309. Delano suggests that in the old days, *dipomu* was actually the method that women used to secure divorces. In cases of ill-treatment, women went to the palace and took hold of one of the pillars. Their husbands could not touch them there, for it was considered an insult to the king to touch a woman in "the land of refuge." See I.O. Delano, *The Soul of Nigeria* (London: T.W. Lauri, 1937), 142.

23. Minutes of Egba Council Meeting, 24 October 1927. ECR 1/1/38 (NAA).

24. Record Book for *Dipomu* from Courts. ECR 1/7/1.

25. ENA Minutes of Egba Council Meeting, 18 June 1925, 17–18, Abe Prof. 2/9–33/25 (NAI).

26. C. Partridge, "Native Law and Custom in Egbaland," *Journal of the African Society* 10, 40 (1910): 422–33.

27. Minutes of Egba Council Meeting, 25 September 1926. ECR 1/1/33, vol. 1 (NAA).

28. Minutes of Egba Council Meeting, 5 July 1928. ECR 1/1/40 (NAA).

29. ENA Minutes of Egba Council Meeting, 18 February 1932, 3. ECR 1/1/54, vol. 1 (NAA). Also see ENA Minutes of Egba Council Meeting, 18 June 1925. Abe Prof. 2/9–33/25 (NAI).

30. At an earlier meeting, one council member reported, "A woman divorced me, but when her seducer could not pay me the high dowry on her as adjudged by the Court, the woman had to return to me." Oluwo of Oko, ENA Minutes of Egba Council Meeting, 18 June 1925, 11. Abe Prof 2/9–33/25 (NAI).

31. Minutes of Egba Council Meeting, 18 February 1932, 4. ECR 1/1/54 (NAA).

32. Ibid., 8.

33. By 1915 bridewealth had reached £50. See Memo from W.F. Sosan, Clerk of Council, 24 July 1915. APP 3/1/13 (NAA).

34. Minutes of Egba Council Meeting, 10 May 1934. ECR 1/1/66, vol. 1; and Minutes of Egba Council Meeting, 7 March 1936. ECR 1/1/74, vol. 1 (NAA).

35. See *Egba Government Gazette*, 27 January 1913. A native of Egbaland was defined as "any person with both parents Egba or of Egba descent; a slave in Egbaland who redeemed himself and intends to reside permanently in Egbaland; or all person of Yorubaland and not of Egba descent who have shown intention of permanently residing in Egbaland." Also see Adebesin Folarin, *The Laws and Customs of Egbaland* (Abeokuta: Balogun Printers, 1928), 15–16.

36. Egba United Government Notice, 29 May 1903. APP 5/1/1 Correspondence Book 1900–04 (NAA).

37. See Minutes of Egba Council Meeting, 14 August 1922, 17 August 1922 and 16 October 1922. Abe Prof. 6/4—ABP 11/22B (NAI).

38. Letter of Lord Lugard to Harcourt, 17 November 1913. CO 520/128 #2176 (Public Records Office, London—hereafter PRO).

39. Minutes of Egba Council Meeting, 14 August 1922, Abe Prof. 6/4—ABP 11/22B (NAI).

40. Minutes of Egba Council Meeting, 3 February 1927. ECR 1/1/33, vol. 1 (NAA). Although the issue would not be resolved for decades to come, it led to the appointment of a commissioner of lands for the whole of Nigeria and a major study of Yoruba land tenure in 1932 by H. Ward-Price. Ward-Price served at numerous stations in eastern and western Nigeria and succeeded Captain W.A. Ross as Resident of Oyo Province in the 1930s.

41. The extent to which women inherited land varied from one city-state to another. In the strongly hierarchical and patrilineal kingdoms such as Oyo, fixed property tended to be passed to men in order to keep it in the patrilineage. Property rights were much more relaxed in Abeokuta, and men and women inherited land from both patrilineal and matrilineal lines. Simi Afonja, "Land Control: A Critical Factor in Yoruba Gender Stratification," in Claire Robertson and Iris Berger, eds., *Women and Class in Africa* (New York: Africana, 1986), 81–83.

42. Kristin Mann, "Women, Landed Property, and the Accumulation of Wealth in Early Colonial Lagos," *Signs: Journal of Women in Culture and Society* 16, 4 (1991): 705.

43. Minutes of Egba Council Meeting, 20 February 1936, 11. ECR 1/1/70, Vol. I (NAA).

44. Mann, "Women, Landed Property," 705.

45. See Judith Byfield, "Pawns and Politics: The Pawnship Debate in Western Nigeria," in Toyin Falola and Paul Lovejoy, eds. *Pawnship in Africa: Debt Bondage in Historical Perspective* (Boulder, CO: Westview Press, 1993).

46. Minutes of Egba Council Meeting, May 1924. Abe Prof. 6/4, ABP 6/22B.

47. See Minutes of Egba Council Meeting, 19 March 1925 and 23 March 1925. Abe Prof. 2/9–33/25 (NAI). This system was a modified version of the system the colonial government had tried to impose in 1918. This measure helped spark the tax revolt because the township chiefs still carried significant authority at that time, and the creation of district heads usurped the authority of township chiefs in their rural satellites. The fact that they were able to reintroduce the system seven years later attests to the declining authority of these chiefs as the colonial state consolidated its power.

48. Minutes of Egba Council Meeting, 26 April 1934. Abe Prof. 1/1, ABP 236, vol. 3 (NAI).

49. F.C. Royce, Report of the Re-Assessment of Abeokuta Town, 1926. CSO 26/19855 (NAI).

50. Minutes of Egba Council Meeting, 16 May 1934. Abe Prof. 1/1, ABP/236, vol. 2 (NAI).

51. I.W.E. Dods, Report on Tax Collection in the Egba Division, for the Year 1938–39. ECR 1/1/12 (NAA).

52. Further research will be needed to confirm these figures. But the Resident in 1933, A.E. Murray, who had questioned the valuation of the industry Captain Royce

had given in the 1926 Assessment—£200,000 representing 80 percent of the cloth trade—was reassured by UAC that the figure was not an overestimation. Besides buying cloth from the firms in Abeokuta, a considerable amount of undyed cloth was purchased in Ibadan and Lagos and brought to Abeokuta to be dyed. Letter from the Resident to the secretary, Southern Provinces, Enugu, 6 June 1933. CSO 28400, vol. 1 (NAI).

53. Proceedings of the *Adire* Cloth Committee, July 1936, 19. Abe Prof. 4—D29 (NAI).

54. By 1932 cloth imports from Japan were adversely affecting English cottons because they were cheaper. Annual Report of Nigeria, 1932, 79 (NAI).

55. Annual Report, Abeokuta Province, 1924. CSO 26/2 11875, vol. 2; Annual Report, Abeokuta Province, 1927. CSO 26/2 11875, vol. 5; Annual Report, Abeokuta Province, 1928. CSO 26/2 11875, vol. 6 (NAI).

56. Annual Report, Abeokuta Province, 1930, 27. CSO 26/2 11875, vol. 8 (NAI).

57. See "Abeokuta News and Notes," (Nigerian) *Daily Times,* 15 February 1930.

58. (Nigerian) *Daily Times,* 5 March 1930.

59. Annual Report, Abeokuta Province, 1931, 40–41. CSO 26/2 11875, vol. 8 (NAI). During a 1936 meeting, one dyer reported that foreign buyers used to come every two weeks, but by that point they were coming every thirty days. See Minutes of Extraordinary Meeting, 3 April 1936, 9. ECR 1/1/77, vol. 2 (NAA).

60. Mohamed Mbodj, personal communication. "Lagos Cloth" referred specifically to cloth made in Nigeria.

61. Proceedings of the *Adire* Cloth Committee, July 1936, 20. Abe Prof. 4—D29 (NAI).

62. Report of the Public Meeting of the Adire Women, 25 July 1927, in the *Egba Administration Bulletin,* 31 August 1927, 109. E.A.B. 6/1/14 (NAI).

63. Ibid. See also Minutes of Egba Council Meeting, 20 September 1928. ECR 1/1/77 (NAA).

64. Report of the Public Meeting of the Adire Women, 25 July 1927, in the *Egba Administration Bulletin,* 31 August 1927, 104. E.A.B. 6/1/14 (NAI).

65. Ibid.

66. Minutes of Egba Council Meeting, 8 October 1931. ECR 1/1/54, vol. 3 (NAA). These women were the wives and sisters-in-law of an Alhaji Saka, with whom Senegalese buyers often stayed when they were in Abeokuta.

67. Report of the Public Meeting of the Adire Women, 25 July 1927, in the *Egba Administration Bulletin,* 31 August 1927, 105. E.A.B. 6/1/14 (NAI).

68. Proceedings of the Adire Cloth Committee, 1936, 4, Abe Prof. 4—D29. (NAI).

69. Interview with Chief Adura Majikodunmi, 28 June 1988, Ikereku, Abeokuta.

70. Interview with Alhaja Munirat Raji, 28 October 1988, National Museum, Lagos.

71. Interview with Adepate Adeniji, 29 June 1988, Ikereku, Abeokuta.

72. Adire Cloth Committee, 1936, 34 (NAI). Also, Report of the Public Meeting of the Adire Women, 25 July 1927, ECR 1/1/42, vol. 2 (NAA). A copy of the minutes of this meeting also appears in the *Egba Administration Bulletin,* 31 August 1927 (NAI).

73. Report of the Public Meeting of the Adire Women, 25 July 1927, *Egba Administration Bulletin,* 31 August 1927. E.A.B. 6/1/14 (NAI).

74. Adire Cloth Committee, 1936, 42 (NAI).

75. Ibid., 35.

76. Ibid., 35.

77. Ibid., 7; also, Minutes of Egba Council Meeting, 26 May 1932. ECR 1/1/56.

78. Minutes of the Egba Council Meeting, 2 April 1936. ECR 1/1/77.

79. The general manager of the Compagnie Française de l'Afrique Occidentale, M. Lancelin, conducted experiments on the dyeing process utilized by Abeokuta dyers. His study indicated that the quality of the cloth was an important factor that could not be overlooked. See the letter from Lancelin to A.E.F. Murray, Resident, Abeokuta, 4 July 1936. ECR 1/1/42, Adire Trade 1928–39, vol. 1.

80. Memo to the chief secretary from the government analyst, A.B. Hobson, 4 May 1933. Abe Prof. 4—D29.

81. See letter from Lancelin to A.E.F. Murray, resident, Abeokuta, 4 July 1936. ECR 1/1/42, Adire Trade 1928–39, vol. 1. Although Lancelin did not refer specifically to direct or vat dyes, it can be inferred from their correspondence that since the reducing agent caustic soda was required with these dyes, they were not identical with the direct dyes the government analyst tested in 1933.

82. Several council members visited other Yoruba towns—Ibadan, Ede, Oshogbo, and Ikirun—to determine whether dyers in these towns used caustic soda. They found that caustic soda was in use by dyers in all these towns. They interviewed several women who claimed that the Egba dyers had introduced the system of using caustic soda. Report to the *Alake,* April. ECR 1/1/77 (NAA).

83. Minutes of Egba Council Meeting, 14 February 1929. ECR 1/1/46 (NAA).

84. Although I was not able to locate the minutes of this meeting, it was referred to in the public meeting with the *adire* dyers on 29 July 1927.

85. Letter from A.E.F. Murray, resident, Abeokuta Province, to the secretary of the southern provinces, 6 June 1933. CSO 28400, vol. 1 (NAI).

86. Report of the Public Meeting of the Adire Women, 29 July 1927, *Egba Administration Bulletin* 31 August 1927 E.A.B. 6/1/14 (NAI).

87. Minutes of Egba Council Meeting, 20 September 1928. ECR 1/1/77, vol. 1 (NAA).

88. Minutes of Egba Council Meeting, 20 February 1936, 11. ECR 1/1/70, vol. 1 (NAA).

89. Minutes of Egba Council Meeting, 20 September 1928. ECR 1/1/77, vol. 1 (NAA).

90. Minutes of Egba Council Meeting, 26 May 1932. ECR 1/1/56, vol. 2 (NAA).

91. One dyer complained that in the old days before a woman began to dye she had to have capital of at least £50. Minutes of Egba Council Meeting, 20 September 1928, 3. ECR 1/1/77, vol. 1 (NAA).

92. Minutes of Egba Council Meeting, 26 May 1932. ECR 1/1/56, vol. 1 (NAA).

93. Minutes of Egba Council Meeting, 3 September 1931. ECR 1/1/77, vol. 2 (NAA).

94. Mrs. Kesiah Jones, in Minutes of Egba Council Meeting, 20 September 1928, p. 4. ECR 1/1/77 (NAA).

95. Ibid., 3. Despite the effort to ban the *iwofa* system, the economic crisis contributed to its continuation.

96. Business Notes, "Sales and Return," *West African Pilot,* 6 October 1938.

97. Minutes of Egba Council Meeting, 20 September 1928, p. 7. ECR 1/1/77, vol. 1 (NAA).

98. Michael C. Atkinson, *An African Life: Tales of a Colonial Officer* (London: Radcliffe Press, 1992), 8. Atkinson remembers that Mason was not well liked by government people, even though he allowed them to take items on credit from UAC. Interview with M.C. Atkinson, 20 July 1997, Winchester, U.K.

99. Minutes of Egba Council Meeting, 14 February 1929, p. 4. ECR 1/1/46 (NAA).

100. Ibid.

101. A similar refusal to address credit and the economy was evident in the debate around pawning. The discussion on pawning, for instance, was much more concerned with whether the institution fit into the colonial government's articulated position on slavery. It did not establish any dialogue on ways to meet the demand for credit. See Byfield, "Pawns and Politics."

102. Jacob, *Report on Taxation,* 87.

5

DOES FATHER KNOW BEST? CONFRONTING THE *ALAKE*

The 1920s was a bruising decade for Abeokuta's indigo dyers. Their struggles to maintain their economic footing revealed deep divisions within their ranks as well as the negative consequences of their political marginalization. The *Alake*'s decision to ban caustic soda and synthetic dyes privileged his interpretation of the difficulties in the *adire* industry and reinforced his authority. In extending the bans he assumed the right to intervene in the production process and to legislate the nature of production. The bans, however, did not address the constraints dyers faced in obtaining reasonable credit terms, labor or natural indigo. In addition, the economic crisis only intensified during the first half of the 1930s.

The bans on caustic soda and synthetic dyes changed the context significantly. They criminalized dyers for using the products on which the viability of the industry had come to rest. Arrests and other sorts of harassment forced dyers to adopt a new set of strategies that also confronted the divisions within their ranks and the *Alake*'s authority to legislate production practices. This chapter examines the sequence of actions and counteractions as the *Alake* and the dyers struggled over this question of authority. The analysis of their actions reveal that this conflict was not just a minor dispute about indigo dyeing. It became a test of colonial power, and in the process it revealed inner workings of the colonial state, its cleavages, and its contradictions. It exposed multiple layers of politics in Abeokuta as well as transformations in political culture under colonialism. Equally important, the records of this conflict offer rare access to aspects of these women's political

Photo 5.1   *Alake* Ademola with British officials. (Copyright The Bodleian Library, University of Oxford. MS. AFR. s. 1863. Reprinted with permission.)

thought. As they defined and clarified their rights as producers, they also defined their expectations of power and authority.

THE BUILDING CRISIS

Although caustic soda and synthetic dyes had been banned in 1929 and 1933 respectively, dyers continued to use both substances. Dyers continued to use these products despite the upheaval they caused because of the depressed condition of the economy. The 1933 Annual Report for Nigeria stated, "Trade continues to be stagnant and the prices of produce are low, with a consequent decrease in the purchasing power of the agriculturalist."[1] The diminished purchasing power of African consumers was reflected in the declining imports of cotton piece goods. The total square yards of cotton piece goods imported into Nigeria fell from 101,093,732 square yards in 1929 to 68,298,992 square yards by 1934.[2]

The Abeokuta annual reports also reflected the generally depressed economy and called continual attention to the state of the *adire* trade and its decline relative to other sectors of the economy. The 1932 Annual Provincial Report for Abeokuta, for example, stated, "The demand for provisions and drinkables has been least affected by the depression, textiles suffering to a greater degree."[3] In the 1933 provincial report, the Resident reported that "the condition of trade has been depressing in the extreme."[4] In reference to *adire* the report elaborated:

> the local dyeing industry has also suffered as the result of low produce prices elsewhere. Buyers from Senegal and the Gold Coast have been fewer. If it retains its quality, however, and avoids the dangers of caustic soda, synthetic indigo and the latest menace of Japanese and other cheap quality material, the situation must improve later on.[5]

In spite of dyers' efforts to cut costs by using less expensive cloth and caustic soda and synthetic dye, the industry fared badly, because dyers were producing for a market that found it increasingly difficult to afford their products.

Economic historians have recently suggested that there may be an inverse relationship between industries that survived the depression well and the extent of their integration into the international economy. Industries with limited exposure to the international economy withdrew or limited their exposure and were thus able to survive or flourish.[6] Abeokuta's dyers could not withdraw in the face of the international economy's cyclical crises because their industry was dependent on it in critical ways. Furthermore, as the depression continued, it cemented dyers' dependence. Dyers were reliant upon the international economy for cost- and labor-saving technology such as caustic soda, as well as their primary inputs, indigo and cloth. Innovation was achieved through increased dependency.

The dyers' position contrasted significantly with that of producers who could diversify or withdraw from the international economy. Farmers, for example, had greater leeway to modify their relationship with the international economy. Although many farmers had begun to raise cash crops, they still grew some food crops. As export prices declined, many farmers increased food production. In Abeokuta, food production actually increased during the 1930s and food prices remained low, a critical advantage as extra-agricultural incomes fell. Egba farmers supplied the local market as well as the Lagos market,

thus supplementing their income from cash crops. The colonial government also assisted farmers by developing citrus crops for export,
in hopes of further diversifying exports.[7] Abeokuta was in some measure more fortunate than other provinces, because its already relatively
diversified economy helped keep some money in circulation. The 1934
annual report trumpeted the fact that "the residents were impoverished
. . . but not penniless."[8] While increased production of food crops
helped mitigate some of the impact of the depression, it was not a
panacea for farmers, who still had to have money to pay their tax
bills and to buy imported items that had become necessities.

A GLIMMER OF RECOVERY

By 1935 it appeared that the worst had passed. There were signs of
improvement in the economy; the prices for produce improved and the
trade in palm oil, which was virtually suspended in 1934, resumed.[9] There
was also a tremendous increase in the volume of cotton piece goods imported into the country. In 1934, as was mentioned earlier, Nigerians
bought 68,298,992 square yards of cloth. In 1935 cotton piece goods
imported into the country nearly doubled—118,883,951 square yards.
Another substantial increase was reported in 1936, when the amount
reached 183,176,054 square yards.[10] It appears that the beginnings of an
economic recovery inspired the *Alake* to turn his attention once again to
the *adire* dyers.

The *Alake* invited dyers from all four quarters of the town to a
special council meeting on 8 August 1935 to discuss the surreptitious
use of caustic soda and synthetic indigo. Many dyers chose to ignore
the summons. During the meeting, the *Alake* essentially lectured the
women, expressing his impatience with the dyers and calling them
stubborn and obdurate. He was also quite incensed that many dyers
chose to ignore his invitation, for only 200 women attended. He lik-
ened the dyers to a son who refused to heed his father's direction and
was on the road to ruin and harshly accused them of using the new
technology because they were "lazy and unlike our industrious mothers of old."[11] In less harsh tones, but laced with an equally negative
attitude, the Resident exhorted the women to heed the advice they
had received because dyeing was the staple industry of Egbaland. He
effectively elevated dyeing over other economic sectors and claimed
that it brought in more money than any other industry. He compared
the *adire* industry to the goose that laid golden eggs and suggested
that dyers were on the way to becoming like the townspeople in the

fable who, overcome by their greed and selfish interests, killed the goose.[12]

Both men urged the women to form associations in their respective quarters in the town and effectively police each other to ensure that no one broke the rules. It was suggested that any member who broke the rules should be exposed, reported to the *Alake*, and expelled from the association. The *Alake* further proposed that the women organize themselves with the assistance of certain general titled chiefs. The dyers from Owu were to work with the Ekerin of the Egbas, those from Gbagura with the Osi of the Egbas, those from Oke Ona with the Otun of the Egbas, while the *Balogun* of the Egbas would assist the *Alake* in organizing the dyers in Egba Alake quarter.[13]

The *Alake* and the Resident clearly felt strongly about the women's actions. They believed in the superiority of the natural indigo method and felt disdain for the women who disobeyed the *Alake*'s laws. They both tried to use the moral weight of their offices to bring the dyers into line. The *Alake* and the Resident positioned themselves as the protectors of the community, legislating for the common good against the dyers' childlike stubborn, greedy, self-centered ways. Their tone was intended to belittle as well as to intimidate the dyers. Both assumed that after the meeting, the dyers would quickly organize as instructed, discard the new technology, and heed the *Alake*'s orders.

In spite of the harsh lecture from the Resident and the *Alake*, dyers continued to disregard the bans, but they paid a high cost. Policemen extorted money from them, demanding 1s. or 2s. in lieu of arrests. In addition, it was reported that a notorious criminal, Yesufu Olorunmo, collected money from them ranging from 5s. to 11s. in the *Alake*'s name. Any woman who refused to pay him was automatically reported to the police for disobeying the rules against the use of synthetic dyes and caustic soda. Once reported, these women were prosecuted and fined 40s.[14]

The conflict between the dyers and the *Alake* climaxed in February 1936 when the police began confiscating *adire* cloths made with the banned chemicals. On 10 February policemen (*olopas*) made several arrests in the night and on 11 February policemen raided *adire* stalls at Itoku market, virtually closing the market simultaneously.[15] The police arrested 200 dyers and seized bundles of cloths allegedly dyed with caustic soda and synthetic dyes.[16] The following morning "thousands of *adire* women traders marched to the palace"[17] and an extraordinary council meeting was called the same day. During the meeting a petition from the Women *Adire* Traders in Abeokuta was read aloud and translated into Yoruba. The petition called on the *Alake* and the council to remove the bans, because they inflicted hardship on the women. They reinforced their displeasure by singing abusive songs to the Alake,

Oba ko jelu. Oba ko soda. Ki Oba pa soda naa mu. (The King rejected the dye and the soda. Let him mix the soda and drink it.)[18]

The accounts of this meeting reflected an attempt to further contain the dyers. Dyers were given very few opportunities to speak for themselves. They were asked a few specific questions such as "Did you all agree to the writing of this petition?" and "Are the thoughts expressed therein your own opinion?"[19] Only one woman was identified in the text of the minutes, Karimu Baba's mother, and she reiterated the value of synthetic indigo and caustic soda to the industry. All the other speakers identified in the minutes were male: the *Alake*, the district officer, and Mr. Mason of United Africa Company. The *Balogun* of Idomapo, whose compound was one of the major dyeing compounds, also spoke, and he was the only man to support the dyers. He acknowledged that chemicals were detrimental to the industry, but he stressed that the chemicals made work easier especially for those dyers who did not have assistance. It allowed them to produce their cloths quickly and attend market regularly. The *Alake*, however, dismissed these points and argued that "You [the dyers] cannot judge . . . what is good for you in the same way as those who are placed in authority over you can."[20] After the protest, the cloths were returned to the women and they were given a thirty-day grace period to get rid of the chemicals they had on hand.

Although the *Nigerian Daily Times* prematurely reported that the matter had been settled "to the satisfaction of all concerned," press interest brought the issue to a wider audience and raised the intensity of the debate.[21] The Legislative Council in Lagos did not play a role in Egba politics, but even they raised questions about the dispute. In the minutes of the Lagos council's meeting on 2 March 1936, Dr. C. C. Adeniyi-Jones, the second Lagos member, requested that the chief secretary of the government respond to a number of questions about the *adire* industry and the *Alake*'s actions. He wanted to know why the dyers were arrested and their cloths confiscated, why an embargo was placed on synthetic dyes and caustic soda in Abeokuta, what role the European firms played in this conflict, and what role the other *Oba*s played.[22] The contest between the *Alake* and dyers was no longer an issue of only local concern.

The *Alake* and the Resident tried to restore the *Alake*'s authority as best they could under the glare of so much observation. On 20 February 1936, the dyers were summoned to the council again. The minutes recorded only the *Alake*'s comments, which began "I invited you before the Council today in order to set your minds at rest."[23] He informed them that nothing in Egbaland was secret from him and he had learned the dyers were collecting 1s./6d. from all involved in the profession, although he did not know the purpose. He strongly advised them to stop collecting money, stop holding meetings on the subject, and instead follow the council's advice.[24] Although the minutes did not offer the dyers' contributions to this meeting, they exposed the state's unease about the situation. The dyers had disregarded the new laws and were clearly organizing themselves. Despite the *Alake*'s warnings, dyers continued to take in these contributions, which they used to establish a defense fund.

The women retained several literate men to assist them. These men, Oladipo Somoye, a former clerk at UAC; M. A. Egberongbe, formerly a clerk for one of the Native Courts and John Holt & Co.; and Alhaji Gbadamosi[25] were made officers of the union and given power of attorney.[26] Little is known about these men to whom the dyers entrusted their struggle, but they all had one important skill in common. They were literate in English. Literacy and fluency in English had become necessary political skills. As a result, professional letter writers flourished in many parts of the country. Colonial officials believed Abeokuta had some of the most prolific letter writers.[27]

Somoye et al. were expected to interpret and represent the women at meetings and conferences where the *adire* trade was discussed, and most important, to "address and reply [to] all communications to the Nigerian Government, The Egba Native Administration, the Newspapers in Nigeria," and to hire a counsel or counsels when necessary. These men did not receive salaries. Their service was voluntary, but the dyers' association defrayed all legal costs and out-of-pocket expenses.[28] Two trained barristers were also brought in—J. K. Doherty, from Abeokuta, who had been disbarred, and William Geary, an English lawyer practicing in Lagos. The decision to seek the assistance of these men was not a light one, because everyone knew that the *Alake* and the Resident strongly opposed the intervention of literate members of the community in local issues. In order to mitigate some of the expected rancor, Doherty sent the *Alake* copies of the letters he received from the dyers so that the *Alake* could ascertain that Doherty had been approached by the dyers and not vice versa. He wrote, "I have been forced to adopt this course judging from your past attitude and that of the Resident that the intercession of any educated man between you and the illiterates is always offensive."[29]

Doherty joined the dyers' struggle through Egberongbe's entreaties, but it is unclear how or why Egberongbe and Gbadamosi were brought into the union. Somoye, on the other hand, had a relationship with the dyers going back at least to 1935. In August 1935 he had written several letters to the *Alake* and council supporting the prohibition of synthetic dyes and caustic soda, as well as some of the dyers' complaints. Although he supported the ban on caustic soda and synthetic dye, he had argued that the monthly credit structure must be replaced by long-term credit, three to six months. He saw that the anxiety created by the short-term credit really forced the women to use the chemicals. Furthermore, he had insisted that long-term credit would enable the women to form a market pool and better maintain uniform prices. He also suggested that credit should be structured on a cooperative basis,

> for example, one leading woman in each compound or a leading woman in each township should have an account with the trading firms and the remaining women in the compound or township should receive white shirting from her or him; this is to replace or eliminate individual monthly accounts.[30]

Somoye had proposed that the commission charged by interpreters be absolutely prohibited and that the dyers form themselves into an association with a central body and four sectional branches, one in each quarter.[31] He also volunteered to assist them in drafting a constitution.

After his initial letters to the *Alake*, Somoye changed his position on synthetic dyes and caustic soda. He called for an end to the bans in a letter to the district officer after the arrests of dyers in February 1936. He wrote

> The writer . . . support[ed] the prohibition; and I could not have changed my views but for the fact that I afterwards opened discussions with a good many leading dyers among the women, and not only that, I personally have . . . witness[ed] the preparation of the dyeing pots while in process and ascertained in person how and why the two materials were mixed with our natural indigo.[32]

Somoye came to appreciate the necessity of the new ingredients after observing the preparation of the dye pots. He became convinced that the ban on synthetic dyes and caustic soda was unwarranted and he wrote the *Alake* and council several other letters in September and October 1935 detailing his findings and suggesting that an enquiry be held into the matter. It appears that the *Alake* and council did not respond to his correspondence; rather, they chose to enforce the rules as they stood. Somoye capitalized on the tension created by the arrests by suggesting to the district officer that 90 percent of the people in Egbaland were against this prohibition that he described as "uncalled for, unwarrantable, unnecessary, Unjustified, Oppressive, and not . . . conducive to the welfare, prosperity and best interest of the Egba People."[33] Using a quote from Edmond Burke, he justified the dyers' actions and laid the blame for their response at the feet of government: "When popular discontents have been very prevalent, it may well be affirmed and supported that there has been generally something found amiss in the constitution or in the conduct of the Government."[34]

Sir William Geary, who rounded out the team of representatives, was a high-profile Lagos lawyer. Geary first went to West Africa in 1894 to practice law. He left England because of the depression at the end of the century and the "fact that the silver spoon he had been brought up with had turned silver plated."[35] He chose West Africa rather than India, for it presented "the line of least resistance, also the cheapest passage."[36] Though he was not a career bureaucrat, he served in such posts in West Africa—acting Queen's counsel in Sierra Leone (1895–97) and attorney general of the Gold Coast (1897–99). He left West Africa for ten years, and when he returned in 1909 he went to Lagos rather than the Gold Coast or Sierra Leone. It appears that his decision to go to Lagos was influenced by the fact that the responsibilities of barrister and solicitor were combined in Nigeria. In Lagos, he stayed away from government posts and built up an impressive African and European clientele in private practice. He was a close associate of G.W. Neville, founder of the Bank of British West Africa, and his association with Neville was crucial to his practice among African clients. Neville "had started the bank with 'native' money . . . they trusted Niblio and being so installed and vouched for, I gained their confidence."[37] In many of his cases, he represented both European and African commercial interests against the crown.[38] Thus, Geary was an ideal choice to represent the dyers in their struggle against the state.

Through these men, dyers maintained the pressure on local representatives by sending letters and petitions to representatives at each level of the state—the Resident, chief secretary of government, and the governor. These petitions laid out the facts of the case, their claims about the local government's wanton intervention in the dyers' affairs, and their demands—the removal of the bans, the nullification of the 30-day grace period to dispose of chemicals, and a ruling on the matter by the governor.[39] They also reported their suspicions of the *Alake*'s motives to the chief secretary of the government. Geary informed the chief secretary that the *Alake* banned the use of synthetic dye because he was responding to pressure from some European trading companies, specifically the UAC and the French company CFAO. Geary alleged that these companies wanted to replace the dominant synthetic dye on the market, a German product called Anchor sold by Union Trading Company, with another brand, Cork.[40] The chief secretary's office and the comptroller's office made inquiries into the charges, but it appears that they were not able to document this charge. The comptroller's office did not keep detailed information of the dyes and dyestuffs imported into Nigeria, so they could not discern patterns in the importation of particular brands.[41] This particular charge was dubious anyway, because the bans restricted all synthetic dyes. But the chief secretary's attempt to substantiate the dyers' charges demonstrates that Geary's letters and meeting with the chief secretary were effective. On one of Geary's letters an official wrote, "W. [Geary] is a little impatient. Get the information asked for and . . . as quickly as you could."[42]

While Geary continued to flood the chief secretary's office with correspondence, the *Alake* ordered the women to appear before the council again on 2 April 1936. The dyers, however, chose not to attend the meeting. The council was informed that since the meeting interfered with their work, they had gone to the market and sent their representatives—Somoye, Doherty, and Gbadamosi—in their stead. Once again the *Alake* accused the women of being errant children. He charged

> These people are our children. They have been here several times before, there is no reason why they should not be here today. . . . Their absence is a gross disloyalty, and disobedience to the order of the *Alake*.[43]

Though he was clearly upset at the women's decision not to respond to his summons, the business of the meeting continued. The Resident announced that he had seen the petition that had been sent to the chief secretary of the government and consequently he advised the *Alake* to arrange for the appointment of a select committee of "experts and impartial and reliable persons who have no interest in the dyeing industry."[44] He estimated that the inquiry would take up to six months and ordered that the existing law should be observed until the committee presented its report and recommendations.

To reinforce the wisdom of their earlier decisions, various members of the Egba Council and invited visitors gave statements about the decline of the industry as well as the problems they encountered with cloths produced with caustic soda and synthetic dye. Several pieces of cloth dyed with natural indigo and synthetic indigo were washed to exemplify their statements. The *Alake* concluded the meeting with a threat to the dyers. He promised that until the committee's recommendations were submitted, any dyer caught using chemicals would be dealt with according to the law. Furthermore, he insisted once again that the women meet under the surveillance of the general titled chiefs; he declared anything else was unconstitutional. He impressed on the council members that unconstitutional meetings were contrary to law and native custom and that it was their duty to see that meetings held in their respective quarters were "well conducted and under their guidance."[45] Through this maneuver the *Alake* hoped to discourage the dyers' efforts to meet and plan a course of action contrary to his position.

The following day, 3 April the council held an extraordinary meeting with dyers in attendance. Madam Ramotu of Kemta explained that only the younger women had gone to market and the rest had met in the Moslem school in Ijeun to await word from their representatives who had gone to the council meeting in their place. Although there appears to have been some confusion over whether the women should have been notified by Somoye to attend the meeting, the *Alake* homed in on the point that they disregarded his summons. He charged

> I did not order them to assemble there [the Moslem school], I asked them to come here. If they think they can do whatever they like and kick against the order of the Constituted Authorities, I must tell them that they deceive themselves. (To the Women) If you think that the money which you are contributing can ameliorate matters, you also deceive yourselves.[46]

Apparently incensed that the women had obtained representatives, the *Alake* forbade the men to represent the dyers at the meeting. He declared that the men were merely letter writers and as the council knew them only in their capacity as clerks he could not allow them to speak during the meeting.

Many of the points made in the meeting the previous day were touched on again. Using the same paternalistic language as the *Alake* to blur the edges of this conflict, the Resident attempted to placate the dyers. He told them:

> Do not imagine that your complaints will not be sympathetically dealt with by all those in any way concerned with them. The Alake is your father, and the members of Council, as your fathers, have advised you in your best interests.[47]

He reiterated that the committee to investigate the industry would likely take six months to submit its report. In the meantime, they were to observe the laws on the books. The women were given an additional thirty days to dispose of the chemicals on hand, as well as the cloths prepared with chemicals.

It is evident that the *Alake* did not take the women's actions lightly. Their constant disregard for his suggestions and demands invariably created a dent in the armor of his authority. During the meeting he surmised that if the council closed their eyes to the dyers' actions it was tantamount to showing that there was no authority.[48] Whether accurate or not, Ademola perceived the dyers' actions as an enormous threat to his government. In order to understand why their actions were so threatening, it is necessary to examine the relationship between the *Alake*ship and the colonial state as well as Ademola's relationship to the colonial state.

THE *ALAKE* AND THE COLONIAL STATE

The *Alake*'s arrest of the dyers, his subsequent effort to belittle them into accepting his rulings, and his attacks on their advocates must be understood against the backdrop of how colonial political control and Ademola's relationship to the colonial state were forged in Abeokuta. As we saw in Chapter 2, the relationship was cemented during the era of the EUG. The Lagos government recognized the *Alake*, Gbadebo, as the center of power in Abeokuta, and his office was consciously elevated over that of the other *Obas*. Colonial officials acknowledged "we have placed the *Alake* in a position to which he was not entitled by native law and custom."[49] Furthermore, the Lagos government actively protected the *Alake* by sending a contingent of troops whenever he was threatened or exiling political rivals who did not show proper deference to his authority.[50]

The abrogation of the treaty in 1914 formalized many of the colonial features of the relationship between Gbadebo and the Lagos government. The *Alake* became a functionary in the colonial state, a Native Authority. As a "traditional" ruler he still commanded the respect and authority that was accorded the office. Nevertheless, all his actions were subject to the advisement of the British administrator, the Resident. In general, district officers were the main representatives of British administration, but the Residents played a much more central role in the day-to-day affairs of Abeokuta than was the case in other districts because Abeokuta was both the divisional and provincial headquarters.[51] *Alake* Gbadebo worked very closely with the Residents. He was characterized as "considerably stronger than the majority of native rulers, and progressive. . . . He also believed that it was to the interest of this country to seek the advice and assistance of the Political Officers."[52] Colonial officials labeled any opposition to Gbadebo as "reactionary" and "anti-government." Yet the government's strong support for Gbadebo did not equal popularity; a confidential report after his death claimed that "there is no doubt that he was poisoned."[53] The records do not indicate that anyone was formally charged or arrested for his death.

Gbadebo's untimely death in 1920 created a great deal of apprehension in the colonial government that was faced with the task of forging a working relationship with a new *Alake*. Ademola II was put forward as the major candidate and cautiously accepted by the colonial government.[54] Colonial officials did not trust him. There were allegations that he was involved in fraud when he was an adviser to *Alake* Gbadebo. Furthermore, he was supported by key members of the educated elites, whom officials did not trust, as well as Subuola, the trader suspected of playing a role in Gbadebo's death.[55]

The 1920 half-yearly report suggested that the political prospects were far from good.

There were manifestations of anti-European feelings (the singing of abusive songs to Europeans). . . . chiefs were completely roused from their former contentment by the hope of regaining lost privileges. . . . The group of disaffected educated natives, that was always ready to engineer and foster anti-Government intrigues, regained, through the success of the Ademola campaign, the influence they had lost in the preceding months.[56]

Colonial officials held a longstanding antipathy toward educated elites,[57] and the Resident anticipated that educated persons would take chieftancy titles and try to influence the council of chiefs that ruled in conjunction with the *Alake*. Ademola himself was described as "avaricious and treacherous . . . his two principal objects are to enrich himself and to pose as an independent Sovereign free of Government control. He never or seldom speaks the truth."[58] Colonial officials feared that any attempt by Ademola to present himself as independent and not under the control of colonial officials would encourage those segments of the community, particularly the *Ogboni*, that were opposed to British control.

The relationship between Ademola and the colonial state was tenuous in the early years. The 1921 annual report described Ademola as "independent of outside influences . . . [and] increasingly ready to cooperate with Political Officers."[59] In spite of this, he delivered a speech in which he suggested that the Egbas would conduct their affairs with little interference from the political officers. He was reprimanded. The Residents fretted over details that could in some way compromise the authority of the colonial state. For example, a draft concert program in which the chairman was designated as "His Highness the Alake, supported by C.W. Alexander Esq." became an issue. In addition to their fear that Ademola would attempt to pose as "an independent" sovereign, "thereby causing friction and disunion," they were also afraid that the Egba authorities would use their "great freedom of initiative . . . to lessen the prestige of the Resident and Political Officers, and thereby of the Nigerian Government."[60] The Resident argued that under such circumstances even petty matters had to be addressed because of their "effect on the native mind," and he went to great lengths to impress on the *Alake* that

> the Resident as the representative in the Province of the Governor of Nigeria, must not be subordinated in any way to any Oba or Chief. . . . an attempt to exalt themselves by slighting the Government representatives is not only undignified and childish but is likely to impair the prestige of all, and make very difficult the real cooperation with and support of the Egba Administration.[61]

The initial trepidation about Ademola gradually lessened. By 1924 the relationship between Ademola and the political officers had improved. In the annual report they stated:

The Alake had given the political staff willing assistance. He has interest and enthusiasm and takes an active part in the work which now falls to him. He personally sees that the minor details are observed. The support of his brother Obas, and Councilors appears to be passive rather than active.[62]

By the mid-1920s, the defining characteristics of the political relationship between Ademola and the colonial government and Ademola and Egba society were well established. Ademola had clearly come to appreciate the subordination of his office to the colonial state, euphemistically rendered as "working closely with the political officers." Nonetheless, there were nuances to his relationship with the political officers. Atkinson recalled that Ademola's

relationship with members of the Administration depended very much on the individual's rank. The Governor, as direct representative to the Crown, he recognised as his superior; the Chief Commissioner, Western Provinces, and the Resident of the Province, he looked on as equals; the District Officer, he was obliged to pay attention to at times although as a First Class Chief he had the right to direct access to the Resident; assistant district officers like myself hardly merited his consideration although he was always polite, if distant.[63]

As a part of the colonial state, he too shared the general anxiety about insubordination.[64] Challenges to the *Alake* or his policies were interpreted as challenges to the state, and the first line of defense to any such challenge included ridicule and assertions of immaturity.

In theory Ademola administered the Native Authority in conjunction with the Egba Native Council. But in practice he dominated the council even though it was continually expanded to make it more representative. By 1933, when the council had reached thirty-two members, twelve of whom were elected for life and twenty of whom served three-year terms, there were still constant references to the *Alake*'s autocracy. In spite of Residents' rhetorical misgivings about Ademola's autocracy, it was clear that his strong hold over Egba politics worked in their interest. The 1927 annual report, for example, stated that the *Alake* has taken on too much of the administration, from signing vouchers to being involved in all the details of administration. At that time, however, only two members of council could read, write, and speak English. Since the majority of the members of the government were not literate, they

> could not understand Estimates, Prison Books, or many of the modern problems with which the Native Authority had to deal . . . [and] a natural tendency developed for Administrative officers to discuss affairs with the *Alake* alone, leaving him to bring them to the notice of the Council.[65]

Ademola was rewarded for his control of the Native Administration. In 1934, he was made an Honorary Commander of the Order of the British Empire. The Resident at the time, E.J.G. Kelly, felt Ademola richly deserved this award. In the annual report he wrote,

> A man of strong personality, the Alake is an extremely hard worker and no detail of administration is too small for his personal attention. During his fourteen years of office he has devoted his whole time without rest or holiday to the service of his country. To him is due the development of the Egba Council to its present state. . . . Education, farming and marketing . . . the improvement of the Native Courts, sanitation, health measures, social services, in all these his interest, initiative and energy are to be seen. Naturally such a man must have enemies, but in spite of this, he enjoys the support and confidence of the great majority of his people.[66]

Kelly's characterization mirrored Ademola's own perception of himself as the visionary and paternalistic caretaker of the Egba community.

The conflict between the dyers and the *Alake* exposed the existing model of subordination—Ademola was subordinate to the colonial state and Abeokuta was subordinate to Ademola. That subordination was dressed up as paternalism. By portraying the dyers as errant children disobeying their father, the *Alake* and the Resident were attempting to reinforce that existing model of subordination and control. While they had a material interest in the fate of the *adire* industry, it was equally important that the crisis be handled in a manner that did not compromise the lines of authority.

GENDER AND POLITICS IN COLONIAL ABEOKUTA

In the face of the threats made by the *Alake* and the Resident, it is significant that the dyers held their ground and in fact found the will to organize themselves into an effective body. Theirs is an unusual instance of artisans mobilizing during the colonial period. It is important also to appreciate that although the dyers' protests challenged the *Alake*'s authority, it was not an explicitly anticolonial protest. Dyers were not trying to overthrow the *Alake* or the colonial state. Nonetheless, their dispute had political implications because their actions called into question the existing model of authority and representation. Dyers disputed the reach of the *Alake*'s power, which was an outgrowth of the centralization of the colonial state. They also assumed the right to be represented by spokesmen of their choice. Ultimately they questioned the nature of colonial rule in Abeokuta.

John Blair, the author of an intelligence report on Abeokuta noted

A matter like the "*adire*" (dyed cloth) industry, in which for some years there have been disputes about the use or prohibition of caustic soda and synthetic dyes, and which is discussed directly between the *Alake* and the women dyers themselves, would in the old days have been a matter for the *Parakoyi* (trade chiefs) to settle in each township, or if the whole town was concerned in a joint meeting of the township *Parakoyi*s called by the *Olori Parakoyi* of Ibore, who is head of all the *Parakoyi* of the Egbas.[67]

This statement in many ways accurately captured the nature of the political transformation that had occurred. Although some of the old *Ologun* (military), *Ogboni* (civil), and *Parakoyi* (trade) offices still existed and their holders sat on the council, they held no independent base of power, since in practice they all answered to the *Alake*. The *Parakoyi* chiefs as a group did not hold any real power under the new structures and could not mediate an issue in which the *Alake* was already personally involved.

In addition, women's representatives did not get official recognition under colonialism. When colonial officials reconstituted the Egba Council after the 1918 tax revolt in Abeokuta, the Resident specified that members "must be men whom every Egba man knows and respects and be men whose decision in council would not be ignored by the people."[68] The state relied on gender as one criterion for political office. Egba women recognized that they were marginalized and that they needed more formal representation in the council. In a telling discussion during the council meeting on 22 April 1920, members discussed Madam Jojolola's desire to be a member of the council. She had also expressed an interest in having J.K. Coker, the *Olori Parakoyi* of the Christians, create titles for women.[69] The council tabled the discussion of both issues and no action followed.

The issue of title holding was a significant social as well as political concern. Taking titles indicated social and economic status, but titles were also critical in the local political structure. The colonial state recognized certain title holders as legitimate representatives of various townships and constituencies in Abeokuta. The title structure was not static; some titles lapsed and new ones were created. It does not appear that the *Alake* conferred all titles, but he had to sanction the creation of new titles, and the Resident held final approval. In 1919 the Christian community had applied to hold title-giving ceremonies in the palace square. The Resident rejected their application because he viewed these appointments as "church matters," hence private. The appointees were not recognized chiefs who would warrant a public function.[70] Obtaining permission from the *Alake* and the Resident was unpredictable. In fact, Coker claimed that he did not assist the *Iyalode* in creating new titles for women because they did not have the *Alake*'s sanction.[71]

An effort was made to rectify this in 1930 when a number of women's titles were conferred at the town's centenary celebrations.[72] Still, after Madam Jojolola's death in 1932, her title *Iyalode of the Egbas* lapsed until 1973. In the interim, some of the township *Iyalode*s still existed and there was an *Iyalode* of the Christians, but these women did not participate in the formal political structure. Each time the council was expanded, additional seats went to male title holders.

Under colonial rule, male control of the council was reinforced, as was the *Alake*'s position. Since power was centralized in the *Alake* and all major issues were brought to his attention, he was effectively the first and last court of appeal. In order to appeal the *Alake*'s decisions, especially decisions that had the support of the political officers, one had to circumvent the political structure in Abeokuta. In spite of Ademola's attempt to paint himself as synonymous with British power and the colonial state as monolithic, wedges could be created between the layers of power. Literacy was a prerequisite to engage in this tactic. Aggrieved parties attracted the attention of the upper echelons of the colonial bureaucracy by writing letters and petitions either to them or to the press and by hiring letter writers or solicitors to act on their behalf. For example, a dispute between the *Alake* and the *Ogboni* over the reinstatement of the *Oshile* went to the supreme court, for the chiefs were advised by their solicitor to undertake proceedings against the *Alake* and the Resident.[73] The dyers' actions fell well within an established pattern of resolving grievances, though one that invariably earned the *Alake*'s hostility.

Dyers' choice of male advocates reflected another political reality of the period. While there were certainly educated women in Abeokuta during this period, these women did not participate in this type of advocacy. No women were mentioned among the known letter writers and solicitors that the *Alake* and Resident disparaged as agitators. The first women's political association in Abeokuta did not emerge until the 1940s.[74] The absence of women political advocates was a direct outgrowth of the type of education that girls received. Missionaries ran all the schools in Abeokuta, and instruction for girls concentrated on domestic science. The primary goal of girls' education was to in-culcate good morals, modest behavior, and training in selective ideas of modern hygiene and consumption. The ideal occupations for edu-cated women were teaching, dressmaking, and baking.[75] Education was not intended to prepare women to do work of a political nature. There were no literate female advocates to whom the dyers could have turned to pursue the conflict with the *Alake*.

The decision to circumvent the *Alake* in 1936 signaled an impor-tant shift in the dyers' thinking and provides insight into how these women understood their political relationship to the *Alake*. The *Alake* represented the state, both the Egba state of the past and the colonial state. Both the dyers and the *Alake* expected the state to be paternal-istic. The dyers, who at the end of the 1920s initiated the first discus-sions on the crisis in the industry, expected the *Alake* to assist them with their struggle against the European trading firms and the inter-lopers. Furthermore, they expected to play a role in shaping the *Alake*'s response to the crisis. Ademola, on the other hand, had a dif-ferent view of paternalism. For him paternalism included a healthy dose of authoritarianism. He felt justified in dictating the production process. It is also clear that he understood the limits of his authoritarianism. He could legislate against the dyers, but he knew he could not legislate against the European trading firms.

Yet in spite of his dictatorial stance, the dyers were not trying to de-pose the *Alake*.[76] They were trying to regain their autonomy to produce cloths in ways they thought best, an autonomy he had usurped. The peti-tions that the lawyers generated were specific regarding their right to use the new technology. Autonomy also framed their decision to organize the dyers' association independently of the general titled chiefs in their town-ships. These chiefs rubber-stamped the *Alake*'s position and would work only to enforce the *Alake*'s will on the women. Organizing the associa-tion independently of the chiefs gave the women a base on which they could mobilize to challenge the *Alake* rather than acquiesce to him.

In order to resolve the conflict, one side had to shift. The *Alake* had to accept the women's claims that the new technology was not the problem and lift the bans, or the women had to accept his right to act unilaterally. Once it was obvious that neither was willing to give up ground, the location of the conflict shifted. Consequently, it stopped being a matter between the *Alake* and the dyers and became a matter for the central government. By retaining lawyers who went over the *Alake*'s head, the dyers forced the Lagos government to take action in this local dispute and walk a balance between supporting a loyal local ruler and treating these women's grievances with some impartiality.

THE CENTRAL GOVERNMENT

The Lagos government was faced with a dilemma they would have preferred to avoid. The petitions and letters to the governor and chief secretary and the queries from the legislative council kept the dyers on the central government's agenda, while the bureaucracy tried to shift it back to Native Administration in Abeokuta.

The central administration did not welcome the legislative council's interest in the *adire* dispute. As mentioned earlier, the council member Dr. Adeniyi-Jones sent a series of questions to the chief secretary about the embargo of caustic soda and synthetic dye and the subsequent arrest and harassment of the dyers. Acting on the theory that the council was to play a role in the decision making process, African men who sat on the council often used their position to question or criticize government actions and policies. The legislative council was not a strong body and in practice did not have the power to alter government actions. But by calling attention to certain issues it could influence the outcome. Adeniyi-Jones's questions added to the central government's determination to appear impartial. In response to his query about the reasons for the embargo, the government replied:

> Though there are strong grounds for holding that opinion (caustic soda and synthetic dye are detrimental to the industry) to be correct a Committee is being appointed to make a further investigation of the matter in view of representations against the rule.[77]

The central government attempted to further dim the spotlight and reinforce their strong commitment to the *Alake* by redirecting Geary's letters and petitions to the Native Authority. In response to a letter Geary sent to the governor, the chief secretary wrote

I am directed by the Governor to inform you that His Excellency
has made enquiries locally and is satisfied that the question is being handled perfectly adequately by the *Alake*, with whose discretion His Excellency at present sees not the slightest need to
interfere.[78]

Geary was also directed not to address any further representations to the
chief secretary; all communications were to be sent to the *Alake*.

The governor also met with a delegation of dyers during his visit to
Abeokuta on 7 April 1936. Although the reason for this state visit is
unclear, Governor Bourdillon used the occasion to impress upon the
women his support of the *Alake*. The *Alake* reported to the council that
the women promised the governor that they would be obedient, loyal,
and faithful to the orders of the *Alake* and Council. They also promised
they would convene regular meetings with the titled chief of their respective quarters. In the event gentle prodding did not work, the governor reminded the women that whether or not they kept their promise,
there was a law to punish those who disobeyed the order-in-council for-
bidding the use of caustic soda and synthetic dye.[79]

The central government was also uncomfortable with this conflict
because it evoked memories of the women's wars in Igboland in 1929.
More than sixty women were killed as they protested against the actions of warrant chiefs and the counting of their livestock, which they
thought was the precursor to taxation.[80] Geary capitalized on the
memories of the Igbo women's protests when he ended one of his
letters: "I hope there will not be a repetition of the tragic events at
Owerri." His reference to the events in Owerri was intended to pressure the chief secretary to meet with him. The message he meant to
convey was that he hoped they could resolve the conflict between the
dyers and the *Alake* before an event of a similar magnitude unfolded.
His strategy was successful, because the chief secretary did meet with
him.

Although the chief secretary did not respond directly to Geary's
reference to the Aba Women's War, officials were concerned about
the possibility of trouble. In a note to the governor in which he discussed the dyers' conflict and his meeting with Geary, the chief secretary suggested that there was someone at the back of the agitation.[81]
The chief secretary advised the Resident to explore the matter thoroughly and, if there was any possibility of trouble, to take the necessary action at once.[82] He did not mention what specific actions should
be taken, but it is clear that he too found the dyers' actions ominous.

The device of the Commission of Enquiry allowed the central government to fully explore the dispute and show a measure of impartiality without publicly compromising their support of the *Alake*.

THE COMMISSION OF ENQUIRY

By the end of April 1936, the government had arrived at the composition of the commission. On the surface it appeared balanced in favor of the *Alake*. The commission members were Mr. A. Alakija—the *Alake*'s brother-in-law; Mr. H.W. Long—Cassleton Elliot & Co.; Mr. J.L. Irvine—Irvine and Bonnar and late of the Standard Company, a cloth expert; Reverend E.K. Ajayi Ajagbe—Methodist Mission, Ogbe, Abeokuta; Mrs. Modupe Moore; Mr. W. Jones—Co-operative Wholesale Society, Lagos; Mrs. Shyllon; Captain E.F.G. Haig—cooperative officer, Moore Plantation, Ibadan; and Mr. J.H. Ellis—assistant district officer, secretary of the committee.[83]

Geary objected to two members of the commission, Mr. Alakija, the *Alake*'s brother-in-law, and Mrs. Moore. Nonetheless, the government kept them on the commission.[84] The terms of reference, as suggested by the attorney-general, were

1. To examine the representations made in a petition dated the 6th of March, 1936, addressed to the Honorable Chief Secretary to the Government by certain women engaged in the dyeing industry at Abeokuta.
2. To study, compare, and report on the various methods of dyeing referred to in the said petition.
3. To make recommendations with regard to the method or methods that should be adopted and the manner in which the dyeing industry should be organized and conducted in the best interests of the women dyers and the future prosperity of the industry and such other recommendations as the Committee may deem it fit to make.[85]

The commission began hearings on 5 July 1936 in Centenary Hall in Abeokuta. Mr. Long was chosen as chair by a vote of the commission. The members of the commission were joined also by the government analyst, Mr. R.K. Hardy. During the first day, they heard testimony from Somoye and Egberongbe, several dyers, and an interpreter who lodged Senegalese merchants. The first day's proceedings were dominated by Messrs. Jones, Alakija, and Hardy. They dismissed much of the testimony from Somoye and Egberongbe, who were unable to answer many of the questions involving the cost of production.

The dyers selected three women to represent them before the Commission of Enquiry—Mesdames Ramotu from Kemta, Asimowu of Ago Owu, and Asimou Bolajoko.[86] As they interviewed the dyers, it appeared that the commission was most interested in identifying dyers as the main contributors to the problem. The women had to both defend their reputations and explain the complexity of the problem. For example,

> *Q.*   If caustic soda and synthetic indigo continue to be used, do you think that the people from the far bush will continue to take the trouble to come to Abeokuta?
>
> *A.*   We are still the best known dyers and best designers, although our natural indigo is not as good as in olden days.
>
> *Q.*   Is that because when you started to use caustic soda and synthetic indigo farmers ceased to cultivate natural indigo?
>
> *A.*   The young leaves of indigo are no longer obtainable and the soil has become barren and does not produce. [87]

On the second day of testimony, 13 July, commission members tried to explore the debate about the new and old method that had pitted dyer against dyer a decade before. They specifically called dyers like Asimawu of Oke-Solori, who had been against the new method in the 1920s.

> *Q.*   Were you present at the [council] meeting in 1928?
>
> *A.*   Yes.
>
> *Q.*   At that meeting you voted against caustic soda?
>
> *A.*   Yes, but then caustic soda was just imported to Abeokuta and Mr. Sheldon introduced the matter to the Alake. I told him then that it was a new import to Abeokuta and that we had not tried it; now that we have tried it and found it is good we cannot do without it.
>
> *Q.*   At the meeting of Council of September, 1928, you talked about a lot of young women entering into the trade and spoiling it and at the meeting it was decided that young women should be trained. Has that been carried out?
>
> *A.*   Yes, all the apprentices have been taught, also the wives of our sons.

Q.   We have been told that the amount of trade has fallen during the last 9 years to about half. Is that a fact?

A.   The cause of that is that there are not so many customers as before; then there was competition to buy.[88]

The women discussed the way in which the changing availability of labor, particularly pawn labor, affected them and the importance of caustic soda as they relied on fewer workers. They also related caustic soda to their ability to manage their indebtedness to the European firms. The dyers' answers forced the committee to factor the depression into the crisis and to ask many more detailed questions about the quality and availability of indigo and ashes as well as cloth. At the second session, the commission also took testimony from interpreters and traders from Ibadan who sold *adire* in Accra. They obtained important details of how the relationship between long-distance traders and interpreters operated and the changing structure within the dyeing industry as new people entered and competition increased.

On the third and final session, 20 July, they heard from Messrs. Sheldon, Mason, and Lancelin, agents of G.B. Ollivant, UAC, and CFAO, respectively. Egba farmers also addressed the commission during this final session. Sheldon, like the other agents, supported the ban on synthetic dyes and caustic soda, but he also offered critical testimony that supported some of the dyers' complaints. He concurred that the quality of the indigo that was available to them was poor and charged that the Native Authority had done very little to encourage the industry.[89]

The testimonies from the individuals involved in the dyeing industry provided the commission with a fairly comprehensive overview. The context of the discussion was very focused on Abeokuta and in no way invited even the possibility that the constraints the dyers experienced were connected to larger economic developments, specifically the depression. Although debt came up once, credit was not discussed at all during the hearings. Credit had been one of the most important issues during the council meetings held with the dyers in 1928 and 1929, and Somoye's letters in 1935 suggested that the difficulties had not been resolved.

In spite of its composition, which appeared to favor the *Alake*, the commission independently arrived at the conclusion that the new technology was not harmful to the industry. These conclusions rebutted the *Alake*'s and council's assertions that the chemicals had been detrimental to the industry. The Commission of Inquiry agreed with those who favored the use of caustic soda and synthetic dye. They emphasized that *"as used now"* the chemicals did not have a sufficiently deleterious effect to have had an adverse impact on the volume of trade.[90] They even argued that trade had not decreased, but rather had increased. They highlighted several positive outcomes from using the chemicals—fewer losses through failure of dye-pots, greater production of dye and therefore of dyed cloth per pot, and a considerable time saving.

The commissioners felt that the prohibitions, on the other hand, had been both useless and injurious to the industry. The prohibitions had been ineffective because practically no dyers at the time used or desired to use the old method. Enforcement would have definitely placed Abeokuta dyers at a disadvantage with respect to dyers in other centers, where the new chemicals were not prohibited. In view of these considerations, the commission called for the suspension of the prohibitions against caustic soda and synthetic dyes. Nonetheless, they envisaged several dangers attendant on the use of the chemicals—the complete displacement of natural indigo by synthetic indigo; the difficulty for the trained dyer, the craftswoman, to compete with interlopers; and the potential for a commercial concern to develop dyeing along industrial lines with the new chemicals and undercut local dyers. They argued that these dangers were still remote judging from the fact that none of them had materialized in Ede or Ibadan, other major dyeing centers. Furthermore, they noted that the exceptional stitching and tying designs of Abeokuta *adire* makers could not be reproduced by a mechanical process.

The commission members felt that the dyeing industry was sufficiently organized and governed by its own customs and traditional practices. Therefore it was not necessary to impose any form of organization, such as registration, on the dyers. But if the dyers wanted some form of organization, then the commission suggested that the Native Authority assist and advise them. The commission concluded that the 6d. commission on each cloth charged by the Senegalese interpreters was being paid by the Senegalese buyers and not by the dyers. The final recommendations were directed toward the Native Authority. They encouraged the Native Authority to promote the production of local natural indigo. The commissioners noted the number of complaints from dyers about the difficulty they experienced in trying to obtain sufficient quantities of natural indigo. The commission also recommended that the Native Authority provide amenities such as improved market accommodations and market stalls, as well as other assistance that could be reasonably accorded.[91]

Along with its conclusions and recommendations, the commission also submitted a report prepared by the government analyst, R.K. Hardy. This report mirrored the tone of the commission's conclusions. Hardy's report presented some interesting contrasts to the report prepared by the government analyst A.B. Hobson in 1933 when the *Alake* first took action against synthetic dyes. Hobson's report had projected doom for the industry if dyers continued to use synthetic dyes. He had noted that they were using a type of synthetic dye that was a direct dye dissolved in water rather than a vat dye. Hardy's report, however, carried no mention of a synthetic direct dye being used. This discrepancy suggests that the context under which the women were dyeing had significantly changed in the intervening years and supports Hardy's hypothesis that many dyers, taking their cues from the number of complaints about synthetic dyes, had perfected the process of using both the natural indigo and synthetic indigo.

Although the commission held hearings in July 1936 and Hardy's report was completed by September 1936, it was almost six months before the commission's recommendations were acted on. When Dr. Adeniyi-Jones, the second Lagos member in the legislative council, requested an update of the situation in Abeokuta in February 1937, he was informed that the commission's report had not been submitted until 19 February and had not reached the government as yet. It was another month before the report was forwarded to the chief secretary in Lagos. In the accompanying correspondence, he was asked to approve the repeal of the rules banning caustic soda and synthetic dye in Abeokuta.[92] Finally, in March the dyers were informed of the commission's conclusions. On 10 March 1937, approximately one hundred dyers attended the council meeting where the commission's conclusions and recommendations were translated into Yoruba and read to the group. At the end of the reading, the *Alake* announced the suspension of the rules prohibiting the use of caustic soda and synthetic dye.

CONCLUSION

The issues around which this conflict evolved were fairly limited. Dyers were protecting their livelihood. The battle crystallized around caustic soda and synthetic dyes because these products had become necessary to their economic survival. Nonetheless, the conflict is important because it provided critical insight into the relationship between women and the colonial state.

The dyers' successful challenge against the *Alake*'s authority had larger political ramifications that were not lost on Ademola or the political officers. The victory contradicted the state's efforts to present Residents and local leaders, like the *Alake*, as the ultimate source of power in their communities. It also showed that the colonial state had its own internal paradoxes which could allow an aggrieved group to use one arm of the state against another.

Equally important, this conflict and its resolution illuminated the ways in which colonial state formation had been gendered. The exercise of political power became a male activity. Titled women, such as the *Iyalode*, were ignored as the colonial apparatus was installed at the local level. Women, however, were not the only interest group excluded from colonial politics. Many educated men were also excluded from direct political participation, but they could participate indirectly by providing services as letter writers and legal advocates. Some of these men clearly brought more than literacy to the task. They possessed a knowledge of British political culture that could be used to support their arguments. This avenue of indirect political participation was closed to most women. Fewer women gained access to these important skills, and those who did were directed away from public roles. However, as the conflict made clear, women could hire literate personnel and legal expertise.

Although Egba women lost their formal political role, institutions such as commodity associations provided an organizational base from which they could assert themselves in the political arena. The dyers' victory was in part based on the fact that they were able to put aside the competition and differences that had made it impossible for them for work collectively in the 1920s. That organizational base assumed political importance because it allowed the women to quickly marshal their financial resources and to act collectively. As they organized, the association became yet another site of contention in the struggle over control and autonomy. While the dyers were not trying to depose Ademola or end colonial rule, they had very clear ideas on where the boundaries of state control should lie. If the state could not use its power to protect and guard the women's economic well-being, at least it refrained from using its power to undermine their livelihoods.

NOTES

1. See Annual Report on the Social and Economic Progress of the People of Nigeria, 1933 (NAI).

2. Annual Report on the Colony for the Year 1933, 67 (NAI); and Annual Report on the Southern Provinces of Nigeria for the Year 1936, 76. (NAI).

3. Annual Report, Abeokuta Province, 1932, 52. CSO 26/2 11875, vol. 9 (NAI).

4. Annual Report, Abeokuta Province, 1933, 9. CSO 26/2 11875, vol. 10 (NAI).

5. Ibid., 14.

6. Industries which survived best seemed to be those which depended on the local economy for raw materials and sold to the local market. In Egypt and the Belgian Congo, local protectionist initiatives in the wake of the collapse of commodity prices helped spur industrialization. In Egypt particularly, cotton exports declined in favor of the local market as textile plants were developed. By 1939 Egyptian textile factories were able to meet at least half of local demand. See Roger Owen, "Egypt in the World Depression: Agricultural Recession and Industrial Expansion," David Anderson and David Throup, "The Agrarian Economy of Central Province, Kenya 1918–1939," and Gervase Clarence-Smith, "The Effects of the Great Depression on Industrialisation in Equatorial and Central Africa"— all in Ian Brown, ed., *The Economies of Africa and Asia in the Inter-war Depression* (London: Routledge, 1989).

7. The Agricultural Department worked with the Native Administration to arrange regular fortnightly shipments of one hundred cases of pineapples to England. They were also positive that a vigorous trade in West African oranges from Abeokuta could also be established. Annual Report, Abeokuta Province, 1934, 21. CSO 26/2 11875, vol. 11 (NAI).

8. Annual Report, Abeokuta Province, 1934, 23–24. CSO 26/2 11875, vol. 11 (NAI). Also see Annual Report, Abeokuta Province, 1935, 28. CSO 26/2 11875, vol. 12 (NAI).

9. Annual Report, Abeokuta Province, 1935, 27. CSO 26/2 11875, vol. 12 (NAI). The 1933 report noted that with the sudden fall in the price of palm oil, more oil was being consumed locally for illumination and exported to the northern provinces than to Europe. Low prices continued into 1934, resulting in the "virtual cessation of the export of this product." Annual Report, Abeokuta Province, 1934, 10. CSO 26/2 11875, vol. 11 (NAI).

10. Annual Report on the Southern Provinces of Nigeria 1936, 76 (NAI).

11. Extract from Minutes of Egba Council Meeting, 8 August 1935, 1. ECR 1/1/42, vol. 2 (NAA).

12. Ibid., 4.

13. Ibid., 6.

14. Letter from Oladipo Somoye to the *Alake*, 28 February 1936. ECR 1/1/46 (NAA). Somoye, who was described by the Resident in a confidential letter as a former clerk at UAC and a man who interests himself in any current agitation, was later hired by the dyers to represent them before the council. See letter from Resident to the secretary of the southern provinces, 24 April 1936. ECR 1/1/46 (NAI).

15. *Nigerian Daily Times,* 13 February 1936. CSO 28400, vol. 1 (NAI).

16. Letter from Oladipo Somoye to the *Alake*, 28 February 1936. ECR 1/1/46 (NAA).

17. *Nigerian Daily Times,* 13 February 1936. CSO 28400, vol. 1 (NAI).

18. Afusatu Arogundade, 28 August 1996, Kemta, Abeokuta.

19. Minutes of Extraordinary Meeting of Egba Council, 12 February 1936. ECR 1/1/46 (NAA).

20. Ibid.

21. *Nigerian Daily Times,* 13 February 1936, and Extract from Legislative Council Meeting, 2 March 1936. CSO 28400, vol. 1 (NAI). The *Nigerian Daily Times* was one of the earliest Lagos dailies to provide countrywide coverage. It began publishing in June 1926 and dominated until the *Daily Service* and the *West African Pilot* came on the scene in 1933 and 1937 respectively. The latter two papers were strongly affiliated with the nationalist movements, while the *Daily Times* was seen as the conservative paper presenting the side of government. The *Daily Service* became the organ of the Nigerian Youth Movement, while the *Pilot* was owned by Nnamdi Azikiwe, one of the central members of the National Council of Nigeria and the Cameroons. See Increase Coker, *Seventy Years of the Nigerian Press* (Lagos: Daily Times, 1952).

22. Extract from Legislative Council Meeting, 2 March 1936. CSO 28400, vol. 1 (NAI).

23. Minutes of Egba Council Meetings, 20 February 1936. ECR 1/1/70, vol. 2 (NAA).

24. Minutes of Council Meetings, 20 February 1936. ECR 1/1/70, vol. 2 (NAA).

25. Information on these men was discussed in a letter from the Resident to the secretary of the southern provinces, 24 April 1936. Alhaji Gbadamosi was cited only as "one of the unemployed." ECR 1/1/46 (NAA).

26. The men were given power of attorney on 22 February 1936, and the decision was ratified by 258 women in a meeting on 16 March 1936. See the letter from Doherty to Sir Bernard H. Bourdillion, Governor of Nigeria, 9 April 1936. CSO 28400, vol. 1 (NAI).

27. Michael C. Atkinson, ed. "Nigerian Tales of the Colonial Era" (unpublished manuscript, 1988), 19.

28. See the letter from the *adire* traders to Messrs. Alhaji Gbadamosi, Mustafa Egberongbe, and Oladipo Somoye, 22 February 1936. CSO 28400, vol. 1. See also Minutes of Egba Council Meeting, 19 August 1937. Abe Prof. 1/1 ABP 236, vol. 4 (NAA).

29. Letter from Doherty to the *Alake,* 17 March 1936. ECR 1/1/46 (NAA). The colonial government disliked and distrusted African lawyers. Lawyers were excluded from the provincial and "native" courts on the grounds that illiterate litigants had to be spared lawyers' excessive fees. The more germane concern was that lawyers would challenge the activities of political officers and undermine the officers' authority and effectiveness. See Omoniyi Adewoye, *The Judicial System in Southern Nigeria, 1854–1954* (Atlantic Highlands, NJ: Humanities Press, 1977), 107–70.

30. Letter from Oladipo Somoye to the *Alake,* 27 August 1935. ECR 1/1/46 (NAA).

31. Ibid.

32. Letter from Oladipo Somoye to the district officer, Egba Division, 21 February 1936. CSO 28400, vol. 1 (NAI).

33. Ibid., 2. (His capitals)
34. Ibid., 3.
35. Sir William N. Geary, *Nigeria Under British Rule* (London: Frank Cass, 1965), 9.
36. Ibid., 10.
37. Ibid., 11.
38. Ibid., 12.
39. Letter from Somoye to the chief secretary of the government, 6 March 1936. CSO 28400, vol. 1 (NAI).
40. Letter from Geary to the chief secretary of the government, 20 April 1936. CSO 28400, vol. 1 (NAI).
41. Letter from the comptroller to the chief secretary of the government, 17 April 1936. CSO 28400, vol. 1 (NAI).
42. Minute on letter from Geary to the chief secretary of the government, 30 April 1936. CSO 28400, vol. 1 (NAI).
43. Minutes of Egba Council Meeting, 2 April 1936. ECR 1/1/77, vol. 2 (NAA).
44. Ibid.
45. Ibid.
46. Minutes of Extraordinary Meeting of Egba Council, 3 April 1936. ECR 1/1/77, vol. 2 (NAA).
47. Memo from the Resident, Abeokuta Province, to the secretary of the Southern Provinces, 12. 24 April 1936. CSO 28400, vol. 1 (NAI).
48. Minutes of Extraordinary Meeting of Egba Council, 3 April 1936. ECR 1/1/77, vol. 2 (NAA).
49. Memo to governor, 19 April 1922. CSO 21/N309 (NAI).
50. See T.N. Tamuno, *The Evolution of the Nigerian State: The Southern Phase, 1898–1914* (New York: Humanities Press, 1972), especially ch. 3 and 7. Troops were sent to protect the *Alake* in 1901, in 1907, and again in 1914 when the treaty of independence was abrogated. Gbadebo was rewarded for his loyalty with a trip to England in 1903 arranged by Governor MacGregor.
51. Michael Crowder, *West Africa Under Colonial Rule* (Evanston, IL: Northwestern University Press, 1968), 205. Also see Michael C. Atkinson, *An African Life: Tales of a Colonial Officer* (London: Radcliffe Press, 1992), 5.
52. Abeokuta Province Reports, 1 January 1920 to 31 March 1921, 3. CSO 21/309 (NAI).
53. Confidential memorandum. Addendum to political report on Egba division contained in the Abeokuta Province Report, 1 January 1920 to 31 March 1921, 2. CSO 21/309 (NAI). The Resident, C.W. Alexander, speculated that a wealthy Moslem woman trader, Subuola, and her father were behind his death.
54. Ademola was the first Christian and educated Egba king. He had a direct claim to the kingship, for his father was *Alake* Ademola I (1869–77). He was trained as a printer in Lagos and became the head printer for the *Lagos Weekly Record* in 1890, but he later gave up printing and moved into trade. Ademola first became involved in Abeokuta politics in 1898, when he participated in the reorganization of the EUG. He continued to serve *Alake* Gbadebo in various advisory capacities until 1904. In 1899, for example, he helped negotiate the Egba Railway Agreement; in 1901 he served as ambassador to the British government

in Lagos; and in 1904 he accompanied Gbadebo and Edun to England. He disappeared for a number of years, and it is unclear what he did during that time. See A.K. Ajisafe, *History of Abeokuta,* 3d ed. (Lagos: Kash and Klare Bookshop, 1948), 124–25.

55. The British claimed that during the period Ademola had disappeared he was really in hiding in the Egba bush, and an audit of the EUG showed he had been engaged in some fraud. Confidential memorandum. Addendum to political report on Egba division contained in the Abeokuta Province Report, 1 January 1920 to 31 March 1921, 2. CSO 21/309 (NAI).

56. Confidential memorandum. Addendum to political report on Egba division contained in the Abeokuta Province Report, 1 January 1920 to 31 March 1921, 13–14. CSO 21/309 (NAI).

57. Crowder, *West Africa,* 199. This antipathy was nurtured by the involvement of the Lagos Egba community in conflicts in Abeokuta. They were often branded "agitators, and busy-bodies leading their gullible countrymen astray." See Annual Report for Abeokuta Province 1927, p. 4. CSO 26/2 11875, vol. 5 (NAI). Excluding educated elites also became a part of colonial policy under Indirect Rule. See Mahmood Mamdani, *Citizen and Subject: Contemporary Africa and the Legacy of Late Colonialism* (Princeton, NJ: Princeton University Press, 1996), 76.

58. Confidential memorandum. Addendum to political report on Egba division contained in the Abeokuta Province Report, 1 January 1920 to 31 March 1921, 14. CSO 21/309 (NAI).

59. Annual Report, Abeokuta Province, 1921, 11. CSO 21//309 (NAI).

60. Annual Report, Abeokuta Province, 1922. Confidential memorandum amplifying "Political and Administrative" Egba division, 5. CSO 26/1 09104 (NAI).

61. Ibid., 5–6.

62. Annual Report, Abeokuta Province, 1924, 2. CSO 26/2 11875, vol. 2 (NAI).

63. Atkinson, *An African Life,* 7.

64. In 1926 certain *Ogboni* chiefs were agitating for the reinstatement of one of their members. In the annual report the Resident, E.A. Brackenbury, characterized the *Ogboni* as representing the old forces of fetish, intimidation, extortion, and oppression, while the *Alake* and council and the British government represented civilization, reform, and progress. Annual Report, Abeokuta Province, 1926, p. 2. CSO 26/2 11875, vol. 4 (NAI).

65. Annual Report, Abeokuta Province, 1927, 8–9. CSO 26/2 11875, vol. 5 (NAI).

66. Annual Report, Abeokuta Province, 1934, 6. CSO 26/2 11875, vol. 11 (NAI).

67. John Blair, intelligence report on Abeokuta, 1938, 18. CSO 26/4 34231 (NAI).

68. Minutes Book of Interest, 1918. ENA Minutes of Egba Council Meeting, 30 January 1919. ECR 1/1/10 (NAA).

69. Ibid., 22 April 1920.

70. Ibid., 12 June 1919.

71. Ibid., 22 April 1920.

72. Minutes of Abeokuta Women Centenary Celebration Committee. ECR 1/1/49 (NAA).

73. Annual Report, Abeokuta Province, 1928, 1. CSO 26/2 11875, vol. 6 (NAI). The *Oshile* was the *Oba* of Oke Ona section.

74. The Abeokuta Ladies Club, which launched the first all-women's organized protest linking market women and educated women, was not formed until 1944. See Nina Emma Mba, *Nigerian Women Mobilized: Women's Political Activity in Southern Nigeria, 1900–1965* (Berkeley: University of California Press, 1982), 143. Also see Cheryl Johnson-Odim and Nina Emma Mba, *For Women and the Nation: Funmilayo Ransome-Kuti of Nigeria* (Urbana: University of Illinois Press, 1997).

75. LaRay Denzer, "Domestic Science Training in Colonial Yorubaland, Nigeria," in Karen Tranberg-Hansen, ed., *African Encounters with Domesticity* (New Brunswick, NJ: Rutgers University Press, 1992), 120–22. Also Oyeronke Oyewumi, *The Invention of Women: Making an African Sense of Western Gender Discourses* (Minneapolis: University of Minnesota Press, 1997), 128–36.

76. It was claimed that the *Ogboni* chiefs who took the *Alake* to court over the disputed *Oshiele*ship were trying to depose him. Annual Report, Abeokuta Province, 1928, 1. CSO 26/2 11875, vol. 6 (NAI).

77. Letter from K.A. Sinker, clerk, Lagos Council, to Dr. Adeniyi-Jones, 14 May 1936. CSO 28400, vol. 1 (NAI).

78. Letter from chief secretary to the government to Sir William Geary, 11 April 1936. CSO 28400, vol. 1 (NAI).

79. Decisions of Egba council meeting held 16 April 1936. Abe Prof. 1/1 ABP 236, vol. 4 (NAI).

80. See Susan Martin, *Palm Oil and Protest: An Economic History of the Ngwa Region, South-eastern Nigeria, 1800–1980* (Cambridge: Cambridge University Press, 1988); Judith Van Allen, "'Aba Riots' or Igbo 'Women's War'? Ideology, Stratification and the Invisibility of Women," and Kamene Okonjo, "The Dual-Sex Political System in Operation: Igbo Women and Community Politics in Midwestern Nigeria"—both in Nancy Hafkin and Edna G. Bay, eds., *Women in Africa: Studies in Social and Economic Change* (Stanford, CA: Stanford University Press, 1976), for discussions of the Aba women's protest.

81. In a similar manner, colonial officials assumed that men had directed the Igbo women's war and that women could not have organized protests on their own initiative. See Van Allen, "Aba Riots."

82. See Continuation Sheet no. 45, 3 April 1936. CSO 28400, vol. 1 (NAI).

83. Letter from Resident A.E.F. Murray to commission members, 8 May 1936. CSO 28400, vol. 1 (NAI).

84. Letter from Geary to the chief secretary, 15 June 1936. CSO 28400, vol. 2 (NAI). Dyers initially objected to Mrs. Moore because they feared that she was Modeefe Moore, a wife of the *Alake*. Unfortunately, no further information was uncovered about Mrs. Moore.

85. Letter from the Resident, Abeokuta to the members of the Special Committee on Adire Trade in Abeokuta, 8May 1936. CSO 28400, vol. 1 (NAI).

86. Proceedings of the Adire Cloth Committee, 6. Abe Prof. 4—D29 (NAA). Madam Bolajoko's township was not identified.

87. Ibid., 10.
88. Ibid., 24.
89. Ibid., 36.
90. Underlined in original. See "Conclusions and Recommendations of the Committee Appointed to Enquire into the Abeokuta Adire Cloth Industry," 2 September 1936. ECR 1/1/42, vol. 1 (NAA).
91. Ibid.
92. See Memo from the secretary of the Southern Provinces to the chief secretary of the government. CSO 28400, vol. 2. The rules were formally repealed by the *Alake* on 25 November 1937 and approved by Governor Bourdillon on 11 February 1938. CSO 28400, vol. 3 (NAI).

6

THE COLLAPSE OF
THE *ADIRE* INDUSTRY,
1937–1939

Although economic decline characterized much of the interwar years, there were moments when the conjuncture of several interrelated factors intensified the crisis. The period between 1937 and 1939 represented one of these intensified phases in this period of economic decline. The factors at play were multidimensional—local, regional, international—and well beyond the dyers' scope of control. The severity of the decline between 1937 and 1939 was magnified by the fact that trade had improved significantly in 1936. It is probably not coincidental that the conflict between the *Alake* and the dyers erupted during 1936, since 1936 and the first half of 1937 were high points of recovery.

This chapter has multiple tasks. It examines changes in the industry that built on the momentum of the economic recovery and the removal of the bans. Dyers used that momentum to construct a new type of dyers' association that mirrored their recently realized solidarity. Reconstructing the history of the association and its impact on the industry has been difficult because both the archival and oral data were quite fragmentary. Few key documents survived, and the association was discussed in two council meetings only. Oral sources did not provide a great deal of information, because few informants remembered the association from this era in any great detail. Most recalled the social roles that the association played, such as contributing to members who were celebrating marriages or births. Few remembered who had been president or what issues divided the community of dyers.

Nonetheless, enough evidence survives to appreciate distinctive features in the new association.

The economic recovery and the momentum it generated ground to a halt by the second half of 1937. The severe economic downturn led some officials to declare that the *adire* industry had collapsed. The industry lost its flagship position in the economy, and this was reflected in its virtual disappearance from colonial records. *Adire*'s precipitous decline was explicitly connected with the decline in cocoa prices and the cocoa holdups in the Gold Coast. The juxtaposition of *adire* and cocoa allow us to once again examine the gender implications of this moment and to consider the crisis from a regional perspective.

The dyers' universe was never restricted to economic developments; fashion and consumer tastes always shaped the industry. Taste and patterns in consumption did not remain static during the early and midcolonial period. This chapter also examines the changes in styles and fashions and their implications for the *adire* industry in the midst of economic upheaval.

THE DYERS' ASSOCIATION

Interviews with dyers about their association provided interesting contrasts with the documentary evidence about the association. The documentary evidence primarily stressed the economic presence of the association, while dyers revealed that the association played a role in their social life as well. Describing the association, Wosinatu Adeniji recalled, "If there is any ceremony like marriage ceremony of a daughter or burial ceremony, the members would contribute some money to give the celebrant."[1]

Several dyers insisted that the association did not have fixed meeting times or places. Alhaja Bakare reported, "There was not time for us to meet, for any meeting we only met at any member's house who has something to celebrate."[2] Madam Sidikat Ayinde concurred, adding, "We don't have a meeting place, but when there is going to be a social function people from Jojo's compound would go round to tell dyers and we would all go."[3] However, Alhaja Falilat Tukuru, offered a different recollection: "On meeting days nobody should work until after the meeting. . . . [we met] every fifteenth day at the president's house and at times at Nawal-nu-deen."[4]

All concurred that the association was very inclusive. Alhaja Bakare noted that "The association has one main body. . . . All the compounds form the main body of the association, while compounds form the branches."[5] Alhaja Tukuru added, "Everybody is a member. Once you are involved in the business you are a member."[6]

Most dyers did not remember when the association began. Alhaja Bakare dated it to the time of their great-grandmothers, and Alhaja Soetan and Alhaja Tukuru to the time that the *Alake* banned caustic soda.[7] Alhaja Tukuru suggested that Madam Jojolola was the first president of the association. It is likely that the differences in their recollections reflect different periods in the organizational strength and strategies of the dyers' association.

Traders and producers in Yoruba society have a long history of forming commodity associations, such as the pepper sellers' association, and thus it is more than likely that dyers also had their own association before the 1930s as Alhaja Bakare insisted. One of the most important functions of commodity associations was to help regulate trade by discouraging competition among women trading in the same commodity. Scholars in the past have suggested that these associations were able to control their membership and effectively regulate trade. Kenneth Little, for example, argued

> Each such section (for each commodity) has its own association, or egbe, which discourages competition between women trading in that particular article. Such is the sense of solidarity . . . that it is said to be unthinkable for a trader to disobey her market egbe in this matter. Any woman undercutting is ostracized by her fellows, who may even take a case against her . . . to the leader of the egbe, and if necessary to the Iyalode.[8]

The evidence from the *adire* industry suggests that Little's conclusions may have been idealized. The theoretical roles of commodity associations did not necessarily manifest themselves in practice, for their ability to enforce sanctions and regulate trade varied over time. It is clear that in the 1920s and early 1930s, the Abeokuta dyers' association as it existed could not regulate competition among dyers. The sanctions that previous generations of dyers may have used effectively to control their members had lost their currency, and their inability to regulate the industry had propelled the first group of dyers to seek the *Alake*'s assistance in 1927.

Thus, when the *Alake* encouraged the women to form associations, he was not encouraging an innovation in Yoruba commercial practice. Instead, he was urging them to create an effective body that could control its members. He was also willing to put the support of the state behind this body by upholding the expulsion of members who disobeyed the rules. The *Alake*'s support was fraught with contradictions. He promised to support the dyers' association as long as dyers organized under the guidance of a general titled chief from their respective quarters. The dyers' association that crystallized during the conflict with the *Alake* had to address two potentially contradictory objectives: (1) establishing solidarity and control over its members, while (2) maintaining autonomy.

It appears that in spite of the many differences and tensions that existed among dyers, they were able to put them aside while they focused their attention on removing the bans on caustic soda and synthetic dye. Solidarity was quite comprehensive in 1936 and the association was close to the model Little described. The dyers' association was certainly a reinvigorated and palpable force among dyers by 1936, because the bans had galvanized dyers into action. This sequence of events could explain Alhajas Soetan and Tukuru's claim that the dyers' association began at the time of the bans.

After the Commission of Enquiry, the dyers tried to capitalize on this heightened solidarity and put it on a much more secure footing by organizing the association along more formal lines. In January 1937 the dyers approved a constitution and formed the Egba Women Dyers and *Adire* Trading Union. The resolutions that became the bylaws of the union were signed by 294 women from the four main quarters of the town.[9] The union claimed a total of 1,627 members.[10]

Membership was open to anybody in Egbaland—the towns and the rural districts—involved in the manufacturing and sale of *adire*. Members had to pay an admission fee of two guineas (£2/2s.) and a monthly subscription fee of 6d. The money was placed in a bank account. The registered office of the Union was to be located in Ijeun and a special branch office was to be opened in another part of town for the union's clerks. Members nominated six members as trustees, who were to manage all matters of vital importance on behalf of the union. In addition to the trustees, the constitution called for eight officers: patron and vice patron, president, lady president, vice lady president, secretary, treasurer, and auditor. It is unclear whether all these offices were ever filled. Alhaja Soetan remembered only three major posts: *Iya Egbe Alaro* (President), *igba keji iya egbe* (vice president), and *baba isale* (advisor).[11] The association also gave honorary titles. Alhaja Bakare was named *iyalajed*.[12]

The union had five major purposes:

1. To carry out the business of dyers and *adire* cloth sellers in Egbaland

2. To protect and promote the trade welfare in Egbaland by guarding against adulteration of dyes used in the manufacture of *adire* cloths, etc.

3. To protect the rights and interests of all dyers in Egbaland in a legitimate course, and to establish firmly the sales and manufacture of *adire* cloths in Egbaland

4. To protect the sales of *adire* cloths and cooperation in all the public markets in Egbaland, in order to equalize the selling prices of these cloths

5. To hold or promote competition of any descriptions of *adire* cloths authorized by the union which may be calculated to increase the business from time to time[13]

From their regulations it was clear that the dyers wanted to protect and promote the interests of the industry as a whole. They also wanted to establish mechanisms to set and enforce adherence to uniform prices and fair market practices. For example, on special meeting days, no member of the union was to sell her goods directly or indirectly or attend any public markets. If a member violated these rules, other members could seize her goods and take them to the house of the lady president until the entire membership decided on an appropriate penalty. Members were not to conduct house-to-house sales; instead, all sales were to be conducted in the public markets. No member was to leave her stall to "rush against buyers" in order to persuade them to buy from her. Rather, they were to sit in an orderly way in their stalls awaiting customers. Members were not to dye cloths for non-members who intended to sell them. Prices would be determined by the Trustees and announced in the public market. Any member who resigned from the union or who was dismissed was not permitted to dye, manufacture, or trade *adire* cloth. If she did not change her trade, the union would begin court action against her. The constitution also called for the appointment of clerks to protect the interests of the union in any public market. The clerks were to wear uniforms and badges when on duty and visit members at their places of business from time to time.[14]

The dyers tried to obtain official backing of their newly established union and constitution by applying for incorporation. They applied under the Land (Perpetual Succession) Ordinance and received a certificate of incorporation signed by the governor on 21 July 1937.[15] Dyers thought that such certification gave them legal recognition and their rules and regulation the force of law. However, the attorney-general advised the Resident that these certificates did not grant government approval or sanction of their bylaws. They only signified that since the union had appointed trustees, it could hold land. Under the law, the union was an unregistered association with the same status as a club. Members were not liable to punishment either by a fine or imprisonment for noncompliance with its rules and regulations. Nonetheless, the union could launch civil proceedings against members who broke their contractual obligations.[16]

Though incorporation did not provide the type of state support the framers of the constitution anticipated, it is important to examine the implications of their actions. The provisions of the constitution gave the leadership strong control over prices, restricted participation in the craft to those who were recognized members, and provided for enforcement. The provisions specifically addressed the issues that had undermined the industry in the 1920s. The concern with compliance and enforcement was also evident in the union's creation of market masters in the latter half of 1937. The union employed clerks who were appointed market masters and given uniforms and badges. They were to circulate through the market and prevent anyone who did not abide by the union's rules and regulations from selling.

In spite of the desire to have a strong organization, the union was torn apart by conflict as early as August 1937. Dyers from Oke-Ona quarter resigned. They charged that the Union held private consultations without inviting a representative from Oke Ona.[17] In addition, they were not kept informed about the union's accounts and alleged that the leadership made frivolous disbursements. Since the union intended to exercise a much more controlling presence in the industry, the Oke Ona women were clearly upset by their exclusion from financial and policy meetings.

After their decision to resign, Oke Ona dyers arranged a public hearing of their grievances, because under the constitution withdrawal from the union was now tantamount to a withdrawal from the trade. Fearing that the union would enforce strictures against ex-members, especially after the appointment of the market masters, the Oke Ona women enlisted Somoye's assistance.[18] Somoye's relationship with the union had been severed by this time. He advised the Oke Ona dyers to go as usual to the market, and he wrote to the *Alake* on their behalf questioning the legality of the union's market masters.[19] This issue brought the *adire* dyers and makers back before the council. Two extraordinary council meetings on 19 and 21 August provided information about this and other important developments since the Commission of Enquiry.

One of the most striking developments was the strained relationship between the union and the literate men who had represented them during their struggle with the *Alake*. Somoye was the first person from that important coalition to depart. Dyers charged that he had represented himself as the leader of the *Adire* Women Dyers Union and approached the manager of the Union Trading Company for money. It does not appear that the union was consulted about his intention to use its name to acquire a loan, or that the loan was to be used by the union. If he had been successful in obtaining the loan, the union might have been liable in the event of a default. As a result of his actions, the women dismissed him.[20]

Doherty, the disbarred lawyer, left after the union refused to give him a loan.[21] Egberongbe was still serving the union as its secretary, though Somoye charged that he too had taken money from the *adire* women under false pretenses. It appears that these men had attempted in pursuit of credit to exploit their relationship with the dyers' association. Though Somoye and Doherty had played crucial roles in the dyers' struggle against the bans, their position was based on the dyers' temporary need for literate personnel, services not crucial to the long-term functioning of the association. The men's actions suggest that their continued relationship could have been draining, and thus a liability to the association.

While the dyers' relationships with Somoye and Doherty ended poorly, their relationship with the *Alake* had improved significantly. He was made the patron of the union. During one of the council meetings, Doherty challenged the appropriateness of this appointment, since the dyers had fought the *Alake* and council and won.[22] This set in motion a fascinating exchange in which the history of the conflict was essentially rewritten. The *Alake* rejected Doherty's characterization of the previous year's events as a confrontation. He informed Doherty that it was improper to say that they had fought the Native Administration and won. He asserted that it was a lack of etiquette for anyone to use the word "fight" when addressing the government. In correct terminology, they had had a grievance and they approached him as their "father" and petitioned the administration. He also pointed out that the Commission of Enquiry into the *adire* trade had been appointed by the *Alake* and council, not by the British government.[23] He exalted his role with the colonial bureaucracy, suggesting that his local bureaucracy could have undertaken such an important event as the Commission of Enquiry without the explicit support of the upper echelons of the colonial government in Lagos.[24] Casting his actions in a paternalistic framework also secured certain points. It underscored his position as the head of the community, and therefore, the one to whom all issues ultimately had to be addressed. It also underlined his view of his reign as that of a sympathetic, benevolent father who ruled in the best interest of his family. With rhetoric calculated to submerge real conflict and invite analysis at the level of personalities and characters rather than structures, the *Alake* charged that the conflict was the result of bad advice that the dyers received. He blamed the agitation on the educated men.

This paternalistic rendition of past events was not exclusive to the *Alake*. It was used equally effectively by certain dyers. One of the dyers who spoke during the council meeting, Madam Asimowu Apampa of Ago-Owu, was among the group of representatives selected by dyers to speak for them on the first day's hearing before the 1936 Commission of Enquiry. She was obviously highly regarded by her peers, and that enhanced her fascinating portrayal of their relationship with the *Alake* as she recounted their history.

> The first meeting was about the Senegalese; previous to that they were already in a body and used to come to the Alake for any matter they desired. When their visits became frequent the Alake gave them a present of £5 and told them that he was their "father" and ready to assist them. . . . They were united from the beginning up to the time of Adubi Rising [1918] and used to assemble till then in the house of the late *Iyalode* of the Egbas [Madam Jojolola]. There, during the Rising, they decided to call a truce, which was successful; during all the time no one was considered too little among them and they were united. As it was the Alake alone . . . [who] could improve their condition, they appointed him their Patron.[25]

Her statement was interesting for a number of reasons. It pointed out the active role that Madam Jojolola played among dyers, an important segment of her constituency, and suggests that dyers had a much longer history of association than exists in any surviving record. Her statement suggests that there had been a high degree of solidarity among dyers, "no one was considered too little," yet there were instances of tension, i.e., "they decided to call a truce." Her rendition managed both to recast the acrimonious conflict over interlopers and hint at periods of disunity. Her discussion also painted the relationship between the dyers and the *Alake* in a very positive, mutually supportive light. It excluded their disappointment with him in 1929 when he dismissed their arguments about the debilitating impact of the credit crisis as well as their anger around the arrests in 1936.

The proceedings indicated that most of the tension from the previous year's events had been put to rest. Also embedded in these exchanges was a political realignment. During the conflict, the dyers had sought the assistance of educated men to circumvent the *Alake*'s authority and overturn his rulings. But the conflict did not permanently embitter the relationship between the *Alake* and the dyers, nor did it transform the women's general ideological support of patriarchal relations. Both Ademola and the women were engaged in the process of restoring their political relationship and the ideological hegemony of patriarchy represented by the image of the *Alake* as the benevolent father of the community. At the same time that the political order was being reaffirmed, all were cognizant of the fact that certain boundaries had been established during the conflict. Dyers had successfully overturned the *Alake*'s attempt to legislate the production process.

The central issue that brought the parties together again, the market masters, was cast in a larger discourse about boundaries. Members of the council were especially concerned about the posting of market masters and the fact that such actions had been taken without the knowledge and consent of the *Alake*. As the *Alake* himself argued, "the market belonged to the Oba as [a] public market and it was the Oba alone who could invest people with authority to watch people's interest in the markets."[26] Another member of the council declared that "if such practice was allowed in Egbaland there was nothing else that other Egbas could not do in the markets."[27] Others pointed out that groups such as Produce Buyers and the Motor Transport Union had employed uniformed men to watch their interests in the past. The association's action was consequently not unique. Nevertheless, the other groups had been discouraged from using uniformed men. Although the *Alake* wanted to see the women police themselves, he had to balance their enforcement measures against his control of the market. The *Alake* and council ultimately acted to protect their monopoly of the dispensation of symbols of authority—uniforms and badges.

Despite earlier promises to enforce the association's regulations, the *Alake* and council advised the women to suspend the enforcement of rules and regulations until they had reconciled their differences. The Resident also wrote to the union, advising them to "be very careful to offer no provocation to non-members of [the] Union such as might lead to any breach of the peace."[28] The outcome of this dispute did not appear in the minutes of following council meetings. It is possible that after the council meetings, the dyers resolved the dispute among themselves and therefore did not have to return to the council. The direction of the government's advice suggests that reconciliation may have occurred at the expense of a strong association.

The dyers' experience was extremely illuminating on a number of levels. It demonstrated that our analysis of women's associational life needs to be historically grounded. In this instance, the authority of a commodity association to act effectively changed over the lifetime of the association. Second, the dyers' new constitutional apparatus seemed to borrow from the colonial political order. The effort to codify laws and sanctions rigidly suggests that state practice and its corresponding legal system had permeated organizational space. These new bylaws were intended to supersede custom.

Dyers' application for state recognition is also informative. In applying for state recognition, the dyers' association hoped to use the sanction, and therefore the power of the state, to enforce its regulations. In the past, commodity associations had utilized different types of power to keep colleagues in check. Fadipe noted that there was not much open jealousy among rival traders, but there was a case involving cloth dealers, who "in order to prevent what they thought cut-throat competition, banded together and laid a conditional curse upon anyone who should resort to undercutting of prices."[29] This suggests that moral persuasion, imposing a curse, or other socially recognized sanctions that may have been used in the past to condemn inappropriate actions were no longer effective. Or else that dyers were maximizing their resources by drawing on codified bylaws and the colonial state, to ensure control and harmonious relations within the industry.

Whether or not reconciliation was achieved, after the dyers' final meeting with the *Alake* and council in 1937, the economic changes that surfaced between the latter half of 1937 and 1939 undermined dyers' efforts to safeguard their industry. Once again *adire* producers were left vulnerable and exposed as other segments of the economy struggled to protect their interests. *Adire* producers were most critically affected by the strategies of Gold Coast cocoa producers.

COCOA AND *ADIRE*

In 1936 the *adire* industry and the overall economy rebounded from the slump that characterized the first half of the decade. The annual report for the province stated that the industry was thriving and that the value of the shirting sold for dyeing was at least £70,000. Consumer purchasing power had increased so much so that the retail trade was lively and the turnover by the European firms had increased by 35 percent.[30] The picture the following year was dramatically different.

High cocoa prices carried over from 1936 into January 1937, but as the year progressed Egba farmers saw the price of exports decline steadily, reaching very low levels in December. The average price of cocoa in 1937 was £27 per ton; in 1938 the average price of cocoa was £13 per ton.[31] Colonial officials acknowledged that the average price did not tell the entire story, for it did not reflect the dramatic decline that occurred in the last few months of 1937.[32] Prices, for example, fell 25 percent between August and December 1937.[33] The downturn was further exacerbated by the high price of manufactured goods from Europe. This decline in farmers' income was immediately reflected in the volume of *adire* sales. The 1937 annual report noted that the *adire* industry shrank to "a fraction of its previous volume."[34] The decline of the *adire* industry was in large measure due to the cocoa holdups in the Gold Coast, where producers refused to sell their crop. As farmers refused to sell their cocoa, merchants who usually visited Abeokuta to buy *adire* ceased to come, because Gold Coast consumers could not afford to buy cloth.

The 1937–38 cocoa holdup was not the first; Gold Coast farmers had refused to sell their crop in 1908 and again in 1930–31, but this holdup was the most organized and the longest—seven months.[35] In 1937 the major buying firms came together at UAC's urging to set prices for that season's cocoa. The firms argued that the price agreement was intended to limit competition between them. As word of the agreement spread, cocoa producers refused to sell their cocoa. This price fixing occurred concurrently with the falling cocoa prices, and many people associated the collusive agreement with the downward price movements.[36]

As the boycott continued, trade with the Gold Coast was affected severely. Lancashire textile manufacturers' associations lobbied the Colonial Office and Parliament asking for the removal of the buying agreement.[37] Retail sales were also affected by a producer boycott of nonessential imported merchandise distributed by the firms that dominated cocoa buying. Farmers were especially embittered against UAC, which dominated cocoa buying in the Gold Coast.[38] It is likely that this boycott also affected *adire* sales in the Gold Coast because UAC had become an important distributor of Abeokuta *adire*.

The records do not explicitly link the boycott against UAC with the decline in *adire* sales. Nonetheless, there was a significant drop in UAC's sales of *adire* between 1937 and 1938. UAC reported that the value of cloth exported to Ghana between 1936 and 1938 was

Year	Yardage	Declared Value
1936	1,500,000	£63,000
1937	1,600,000	£66,000
1938	600,000	£24,000[39]

As the trade reached this low point, the company petitioned the colonial government for relief from the double duty that was imposed on *adire* exported to the Gold Coast. There was an import duty of 1d. per square yard on cloth imported into Nigeria and another 1d. per square yard on cloth going into the Gold Coast.[40] UAC argued that a refund of the reexport duty would help the dyers considerably, especially since the decline would continue in the foreseeable future.

As the UAC request for a waiver of the reexport tax went through the various levels of government, there was a fair amount of ambivalence toward the proposal. The comptroller pointed out that the UAC figures for 1938 were incorrect. Imports into the Gold Coast from Nigeria had totalled 872,490 square yards of cloth and produced a total duty of £3,630, a sum he did not feel the government would be in favor of relinquishing. Furthermore, he wondered who would receive the refund—the original importer, the actual dyer, the middleman or exporter?[41] One commentator felt that they were obligated to encourage export trade and should help the *adire* trade as long as possible in spite of its uneconomic nature as a result of "the wasteful transport involved."[42] Another expressed surprise that the dyeing industry was able to exist at all since "It is hopelessly uneconomic in modern conditions."[43] Refunding the reexport duty would also have necessitated the approval of new tariff regulations. Ultimately UAC's appeal was denied because "the objections both economic and administrative . . . outweigh[ed] the possible advantages."[44] Although it was unclear whether dyers would have benefited, it was clear that the government was not prepared to assist the European firms at the expense of the colonial treasury either.

The Gold Coast cocoa holdup was still one of several factors that contributed to *adire*'s falling demand. The industry had not recovered fully from the dyeing difficulties of the 1920s. Although they improved their techniques, the synthetic dyes did not have the fastness of the dye produced through the old fermentation method, and thus cloths still faded more quickly, and the indigo residue turned consumers' skin blue.[45] Dyers also faced competition in their regional markets. The population of the Yoruba community in the Gold Coast had increased substantially during the 1920s, reaching approximately 10,000 by the end of the decade. Fewer men made the circulatory trip between Nigeria and the Gold Coast and more women arrived, encouraging the development of a settled community.[46] Members of this community produced *adire* and competed with *adire* producers in Nigeria. They enjoyed certain advantages due to the tariff structure and their proximity to Gold Coast consumers. The import duty on cloth brought into the Gold Coast from England was only $^3/_4$d. per square yard and they did not have additional reexport duties.[47] Transportation cost was also much less for *adire* producers in the Gold Coast, since they lived in or near their markets.

Egba dyers were also losing their market in the Congo at the same time that they were losing their market in the Gold Coast. A textile mill, which the UAC reported made good reproductions of Abeokuta *adire*, had opened in Léopoldville in 1929.[48] The factory was a modern integrated spinning and weaving plant, run by hydroelectric power. The plant as well as *adire* producers faced stiff competition from Japanese textile imports, including Japanese manufactured *adire*. Nonetheless, the plant was able to make inroads in the regional market especially after 1936 by reducing prices and making them more competitive with Japanese imports.[49] Thus in the Congo, Abeokuta dyers were competing with local and Japanese industrially manufactured *adire* as well as genuine (hand-made) *adire* produced by Yorubas living in the Congo.[50] The silence in the colonial records about Senegalese merchants during this period suggests that trade with Senegal also declined. It appears that after 1936 *adire* lost a significant portion of its export markets.

Adire's local market was also jeopardized by the renewed economic crisis in 1937. The fall in cocoa prices led to increased economic hardship for cocoa producers in Nigeria as well. There were reports of scattered produce holdups and calls for farmers around the country to organize and demand a government inquiry into the produce trade, but nothing comparable to the Gold Coast protests developed.[51] Cocoa production increased in Nigeria during the 1937–38 season as farmers tried to maintain their income.[52]

Despite producers' efforts, money was scarce. Many firms found it difficult to sell their stocks on hand, and some even resurrected the barter system, exchanging produce for manufactured goods.[53] Cloth sales, of course, reflected the poor economic state. Newspapers called attention to the fact that although the Muslim festival of Eid-el-Fitri and the Christian Christmas season were usually occasions when families bought cloth for new outfits, sales were considerably less as a result of the low produce prices.[54] *Adire* producers suffered equally under these conditions. The annual report of 1938–39 noted that

> As the direct result of the depressed cocoa prices the *adire* industry . . . dwindled away almost entirely, and the export trade to the Gold Coast became negligible.[55]

Once again, the difficulties dyers experienced were compounded by the actions of other social and economic sectors. As cocoa producers and European trading firms struggled to gain leverage over each other, *adire* producers were trammeled in the process.

It appears that the decline precipitated by this cycle of falling commodity prices, cocoa holdups, and increased competition was qualitatively different from the earlier declines. In the late 1920s, it was clear that the *adire* industry still held an important place in the town's economy. The trading firms and the *Alake* and council were willing to challenge *adire* producers over the incorporation of caustic soda and synthetic dyes into the production process. The absence of discussion about the further demise of the industry after 1937 suggests that *adire* was no longer considered a major industry.

The last brief exchange between the *Alake* and the dyers in 1939 sounded like a death knell. As the *Alake* inquired into the state of their affairs, the women told him that the present level of trade was "most discouraging."[56] Ademola expressed no greater depth of understanding of the constraints that the industry faced. As was his standard practice, he blamed the decline entirely on the dyers' use of caustic soda and synthetic dye and insisted that if they wanted their trade to recover, they must return to the old method.[57] It appears that the women finally gave up hope of receiving any help from the *Alake* and council. After this meeting, the dyers submitted a petition to the *Alake* stating that there was no demand for cloth dyed by the old method and that they were satisfied with their present small profits. They also asked to be left alone. The council informed them that they were free to do as they pleased.[58]

PROTECTING THE TREASURY

The renewed economic crisis reverberated in the treasury as well, and the colonial state took new steps to maintain revenue collection.

In Abeokuta a special political officer was brought in to improve tax collection, I.W.E. Dods. Dods arrived in Abeokuta on 25 August 1938 and immediately began an assessment of the existing tax system. He leveled his most severe criticism at compound heads (usually the eldest male in the compound), who were supposed to be the first link in the chain of collection. In order to stimulate compound heads to pursue tax collection more vigorously, Dods recommended that they be appointed "village headmen" under the Native Revenue Ordinance.[59] Under the ordinance, village headmen were recognized as government agents for collecting taxes. If they failed to carry out their duty, they could be liable for prosecution.[60] They also received a minimum of 5 percent of the taxes they collected.[61] Dods also recommended that compound heads receive the 5 percent remuneration only on the taxes they personally brought to the treasury. They were not to be credited for taxes brought in by individual members of their compounds. These changes represented a significant concession, for in previous years compound heads received a percentage only of the taxes they collected during the first month. Dods hoped that by giving compound heads the force of law and greater financial rewards they would enforce tax collection.

In spite of the potential financial gain, the social costs of enforcing tax collection may have been much greater than Dods appreciated. He expressed bitter disappointment that "daily receipts . . . far from increasing fell [from £5] to an average of little over £3 for the period the 8th September to the 30th of November."[62] He ascribed this "apathy" to three factors: (1) the compound head is usually the head of a family or extended family; there were few large compounds; (2) prices for produce had fallen and money was scarce; and (3) in recent years tax defaulters had not been summoned to court. His first theory is quite intriguing, because it suggests that the sizes of households or compounds may have changed significantly. Rather than the large compounds of the nineteenth century that included husband, wives, children, and an assortment of dependents—slaves, pawns, and clients—a more nuclear pattern may have emerged. Smaller compounds also suggest that the economic base of the compound head had shrunk, so that both the social and material cost of appropriating their limited resources for the benefit of the colonial state was quite high. Regardless of his insights, Dods was committed to following through on his charge, and he began issuing court summonses.

The court summonses had the desired effect. Tax collection increased to an average of £42 per day.[63] Yet by January tax collection slowed again. Dods reported that many of the people who came to the tax office came not to pay taxes but to report that they had moved from Abeokuta town and paid their tax to one of the district collecting centers. It appears that this outmigration from Abeokuta was shaped by the depression as well as the tax structure. Since trade was so poor, many who may have been small traders returned to farming or left to live with relatives in the rural areas.[64] In addition, urban residents had a slightly higher tax bill than rural residents because they paid a flat water rate of 1 s. per person. Rural residents were not subject to this additional tax because the waterworks system did not yet extend beyond the town.

Further research is needed before any definitive conclusions can be drawn about the relationship between the depression, taxes—specifically the water rate—and migration to the rural areas.[65] Nonetheless, it may in part account for Abeokuta's large rural population in relation to other Yoruba towns. The 1952 census showed that Abeokuta's urban population was the lowest among the major Yoruba towns, 21.6 percent. Ibadan's urban population was 68 percent, Oyo's 64 percent, and Ijebu's 40 percent. Magbogunje attributed much of the migration in the 1950s to the establishment of new cocoa farms in the northeast and northwest sections of the division, but it is possible that the economic crisis during the depression contributed significantly to the crystallization of this pattern. If indeed migration was a response to the higher tax burden in Abeokuta town, it was a passive form of resistance. Some taxpayers chose more direct ways to confront their tax burden.

There was a minor agitation among certain artisans against paying special assessments. Adults who earned a minimum of £40 per year paid a special assessment tax of 1 percent. Income from rents was assessed at 5 percent. The Resident, in conjunction with the *Alake* and chiefs who made up the assessment committee, estimated the annual value of profits from trade and manufacturing and then recommended the sum which each person should be assessed.[66] Two master carpenters who had been assessed in the high tax bracket by the assessment committee refused to pay their 1937–38 tax, arguing that the assessment was too high and the Resident had not approved it.[67] The men had journeymen and apprentices working with them and had been assessed £50. Though they were convicted as tax defaulters in a lower court, they carried their case to the High Court of Appeal, where Sir William Geary successfully defended them.[68]

In 1938 the two master carpenters who had won the Appeals case were again assessed for £50. Again they protested their assessment, but on this occasion their protest did not get very far. A petition claiming to represent "Artisans in Abeokuta" was circulated on behalf of these two carpenters. The petition was written by Doherty, the letter writer. In it, he stated that assessments were too high and that tradesmen in Abeokuta could not pay more than the minimum rate flat tax, 5s. However, before the petition was sent to Dods for his action, the men paid their taxes and the matter lapsed.[69] It is unclear whether this was an aborted attempt to organize a concerted protest against the special assessment. Even without any organized action, the financial situation was such that the number of people in the higher tax bracket decreased between the 1937–38 tax year and the 1938–39 year. More people paid the minimum flat rate.[70] In several cases, officials reduced taxes on entire occupational groups. For example, the special assessment on corn-mill owners was reduced from 10s. to 7s./6d., while kola sellers were exempted from special assessment altogether.[71]

Many individuals resisted by not paying taxes at all. In the past, tax defaulters were not pursued aggressively by tax collectors, but during Dods's tenure a greater percentage of defaulters were brought into court. Increasingly they were being imprisoned for up to one month. Defaulters who were determined to be able to pay their taxes were also fined court fees up to £5.[72] The record of tax default suggests that women were experiencing greater financial hardship than men during this period. By January 1939, summonses for failure to pay taxes had been issued to 791 women and 324 men. A similar ratio was evident in cases of tax exemptions. Exemptions were granted to 267 females and to 134 males as a result of "old age, infirmity, or some other reason that prevents them from earning more than the bare means of subsistence."[73]

The struggle to collect taxes reflected the profound downturn in the economy. In the 1938 annual report the Resident lamented

> These poor trade conditions have been reflected in the revenue of the Native Treasuries. . . . [the] collection of the annual tax was so delayed that the resources of the treasury were subjected to very severe strain. . . . If . . . the general situation does not improve at a fairly early date, drastic economies will be absolutely necessary.[74]

He elaborated on the state of the economy:

> As the direct result of the depressed cocoa prices the *adire* industry
> . . . dwindled away almost entirely, and the export trade to the Gold

Coast became negligible. . . . The kola trade which is of great importance in the southern part of Egba division, did nothing to relieve the situation, prices are being depressed almost to vanishing point.[75]

The year 1939 began as bleakly as the preceding year ended. Prices for produce for export and for local consumption were extremely low. In July cocoa prices dipped to £8/7s./6d. per ton. The annual report acknowledged that the peoples' standard of living was in danger of being seriously affected. The district officer of Egba division summed up the economic picture as follows:

Internal trade is not in a satisfactory condition. Now that the *Adire* cloth industry has to all intents and purposes collapsed and the bottom has fallen out of the kola trade, the Egbas have little to fall back upon save farm produce. . . . Efforts are being made to stimulate rice growing and livestock breeding, to go some way towards making the Division eventually self sufficient and in a position to balance up drops in external trade with internal profits.[76]

Once again tax collection was extremely difficult, particularly since officials were trying to collect arrears from 1938 as well as taxes for the 1939–40 tax year. Tax collection virtually came to a standstill in August, and as the *Alake* and council prepared the first draft of the 1940–41 estimates, they agreed to a 10 percent cut in their own salaries. In order to stave off bankruptcy, the *Alake* and the district officer visited all the district headquarters exhorting people to pay their taxes promptly and in full. Those visits did not have the desired effect, so by the end of September the state began to prosecute defaulters severely.[77]

While the officials in the field pursued tax defaulters, it became clear within the central administration that the colonial government had to reconsider its laissez-faire attitude toward the produce trade.[78] During the earlier phases of the depression, the colonial government had done little to assist African producers. After 1922 the Agricultural Department encouraged the formation of farming societies, especially among cocoa producers, in order to improve agricultural and fermentation methods and to serve as useful links between European buyers and peasant farmers.[79] By the early 1930s, they tried to develop overseas markets for citrus fruits in order to diversify exports. The 1932 annual report noted that

Agricultural Officers from Ibadan and Agege frequently visited the Province during the year. The Agricultural Department has advised and encouraged growers of pine apples in the Otta district in connexion with the export of this fruit. The names of farmers supplying fruit for export have been registered. The United Africa Company are now taking an interest and pine apples purchased by them are kept in cold storage pending shipment.[80]

Pineapples and other citrus crops were nonetheless secondary to the area's main export, cocoa.

The political tensions around the cocoa holdup, and fear of renewed tensions at the start of World War II, forced the colonial government to intervene.[81] In 1939 the government purchased the entire Nigerian cocoa crop. In the Egba Division the price was approximately £15/ 12s./6d. The Resident acknowledged that the price did not provide fabulous profits, but it was a welcome relief because it "assured a reasonable return to both the producer and the purchaser."[82] Although Fieldhouse highlights the war as a compelling factor, it is clear that officials on the ground were equally concerned about the stagnation in income and livelihoods.

While the state intervened in the interest of cocoa producers, *adire* producers were left to fare according to unregulated market conditions. In 1935 the acting director of education participated in a discussion about the development of local industries. Officials began a survey of indigenous blacksmithing, shoe production, dyeing, basketry, and a range of other crafts. They considered several options to assist craft producers but recognized that they had to learn much more about these industries before any plans could be adopted.[83]

The most concrete proposal that emerged from the discussions was a plan to conduct a more detailed and systematic survey of local crafts. They specified the areas to be investigated during the survey: materials and where obtained; tools; processes, step by step; workers—man's or woman's work, how apprentices are taught; history and traditions; religious meaning and symbolism; organization and how goods are marketed; vocabulary in local language of technical terms.[84] The discussion is insightful because it revealed how poorly colonial officials understood the critical role these industries played in the colonial economy. For example, they argued that

> Crafts are not practised solely to make money. They please the people
> and fill in their time profitably. It is not to be assumed that labour-

saving devices are wanted at all. Commercialism is as yet a comparative stranger here.[85]

The discussions reflected many prevailing stereotypes about African artisans—for example, that they were conservative and their industries static. The participants expressed little appreciation of the
range of innovations that craft producers could and did employ. They
were correct that crafts were not practiced only to make money, but
neither were crafts a hobby. Certain crafts like dyeing were occupational niches. Dyers relied on this industry to generate an income that
allowed them to meet their social and familial obligations and pay
their taxes. Thus, like other producers, craftsmen and women worried
about markets, credit, and labor. The economic importance of certain
craft sectors extended well beyond a quaint hobby. The state's failure
to recognize the importance of craft production to the colonial
economy contributed to a perception that craft producers did not require urgent assistance even during the depression.

ADIRE IN A WIDER SOCIAL CONTEXT

Adire's position was not defined only by the economic context in which
the dyers operated. Cultural preference and taste helped create the markets which *adire* producers satisfied. As we saw in preceding chapters,
adire producers incorporated imported textiles in order to create products
that catered to the social and economic demands of an expanding consumer society. These cloths, with their innovative patterns and highly valued indigo color, helped fill the demand for relatively inexpensive cloths
in a fashion-conscious society. But taste and styles underwent constant
change. *Adire* producers thus always competed in a larger cultural and
aesthetic context in which a wide array of changes were being introduced
and incorporated.

From the mid nineteenth century onward, styles of dress were borrowed from European as well as other African cultures. The Elder
Dempster shipping line stopped in Sierra Leone, the Gold Coast, and
Nigeria, facilitating an exchange of goods and people along the West
African coast. Saro dress styles from Sierra Leone as well as styles
from the Gold Coast became popular in Lagos. The Saro styles included a basically western dress with intricate decorative detail on the
bodice. The *Agaayin* style from the Gold Coast was a fitted bodice
ending in a peplum that was worn over an ankle-length wrapper.[86] In
the mid-1930s, Yoruba women in Lagos also adopted the Fanti (Gold

Coast) women's style of wrapping their cloths. This trend, called "Going Fanti," erupted into a controversy. Even though it was recognized that the method Fanti women used was more efficient in keeping their garments together, opponents felt that the Yoruba women should devise their own innovation rather than copy another.[87]

The expansion of the colonial bureaucracy and education also contributed to changing fashions, for they increased the number of venues and experiences where European dress was certainly preferred if not mandatory. A former missionary in southern Nigeria writing in 1937 captured the advancing trend toward European clothing he had observed:

> Up to the time when the Government began to take an active interest in education the schools were simple and homely. The teachers generally wore African dress, and the older scholars did the same, and looked well in the gracefully draped, coloured cloths. The small children often wore nothing—and looked sweet in their innocence. The School syllabuses did not go beyond Standard IV, and most of the instruction was given in the vernacular.

> Today, English dress for teachers and scholars in Government-aided schools is practically compulsory; school methods follow closely those of Europe; "Native" buildings are replaced every where by those with iron roofs and concrete floors; European school apparatus is used as far as means allow; boys have little chance of employment unless they pass Standard VI and can speak English and examinations organised in England are popular with teachers and scholars.

> In boarding schools and training colleges the influences are much stronger. . . . A uniform is generally insisted on, and is certainly not African in character—including a cap or hat with a distinctive badge or band.

> In social life, outside school, the forces in the direction of "Europeanisation" are equally strong. . . . When young Africans take up English sports . . . and get up dances in European style—where men and women wear evening dress—they receive an amount of attention from Europeans that they would never arouse by doing something purely "African."

> . . . Government Departments . . . act as stimulants to "Europeanisation." . . . English dress is universal amongst Government clerks.

Soldiers, police, interpreters, messengers and employees of the Marine are all dressed compulsorily in uniforms anything but "Native" and designed and manufactured in Europe.[88]

European dress became integrated into the symbolic representation of education, Christianity, and social mobility. European dress was particularly emphasized among Christian, educated elites. In a study of Yoruba dress, which examined five generations of a Christian Lagos family in which a number of descendants became professionals, Wass found that western modes of dress predominated during the period 1900–39.[89] European clothes were also promoted in the press. Pictures of people in the news showed a range of clothing styles, but even in the *West African Pilot*—that symbol of increased political awareness and sophistication[90]—the fashion pages almost exclusively focused on European dress. In a section designaed to be of interest to women, "Milady's Bower," readers could find pictures of a "nice alpine dress . . . in white woolen material," an "elegant summer coat . . . in black crepe georgette,"[91] knitted frocks,[92] and the latest hats worn by spectators at the races.[93]

Despite the popularity of European dress, elite Christian women still wore the classic *iro* and *buba* in numerous social settings. They were credited with establishing the popularity of *aso-ebi*. *Aso-ebi* derived from *aso ti ebi da jo,* which were the various cloths family members contributed as grave goods for the dead. In the 1920s, bereaved family members began to use uniform handwoven fabrics for easy recognition within the church congregation.[94] They adopted the term *aso-ebi* to describe these matching fabrics worn by family members during burials. Elite churches restricted the use of traditional dress at funerals, but Christian women adapted and expanded the *aso-ebi* practice that had developed for these occasions. These women used imported cloth, baptized it with a ritual name, made it into local garments, and wore them for important Christian events.[95] *Aso-ebi* extended to ceremonies beyond the church and to the general population as it moved inland from Lagos. It was used to mark birthdays, and young girls even began to demand it as part of their engagement presents. Many women became indebted because they needed a new *aso-ebi* for every event. The practice came under severe criticism from men as well as from the colonial state, and by the 1940s there were attempts to ban it.

Among the educated elites, there was an inverse relationship between nationalist sentiment and the popularity of European dress. The use of traditional dress increased during the nationalist periods. As we saw in Chapter 2, there was a cultural nationalist movement at the turn of the century that advocated a return to traditional styles. A similar effort emerged during the worst moments of the depression in 1931, when many adopted the slogan "Back to the Land." Advocates argued that in order to stabilize the country's economic situation, Nigerians needed to improve farmlands and patronize local industries. They encouraged the use of "native" attire and "the whole country seemed to become crazy for Native dress. . . . Everybody at the least opportunity, went into costly dresses cut into Native fashion but made of foreign stuffs."[96] The commentator's exasperation was evident when he pointed out that wearing "native" fashion made with imported cloth defeated the main objective of the movement.

Aesthetic changes were not limited to educated elites. There was an increasing preference for brightly colored materials.[97] This preference for brighter colors was a much more pervasive change, and it did not have the social connotations that came with Western dress. The market for brighter colors did not begin with colonialism. As early as the fourteenth century, Indian textiles found a niche in West Africa, especially parts of eastern Nigeria, because they were colorful and light. Indian cloths such as madras dominated the West African market until the nineteenth century and continued to be very popular into the twentieth century.[98] Waxprints made in Japan, the Netherlands, England, and Switzerland for the West African market also satisfied this desire for light, brightly colored cloths. Importation of wax prints increased significantly after 1890, despite import restrictions during both world wars and the 1930s.[99] These cloths combined a variety of colors with motifs taken from Indian cloths, Javanese batiks, European prints, and African indigenous cloths, as well as traditional African objects and symbols. African traders, especially market women, also suggested designs. The most popular cloths were given names and were incorporated into a network of cultural associations. A successful cloth would be in demand for several years.[100] While other cloths grew in popularity and stature, *adire* increasingly became the cloth of last resort. Betty Oyeboyejo recalled that when she first moved to Nigeria in 1963, *adire* was considered "poor people's cloth, made by poor people for poor people."[101]

Despite their waning popularity, *adire* producers held onto a share of the market. By the 1960s *adire* producers also began to experiment with different colors.[102] An excursion into the dyeing compounds and markets today reveal a wide array of colors from the traditional indigo to bright yellows and reds. Color combinations have become as integral to *adire* as the patterns on the cloth. These changes in popularity, fashions, and styles reflect the dynamic economic and cultural contexts in which *adire* producers have always had to operate. Ultimately, 1939 was a dire moment in the history of *adire* production in Abeokuta, but not its demise.

CONCLUSION

In literal terms, collapse is not synonymous with disappearance. Nonetheless, this phase of the depression dramatically changed the *adire* industry. *Adire* producers lost a substantial share of their export markets. This transition entailed a dramatic decline in the overall volume of production and the loss of the industry's strategic importance in relation to other sectors of the economy, as well as a loss of income. The collapse of *adire*'s export market coincided with its disappearance from official notice. Colonial officials were most concerned with the industry when it competed on a regional level. Dyeing for a local market was not "seen" and was not of statistical interest to colonial officials.

Adire's reduction to a local industry was the outcome of several critical economic developments. The fall in cocoa prices was just one dimension of the changes that adversely affected the industry, yet it was probably the major contributor to the demise of the industry during the period. Abeokuta dyers also lost their dominant position at the center of production. Improvements in transportation that had facilitated the movement of buyers to Abeokuta also favored the establishment of Yoruba diasporas in the Gold Coast and the Congo, where expatriate communities became new centers of production. Proximity to these foreign markets gave them advantages over producers resident in Abeokuta. Similarly, machine-produced *adire* had pricing advantages against which dyers in Abeokuta could not compete.

Dyers in Abeokuta had no control over these factors. In addition, they did not have the economic base or the political support to compete for the retention of their export market. Contraction and impoverishment did not favor cohesion and impeded their efforts to regulate trade in Abeokuta. Within a few decades the international and regional economy that had facilitated the rise of the *adire* industry now contributed to its decline. Nonetheless, neither dyeing nor *adire* production disappeared from Abeokuta's economic or social landscape. A market for *adire* remained and provided a livelihood for those women who continued to dye.

NOTES

1. Interview with Wosinatu Adeniji, 1 June 1988, Ikereku, Abeokuta.
2. Interview with Alhaja Bakare, 27 June 1988, Hoku Market, Abeokuta.
3. Interview with Madam Sidikat Ayinde, 5 August 1988, Itoku, Abeokuta.
4. Interview with Alhaja Falilat Tukuru, 23 August 1988, Kemta, Abeokuta.
5. Interview with Alhaja Bakare, 27 June 1988, Itoku Market, Abeokuta.
6. Interview with Alhaja Falilat Tukuru, 23 August 1988, Kemta, Abeokuta.
7. Interview with Alhaja Bakare, 27 June 1988, Itoku Market, Abeokuta; with Alhaja Soetan, 1 September 1988, Kemta, Abeokuta; with Alhaja Falilat Tukuru, 23 August 1988, Kemta, Abeokuta.
8. Kenneth Little, *African Women in Towns: An Aspect of Africa's Social Revolution* (Cambridge: Cambridge University Press, 1973), 50. Also see Gloria Marshall, "Women, Trade, and The Yoruba Family," Ph.D. diss., Columbia University, 1964.
9. Minutes of Council Meeting, 19 August 1937. Abe Prof. 1/1-ABP 236, vol. 4 (NAI).
10. Minutes of Extraordinary Meeting, 21 August 1937. Abe Prof 1/1 ABP 236, vol. 4 (NAI).
11. Interview with Alhaja Soetan, 1 September 1988, Kemta, Abeokuta. *Baba* is the equivalent of father in Yoruba. Thus it appears that the adviser was male.
12. Interview with Alhaja Bakare, 27 June 1988, Itoku, Abeokuta. She explained that this was an honorary title that did not require official duties.
13. Constitutional Rules and Regulations of the Egba Women Dyers and Adire Trading Union. CSO 26 28400, vol. 3 (NAI).
14. Minutes of Egba Council Meeting, 9 August 1937. Abe Prof. 1/1/ ABP 236, vol. 4 (NAI).
15. Continuation Sheet 252. CSO 26 28400, vol. 3 (NAI).
16. Continuation Sheet 259, note from the attorney-general to the chief secretary, 21 August 1937. CSO 26 28400, vol. 3 (NAI).
17. Minutes of Extraordinary Meeting, 21 August 1937, 10. Abe Prof. 1/1 ABP 236, vol. 4 (NAI).
18. Minutes of Extraordinary Meeting, 21 August 1937. Abe Prof. 1/1 ABP 236, vol. 4 (NAI).
19. Minutes of Council Meeting, 19 August 1937, p. 4. Abe Prof. 1/1 ABP 236, vol. 4 (NAI).
20. Minutes of Council Meeting, 19 August 1937, p. 4. Abe Prof. 1/1 ABP 236, vol. 4 (NAI).
21. Minutes of Egba Council Meeting, 21 August 1937, 5. Abe Prof. 1/1 ABP 236, vol. 4 (NAI). He had received small loans for £2 and £4 on earlier occasions. He approached them for a third loan of £8 to pursue a case against the Native Administration in which dyers were not involved.
22. Ibid., 2.
23. Ibid., 2–3.
24. The committee received the endorsement of the governor, secretary of the Southern Provinces as well as the chief secretary of the government. See letter from

A.R.A. Dickens, acting secretary, Southern Provinces to the chief secretary of the government, 11 May 1936. ECR 1/1/46 (NAA).

25. Minutes of Egba Council Meeting, 21 August 1937, 9–10. Abe Prof. 1/1 ABP 236, vol. 4 (NAI).

26. Ibid., 12.

27. Ibid., 11.

28. Ibid., 13.

29. N.A. Fadipe, "A Yoruba Town: A Sociological Study of Abeokuta in the British Colony and Protectorate of Nigeria, West Coast of Africa," M.A. thesis, Columbia University, 1931, 58.

30. Annual Report, Abeokuta Province, 1936, 25. CSO 26/2 11875, vol. 13 (NAI).

31. Annual Report, Abeokuta Province, 1938, 31–32. CSO 26/2 11875, vol. 14 (NAI).

32. Annual Report, Abeokuta Province, 1937, 22. CSO 26/2 11875, vol. 13 (NAI). Palm oil, for example, began the year at £20 per ton and ended the year at £7/19/3 per ton.

33. Rod Alence, "The 1937–1938 Gold Coast Cocoa Crisis: The Political Economy of Commercial Stalemate," *African Economic History* 19 (1990–91): 8. The fall in the cocoa price was partly due to a sharp decline in American demand.

34. Annual Report, Abeokuta Province, 1937, 8. CSO 26/2 11875, vol. 13 (NAI).

35. John Miles, "Rural Protest in the Gold Coast: The Coca Holdups, 1908–1938," in Clive Dewey and Anthony G. Hopkins, eds., *The Imperial Impact: Studies in the Economic History of Africa and India* (London: Athlone Press, 1978).

36. Alence, "1937–1938 Gold Coast," 88. For a discussion of UAC's role, see D.K. Fieldhouse, *Merchant Capital and Economic Decolonization: The United Africa Company 1929–1989* (Oxford: Clarendon Press, 1994), 124–75.

37. Alence, "1937–1938 Gold Coast," 99.

38. Miles, "Rural Protest," 157.

39. Letter from the general manager, UAC, to the chief secretary of the government, 13 April 1939. CSO 26 28400, vol. 3 (NAI).

40. Letter from the acting comptroller, K. S. Martin, to the financial secretary, Lagos, 27 April 1939. CSO 26/2 228400, vol. 3 (NAI).

41. Ibid.

42. Minutes to letter from the acting comptroller to the financial secretary, 27 April 1939. CSO 26/2 28400, vol. 3 (NAI).

43. Ibid.

44. Letter from the acting financial secretary, S.R. Marlow, to the general manger, UAC, 26 June 1939. CSO 26 28400, vol. 3 (NAI).

45. Carolyn Keyes, "*Adire:* Cloth, Gender and Social Change In Southwestern Nigeria, 1841–1991," Ph.D. diss., University of Wisconsin–Madison, 1993, 31.

46. Niara Sudarkasa, "The Economic Status of the Yoruba in Ghana Before 1970," *Nigerian Journal of Economic and Social Studies* 17, 1 (March 1975): 98.

47. Letter from the acting comptroller, K.S. Martin, to the financial secretary, Lagos, 27 April 1939. CSO 26/2 28400, vol. 3 (NAI).

48. Letter from the general manager, UAC, to the chief secretary of the government, 13 April 1939. CSO 26 28400, vol. 3 (NAI).

49. Gervase Clarence-Smith, "The Effects of the Great Depression on Industrialisation in Equatorial and Central Africa," in Ian Brown, ed., *The Economies of Africa and Asia in the Inter-war Depression* (London: Routledge, 1989), 193.

50. Letter from the general manager, UAC, to the chief secretary of the government, 13 April 1939. CSO 26 28400, vol. 3 (NAI).

51. See "Import Trade," *West African Pilot*, 17 September 1938, and "Our Produce Trade," *West African Pilot,* 28 October 1938. There were holdups in Warri as well as in Ibibio and Urhobo districts in eastern Nigeria. Producers in Warri also organized a boycott of foreign goods.

52. Alence, "1937–1938 Gold Coast," 100.

53. "Import Trade," *West African Pilot,* 17 September 1938.

54. See "Business Notes," *West African Pilot,* 14 November 1938, and "Business Notes" *West African Pilot,* 1 December 1938.

55. Annual Report, Abeokuta Province, 1938–39, 16. CSO 26/2 11875, vol. 14 (NAI).

56. *Nigerian Daily Times,* 5 May 1939.

57. Ibid.

58. Letter from the secretary, Western Province, to the financial secretary, Lagos, 13 June 1939. CSO 28400, vol. 3 (NAI).

59. I.W.E. Dods, Report on Tax Collection in the Egba Division for the Year 1938–39, 3. ECR 1/1/12 (NAA).

60. I.W.E. Dods, "Tax Collection in Abeokuta," *Nigerian Daily Times,* 12 October 1938. Abe Prof. 1/1 ABP 1240 (NAI).

61. Frederick Lugard, *Political Memoranda: Revision of Instructions to Political Officers on Subjects Chiefly Political and Administrative, 1913–1918,* 3d ed., A.H.M. Kirk-Greene, ed. (London: Frank Cass, 1970), 184, 195.

62. I.W.E. Dods, Report on Tax Collection in the Egba Division for the Year 1938–39, 4. ECR 1/1/12 (NAA).

63. Ibid., 6.

64. Ibid., 8.

65. Mabogunje, "The Changing Pattern of Rural Settlement and Rural Economy in Egba Division, South Western Nigeria," M.A. thesis, University of London. Mabogunje attributes the urban to rural migration in Egba Division to the development of cocoa farms in new parts of the division. As the trees in the first areas brought under cocoa cultivation and in areas closer to the town died by the end of the 1930s, farmers opened new cocoa farms in the northeast and northwest sections of the division.

66. I.W.E. Dods, Report on Tax Collection in the Egba Division for the Year 1938–39, 10–11. ECR 1/1/12 (NAA).

67. Annual Report, Abeokuta Province, 1937. CSO26/2 11875, vol. 13 (NAI).

68. I.W.E. Dods, Report on Tax Collection in the Egba Division for the Year 1938–39, 11, 13–15. ECR 1/1/12 (NAA).

69. Ibid., 13-14. ECR 1/1/12 (NAA). The actual petition was not located. It was discussed at length in Dods's report, which stated that Doherty's was the only signature on the petition. Doherty was well known to Dods, for they had a lengthy dispute over Doherty's own tax assessment. Doherty's income was assessed at £50,

which Dods thought was accurate, given the number of letters he wrote on behalf of nonliterate members of the community.

70. Ibid., 15.

71. Assessment Committee Meetings and Deliberations, 1937–1940. Abe Prof. 1/ 1 ABP 1208 (NAI).

72. Minutes of Egba Council Meeting, 30 November 1939. ECR 1/1/97, vol. 1 (NAA).

73. I.W.E. Dods, Report on Tax Collection in the Egba Division for the Year 1938–39, 28. ECR 1/1/12 (NAA).

74. Annual Report, Abeokuta Province, 1938–39, 16. CSO 26/2 11875, vol. 14 (NAI).

75. Ibid., 15–16.

76. Egba Division Annual Report, 1939–40, 9. ECR 1/1/12 (NAA). He was obviously equating farm produce with foodstuffs.

77. Ibid, 5–7. ECR 1/1/12 (NAA).

78. C.E.F. Beer, *The Politics of Peasant Groups in Western Nigeria* (Ibadan: University of Ibadan Press, 1976), 25.

79. Beer, *Politics of Peasant,* 20.

80. Annual Report, Abeokuta Province, 1932, 47. CSO 26/2 11875, vol. 9 (NAI).

81. The Nowell Commission, which investigated the cocoa holdup, proposed in 1938 the creation of a statutory association to assemble and sell the entire cocoa crop. The association was to be run by a board made up of colonial government officials and African members. European firms as well as African producers were against it. When the war began, the firms changed their objection and appealed to the state to intervene, since the loss of enemy markets meant that prices would remain depressed and possibly result in political crisis. Fieldhouse argues that this logic was very effective with the colonial government and compelled them to finally act. Fieldhouse, *Merchant Capital,* 229–33.

82. Annual Report, Abeokuta Province,1 939, 3–4. CSO 26/2 11875, vol. 14. These prices stand in stark contrast to the pre–World War I era. Miles argues that the "highest average annual price in the 1930s was only slightly above the lowest pre-1914 price." See Miles, "Rural Protest," 155.

83. Stanley Milburn, "Notes on the Development of Local Crafts and Industries," 4. MSS AFR.S.1167. Rhodes House.

84. Ibid., Appendix, 5.

85. Ibid., 4.

86. Betty Wass, "Yoruba Dress: A Systematic Case Study of Five Generations of a Lagos Family," Ph.D. diss., Michigan State University, 1975, 68–69.

87. N.A. Fadipe, "Stirring Up West Africa," *West Africa,* 26 September 1936. This controversy evolved from a larger discussion on the problems of "detribalization." Anthropologists, colonial officials, and nationalists concurred on the evils of "detribalization," though from different positions. Also see *West Africa,* 19 September; 3, 10, 17, and 24 October.

88. Anonymous, "'Europeanisation' in West Africa: A Continuous Process in Southern Nigeria," *West Africa,* 20 March 1937.

89. Betty Wass, "Yoruba Dress in Five Generations of a Lagos Family," in Justine M. Cordwell and Ronald A. Schwarz, eds., *The Fabrics of Culture: An Anthropology of Clothing and Adornment* (New York: Mouton, 1979), 334.

90. Omu, *Press and Politics in Nigeria*, 240. The *Pilot* was launched in 1937 by Nnamdi Azikiwe.

91. "Milady's Bower," *West African Pilot,* 28 August 1938.

92. Ibid., 11 September 1938.

93. Ibid., 12 August 1938.

94. Akinwumi, "The Commemorative Phenomenon of Textile Use among the Yoruba," 171–73.

95. Keyes, "Adire," 326–27.

96. "Business Notes," *West African Pilot,* 30 August 1938.

97. Letter from the general manager, UAC, to the chief secretary of the government, 13 April 1939. CSO 26 28400, vol. 3 (NAI).

98. Ruth Nielsen, "The History and Development of Wax-Printed Textiles Intended for West Africa and Zaire," in Justine M. Cordwell and Ronald Schwarz, eds., *The Fabrics of Culture: The Anthropology of Clothing and Adornment*, ed. (New York: Mouton, 1979), 471. In some communities Indian madras was incorporated into their culture to mark both ethnicity and status. See Joanne Eicher and Tonye Erekosima, "Why Do They Call It Kalabari? Cultural Authentication and the Demarcation of Ethnic Identity," in Joanne Eicher, ed., *Dress and Ethnicity* (Oxford: Berg Press, 1995): 139–64.

99. Nielsen, "History and Development of Wax-Printed," 474; Fieldhouse, *Merchant Capital,* 109.

100. Nielsen, "History and Development of Wax-Printed," 481–82.

101. Interview with Betty Oyeboyejo, 24 September 1988, Maryland, Lagos.

102. Justine Cordwell, "The Art and Aesthetics of the Yoruba," *African Arts* 16, 2 (1983): 56–59, 93–94.

CONCLUSION

This study illuminates several important considerations in women's socioeconomic and political history in Abeokuta specifically, and West Africa in general. It contextualizes the lives of the craftswomen who were its central focus, and locates them within the currents of events and processes that transformed their society from the end of the nineteenth century until the beginning of World War II. It delineates the very specific ways in which these women became integrated into the international economy. As purchasers and finishers of imported cloth, they became important players in the circuits of commodity and capital between metropole and colony. The study also illustrates their active engagement with those processes. Dyers cultivated extensive relations with creditors and consumers who were vital to the health of the industry. Many flourished as a result of the enhancement of their structural position and became autonomous owners, managers, and credit brokers. But the decline of the international economy in the 1920s and 1930s undermined their success. When international and regional markets collapsed, their economic position was ruined. Yet they were not passive victims. They used a variety of economic and political measures in their attempts to hold onto their livelihood.

This study conveys the complex milieu in which these women operated. It captures the dynamic and fluid relationship between dyers and other segments of the economy and between dyers and their allied and dependent workers and puts these relationships in historical perspective. In the wider arena, dyers competed with other producers and traders for credit, labor, and the state's assistance. Gender clearly shaped their access to resources and put them at a distinct disadvantage with their European and Egba male counterparts. The state was an equally active variable in this complex. Officials often put concerns about revenue collection above the circumstances of the people or certain industries. Thus, dyers had to struggle to protect their interests from the encroachment of European and Egba male traders as well as the state. Dyers were not just an amorphous group fending off competing interests from external protagonists. They were a stratified and internally contested group. Their ranks reflected distinctions of age, religion, wealth, and social status that generated competing interests, as well as multiple strategies and options in the evolving political economy.

For all that it illuminates, this study simultaneously raises questions that call for further research and critical analysis of the processes and events that shaped women's lives in Abeokuta. New questions must be asked about the development of the regional economy, particularly during the colonial period, the relationship between women and the colonial state, and the nature of changing gender relations. These conclusions summarize the findings on a series of topics and point to the necessary steps forward.

ABEOKUTA AND THE REGIONAL ECONOMY

Most studies on trade and economic development in Abeokuta during the colonial period focus on the development of cash crops and the town's integration into the schemes of the British empire. Although trade with Britain was paramount in the minds of colonial officials, it is clear that West African traders forged and reinforced economic relations between colonies. Some overland trade routes, such as the trans-Saharan, declined precipitously, but others continued to thrive. Sea routes became more important as male and female African traders plied the coast in steamers. Research on waterborne trade, particularly on the African customers of European and African vessels, will contribute greatly to our understanding of the regional trade networks that were created or continued under colonialism.

The movement of goods between colonies by African traders was not always reflected in economic indices, but they formed an important part of local economies. The movement of *adire* between the Gold Coast, Senegal, and Abeokuta is a striking example of a poorly documented but important trade that linked producers and traders from these colonies to each other and to the international economy. Since colonial officials primarily recorded the movement of cloth from England to Nigeria, significant elements of the industry were invisible to data collectors. Colonial records have told us very little about the Senegalese traders who visited Abeokuta or the Yoruba traders who took cloth to the Gold Coast. Clearly, more information about these traders will provide important insights about capital accumulation and the commercial networks that spanned these great distances.

Further analysis of regional trade is also important because much more than goods moved across borders. People, fashions, ideas, and technology also migrated. A different social history of towns like Lagos and Abeokuta that received these goods and people may emerge if we have a fuller picture of the range of influences that were borrowed, assimilated, and transformed from one colony to another.

Abeokuta was also part of a Yoruba regional economy. A variety of sources provide a broad outline of the extensive economic relations between the Yoruba states, especially after the fall of the Oyo empire. Nonetheless, far greater attention has been focused on the political relationship between these states and the colonial state. Equal attention needs to be directed to economic relations between Yoruba states during the nineteenth century and the colonial period. As this study demonstrates, trade relations between Yoruba towns remained quite important. Traders from other Yoruba towns helped expand Abeokuta's integration into the wider West African regional economy.

WOMEN ENTREPRENEURS AND ECONOMIC CHANGE

The political and economic fluidity that characterized Abeokuta's political economy during much of the nineteenth century created opportunities for women with sufficient capital to engage in both internal and external trade. Dyers' commercial success appears to have continued a pattern of greater female engagement in the international economy since the mid nineteenth century. The nature of women's involvement in international trade underwent important shifts as trade relations between Europe and Africa changed. Madam Tinubu, the first *Iyalode* of Abeokuta, made her fortune by trading slaves, ammunition, and later palm oil. Her successor, Madam Jojolola, raised foodstuffs, especially corn, and was an important cloth trader and *adire* producer.

The commodities on which Madam Tinubu's and Madam Jojolola's fortunes were based also reflected changes in the social composition of traders in external trade. Trade in slaves and ammunition required a substantial capital base. *Adire* production, on the other hand, was within reach of many more women, though it certainly required more capital than trade in foodstuffs. It appears that as the cloth trade and the production of *adire* succeeded trade in slaves and palm oil, they increased the opportunity for women with smaller capital bases to become involved in international trade.

The scale of production of women entrepreneurs changed over the period of this study. The number of dependents and the size of one's labor force were signs of wealth. Madame Tinubu, like her male counterparts, employed numerous slaves in her trading operations and in her private army. Her army allowed her to participate in Egba politics in a very forceful manner. Madame Jojolola also employed slaves as well as pawns, but sources suggest that she did not have as extensive a labor force as the previous generation of entrepreneurs. Slavery declined significantly after the imposition of colonial rule, and she did not and could not have had a private army because the colonial state monopolized military power. The next generation of traders took advantage of the available opportunities, and some did become quite wealthy, but it does not appear that they were able to achieve the same economic or political stature as their nineteenth-century predecessors.

The new social structure and women's position in the evolving economy shaped the declining scale of women's entrepreneurial enterprises. There were important distinctions between the way Egba men and Egba women were integrated into the international economy by the end of the nineteenth century. Men predominated in the production and export of cash crops, the most lucrative sectors of the new economy, while women concentrated on imports. Men's better access to land and labor facilitated their predominance in cash crop production. Even though male entrepreneurship also declined during this period, they still had the resources to support entrepreneurial activities of a larger scale.

The study also shows that the 1930s depression was a critical moment in women's economic history. It demonstrates that although the crisis was general, it had different ramifications for women than for men, and different socioeconomic classes experienced it differently. In the *adire* industry, the depression was a watershed. It contributed to the demise of regional trades that had thrived in conjunction with the early colonial economy. It intensified the *adire* industry's dependence on the international economy.

The depression also transformed the socioeconomic composition of the industry. Many dyers left the industry altogether. In the 1936 Commission of Enquiry, dyers testified that many women who had become impoverished left the industry. However, as the industry adjusted to its new position, wealthy women also left. One no longer finds large-scale producers like those of old who had eight pots or more in operation simultaneously. The old oligarchy represented by dyers like Madame Jojolola had dissolved. Many of the large dyeing compounds had ceased operating by the 1980s. Difficulties in obtaining labor and favorable credit terms may have contributed to their decision to leave the industry, but new economic opportunities may have influenced their decision as well. Many sent their children to school instead of preparing them to become dyers. This suggests that not only did the socioeconomic profile of the industry change, but the relationship between trade and production also changed, especially for poorer dyers. Many more of these women left dyeing and turned to trade in other commodities such as foodstuffs that do not require as much capital or labor. The example of the *adire* industry suggests that women's role in trade grew as the economics of production became increasingly difficult.

Developing a fuller picture of women's commercial history, particularly during the depression, will provide greater insight into class formation and the ways in which class mediated women's economic options. Access to resources, especially capital, labor, and technology had a tremendous bearing on a dyer's capacity to respond to economic change. Further research will allow us to identify women who were able to make transitions both temporally, from one era to another, and structurally, from one lucrative trade to another. It is important to contrast their lives with those of women whose life experiences show little mobility or downward mobility.

The depression also had a significant impact on wider social and gender relations. The economic changes during the depression, particularly the severe limitations on credit, strengthened the position of the European trading firms at the expense of both African producers and African entrepreneurs. The commercial realignments also encouraged changes in land tenure and ownership as African entrepreneurs pressed claims for individual ownership of land so that they could use property as collateral for credit. This drive for property-based credit threatened women's access to land that was not secured in practice even though Yoruba culture recognized women's right to own property. The depression also reshaped divorce practices. Men, who often went into debt to obtain marriage fees, attempted to limit the ease with which women could obtain divorces. Supporters of these attempts to limit divorce wanted to give men greater control over their wives' service or at least ensure that husbands were refunded the bride-wealth.

The periodization of the history of *adire* adds depth to our under-standing of what some social scientists regard as the "informal economy," the largely self-employed sector where labor is not re-cruited on a permanent or regular basis for fixed rewards.[1] *Adire*, like most other women's trades, are today cataloged in this sector of the economy. This examination of the *adire* industry has shown that ac-tivities in the informal economy must be analyzed in relation to larger historical changes and in relation to other sectors of the economy. This "traditional" activity was dynamic and continually shaped and re-shaped as conditions and opportunities in the wider political economy changed. While some social scientists consider what role the informal economy can play in development, this analysis demonstrated that the informal economy did not exist outside development agendas. This divide between formal and informal sectors obscures the critical role that craft producers and market women played in simultaneously lim-iting and extending capitalist commercial and social relations.

Adire contributed significantly to the development of the colonial economy. Colonial officials, however, did not acknowledge or recog-nize women's contributions in sustained ways. While agricultural sta-tions were built and official support (though limited) was given to cash crop production, women's production was taken for granted. *Adire* received official attention usually reserved for the formal sectors of the economy only when it began experiencing difficulties. The fear of losing this central feature of European commercial expansion in Abeokuta propelled officials to attempt to bring this industry under their direction and supervision. But once the regional markets col-lapsed and *adire* ceased to be a major revenue earner, it returned to obscurity.

The study also raises important questions about the relationship be-tween socioeconomic change and religion. Scholars have documented the relationship between cocoa and Christianity. Evidence from this study suggests that we also need to explore the relationship between craft production more generally and Islam. In the early decades of the twentieth century women of all religious beliefs produced *adire*. By the 1960s, observers noted that most producers were Muslim. It is important to quantify this observation and determine what role Islam may have played in the survival of craft production and knowledge. Euba argues, for example, that Islam did much to promote traditional Yoruba arts such as weaving, dyeing, music, and dancing.[2]

SOCIOECONOMIC CHANGE, POLITICS, AND CONSCIOUSNESS

The centrality of politics to the dyers' response to the depression has offered an important opportunity to begin periodizing and analyzing women's political history. This study demonstrates that politics is best understood when situated in the larger social and economic context of people's lives. Failure to understand the intersections between women's exclusion from politics, the specifics of the dyers' economic decline, and the changing nature of the *Alake*ship would have hidden the most compelling transformations of women's political consciousness. The dyers' decision to include the *Alake* in their strategy to protect the industry forced us to consider the link between socioeconomic change, political action, and consciousness, as well as women's relationship to the state.

Women's changing economic role, particularly during the nineteenth century, was reflected in the evolving Egba polity after 1860. New titles were created and bestowed upon female entrepreneurs. The *Iyalode*, the most significant of these titles, recognized women as a distinct interest group in Egba politics. Recognizing women as a distinct interest group does not entail suggesting that women acted as a solid interest group vis-à-vis the state. Class mediated women's access to the state. The titles created in the nineteenth century all privileged wealth as well as age. Wealthy dyers cognizant of their differential access to the state attempted to use it in their interest when they sought the *Alake*'s help against the "interlopers." Self-interest propelled their overture to the *Alake* at the end of the 1920s. Their overture was also propelled by the assumption that the state, personified in the *Alake*, would be responsive to their interests. Ademola had a personal involvement with the industry through his mother and his wives.

Comparisons of the first set of meetings at the end of the 1920s and the confrontation in 1936 provide insight into how the women dyers defined their interests and how their political consciousness shifted during that period. In 1928 the prominent dyers who approached the *Alake* defined their interest in terms of access to long-term credit and protection from new people entering the industry. Their concerns were limited primarily to protecting their economic status within their occupational group. In 1936 interests were defined quite differently. Central to this development was the fact that the *Alake* was no longer seen as a possible ally; his actions had become ob-

stacles. The conflict between the *Alake* and the dyers was partly based
on the transformation of the *Alake*ship under colonial rule. The *Alake*s
had become increasingly autocratic and less responsive to the concerns of their constituents. This was particularly true during Ademola's
tenure. The *Alake* was a functionary of the colonial state and had an
overriding responsibility to ensure the interests of the colonial state
and European capital. The European firms demanded control and regulation of the industry in order to safeguard their interests. The *Alake*
fulfilled his responsibility to the European trading firms by privileg-
ing their interests. Ademola also had a personal stake in the *adire*
industry, thus, his actions were shaped by the conjunction of his
knowledge and understanding of *adire* and his political role.

The dyers' primary concern in 1936 was to end the bans the *Alake*
had imposed on caustic soda and synthetic dye. The issue was central
to all dyers regardless of economic status, for the very survival of the
industry was at stake. Thus, they were able to put forward a show of
solidarity in 1936 that they could not even pretend in 1928. In addition, they formed critical alliances with literate men who gave them
access to the upper echelons of the colonial bureaucracy. By hiring
lawyers and letter-writers, they secured the means—literacy—to circumvent the *Alake* and the Resident. They took a political path that
was primarily traveled by men and they succeeded in establishing
boundaries that limited state control and protected their autonomy as
dyers.

This was a significant victory for the dyers, but once again their
interests were entirely defined by their occupational concerns. Dyers
were not party to any of the larger discussions on land titles or divorce that would have had a significant impact on both their social
and their economic positions. Dyers' silence on these issues reflected
women's exclusion from the political structure. The colonial state did
not recognize women as a political interest group that warranted in-
clusion in the Egba Native Council. Even though the Egba Council
was continually expanding to give specific social groups or sections
of the town input in the political process, no woman was ever invited
to sit on the council.

The dyers' silence on the debates around land and divorce, and even
on women's exclusion from the political process, reflected a fairly nar-
rowly defined political consciousness. The changing economic context
forced the creation of new forms of cohesive political actions; still,
dyers were not prepared to make larger political demands. The study
has demonstrated that political action and consciousness must be understood in their historical context. The elements for larger concerted

action existed. Dyers could have mobilized support from other commodity associations such as the cloth sellers. There were literate women who eventually would replace male lawyers. However, the institutional mechanism to bring these factions together had not yet emerged. One of the significant differences between the dyers' political action of 1936 and that of the tax revolt in 1947 was that an institutional mechanism had been created, the Abeokuta Women's Union. The union matched elite nationalist women, those with the skills to operate through political channels that demanded literacy, with the more numerous women for whom taxation was a heavy burden. Comparing the 1936 and 1947 protests helps us appreciate how thoroughly Egba women had coalesced into a strong constituency. There was new leadership in the form of Mrs. Ransome-Kuti, a highly educated woman, but her leadership did not exclude the leaders of the various groups of market women. In fact, the Abeokuta Women's Union built on the preexisting base of women's leaders and associations.

The importance of commodity associations to later political action underscores the need for more research on women's commercial associations. The history of the dyers' association reveals that the structure and effectiveness of these associations were responsive to changes in the larger society. Furthermore, we cannot assume that, because these associations shared a set of commercial concerns, political mobilization was a natural occurrence. It is important to understand how periods of collective political action were forged. The 1936 dyers' protest was an important gauge in the historical development of political consciousness and political action among women in Abeokuta. The continual economic decline which women experienced during World War II, the colonial state's indifference to their economic circumstances, and the emergence of the nationalist movement set the stage for larger cohesive political action in 1947.

CLOTH, ARTISANS, AND THE CONTEMPORARY ECONOMY

This study has shown that textiles and their production embody a rich source of data from which we can document, gauge, and distill historical change. By the 1920s the development of cash crop production as well as the colonial economy stimulated changes that contributed to a decline in dyeing industry. In spite of predictions that *adire* production would disappear, dyers continue to play an important role in Abeokuta's economy, and the industry experienced a resurgence in the 1980s. This resurgence was shaped by a ban on imported cloth in 1978 and the massive devaluation of Nigeria's currency, the *naira*, in the 1980s. These factors forced Nigerian consumers to rely on locally produced cloth and helped to breathe new life in the local textile sectors.

A growing pool of local designers and boutique owners sponsored fashion shows which featured new garments made from local cloths. Newspapers and magazines reported that more Nigerian women were turning to local designers for their dress and shunning Christian Dior, Nina Ricci, Chanel, Gucci, and other foreign designers.[3] Although only a small fraction of Nigerian women routinely bought the clothes of these foreign designers, the fashion shows, competitions like the Miss *Adire* Carnival,[4] and innovative styling extended the appeal for fashions made from *adire* or locally woven cloth.

Once again, *adire* became very lucrative and the increasing demand brought many new people, primarily women, into the industry. Older dyers taught this new generation of students, but some learned the craft in both government-sponsored and private schools like the Consty Institute of Fashion Design in Lagos. Students at Consty learned dyeing, textile design, and textile technology as well as clothing construction. Graduates were being prepared to complete all the stages of production right up to the finished garment, since they could dye, design, and sew.[5] In the 1980s *adire* had shed its characterization as an industry practiced primarily by old, non-literate Muslim women.

The renaissance in *adire* production also coincided with the implementation of Nigeria's structural adjustment program. As many people's buying power shrank with each devaluation or because of job loss or extended unemployment, *adire* offered an important economic alternative. It could be produced intermittently or combined with other economic activities. It was not uncommon to find women who were engaged in salaried jobs who also produced *adire* on the side. Their income from *adire* supplemented their salaries and in the case of government workers was often more reliable.

Nigeria's present economic crisis and the search for income-generating activities have contributed to a widespread dissemination of knowledge and information about dyeing. Women's church groups, for example, sponsor events to which dyers were invited to teach other women the basics of dyeing.[6] Similarly, the Lagos Museum was developing a program to train people to make *adire* so that they could go to museums around the country to teach others. This project was seen as a strategy for addressing the country's large unemployment problem.

Adire's renaissance in the 1980s did not reflect the mere survival of a traditional craft. It was rooted in the economic and political developments of the contemporary period. The economic position of *adire*, like that of other artisan-based crafts, encapsulates a critical dimension within current debates about job creation, incomes, and economic development. As a result of those discussions, *adire* producers in Abeokuta have received some support from government programs such as the Better Life Program during the Babangida regime (1985–93).[7] Many dyers noted that the support was inadequate in relation to the crisis posed by the poor state of the economy.[8] Some complained about the high cost of cloth,[9] the lack of electricity and pipe-borne water, and the need for some form of financial support.[10] Clearly any analysis of *adire* production since the 1980s must be contextualized by the present conditions of the Nigerian political economy. A full appreciation of where *adire* fits into the present economy also requires an analysis of the industry in relation to other textile sectors—hand weaving, tailoring, and Nigerian textile factories.

CHANGING GENDER RELATIONS

Throughout this study, there has been a concern with the ways in which social, economic, and political changes were gendered. It has demonstrated that the rise of the colonial state and even the depression had different ramifications for men and women. Gender roles and expectations opened different options and opportunities for men and women as they struggled to remain solvent during the economic crisis. The depression was also an era when men in pursuit of economic redress could use their access to the state to address aspects of patriarchy and seniority that had been undermined by the early decades of economic expansion. Thus, the Egba Council's efforts to limit access to divorce was directed at both women and young men. Yet this study does not capture many of the more nuanced changes in gender relations because of its focus on the industry and the dyers' wider external economic and political relations. Questions about household and family will, in due course, bring gender relations into clearer focus and shed light on more incremental social and economic changes.

The present study has, however, opened new perspectives on Abeokuta, its women as producers and traders of *adire*, and its politics in the era of indirect rule and a worsening international economy. It honors the agency and determination of the Abeokuta craftswomen and suggests that social and economic history of craft producers cannot hereafter be written without detailed attention to gender, power, and production.

NOTES

1. Keith Hart, "Informal Income Opportunities and Urban Employment in Ghana," *Journal of Modern African Studies* 11, 1 (1973): 68. For an important discussion of the theoretical models applied to this sector, see Gracia Clark, *Onions Are My Husband: Survival and Accumulation by West African Market Women* (Chicago: University of Chicago Press, 1994), 73–125.

2. Titilola Euba, "Dress and Status in 19th Century Lagos," in Ade Adefuye, Babatunde Agiri, and Jide Osuntokun, eds., *History of the Peoples of Lagos State* (Lagos: Lantern Books, 1987).

3. "Good-bye, Gucci," *Newswatch,* 10 June, 1991.

4. "Enter Miss Adire Carnival '93," *Poise,* 15 November 1993. The carnival was sponsored by the Ogun State Broadcasting Corporation. I am thankful to LaRay Denzer for bringing this article to my attention.

5. Interview with Olanike Oladunjoye, 21 July 1996, Lagos.

6. I attended such an event in Lagos in 1994, where a dyer as well as a seamstress were on hand to conduct demonstrations at a women's church retreat.

7. The program tried to assist women's industries and crafts, especially those of rural women. A number of trade shows were held around the country to promote women's crafts.

8. In Jojolola's compound dyers received a water tank. Since the compound was made a showcase of the Better Life Program, many people now refer to it as the Better Life compound rather than Jojo's compound.

9. Interview with Afusatu Agogundade, 28 August 1996, Kemta, Abeokuta.

10. Interview with Alhaja Biliahu, 30 August 1996, Kemta, Abeokuta; and Wasilat Animasaun, 1 September 1996, Kemta, Abeokuta.

BIBLIOGRAPHY

INTERVIEWS

Chief E.A. Adeboya, Ibara, Abeokuta, 11 November 1988.
Rafatu Adegbeno, Kemta, Abeokuta, 28 August 1998.
Madam Adepate Adeniji, Ikereku, Abeokuta, 25 May, 1 and 29 June 1988.
Madam Wosinatu Adeniji, Ikereku, Abeokuta, 30 May, 13, and 29 June 1988.
Afusatu Arogundade, Kemta, Abeokuta, 28 August 1996.
Madam Wasilat Animasaun, Kemta, Abeokuta, 1 September 1 1996.
Madam Aroga, Ikereku, Abeokuta, 22 and 23 June 1988.
Mr. Michael Atkinson, Winchester, England, July 1997.
Madam Sidikat Ayinde, Itoku, Abeokuta, 21 June and 5 August 1988.
Alhaji Samshedeen Bada, Kemta, Abeokuta, 2 September 1996.
Alhaja Bakare, Itoku Market, Abeokuta, 27 June, and 8 August 1988.
Alhaja Biliahu, Kemta, Abeokuta, 30 August 1996.
Chief T. Coker, Ibara, Abeokuta, 11 November 1988.
Mrs. Runke Doherty, Ibara, Abeokuta, 3 October and 12 November 1988.
Mr. Anthony Ingelsdorf, London, England, July 1997.
Afusat Karimu, Kemta, Abeokuta, 1 September 1996.
Dolupo Kuti, Sapon, Abeokuta, 7 September 1988.
Alhaja Falilat Lasaki, Totoro, Abeokuta, 8 and 31 August 1988.
Chief Adura Majekodunmi, Irereku, Abeokuta, 14, 21, and 28 June 1988.
Betty Oyeboyoje, Maryland, Lagos, 24 September 1988.
Miss Olanike Oladunjoye, Lagos, 21 July 1996.
Alhaji Olumiran, Kemta, Abeokuta, 2 September 1996.
Alhaja Owomipe, Kemta, Abeokuta, 28 August 1996.
Alhaja Raji, Lagos, 28 October 1988.
Miss Oludulupo Ransome-Kuti, Isaba, Abeokuta, 7 September 1988.
Mr. Salawu Sadiku, Kemta, Abeokuta, 29 August 1996.
Alhaja Ajoke Soetan, Kemta, Abeokuta, 1 and 6 September 1988, 11 November 1988,
        and 20 August 1996.

Alhaji Oladunwo Soetan, Kemta, Abeokuta, 9 August and 11 November 1988.
Chief E.B. Sorunke, Ibara, Abeokuta, 11 November 1988.
Alhaji Murana Surakatu, Ketu compound, Igbein, Abeokuta, 28 June and 8 August 1988.
Alhaja Suri, Itoku, Abeokuta, 11 November 1988.
Alhaja Falilat Tukuru, Kemta, Abeokuta, 23 August and 6 September 1988.

UNPUBLISHED SOURCES

Government Archives in Nigeria

Nigerian National Archives, Ibadan

CSO 21: Annual reports, Abeokuta Province, 1920–53.
CSO 26: Official communications, 1914–52.
CSO 26/1: Files of the Egba Judicial Council, Tribal Customs and Superstitions of Southern Nigeria (Pawning).

Abeokuta Provincial Office Papers

Abe Prof. 1/1 : Income tax ordinance, annual reports, assessments reports, and Minutes of Egba Council Meetings, 1933–56.
Abe Prof. 2/1: Quarterly reports, reports on road construction, and circulars from secretariat, southern provinces, 1925–32.
Abe Prof. 3: Annual reports and financial statements.
Abe Prof. 4–D29: Proceedings of the Adire Cloth Committee, 1936.
Abe Prof. 5: Administrative officers' traveling reports and correspondence.
Abe Prof. 6/2: Annual reports and reports on tax collection.
Abe Prof. 6/4: Minutes of Abeokuta Council Meetings.
Abe Prof. 8/2: Intelligence Report 1938.
Abe Prof. 8/3: Report book on Egba affairs, 1900–1906.
Abe Prof. 9/2: Letter books.
Abe Prof. 9/3: Minute books.

Papers of the Secretariat, Western Province

SWP 1/15: Lease agreements, Abeokuta.
SWP 1/16: Lease agreements, Abeokuta.
DCI: Department of Commerce and Industries, Lagos

Egba Archives, Abeokuta

Egba Council Records (Ake Palace Papers), 1898–1973:

ECR 1/1: Minutes of Egba Council Meetings, annual reports, and files on the *adire* trade, *dipomu*, land tenure, and the Abeokuta Women's Union.
ECR 2/1: Judicial complaints books, 1901–52.

ECR 3/1: Correspondence books, 1899–1949.
ECR 5/1: Correspondence books, 1900–53.
ECR 6/1: Egba Administration Bulletin, 1925–50.
ECR 7/1: *Alake* Ademola's personal papers, 1919–50.
ECR 8/1: Egba Government Gazette.

Government Archives in U.K.

Public Records Office, London

CO 659: Customs and Trade Journal.
CO 520: Original correspondence.
CO 583: Original correspondence.
CO 820: Economic files.

Collections of Private Papers

CMS Yoruba Mission Papers (NAI)

J.K. Coker
Samuel Crowther, Jr.
Rev. James Johnson
Rev. J.B. Macaulay
Rev. A.C. Mann
William Marsh
Rev. Henry Townsend
Rev. J.B. Wood

Africana Collection, University of Ibadan Library, Ibadan

Funmilayo Ransome-Kuti Papers.
Report of the Commission of Enquiry into the disturbances in Abeokuta Province, 1918.

Rhodes House, Oxford

James Deemin Papers.
Rev. Ernest and Mrs. Phillis Fry, Missionary Letters.
John Holt Papers.
Frederick Lugard Papers.

Reports (Rhodes House)

S.M. Jacob. Report on the Taxation and Economics of Nigeria, 1934.
Alfred Moloney. "Cotton Interests, Foreign and Native in Yoruba, and Generally in West Africa." Address to Members in the Mayor's Parlour, Friday, 15 November 1889.
Cyril Punch. "A Report on the Native Law of Egbaland 1906."

Government Publications

H.F. Gurney. Department of Overseas Trade, Report on Economic and Commercial Conditions in the British Dependencies in West Africa (The Gambia, Sierra Leone, The Gold Coast and Nigeria), London: H.M. Stationery Office, 1937.

Durant Ferson Ladd. Trade and Shipping in West Africa, Senegal, Gambia, Ivory Coast, Gold Coast, Nigeria, Cameroons (Washington, DC.: Government Printing Office, 1929).

Newspapers

Christian Science Monitor
Daily Times (Nigeria)
Egba Administrative Bulletin
Egba National Harper
Iwe Irohin
Lagos Standard
Lagos Weekly Record
West African Pilot

UNPUBLISHED WORKS

Afolabi, Adesola. 1981. "The Origin, Development and Impact of 'Adire' Dyeing Industry in Abeokuta." B.A. honors essay, University of Ibadan.

Afolabi, Esther. 1983. "Yoruba Adire, Its Potentials and Future." B.A. honors essay, University of Ife.

Agiri, Babatunde A. 1972. "Kola in Western Nigeria, 1850–1950: A History of the Cultivation of Cola Nitida in Egba-Owode, Ijebu-Remo, Iwo and Ota Areas." Ph.D. diss., University of Wisconsin.

Akinwumi, T.M. 1990. "The Commemorative Phenomenon of Textile Use Among the Yoruba: A Survey of Significance and Form." Ph.D. diss., Institute of African Studies, University of Ibadan.

Ashiru, M.O. 1988. "Silkworms As Money Spinners: Anaphe vs. Bombyx—A Status Report on Nigeria." Unpublished paper presented at the Nigerian Field Society, Ibadan, 13 April.

Atkinson, Michael C., ed. 1988. "Nigerian Tales of the Colonial Era." Unpublished manuscript.

Badejogbim, O.A. 1983. "The Relationship Between Environment and Culture: Adire Industry in Southern Nigeria As a Case-Study." B.A. honors essay, Department of Archaeology, University of Ibadan.

Byfield, Judith. 1990. "Constructing the Colonial State: Sanitation Enforcement and Forced Labor in Abeokuta During the First World War." Unpublished paper presented at the Berkshire Conference of Women Historians, 10 June.

———. 1993. "Women, Economy and the State: A Study of the Adire Industry in Abeokuta (Western Nigeria), 1890–1939." Ph.D. diss., University of Wisconsin–Madison.

Dilley, Roy M. 1984. "Weaving Among the Tukolor of the Senegal River Basin: A Study of the Social Position and Economic Organization." Ph.D. diss., Keble College, Oxford.

Fadipe, N.A. 1931. "A Yoruba Town: A Sociological Study of Abeokuta in the British Colony and Protectorate of Nigeria, West Coast of Africa." M.A. thesis, Columbia University.

Gertzel, Cherry. 1959. "John Holt: A British Merchant in West Africa in the Era of Imperialism." Ph.D. diss., Oxford University.

Haynes, Douglas, and Judith Byfield. 1994. "Artisans, Cloth, and the World Economy: Textile Production and Distribution in Africa and India." Unpublished manuscript.

Keyes, Carolyn. 1993. "*Adire*: Cloth, Gender and Social Change in Southwestern Nigeria, 1841–1991." Ph.D. diss., University of Wisconsin–Madison.

Lennihan, Louise. "Critical Historical Conjunctions in the Emergence of Agricultural Wage Labor in Northern Nigeria." Unpublished manuscript.

Mabogunje, Akin L. 1958. "The Changing Pattern of Rural Settlement and Rural Economy in Egba Division, South Western Nigeria," M.A. thesis, University of London.

Marshall, Gloria. 1964. "Women, Trade and the Yoruba Family." Ph.D. diss., Columbia University.

Mba, Nina. 1978. "Women in Southern Nigeria Political History." Ph.D. diss., University of Ibadan.

Mikell, G., and E.P. Skinner. 1989. "Women and The Early State in West Africa." University of Michigan, Working Paper #190.

Oroge, E.A. 1971. "The Institution of Slavery in Yorubaland with Particular Reference to the Nineteenth Century." Ph.D. diss., University of Birmingham, U.K.

Pallinder-Law, Agneta. 1973. "Government in Abeokuta 1830–1914: With Special Reference to the Egba United Government 1898–1914." Ph.D. diss., Götesborgs University.

Pitts, Delia C. 1978. "An Economic and Social History of Cloth Production in Senegambia." Ph.D. diss., University of Chicago.

Renne, Elisha. 1990. "Wives, Chiefs and Weavers: Gender Relations in Bunu Society." Ph.D. diss., New York University.

———. 1993. "The Decline and Resurgence of Women's Weaving in Ekiti, Nigeria." Paper presented at the conference Artisans, Cloth and the World Economy: Textile Manufacturing and Marketing in South Asia and Africa. Dartmouth College, 23–25 April.

Shea, Philip J. 1975. "The Development of an Export Oriented Dyed Cloth Industry in Kano Emirate in the Nineteenth Century." Ph.D. diss., University of Wisconsin–Madison.

Turner, J. Michael. 1975. "Les Brésiliens—The Impact of Former Brazilian Slaves upon Dahomey." Ph.D. diss., Boston University.

Vincent, Brian. 1977. "Cotton Growing in Southern Nigeria: Missionary, Mercantile, Imperial and Colonial Government Involvement versus African Realities, from 1845 to 1939." Ph.D. diss., Simon Fraser University, British Columbia, Canada.

Wass, Betty. 1975. "Yoruba Dress: A Systemic Case Study of Five Generations of a Lagos Family." Ph.D. diss., Michigan State University.

PUBLISHED SOURCES

Adewoye, Omoniyi. 1977. *The Judicial System in Southern Nigeria, 1854–1954.* Atlantic Highlands, New Jersey: Humanities Press.
———. 1986. "Land Control: A Critical Factor in Yoruba Gender Stratification." Pp. 78–91 in Claire Robertson and Iris Berger, eds., *Women and Class in Africa.* New York: Africana.
———. 1986. "Women, Power and Authority in Traditional Yoruba Society." Pp. 137–57 in Shirley Ardener et al., eds., *Visibility and Power—Essays on Women in Society and Development.* Oxford: Oxford University Press.
———. 1988. "Historical Evolution in the Sexual Division of Labour in Nigeria." Pp. 133–47 in Jay Kleinberg, ed., *Retrieving Women's History: Changing Perception of the Role of Women in Politics and Society.* Oxford: Berg Press.
Agiri, Babatunde A. 1974. "Aspects of Socioeconomic Changes Among the Awori Egba and Ijebu Remo Communities During the Nineteenth Century." *Journal of the Historical Society of Nigeria* 7, 3: 465–83.
Ajayi, Jacob F. Ade. 1981. *Christian Missions in Nigeria, 1841–1891: The Making of a New Elite.* London: Longman.
———. 1984. "Samuel Johnson: Historian of the Yoruba." *Nigeria Magazine* 81: 141–46.
Ajayi, Jacob F. Ade, and R.S. Smith. 1964. *Yoruba Warfare in the Nineteenth Century.* Cambridge: Cambridge University Press.
Ajisafe, A.K. 1948. *History of Abeokuta,* 3d ed. Lagos: Kash and Klare Bookshop.
Akintoye, S.A. 1971. *Revolution and Power Politics in Yorubaland, 1840–1893: Ibadan Expansion and the Rise of Ekitiparapo.* New York: Humanities Press.
Alence, Rod. 1990–91. "The 1937–1938 Gold Coast Cocoa Crisis: The Political Economy of Commercial Stalemate." *African Economic History* 19: 77–104.
Allman, Jean. 1991. "Of 'Spinsters,' 'Concubines' and 'Wicked Women': Reflections on Gender and Social Change in Colonial Asante." *Gender and History* 3, 2:176–89.
Anderson, David, and David Throup. 1989. "The Agrarian Economy of Central Province, Kenya 1918–1939." Pp. 8–28 in Ian Brown, ed., *The Economies of Africa and Asia in the Inter-war Depression.* London: Routledge.
Aremu, P.S.O. 1979. "Yoruba Adire-Eleko Fabrics." *Nigerian Field* 44, 3/4: 98–106.
———. 1982. "Yoruba Traditional Weaving: Kijipa Motifs, Colour and Symbols." *Nigeria,* no. 140: 3–10.
Arneson, Jeanette Jensen. 1974. *Tradition and Change in Yoruba Art.* Sacramento: E.B. Crocker Art Gallery.
Arnoldi, Mary Jo, Christraud Geary, and Kris Hardin, eds. 1996. *African Material Culture.* Bloomington: Indiana University Press.

Aronson, Lisa. 1980. "History of Cloth Trade in the Niger Delta: A Study of Diffusion." Pp. 89–107 in Dale Idiens and K. G. Ponting, eds., *Textiles in Africa.* Bath, U.K.: Pasold Research Fund.

———. 1982. "Popo Weaving: The Dynamics of Trade in Southeastern Nigeria." *African Arts* 15, 3: 43–47.

———. 1992. "Ijebu Yoruba Aso Olona." *African Arts* 25, 3: 52–63.

Ashiru, M.O. 1979. "Sericulture in Nigeria." *Indian Silk,* 18, 5 (October): 15–17.

Asiwaju, A.I. 1976. *Western Yorubaland under European Rule, 1889–1945: A Comparative Analysis of French and British Colonialism.* London: Longman.

Atanda, J.A. 1973. *The New Oyo Empire: Indirect Rule and Change in Western Nigeria, 1894–1934.* London: Longman.

Atkinson, Michael C. 1992. *An African Life: Tales of a Colonial Officer.* London: Radcliffe Press.

Austen, Ralph. 1987. *African Economic History.* Portsmouth, NH: Heinemann.

Awe, Bolanle. 1973. "Militarism and Economic Development in Nineteenth Century Yoruba Country: The Ibadan Example." *Journal of African History* 14, 1: 65–77.

———. 1977. "The Iyalode in the Traditional Yoruba Political System." Pp. 1144–59 in Alice Schlegel, ed., *Sexual Stratification: A Cross-Cultural View.* New York: Columbia University Press.

Ayandele, E.A. 1970. *Holy Johnson: Pioneer of African Nationalism, 1836–1917.* New York: Humanities Press.

———. 1981. *The Missionary Impact on Modern Nigeria, 1842–1914: A Political and Social Analysis.* London: Longman.

Barber, Karin. 1991. "Oriki and the Changing Perception of Greatness in Nineteenth-Century Yorubaland." Pp. 31–41 in Toyin Falola, ed., *Yoruba Historiography.* Madison: University of Wisconsin, African Studies Program.

Barbour, Jane. 1970. "Nigerian Adire Cloths." *Baessler-Archive,* 18: 363–426.

Barbour, Jane. 1971. *Adire Cloth in Nigeria: The Origin of Some Adire Designs.* Ibadan: Institute of African Studies, University of Ibadan.

———. 1971. "The Origin of Some Adire Designs." Pp. 49–80. in Jane Barbour and Doig Simmonds, eds. *Adire Cloth in Nigeria.* Ibadan: Institute of African Studies, University of Ibadan.

———. 1990. "Adire Cloth in Nigeria." *Nigerian Field* (U.K.) 55, 1–2 (April): 65–69.

Barbour, Jane, and Doig Simmonds, eds. 1971. *Adire Cloth in Nigeria: The Preparation and Dyeing of Indigo Patterned Cloths Among the Yoruba.* Ibadan: Institute of African Studies, University of Ibadan.

Barnes, Ruth, and Joanne Eicher, eds. 1992. *Dress and Gender: Making and Meaning in Cultural Contexts.* Oxford: Berg Press.

Barth, Heinrich. 1858. *Travels and Discoveries in North and Central Africa: Journal of an Expedition, 1849–1855.* London: Longman, Brown, Green, Longmans and Roberts.

Bascom, William. 1951. "Social Status, Wealth and Individual Differences Among the Yoruba." *American Anthropologist* 53: 490–505.

———. 1951. "Yoruba Food." *Africa* 21, 1: 41–53.

———. 1952. "The Esusu." *Journal of the Royal Anthropological Institute* 82, 1: 63–69.

———. 1984. *The Yoruba of Southwestern Nigeria*. Prospect Heights, IL: Waveland Press.

Bastian, Misty L. 1996. "Female 'Alhajis' and Entrepreneurial Fashions: Flexible Identities in Southeastern Nigerian Clothing Practice." Pp. 97–132 in Hilde Hendrickson, ed., *Clothing and Difference: Embodied Identities in Colonial and Post-Colonial Africa*. Durham, NC: Duke University Press.

Bauer, P.T. 1954. *West African Trade: A Study of Competition, Oligopoly and Monopoly in a Changing Economy*. Cambridge: Cambridge University Press.

Beer, C.E.F. 1976. *The Politics of Peasant Groups in Western Nigeria*. Ibadan: University of Ibadan Press.

Beier, Georgina. 1980. "Yoruba Pottery." *African Arts* 13, 3: 48–53, 92.

Belasco, Bernard. 1980. *The Entrepreneur As Culture Hero: Preadaptations in Nigerian Economic Development*. New York: Praeger.

Ben-Amos, Paula. 1978. "Owina N'Ido: Royal Weavers of Benin." *African Arts* 11, 4: 49–53.

Berman, Bruce. 1990. *Control and Crisis in Colonial Kenya: The Dialectic of Domination*. Athens: Ohio University Press.

Berman, Bruce, and John Lonsdale. 1992. "Coping with the Contradictions: The Development of the Colonial State, 1895–1914." Pp. 77–100 in Bruce Berman and John Lonsdale, eds., *Unhappy Valley—Conflict in Kenya and Africa, Book One: State and Class*. Athens: Ohio University Press.

Berman, Bruce, and John Lonsdale, eds. 1992. *Unhappy Valley, Conflict in Kenya and Africa*. Athens: Ohio University Press.

Berry, Sara. 1975. *Cocoa, Custom and Socio-economic Change in Rural Western Nigeria*. Oxford: Clarendon Press.

Biobaku, S.O. 1949. "Ogboni, the Egba Senate." Pp. 257–63 in *Proceedings of the International West African Conference*. Lagos: the Conference.

———. 1952. "An Historical Sketch of Egba Traditional Authorities." *Africa* 22, 1: 35–49.

———. 1956. "The Egba Council 1899–1918: Part 1." *ODU—Journal of Yoruba and Related Studies* 2: 14–20.

———. 1957. *The Egba and Their Neighbors, 1842–1872*. Oxford: Clarendon Press.

———. 1960. "Madam Tinubu." Pp. 33–41 in National Broadcasting Company of Nigeria, eds., *Eminent Nigerians of the Nineteenth Century*. Cambridge: Cambridge University Press.

———. 1992. *When We Were Young*. Ibadan: University Press.

———. 1994. *A Window on Nigeria*. Lagos: Nelson.

Blackett, R.J.M. 1975. "Return to the Motherland: Robert Campbell, A Jamaican in Early Colonial Lagos." *Journal of the Historical Society of Nigeria* 8, 1:133–143.

Blair, John. 1991. *Juju & Justice*. Perth, Australia: Leader Press.

Boahen, A. A. 1962. "The Caravan Trade in the Nineteenth Century." *Journal of African History* 3, 2: 349–59.

————. 1964. *Britain, the Sahara, and the Western Sudan, 1788–1861.* Oxford: Clarendon Press.

Boser-Sarivaxevanis, R. 1975. *Recherche sur l'histoire des textiles traditionnels tisses et teints de l'Afrique occidentale.* Basel: Naturforschenden Gesellschaft.

Bowen, Thomas J. 1968. *Adventures and Missionary Labours in Several Countries in the Interior of Africa from 1849 to 1856,* 2d ed. London: Frank Cass.

Boyer, Ruth. 1983. "Yoruba Cloths with Regal Names." *African Arts* 16, 2: 42–45.

Braudel, Fernand. 1967. *Capitalism and Material Life, 1400–1800.* New York: Harper and Row.

Bray, Jennifer. 1968. "The Organization of Traditional Weaving in Iseyin, Nigeria." *Africa* 38, 3: 270–80.

————. 1969. "The Economics of Traditional Cloth Production in Iseyin, Nigeria." *Economic Development and Cultural Change* 17, 4: 540–51.

Brown, Ian, ed. 1989. *The Economies of Africa and Asia in the Inter-war Depression.* London: Routledge.

Buckley, Anthony D. 1985. *Yoruba Medicine.* Oxford: Clarendon Press.

Burton, Richard F. 1863. *Abeokuta and the Cameroons Mountain: An Exploration.* 2 vols. London: Tinsley Brothers.

————. 1863. *Wanderings in West Africa from Liverpool to Fernando Po,* vol. 2. London: Tinsley Brothers.

Buxton, Thomas F. 1840. *The African Slave Trade.* New York: Anti-Slavery Society.

Byfield, Judith. 1993. "Pawns and Politics: The Pawnship Debate in Western Nigeria." Pp. 187–216 in Toyin Falola and Paul Lovejoy, eds., *Pawnship in Africa: Debt Bondage in Historical Perspective.* Boulder, CO: Westview Press.

————. 1996. "Women, Marriage, Divorce and the Emerging Colonial State in Abeokuta (Nigeria), 1892–1904." *Canadian Journal of African Studies* 30, 1:32–51.

Campbell, J.G. 1918. *Some Thoughts on Abeokuta During the Reign of His Highness King Gbadebo the Alake, 1898–1918.* Lagos: Tika Tore.

Campbell, Robert. 1969. "A Pilgrimage to My Motherland—An Account of a Journey Among the Egbas and Yorubas of Central Africa in 1859–60." Pp. 149–250 in Martin R. Delany and Robert Campbell, eds., *Search For a Place: Black Separatism and Africa, 1860.* Ann Arbor: University of Michigan Press.

Carland, John M. 1985. *The Colonial Office and Nigeria, 1989–1914.* Stanford, CA: Hoover Institution Press.

Chanock, Martin. 1982. "Making Customary Law: Men, Women, and Courts in Colonial Northern Rhodesia." Pp. 53–67 in M.J. Hay and Marcia Wright, eds., *Women and the Law in Africa.* Boston: Boston University.

————. 1985. *Law, Custom and Social Order: The Colonial Experience in Malawi and Zambia.* Cambridge: Cambridge University Press.

Clarence-Smith, Gervase. 1989. "The Effects of the Great Depression on Industrialisation in Equatorial and Central Africa." Pp. 170–202 in Ian Brown,

ed., *The Economies of Africa and Asia in the Inter-war Depression*. London:
Routledge.

Clark, Gracia. 1994. *Onions Are My Husband: Survival and Accumulation by West
African Market Women*. Chicago: University of Chicago Press.

Clarke, Julian. 1981. "Households and the Political Economy of Small-scale Cash
Crop Production in South-western Nigeria." *Africa* 51: 807–23.

Clarke, William H. 1972. *Travels and Explorations in Yorubaland, 1854–1858*, edited by J. A. Atanda. Ibadan: Ibadan University Press.

Cohen, Abner. 1966. "Politics of the Kola Trade: Some Processes of Tribal Community Formation Among Migrants in West African Towns." *Africa* 36, 1: 18–
35.

———. 1969. *Custom and Politics in Urban Africa: A Study of Hausa Migrants in
Yoruba Towns*. Berkeley: University Press of California.

Coker, Increase. 1951. *Seventy Years of the Nigerian Press*. Lagos: Daily Times.

Cookey, S.J.S. 1965. "West African Immigrants in the Congo, 1885–1896." *Journal
of the Historical Society of Nigeria* 3, 2: 261–70.

Coombes, Annie E. 1994. *Reinventing Africa: Museums, Material Culture and Popular Imagination in Late Victorian and Edwardian England*. New Haven, CT:
Yale University Press.

Cooper, Frederick. 1994. "Conflict and Connection: Rethinking Colonial African History." *American Historical Review* 99: 1516–45.

———. 1996. *Decolonization and African Society: The Labor Question in French
and British Africa*. Cambridge: Cambridge University Press.

Cordwell, Justine M. 1983. "The Art and Aesthetics of the Yoruba," *African Arts* 16,
2: 56–59, 92–94, 100.

Cordwell, Justine M., and Ronald A. Schwarz, eds. 1979. *The Fabrics of Culture:
The Anthropology of Clothing and Adornment*. New York: Mouton.

Crowder, Michael. 1968. *West Africa Under Colonial Rule*. Evanston, IL: Northwestern University Press.

Cruise O'Brien, Donal. 1975. *Saints and Politicians: Essays in the Organisation of
a Senegalese Peasant Society*. Cambridge: Cambridge University Press.

Curtin, Philip, ed. 1975. *Economic Change in Precolonial Africa: Senegambia in the
Era of the Slave Trade*. Madison: University of Wisconsin Press.

———. 1984. *Cross-Cultural Trade in World History*. Cambridge: Cambridge University Press.

———. 1997. "Joseph Wright of the Egba." Pp. 317–33 in Philip Curtin, ed., *Africa
Remembered: Narratives by West Africans from the Era of the Slave Trade*,
2d ed. Prospect Heights, IL: Waveland Press.

Dada, S.A. 1986. *J.K. Coker, Father of African Independent Churches*. Ibadan: Aowa
Press.

Daniel, F. 1938. "Yoruba Pattern Dyeing." *Nigeria*, no. 13: 125–28.

Davies, P.N. 1976. *Trading in West Africa, 1840–1920*. New York: Africana.

Davison, Patricia, and Harries, Patrick. 1980. "Cotton Weaving in South-East Africa:
Its History and Technology." Pp. 175–192 in D. Idiens and K.G. Ponting,
eds., *Textiles in Africa*. Bath, U.K.: The Pasold Research Fund.

Delano, I.O. 1937. *The Soul of Nigeria*. London: T.W. Lauri.

————. c.1940. *The Singing Minister of Nigeria: The Life of Canon J. J. Ransome-Kuti.* London: United Society for Christian Literature.

Delany, Martin R. 1969. "Official Report of the Niger Valley Exploring Party." Pp. 27–148 in Martin R. Delany and Robert Campbell, eds., *Search For a Place: Black Separatism and Africa, 1860.* Ann Arbor: University of Michigan Press.

de Negri, Eve. 1962. "Yoruba Women's Costume." *Nigeria Magazine* 72: 4–12.

————. 1962. "Yoruba Men's Costume." *Nigeria Magazine* 73: 4–12.

————. 1966. "Nigerian Textile Industry Before Independence." *Nigeria Magazine* 89: 95–101.

Dennett, R.E. 1916. "The Ogboni and Other Secret Societies in Nigeria." *Journal of the African Society* 16, 1: 16–27.

————. 1968. *Nigerian Studies: The Religious and Political System of the Yoruba.* London: Frank Cass.

Denzer, LaRay. 1992. "Domestic Science Training in Colonial Yorubaland, Nigeria." Pp. 116–39 in Karen Tranberg-Hansen, ed., *African Encounters with Domesticity.* New Brunswick, NJ: Rutgers University Press.

————. 1994. "Yoruba Women: A Historiographical Study." *International Journal of African Historical Studies* 27, 1:1–39.

Dewey, Clive, and Anthony G. Hopkins, eds. 1978. *The Imperial Impact: Studies in the Economic History of Africa and India.* London: Athlone Press.

Dilley, Roy M. 1986. "Tukulor Weavers and the Organization of Their Craft in Village and Town." *Africa* 56, 2: 123–48.

Dorward, D. C. 1976. "Precolonial Tiv Trade and Cloth Currency." *The International Journal of African Historical Studies* 9, 4: 576–91.

Drewal, Henry. 1968. "Art and the Perception of Women in Yoruba Culture," *Cahiers d'Études Africaines* 17, 4: 545–67.

Drewal, Henry, and Margaret Drewal. 1990. *Gelede: Art and Female Power Among the Yoruba.* Bloomington: Indiana University Press.

Drewal, Henry, John Pemberton III, Rowland Abiodun. 1989. *Yoruba: Nine Centuries of African Art and Thought.* New York: Center for African Art.

Drewal, M.T., J. Isaac, and D. Dorward. 1988. *Yoruba Art in Life and Thought.* Bundoora, Australia: African Research Institute, La Trobe University.

Eades, J.S. 1980. *The Yoruba Today.* Cambridge: Cambridge University Press.

————, 1994. *Strangers and Traders: Yoruba Migrants, Markets and the State in Northern Ghana.* Trenton, NJ: Africa World Press.

Eicher, Joanne. 1976. *Nigerian Hand-Crafted Textiles.* Ife, Nigeria: University of Ife Press.

————, ed. 1995. *Dress and Ethnicity.* Oxford: Berg.

————, and Tonye Erekosima. 1995. "Why Do They Call It Kalabari? Cultural Authentication and the Demarcation of Ethnic Identity." Pp. 139–164 in Joanne Eicher, ed., *Dress and Ethnicity.* Oxford: Berg.

Ekejiuba, Felicia. 1967. "Omu Okwei, the Merchant Queen of Ossomari: A Biographical Sketch." *Journal of the Historical Society of Nigeria* 3, 4: 633–46.

Ekundare, R.O. 1973. *An Economic History of Nigeria, 1860–1960.* New York: Africana.

Ellis, A. B. 1894. *The Yoruba-Speaking Peoples of the Slave Coast of West Africa.* London: Chapman and Hall.

Ene, J. Chunwike. 1964. "Indigenous Silk-Weaving in Nigeria." *Nigeria Magazine* 81: 127–36.

Etienne, Mona. 1980. "Women and Men, Cloth and Colonization: The Transformation of Production-Distribution Relations among the Baule (Ivory Coast)." Pp. 214–38 in Mona Etienne and E. Leacock, eds., *Women and Colonization: Anthropological Perspectives.* New York: Praeger.

Etienne, Mona, and Eleanor Leacock, eds. 1980. *Women and Colonization: Anthropological Perspectives.* New York: Praeger.

Ette, Mercy, and K. Akoh. 1991. "Good-bye, Gucci." *Newswatch,* 10 June, 34–35.

Euba, Titilola. 1987. "Dress and Status in 19th Century Lagos." Pp. 143–63 in Ade Adefuye, Babatunde Agiri, and Jide Osuntokun, eds., *History of the Peoples of Lagos State.* Lagos: Lantern Books.

" 'Europeanisation' in West Africa: A Continuous Process in Southern Nigeria." 1937. *West Africa,* 20 March.

Fadipe, N. A. 1936. "Stirring Up West Africa, Part 1—Anthropologists and 'Detribalisation.'" *West Africa,* 19 September, pp. 1302–3.

———. 1936. "Stirring Up West Africa, Part 2—Reaction to Taunts of 'Detribalisation.'" *West Africa,* 26 September, pp. 1340–41.

———. 1936. "Stirring Up West Africa, Part 3—The Position of Africa with Regard to 'Borrowing.'" *West Africa,* 3 October, p. 1375.

———. 1936. "Stirring Up West Africa, Part 4—Filling In the Gaps." *West Africa,* 10 October, p. 1411.

———.1936. "Stirring Up West Africa, Part 5—Encouragement of Art in West Africa." *West Africa,* 17 October, p. 1446.

———. 1936. "Stirring Up West Africa, Part 6—The Employment of Leisure Hours." *West Africa,* 24 October, p. 1482.

———. 1970. *The Sociology of the Yoruba.* Ibadan: University of Ibadan Press.

Falola, Toyin. 1984. *The Political Economy of a Pre-Colonial African State: Ibadan, 1830–1900.* Ife, Nigeria: University of Ife Press.

———. 1989. "The Yoruba Toll System: Its Operation and Abolition." *Journal of African History* 30, 1: 69–88.

———, ed. 1991. *Yoruba Historiography.* Madison: University of Wisconsin, African Studies Program.

Falola, Toyin, and Paul Lovejoy, eds. 1993. *Pawnship in Africa: Debt Bondage in Historical Perspective.* Boulder, CO: Westview Press.

Fieldhouse, D.K. 1994. *Merchant Capital and Economic Decolonization: The United Africa Company, 1929–1987.* Oxford: Clarendon Press.

Fields, Karen. 1997. *Revival and Rebellion in Colonial Central Africa.* Portsmouth, NH: Heinemann.

Folarin, Abedesin. 1928. *The Laws and Customs of Egbaland.* Abeokuta: Balogun Printers.

Forde, Daryll. 1934. *Habitat, Economy and Society.* London: Methuen.

———. 1946. "The Rural Economies." Pp. 29–215 in Margery Perham, ed., *The Native Economies.* London: Faber and Faber.

Freeman, Thomas Birch. 1968. *Journal of Various Visits to the Kingdoms of Ashanti, Aku and Dahomi in Western Africa.* London: Frank Cass. [Originally published in 1844.]

Gailey, Harry A. 1982. *Lugard and the Abeokuta Uprising: The Demise of Egba Independence.* London: Frank Cass.

Galletti, R., et al. 1956. *Nigerian Cocoa Farmers.* Oxford: Oxford University Press.

Gbadamosi, T.G.O. 1978. *The Growth of Islam Among the Yoruba, 1841–1908.* London: Longman.

Geary, William N. 1965. *Nigeria Under British Rule.* London: Frank Cass. [Originally published in 1927.]

Geiger, Susan. 1987. "Women in Nationalist Struggle: Dar es Salaam's TANU Activists." *International Journal of African Historical Studies* 20. 1: 1–26.

———. 1997. *TANU Women: Gender and Culture in the Making of Tanganyikan Nationalism, 1955–1965.* Portsmouth, NH: Heinemann.

Gilfoy, Peggy Stoltz. 1987. *Patterns of Life: West African Strip-Weaving Traditions.* Washington, D.C: Smithsonian Institution Press.

Goody, Esther. 1982. "Daboya Weavers: Relations of Production, Dependence and Reciprocity." Pp. 50–84 in Esther Goody, ed., *From Craft to Industry: The Ethnography of Proto-industrial Cloth Production.* Cambridge: Cambridge University Press.

———, ed. 1982. *From Craft to Industry: The Ethnography of Proto-industrial Cloth Production.* Cambridge: Cambridge University Press.

Guyer, J. 1981. "Household and Community in African Studies." *African Studies Review* 24, 2–3: 87–137.

Hafkin, Nancy, and Edna G. Bay, eds. 1976. *Women in Africa: Studies in Social and Economic Change.* Stanford, CA: Stanford University Press.

Hart, Keith. 1973. "Informal Income Opportunities and Urban Employment in Ghana." *Journal of Modern African Studies* 11: 61–89.

Hay, Jean. 1996. "Hoes and Clothes in a Luo Household: Changing Consumption in a Colonial Economy, 1906–1936." Pp. 243–61 in Mary Jo Arnoldi, Christraud Geary, and Kris Hardin, eds., *African Material Culture.* Bloomington: Indiana University Press.

Hill, Polly. 1966. "Landlords and Brokers: A West African Trading System," *Cahiers d'Études Africaines* 6: 349–66.

Hinderer, Ann. 1872. *Seventeen Years in the Yoruba Country.* London: Religious Tract Society.

Hodder, B.W., and U.I. Ukwu. 1969. *Markets in West Africa: Studies of Markets and Trade Among the Yoruba and Ibo.* Ibadan: University of Ibadan Press.

Hogendorn, Jan, and Paul Lovejoy. 1989. "The Development and Execution of Frederick Lugard's Policies Toward Slavery in Northern Nigeria." *Slavery and Abolition* 10: 1–43.

Hopkins, Anthony G. 1966. "The Currency Revolution in South West Nigeria in the Late Nineteenth Century." *Journal of the Historical Society of Nigeria* 3, 3: 471–83.

———. 1968. "Economic Imperialism in West Africa: Lagos, 1880–92." *Economic History Review* 21, 3: 580–606.

———. 1969. "A Report on the Yoruba, 1910." *Journal of the Historical Society of Nigeria* 5, 1: 67–100.

———. 1973. *An Economic History of West Africa.* New York: Columbia University Press.

———. 1976. "Imperial Business in Africa. Part 1: Sources." *Journal of African History* 17, 1: 29–48.

———. 1976. "Imperial Business in Africa. Part 2: Interpretations." *Journal of African History* 17, 2: 267–90.

———. 1978. "Innovation in a Colonial Context: African Origins of the Nigerian Cocoa-Farming Industry, 1880–1920." Pp. 83–90 in Clive Dewey and Anthony Hopkins, eds., *The Imperial Impact: Studies in the Economic History of Africa and India.* London: Athlone Press.

———. 1995. "The 'New International Economic Order' in the Nineteenth Century: Britain's First Development Plan for Africa." Pp. 240–64 in Robin Law, ed., *From Slave Trade to 'Legitimate' Commerce: The Commercial Transition in Nineteenth-Century West Africa.* Cambridge: Cambridge University Press.

Idiens, D., and K.G. Ponting, eds. 1980. *Textiles of Africa.* Bath, U.K.: Pasold Research Fund.

Inikori, Joseph. 1986. "West Africa's Seaborne Trade 1750–1850: Volume, Structure, and Implications." Pp. 50–88 in G. Liesegang, H. Pasch, and A. Jones, eds., *Figuring African Trade: Proceedings on the Symposium on the Quantification and Structure of the Import and Export and Long Distance Trade of Africa in the 19th Century.* Berlin: Dietrich Reimer.

———. 1992. "Slavery and the Revolution in Cotton Textile Production in England." Pp. 145–81 in Joseph Inikori and S.L. Engerman, eds., *The Atlantic Slave Trade Effects on Economies, Societies and People in Africa, the Americas and Europe.* Durham, NC: Duke University Press.

Inikori, Joseph, and S.L. Engerman. 1992. *The Atlantic Slave Trade Effects on Economies, Societies and Peoples in Africa, the Americas and Europe.* Durham, NC: Duke University Press.

Isaacman, Allen, and Richard Roberts, eds. 1995. *Cotton, Colonialism, and Social History in Sub-Saharan Africa.* Portsmouth, NH: Heinemann.

Jackson, George. 1971. "The Devolution of the Jubilee Design," in *Adire Cloth in Nigeria*, ed. Jane Barbour and Doig Simmonds, 81–94. Ibadan: The Institute of African Studies, University of Ibadan.

Johnson, A.W. 1963. "Abeokuta." *Nigerian Geographical Journal* 6 (2): 89–95.

Johnson, Marion. 1966. "The Ounce in the Eighteenth Century West African Trade." *Journal of African History* 7, 2: 197–214.

———. 1970. "The Cowrie Currencies of West Africa. Part 1." *Journal of African History* 11, 1: 17–49.

———. 1970. "The Cowrie Currencies of West Africa. Part 2." *Journal of African History* 11, 3: 331–53.

———. 1973. "Cloth on the Banks of the Niger." *Journal of the Historical Society of Nigeria* 6, 4: 353–63.

———. 1974. "Cotton Imperialism in West Africa." *African Affairs* 73, 290: 178–87.

————. 1976. "Calico Caravans: The Tripoli–Kano Trade After 1800." *Journal of African History* 12, 1: 95–117.

————. 1978. "Technology, Competition and African Crafts," Pp. 259–379 in Clive Dewey and Anthony Hopkins, eds., *The Imperial Impact: Studies in the Economic History of Africa and India.* London: Athlone Press.

————. 1980. "Cloth As Money: The Cloth Strip Currencies in Africa." Pp. 193–202 in D. Idiens and K.G. Ponting, *eds., Textiles in Africa.* Bath, U.K.: Pasold Research Fund.

Johnson, Samuel. 1973. *The History of the Yorubas from the Earliest Times to the Beginning of the British Protectorate,* 6th ed. London: Routledge and Kegan Paul.

Johnson-Odim, Cheryl, and Nina Emma Mba. 1997. *For Women and the Nation: Funmilayo Ransome-Kuti of Nigeria.* Urbana: University of Illinois Press.

Joseph, Marietta. 1978. "West African Indigo Cloth." *African Arts* 11, 2: 34–37.

Kilkenny, Roberta W. 1981. "The Slave Mode of Production: Precolonial Dahomey," Pp. 157–73 in Donald Crummey and C. C. Stewart, eds., *Modes of Production in Africa: The Precolonial Era.* Beverly Hills, CA: Sage Publications.

Kirk-Greene, Anthony H. 1968. *Lugard and the Amalgamation of Nigeria—A Documentary Record.* London: Frank Cass.

Kitchen, Gavin. 1983. "Proto-Industrialization and Demographic Change: A Thesis and Some Possible African Implications." *Journal of African History* 24: 221–40.

Klein, M., and R. Roberts. 1987. "The Resurgence of Pawning in French West Africa During the Depression of the 1930s." *African Economic History* 16: 23–38.

Kopytoff, Jean H. 1965. *A Preface to Modern Nigeria: The "Sierra Leonians" in Yoruba, 1830–1890.* Madison: University of Wisconsin Press.

Kriger, Colleen. 1993. "Textile Production and Gender in the Sokoto Caliphate." *Journal of African History* 34, 3: 361–401.

————, 1999. *Pride of Men: Ironworking in 19th Century West Central Africa.* Portsmouth, NH: Heinemann Press.

Ladd, Durant F. 1920. *Trade and Shipping in West Africa.* Washington, DC: United States Shipping Board.

Laitin, David D. 1986. *Hegemony and Culture: Politics and Religious Change Among the Yoruba.* Chicago: University of Chicago Press.

Lamb, Venice. 1975. *West African Weaving.* London: Gerald Duckworth.

Lamb, Venice, and Judy Holmes. 1980. *Nigerian Weaving.* Roxford, U.K.: H.A. & V.M. Lamb.

Lamb, Venice, and Alastair Lamb. 1980. "The Classification and Distribution of Horizontal Treadle Looms in Sub-Saharan Africa." Pp 22–62 in D. Idiens and K. G. Ponting, eds., *Textiles of Africa.* Bath, U.K.: Pasold Research Fund.

Lander, Richard. 1830. *Records of Captain Clapperton's Last Expedition to Africa.* 2 vols. London: Henry Colburn and Richard Bentley.

Law, Robin. 1973. "Anthropological Models in Yoruba History." *Africa* 43, 1: 18–26.

———. 1978. "Slaves, Trade and Taxes: The Material Basis of Political Power in Precolonial West Africa." *Research in Economic Anthropology* 1: 37–52.

———. 1983. "Trade and Politics Behind the Slave Coast: The Lagoon Traffic and the Rise of Lagos, 1500–1800." *Journal of African History* 24: 321–48.

———. 1986. "Early European Sources Relating to the Kingdom of Ijebu (1500–1700): A Critical Survey." *History in Africa* 1, 1: 245–60.

———. 1987. "Ideologies of Royal Power and the Reconstruction of Political Authority on the Slave Coast, 1680–1750." *Africa* 57, 3: 321–344.

———. 1995. *From Slave Trade to "Legitimate" Commerce: The Commercial Transition in Nineteenth-Century West Africa.* Cambridge: Cambridge University Press.

———. 1995. "'Legitimate' Trade and Gender Relations in Yorubaland and Dahomey." Pp. 195–214 in Robin Law, ed., *From Slave Trade to "Legitimate" Commerce: The Commercial Transition in Nineteenth-Century West Africa.* Cambridge: Cambridge University Press.

Lawal, Babatunde. 1974. "Some Aspects of Yoruba Aesthetics." *British Journal of Aesthetics* 4, 3: 239–49.

———. 1993. "Oyibo: Representations of the Colonialist Other in Yoruba Art, 1826–1960." Number 24. Boston: Boston University African Studies Center, Working Paper Series.

———. 1996. *The Gelede Spectacle: Art, Gender, and Social Harmony in an African Culture.* Seattle: University of Washington Press.

Leith-Ross, Sylvia. 1939. *African Women—A Study of the Ibo of Nigeria.* London: Faber and Faber.

Little, Kenneth. 1973. *African Women in Towns: An Aspect of Africa's Social Revolution.* Cambridge: Cambridge University Press.

Lloyd, P.C. 1953. "Craft Organization in Yoruba Towns." *Africa* 23, 1: 30–45.

———. 1955. "The Yoruba Lineage." *Africa* 25, 3: 235–251.

———. 1960. "Sacred Kingship and Government Among the Yoruba." *Africa* 30, 3: 221–37.

Lonsdale, John. 1977. "The Politics of Conquest: The British in Western Kenya, 1894–1908." *Historical Journal* 20, 4: 841–70.

———. 1981. "States and Social Processes in Africa: A Historiographical Survey." *African Studies Review* 24, 2/3: 139–223.

Lovejoy, Paul. 1980. *Caravans of Kola: The Hausa Kola Trade 1700–1900.* Zaria, Nigeria: Ahmadu Bell. University Press.

———. 1986. *Salt of the Desert Sun: A History of Salt Production and Trade in the Central Sudan.* Cambridge: Cambridge University Press.

Lovejoy, Paul, and David Richardson. 1995. "The Initial 'Crisis of Adaptation': The Impact of British Abolition on the Atlantic Slave Trade in West Africa, 1808–1820." Pp. 32–56 in Robin Law, ed., In *From Slave Trade to "Legitimate" Commerce: The Commercial Transition in Nineteenth-Century West Africa.* Cambridge: Cambridge University Press.

Lucas, J. Olumide. 1948. *The Religion of the Yorubas.* Lagos: CMS Bookshop.

Lugard, Frederick. 1965. *Dual Mandate in British Tropical Africa,* 5th ed. Hamden, CT: Archon Books.

———. 1970. *Political Memoranda: Revision of Instructions to Political Officers on Subjects Chiefly Political and Administrative, 1913–1918,* 3d ed. London: Frank Cass.

Lynch, Hollis. 1964. *Edward Wilmot Blyden, Pan-Negro Patriot, 1832–1928.* Oxford: Oxford University Press.

Lynn, Martin. 1989. "From Sail to Steam: The Impact of the Steamship Services on the British Palm Oil Trade with West Africa, 1850–1890." *Journal of African History* 30: 227–45.

———. 1995. "The West African Palm Oil Trade in the Nineteenth Century and the 'Crisis of Adaptation.'" Pp. 57–77 in Robin Law, ed., *From Slave Trade to 'Legitimate' Commerce: The Commercial Transition in Nineteenth-Century West Africa.* Cambridge: Cambridge University Press.

———. 1997. *Commerce and Economic Change in West Africa: The Palm Oil Trade in the Nineteenth Century.* Cambridge: Cambridge University Press.

Mabogunje, Akin L. 1959. "The Evolution of Rural Settlement in Egba Division, Nigeria." *Journal of Tropical Geography* 13: 65–77.

———. 1961. "Some Comments on Land Tenure in Egba Division, Western Nigeria." *Africa* 31, 33: 258–269.

———. 1962. *Yoruba Towns.* Ibadan: Ibadan University Press.

———. 1971. *Urbanization in Nigeria.* New York: Africana Publishing Corp. Second printing.

Mabogunje, Akin L., and M.B. Gleave. 1964. "Changing Agricultural Landscape in Southern Nigeria: The Example of Egba Division, 1850–1950." *Nigerian Geographical Journal* 7, 1: 1–15.

Mabogunje, Akin L., and J.D. Omer-Cooper. 1971. *Owu in Yoruba History.* Ibadan: Ibadan University Press.

MacGregor, William. 1904. "Lagos, Abeokuta, and the Alake." *Journal of the African Society* 3, 12: 464–481.

Macmillan, Allister. 1993. *The Red Book of West Africa: Historical and Descriptive Commercial and Industrial Facts, Figures, and Resources,* 2d ed. Ibadan: Spectrum Books.

Mamdani, Mahmood. 1996. *Citizen and Subject: Contemporary Africa and The Legacy of Late Colonialism.* Princeton, NJ: Princeton University Press.

Mann, Kristin. 1985. *Marrying Well: Marriage, Status and Social Change Among the Educated Elite in Colonial Lagos.* Cambridge: Cambridge University Press.

———. 1991. "Women, Landed Property and the Accumulation of Wealth in Early Colonial Lagos." *Signs: A Journal for Women in Culture and Society* 16, 4: 682–706.

———. 1995. "Owners, Slaves, and the Struggle for Labour in the Commercial Transition at Lagos." Pp. 144–71 in Robin Law, ed., *From Slave Trade to "Legitimate" Commerce: The Commercial Transition in Nineteenth-Century West Africa.* Cambridge: Cambridge University Press.

Manning, Patrick. 1982. *Slavery, Colonialism and Economic Growth in Dahomey, 1640–1960.* Cambridge: Cambridge University Press.

Martin, Phyllis. 1986. "Power, Cloth and Currency on the Loango Coast." *African Economic History* 15: 1–12.

Martin, Susan. 1984. "Gender and Innovation: Farming, Cooking and Palm Processing in the Ngwa Region, South-eastern Nigeria, 1900–1930," *Journal of African History* 25, 4: 411–27.

———. 1988. *Palm Oil and Protest: An Economic History of the Ngwa Region,
South-eastern Nigeria, 1800–1980.* Cambridge: Cambridge University Press.

———. 1989. "The Long Depression: West African Producers and the World
Economy, 1914–45." Pp. 74–94 in Ian Brown, ed., *The Economies of Africa
and Asia in the Inter-war Depression.* London: Routledge.

———. 1995. "Slaves, Igbo Women and Palm Oil in the Nineteenth Century." Pp.
172–94 in Robin Law, ed., *From Slave Trade to "Legitimate" Commerce:
The Commercial Transition in Nineteenth-Century West Africa.* Cambridge:
Cambridge University Press.

Matory, J. Lorand. 1994. *Sex and the Empire That Is No More: Gender and the
Politics of Metaphor in Oyo Yoruba Religion.* Minneapolis: University of Minnesota Press.

Mba, Nina Emma. 1982. *Nigerian Women Mobilized: Women's Political Activity in
Southern Nigeria, 1900–1965.* Berkeley: University of California Press.

Mbilinyi, Marjorie. 1989. "This Is an Unforgettable Business: Colonial State Intervention in Urban Tanzania." Pp. 111–29 in Kathleen Staudt and Jane Parpart,
eds., *Women and the State in Africa.* Boulder, CO: Lynne Rienner.

McCaskie, T.C. 1981. "State and Society, Marriage and Adultery: Some Considerations Towards a Social History of Pre-colonial Asante." *Journal of African
History* 22, 4: 477-94.

McPhee, Allan. 1971. *The Economic Revolution in British West Africa,* 2d ed. London: Frank Cass.

Meillassoux, Claude, ed. 1971. *The Development of Indigenous Trade and Markets
in West Africa.* London: Oxford University Press.

Miles, John. 1978. "Rural Protest in the Cold Coast: The Cocoa Hold-ups, 1908–
1938." Pp. 152–170 in Clive Dewey and A.G. Hopkins, eds., *The Imperial
Impact: Studies in the Economic History of Africa and India.* London: Athlone
Press.

Moloney, Alfred C. 1889. "Cotton Interests, Foreign and Native in Yoruba, and Generally in West Africa." *Journal of the Manchester Geographical Society* 5:
255–76.

Moore, Donald, and Richard Roberts. 1990. "Listening for Silences." *History in Africa* 17: 319–25.

Morel, E.D. 1912. *Nigeria—Its Peoples and Its Problems.* London: Smith, Elder.

Morton-Williams, Peter. 1960. "The Yoruba Ogboni Cult in Oyo." *Africa* 30, 4: 362–
74.

———. 1964. "An Outline of the Cosmology and Cult Organization of the Oyo
Yoruba." *Africa* 24: 243–60.

———. 1964. "The Oyo Yoruba and the Atlantic Trade 1670–1830." *Journal of the
Historical Society of Nigeria* 3, 1: 25–44.

Murray, K.C. 1943. "Arts and Crafts of Nigeria: Their Past and Future." *Africa* 14:
155–64.

Newbury, C.W. 1961. *The Western Slave Coast and Its Rulers.* Oxford: Clarendon
Press.

———. 1971. *British Policy Towards West Africa.* Oxford: Clarendon Press.

———. 1971. "Prices and Profitability in Early Nineteenth-Century West African Trade." Pp 91–105 in Claude Meillassoux, ed., *The Development of Indigenous Trade and Markets in West Africa.* London: Oxford University Press.

———. 1972. "Credit in Early Nineteenth Century West African Trade." *Journal of African History* 13, 1: 81–95.

———. 1978. "Trade and Technology in West Africa: The Case of the Niger Company, 1900–1920." *Journal of African History* 19, 4: 551–75.

Nielsen, Ruth. 1979. "The History and Development of Wax-Printed Textiles Intended for West Africa and Zaire." Pp. 467–98 in Justine M. Cordwell and Ronald A. Schwarz, eds., *The Fabrics of Culture: The Anthropology of Clothing and Adornment.* New York: Mouton.

Nwabughuogu, Anthony. 1982. "From Wealthy Entrepreneurs to Petty Traders: The Decline of African Middlemen in Eastern Nigeria, 1900–1950." *Journal of African History* 23, 3: 365–79.

Ofonagoro, Walter. 1976. "The Currency Revolution in Southern Nigeria 1880–1948." Occasional Paper No. 14, African Studies Center, University of California at Los Angeles.

Oguntona, Toyin. 1986. *Basic Textiles: Design Concepts and Methods.* Zaria, Nigeria: Amadu Bello University.

Ojo, G.J.A. 1966. *Yoruba Culture: A Geographical Analysis.* London: University of London Press.

Oke, O.L. 1971. "The Chemistry and General History of Dyeing." Pp. 43–48 in Jane Barbour and Doig Simmonds, eds., *Adire Cloth in Nigeria.* Ibadan: Institute of African Studies, University of Ibadan.

Okonjo, Kamene. 1976. "The Dual-Sex Political System in Operation: Igbo Women and Community Politics in Midwestern Nigeria." Pp. 45–48 in Nancy Hafkin and Edna G. Bay, eds., *Women in Africa: Studies in Social and Economic Change.* Stanford, CA: Stanford University Press.

Omosini, Olufemi. 1975. "Alfred Moloney and His Strategies for Economic Development in Lagos Colony and Hinterland, 1886–1891." *Journal of the Historical Society of Nigeria* 7, 4: 657–72.

Omu, Fred I.A. 1978. *Press and Politics in Nigeria, 1880–1937.* Atlantic Highlands, NJ: Humanities Press.

Oroge, E.A. 1975. "The Fugitive Slave Crisis of 1859: A Factor in the Growth of Anti-British Feelings Among the Yoruba." *Odu,* 12: 47–52.

———. 1985. "Iwofa: An Historical Survey of the Yoruba Institution of Indenture." *African Economic History* 14: 75–106.

Osuntokun, A. 1979. *Nigeria in the First World War.* New York: Humanities Press.

Owen, Roger. 1989. "Egypt in the World Depression: Agricultural Recession and Industrial Expansion." Pp. 137–51 in Ian Brown, ed., *The Economies of Africa and Asia in the Inter-war Depression.* London: Routledge, 1989.

Oyemakinde, Wale. 1974. "Railway Construction and Operation in Nigeria, 1895–1911: Labour Problems and Socio-economic Impact." *Journal of the Historical Society of Nigeria* 7, 2: 303–24.

Oyewumi, Oyeronke. 1997. *The Invention of Women: Making an African Sense of Western Gender Discourses.* Minneapolis: University of Minnesota Press.

Pallinder-Law, Agneta. 1974. "Aborted Modernization in West Africa? The Case of Abeokuta." *Journal of African History* 15, 1: 65–82.

Partridge, C. 1910. "Native Law and Custom in Egbaland." *Journal of the African Society* 10, 40: 422–33.

Pedler, Frederick. 1974. *The Lion and the Unicorn in Africa—A History of the Origins of the United Africa Company, 1787–1931.* London: Heinemann.

Peel, J.D. 1967. "Religious Change in Yorubaland." *Africa* 37, 3: 292–306.

———. 1968. *Aladura—A Religious Movement Among the Yoruba.* Oxford: Oxford University Press, International African Institute.

———. 1978. "Olaju: A Yoruba Concept of Development." Journal of Development Studies 14, 2: 139–65.

Perani, Judith. 1979. "Nupe Costume Crafts." *African Arts* 12, 3: 52–57.

———. 1989. "Northern Nigerian Prestige Textiles: Production, Trade, Patronage and Use." Pp. 65–81 in Beate Engelbrecht and Bernhard Gardi, ed., *Man Does Not Go Naked.* Basel: Swiss Museum of Folklore/Craft.

———, and Norma Wolff. 1999. *Cloth, Dress and Art Patronage in Africa.* New York: Berg Press.

Perham, Margery, ed. 1946. *The Native Economies of Nigeria,* vol. 1. London: Faber and Faber.

Phillips, Anne. 1989. *The Enigma of Colonialism: British Policy in West Africa.* Bloomington: Indiana University Press.

Phillips, Earl. 1969. "The Egba at Abeokuta: Acculturation and Political Change, 1830–1870." *Journal of African History* 10, 1: 117–31.

———. 1970. "The Egba at Ikorodu, 1865: Perfidious Lagos?" in *African Historical Studies* 3, 1: 23–35.

Picton, John. 1992. "Tradition, Technology, and Lurex—Some Comments on Textile History and Design in West Africa." Pp. 9–32 in John Picton, ed. *History, Design, and Craft in West African Strip-Woven Cloth.* Washington, DC: National Museum of African Art.

———, ed. 1992. *History, Design, and Craft in West African Strip-Woven Cloth.* Washington, DC: National Museum of African Art, Smithsonian Institution.

Picton, John, and John Mack. 1989. *African Textiles.* New York: Harper and Row.

Plange, Nii-k. 1984. "The Colonial State in Northern Ghana." *Review of African Political Economy* 34: 29–43.

Pokrant, R.J. 1982. "The Tailors of Kano City." Pp. 85–132 in Esther Goody, ed., *From Craft to Industry: The Ethnography of Proto-industrial Cloth Production.* Cambridge: Cambridge University Press.

Poynor, Robin. 1980. "Traditional Textiles in Owo, Nigeria." *African Arts* 14, 1: 47–51.

Press, Robert M. 1992. "Africa in Blue," *Christian Science Monitor,* 25 September, 10–11.

Polakoff, Claire. 1982. *African Textiles and Dyeing Techniques.* London: Routledge and Kegan Paul.

Ratcliffe, B.M. 1982. "Cotton Imperialism: Manchester Merchants and Cotton Cultivation in West Africa in the Mid-Nineteenth Century." *African Economic History* 11: 87–113.

Rathbone, R. 1978. "World War I and Africa." *Journal of African History* 19, 1: 1–9.

Renne, Elisha. 1995. *Cloth That Does Not Die: The Meaning of Cloth in Bunu Social Life.* Seattle: University of Washington Press.

Roberts, Richard. 1984. "Women's Work and Women's Property: Household Social Relations in the Maraka Textile Industry of the Nineteenth Century." *Comparative Studies in Society and History* 26, 2: 229–50.

———. 1987. *Warriors, Merchants and Slaves: The State and the Economy in the Middle Niger Valley, 1700–1914.* Stanford, CA: Stanford University Press.

———. 1990. "Reversible Social Processes, Historical Memory, and the Production of History." *History in Africa* 17: 341–49.

———. 1996. *Two Worlds of Cotton: Colonialism and the Regional Economy in the French Soudan, 1800–1946.* Stanford, CA: Stanford University Press.

Roberts, Richard and Donald Moore. 1990. "Listening For Silences." *History in Africa* 17: 319–325.

Robertson, Claire. 1984. *Sharing the Same Bowl: A Socioeconomic History of Women and Class in Accra, Ghana.* Bloomington: Indiana University Press.

Robertson, Claire, and Iris Berger, eds. 1986. *Women and Class in Africa.* New York: Africana.

Roy, Tirthankar Roy, ed. 1993. *Artisans and Industrialization: Indian Weaving in the Twentieth Century.* New York: Oxford University Press.

———. 1996. *Cloth and Commerce: Textiles in Colonial India.* Walnut Creek, CA: Alta Mira Press.

Ryder, Alan F.C. 1965. "Dutch Trade on the Nigerian Coast During the Seventeenth Century." *Journal of the Historical Society of Nigeria* 3, 2: 195–210.

Ryder, Alan. 1977. *Benin and the Europeans 1485–1897.* 2d ed. London: Longman Group.

Schmidt, Elizabeth. 1992. *Peasants, Traders and Wives: Shona Women in the History of Zimbabwe, 1870–1939.* Portsmouth, NH: Heinemann.

Schwab, W.B. 1955. "Kinship and Lineage Among the Yoruba." *Africa* 25, 4 (1955): 352–374.

———. 1958. "The Terminology of Kinship and Marriage Among the Yoruba." *Africa* 28, 4 (1958): 301–313.

Scott, Richenda. 1946. "Production for Trade." Pp. 217–91 in Margery Perham, ed., *The Native Economies of Nigeria,* vol. 1. London: Faber and Faber.

Shea, Philip J. 1974–1977. "Economies of Scale and the Indigo Dyeing Industry of Precolonial Kano." *Kano Studies* 1, 2: 55–61.

Shenk, Wilbert R. 1983. *Henry Venn, Missionary Statesman.* Marynoll, NY: Orbis.

Sieber, Roy. 1972. *African Textiles and Decorative Arts.* New York: Museum of Modern Art.

Smith, Robert S. 1973. "Giambattista Scala: Adventurer, Trader and First Italian Representative in Nigeria." *Journal of the Historical Society of Nigeria* 7, 1: 67–76.

———. 1988. *Kingdoms of the Yoruba,* 3d ed. Madison: University of Wisconsin Press.

Smith, Sheila. 1979. "Colonialism in Economic Theory: The Experience of Nigeria." *Journal of Development Studies* 15, 3: 38–59.

Spitzer, Leo. 1974. *The Creoles of Sierra Leone: Responses to Colonialism, 1870–1945.* Madison, University of Wisconsin Press.

Stanfield, Nancy. 1971. "Dyeing Methods in Western Nigeria." Pp. 7–42 in Jane Barbour and Doig Simmonds, eds., *Adire Cloth in Nigeria.* Ibadan: Institute of African Studies, University of Ibadan.

Staudt, Kathleen, and Jane Parpart, eds. 1989. *Women and the State in Africa.* Boulder, CO: Lynne Rienner.

Steiner, Christopher. "Another Image of Africa: Toward an Ethnohistory of European Cloth Marketed in West Africa, 1873–1960." *Ethnohistory* 32, 2: 111–33.

Stoltz Gilfoy, Peggy. 1987. *Patterns of Life: West African Strip-Weaving Traditions.* Washington DC: Smithsonian Institution Press.

Stone, R.H. 1900. *In Afric's Forest and Jungle; or, Six Years Among the Yorubans.* London: Oliphant, Anderson and Ferrier.

Sudarkasa, Niara. 1975. "The Economic Status of the Yoruba in Ghana Before 1970." *Nigerian Journal of Economic and Social Studies* 17, 1 (March): 93–125.

Talbot, A.P. 1921. *The Peoples of Southern Nigeria.* Oxford: Oxford University Press.

Tamuno, T.N. 1972. *The Evolution of the Nigerian State: The Southern Phase, 1898–1914.* New York: Humanities Press.

Thompson, Robert Farris. 1984. *Flash of the Spirit: African and Afro-American Art and Philosophy.* New York: Vintage.

Thornton, John. 1990–1991. "Precolonial African Industry and the Atlantic Trade, 1500–1800." *African Economic History* 19: 1–19.

Thorp, Ellen. 1956. *Ladder of Bones.* London: Jonathan Cape.

Traeger, Lillian. 1987. "A Re-examination of the Urban Informal Sector in West Africa." *Canadian Journal of African Studies* 21, 2: 238–55.

Tranberg-Hansen, Karen. 1989. "The Black Market and Women Traders in Lusaka, Zambia." Pp. 143–60 in Kathleen Staudt and Jane Parpart, eds., *Women and the State in Africa.* Boulder, CO: Lynne Rienner.

———, ed., 1992. *African Encounters with Domesticity.* New Brunswick, NJ: Rutgers University Press.

Trouillot, Michel-Ralph. 1995. *Silencing the Past: Power and the Production of History.* Boston: Beacon Press.

Trowell, Margaret. 1960. *African Design.* London: Faber and Faber.

Tucker, Sara. 1853. *Abbeokuta: Sunrise Within the Tropics: An Outline of the Origin and Progress of the Yoruba Mission.* London: James Nisbet.

Van Allen, Judith. 1976. "'Aba Riots' or Igbo 'Women's War'? Ideology, Stratification and the Invisibility of Women." Pp. 59–85 in Nancy Hafkin and Edna G. Bay, eds., *Women in Africa: Studies in Social and Economic Change.* Stanford, CA: Stanford University Press.

Vaz, Kim Marie. 1995. *The Woman with the Artistic Brush: A Life History of Yoruba Batik Artist Nike Davies.* New York: M.E. Sharpe.

Vernon-Jackson, Hugh. 1960. "Craft Work in Bida." *Africa* 30, 1: 51–61.

Ward Price, H. L. 1939. *Dark Subjects.* London: Jarrolds.

Washbrook, David. 1990. "South, the World System and World Capitalism." *Journal of Asian Studies* 40: 479–508.

Wass, Betty. 1979. "Yoruba Dress in Five Generations of a Lagos Family." Pp. 331–48 in Justine M. Cordwell and Ronald A. Schwarz, eds., *The Fabrics of Culture: The Anthropology of Clothing and Adornment*. New York: Mouton.

Webster, J.B. 1963. "The Bible and the Plough." *Journal of the Historical Society of Nigeria* 4, 2: 418–34.

Weiner, Annette, and Jane Schneider, eds. 1991. *Cloth and Human Experience*. Washington, DC: Smithsonian Institution Press.

Wenger, Susan, and Beier, H.U. 1957. "Adire—Yoruba Pattern Dyeing." *Nigeria,* no. 54: 208–25.

Wilks, Ivor. 1971. "Asante Policy Toward Hausa Trade in the 19th Century." Pp. 124–41 in Claude Meillassoux, ed., *The Development of Indigenous Trade and Markets in West Africa.* London: Oxford University Press.

———. 1975. *Asante in the Nineteenth Century: The Structure and Evolution of a Political Order.* Cambridge: Cambridge University Press.

Williams, D. 1964. "The Iconology of the Yoruba Edan Ogboni." *Africa* 34, 2: 139–66.

———. 1966. "Two Studies of Ifa Divination." *Africa* 36, 4: 406–31.

Yemitan, Oladipo. 1987. *Madame Tinubu, Merchant and King-Maker*. Ibadan: Fastprint.

Young, Crawford. 1994. *The African Colonial State in Comparative Perspective*. New Haven, CT: Yale University Press.

Zachernuk, Philip. 2000. *Colonial Subjects: An African Intelligentsia and Atlantic Ideas*. Charlottesville: University Press of Virginia.

Zeleza, Paul Tiyambe. 1993. *A Modern Economic History of Africa.* Vol. 1, *The Nineteenth Century*. Dakar, Senegal: CODESRIA.

———. 1997. *Manufacturing African Studies and Crises*. Dakar, Senegal: CODESRIA.

INDEX

Aba Women's War of 1929, 177, 188 n.81

Abeokuta, Nigeria: autonomy treaty in 1893, 44, 46; brocade design in, 25, 40 n.165; conflict with Dahomey, 37 n.120; depressed economy, 159; dyers' associations, 144–48, 161, 164, 175, 181, 191–99; dyers owning means of production in, 92–93, 116–17; five crafts in, 13; food production, 159–60; imported cloth volumes, 55–56, 158, 160; migration to rural areas, 205; nineteenth-century textile production, 12–16, 26–27; proportion of dyers in, 104–5, 121 n.75; railroad extension to, 49–50, 53; regional economy and, 220–21; road construction, 50–51, 63, 77 n.45, 77 n.46, 83 n.138; Senegalese buyers in, 114, 125 n.128, 139–40, 146, 154 n.66; settling of, 1, 16–17, 45; slavery in, 21, 111; tax collection, 136–37, 150, 153 n.47, 204–5; traditional political structure, 44–46, 75 n.9

Abeokuta Ladies Club, 188 n.74

Abeokuta Women's Union, 227

Aboaba, 46

Ademola II, 169–72, 175, 186 n.54, 187 n.55

Adenaike, Caroline Keyes, xxiii

Adeniji, Madam Wosinatu, 93, 191

Adeniji, Wosanti and Adepate, 108

Adeniyi-Jones, C.C., 162, 176, 182

Adire-alabere, 90, 118 n.13

Adire cloth: African markets for, 111–15, 123 n.110, 138–39, 220–21; beating of, 109–10, 123 n.105; blue hands as mark of craft, 94; cloth imports, 41 n.181, 55–56, 80 n.87, 107, 158, 160; cocoa trade and, xxvii, 139, 199–203; collapse of industry in 1937–1939, 201–2; credit needs of dyers, 139, 147–49, 164, 180, 223; current popularity of, 228, 230 n.4; current production of, xxii–xxiii, 110, 212–13, 223, 227–29; depression and trade of, 138–40, 159, 213, 222–23; description of, xix, 89; designs, xxiv, 90–91, 108–9; early art historical writings, xxiii; economic linkages of, 103–8; government misunderstanding of importance, 208–9, 224; introduction of, 89; labor needs, xxvi, 64, 67; machine, 119 n.15; production technology,

Punch, Cyril, 50, 63

Racism, 60, 68
Railroad: extension to Abeokuta, 49–50,
    53; judicial control by, 84 n.146;
    land leases, 84 n.146; role of
    European merchants, 53; slavery
    cases judged by commissioners, 66;
    tolls on trade, 82 n.119
Ramotu, Madam, 167, 179
Ransome-Kuti, J.J., 65
Rawlings, H.J., 53–54
Religion: *Egungun*, 7–9, 24, 39 n.161,
    54; *Eshu-Elegba*, 12; indigo and, 12,
    97–98; *Oro*, 15–16; white cloth, 9;
    women tailor prohibition, 15
Resident (British administrator), 163,
    168–72, 198–99
Resist dyeing, xxxv n.2, 89–90, 118 n.7
Richards, Mrs. Coghill, 144, 146, 148
Road construction, 50–51, 63, 77 n.45,
    77 n.46, 83 n.138
Robbin, Henry, 18
Roberts, Richard, xxv
Rotational credit societies, 13

Sale of Land Order of 1913, 134
Samuel, J.H. (Adegboyega Edun), 47,
    85 n.163
Sapara-Williams, C.A., 48–49, 77 n.35
Saros people, 6, 14, 18, 89, 209. *See
    also* Christian population
Scala, Signore, 29
Senegal, *adire* wholesale merchants
    from, 114, 125 n.128, 139–40, 146,
    154 n.66
Sewing machines, 32 n.26
Shea, Philip, xxiii, xxvi
Sheldon, Mr., 144, 180
Shibori cloth, xxxv n.2
Shodeke, 45
Shyllon, Mrs., 178
Silk, Nigerian, 33 n.36
Simmonds, Doig, xxiii
Slavery: *adire* production, 25, 222; ban
    of *iwofa* system, 136, 144, 147, 156
    n.101; debt bondage, 25, 40 n.163,

66–67; demise in Nigeria, 66–67;
    Hausa, 111; by missionaries, 21; by
    Nigerians, 21–22, 38 n.137, 38
    n.140, 39 n.144, 39 n.148, 111;
    railway commissioners judging
    cases, 66; self-redemption, 84 n.148;
    in the United States, 18. *See also
    Iwofas*
Social status: cloth, xxvi; clothing, 3–4,
    6–7, 67–68; imported cloth, 26, 28–
    29, 40 n.170
Société Commerciale de l'Ouest
    Africain (SCOA), 129
Soda Fabrik, 143
Sodipo, Chief, 115
Sodipo, I.A., 141
Soetan, Alhaja, 97, 103, 115, 121 n.73,
    192–93
Sokalu, 46
Somoye, Oladipo, 75 n.12, 163–65,
    180, 184 n.14, 195–96
Sorunke, 44
Sowemimo, D., 133
Spinners, 13, 104
Staudt, Kathleen, xxix
Stencils, 90, 96, 109
Stone, R.H., 6–7, 13, 24
Sucretin cover, 143
Synthetic dyes, 142–44, 148, 179

Tailors, 15–17, 105, 108–9, 123 n.98
Tax collection: during depression, 136–
    37, 150, 151 n.7, 153 n.47, 157 n.7,
    204–7; under Dods, 204–6, 216
    n.69; enforcement, 205–7. *See also*
    Tolls on trade
Tax revolt by women in 1947–48, xxxii
Taylor, Amelia, 21
Tinubu, Madam, 20, 38 n.131, 46–47,
    222
Tolls on trade: to crush local weaving,
    88; EUG collection of, 47, 60;
    exports, 47, 62, 75 n.12; imported
    cloth, 54–55; railway commissioner
    and, 82 n.119; reexport tax on *adire*,
    201; tax collection during depres-
    sion, 136–37, 150, 151 n.7, 153

About the Author

JUDITH A. BYFIELD is associate professor of history at Dartmouth College where she teaches courses in African history. She has also contributed articles to the *Journal of African History*, the *Canadian Journal of African Studies*, and she has edited a special issue on the African Diaspora for the *African Studies Review*.